Identifying Roots

Culture on the Edge: Studies in Identity Formation
Series Editor: Steven W. Ramey, University of Alabama

Culture on the Edge is devoted to studies—both monographs and collections of essays—that explore how social formation involves a series of strategies that present identity as static and uniform. Volumes in this series study identity formation as a sequence of interconnected historical practices, revealing ways that the image of stable selves and groups conceals the precarious and shifting nature of cultures.

Published:

Claiming Identity in the Study of Religion: Social and Rhetorical Techniques Examined
Edited by Monica R. Miller

Identity, Politics and the Study of Islam: Current Dilemmas in the Study of Religions
Edited by Matt Sheedy

Strategic Acts in the Study of Identity: Towards a Dynamic Theory of People and Place
Edited by Vaia Touna

Identifying Roots

Alex Haley and the Anthropology
of Scriptures

Richard W. Newton, Jr.

eQuinox

SHEFFIELD UK   BRISTOL CT

Published by Equinox Publishing Ltd.

UK: Office 415, The Workstation, 15 Paternoster Row, Sheffield,
         South Yorkshire S1 2BX
USA: ISD, 70 Enterprise Drive, Bristol, CT 06010

www.equinoxpub.com

First published 2020

British Library Cataloguing-in-Publication Data
A catalogue record for this book is available from the British Library.

ISBN-13   978 1 78179 546 0   (hardback)
           978 1 78179 547 7   (paperback)
           978 1 78179 548 4   (ePDF)

Library of Congress Cataloging-in-Publication Data

Names: Newton, Richard, 1983- author.
Title: Identifying roots : Alex Haley and the anthropology of scriptures /
  Richard Newton.
Other titles: Alex Haley and the anthropology of scriptures
Description: Bristol, CT : Equinox Publishing Ltd, 2020. | Series: Culture
  on the edge: studies in identity formation | Includes bibliographical
  references and index. | Summary: "This volume presents a cultural
  history of Alex Haley's Roots as a case study in 'operational acts of
  identification.' It examines the strategy and tactics Haley employed in
  developing a family origin story into an acclaimed national history.
  Where cultural studies scholars have critiqued notions of sacrosanct
  'rootedness,' this book shows the fruit of critically identifying those
  claims. It reframes the concept of 'roots' as a theoretical vocabulary
  and grammar for the anthropology of scriptures - a way of parsing the
  cultural texts that seem to read us back"-- Provided by publisher.
Identifiers: LCCN 2020000140 (print) | LCCN 2020000141 (ebook) | ISBN
  9781781795460 (hardback) | ISBN 9781781795460 (paperback) | ISBN
  9781781795484 (ebook)
Subjects: LCSH: Haley, Alex. Roots. | Roots (Television program : 1977) |
  African Americans--Race identity. | Place attachment--Social
  aspects--United States. | United States--Race relations--Philosophy. |
  Roots (Botany) in literature. | Slavery in mass media.
Classification: LCC E185.97.H24 N49 2020 (print) | LCC E185.97.H24
  (ebook) | DDC 305.896/073--dc23
LC record available at https://lccn.loc.gov/2020000140
LC ebook record available at https://lccn.loc.gov/2020000141

Typeset by S.J.I. Services, New Delhi, India

Contents

Acknowledgments

At the root of this book are stories and connections. I am so very grateful for the many people who have taken the time to connect with me and share their stories. They have made this project all the more worthwhile.

First, my sincerest gratitude to Professor Vincent L. Wimbush, my doctoral advisor and mentor. Before beginning my PhD, a former professor of mine described you as "a scholar's scholar," a description that I increasingly find to be true. You challenged me to appreciate the question and equipped me to carry out the work. It continues.

In addition to Professor Wimbush, Professor Monica A. Coleman and Professor Darryl A. Smith graciously served on my dissertation committee. Prof. Coleman, your wisdom and practicality helped me to dream a better, healthier life for myself as a teacher-scholar. Prof. Smith, your excitement about my project and your artful questions helped me to love my project again in the most wearying moments of the process.

I could not begin to imagine this project without the intellectual support provided by the Institute for Signifying Scriptures, the Society for Comparative Research on Iconic and Performative Texts, the Wabash Center for Teaching and Learning in Theology and Religious Studies, and Culture on the Edge. And I could not have completed it without the beneficence of the Albert B. Friedman Grant at Claremont Graduate University and a Doctoral Fellowship from the Forum for Theological Exploration.

This book is an outgrowth of many conversations that I reflect upon often and kindly. Thank you to friends and colleagues at Claremont Graduate University, the Ethnic and Women's Studies program at California State Polytechnic University, the Department of Religious Studies at Elizabethtown College, and the Department of Religious Studies at the University of Alabama (Roll Tide!). Additionally, my investigation was greatly advanced by visits to the Special Collections at the University of Tennessee—Knoxville, Hamilton College's Special Collections, and the Alex Haley Museum and Interpretive Center. These archives of "Haleyalia" were most helpful, as were the skillful and welcoming staffs at these institutions.

I was fortunate to have a wonderful set of anonymous readers share their insights to help me refine my argument. As well, I owe a debt of gratitude to Kevin McGinnis, Lalruatkima, Shayda Kafai, S. Brent Plate, Ed Blum, and Kelly J. Baker—all busy and accomplished scholars—who took time to critically read earlier versions of my work.

To Janet Joyce and Val Hall, I continue to be inspired by so many of the works you have shepherded at Equinox. I am honored that you would count this book among that number. Thanks to the editors at *Postscripts: The Journal for Sacred Texts and Contemporary Worlds* (published by Equinox) who have allowed me to revise a prior article for inclusion in the fourth chapter of this volume. And to Steven Ramey—my colleague, friend, and editor—your sharp insights never cease to amaze me.

Finally, to my family, whose sacrifices, faith, and patience empowered me to start and finish this. All my love.

Introduction: The Anthropology of Scriptures

On January 21, 2013, Barack Obama publicly inaugurated his second presidential term in a ceremony themed "Faith in America's Future" (Joint Congressional Committee on Inaugural Ceremonies 2013). The Joint Congressional Committee on Inaugural Ceremonies (JCCIC) sought to convey an American story that celebrated the promise of the Emancipation Proclamation issued in 1862. With his left hand upon the Bibles of Abraham Lincoln and Martin Luther King Jr., President Obama took the oath of office, affirming the tenability of the American Dream.

Historically-minded skeptics were to be assuaged by the introductory remarks of JCCIC co-chairman, Senator Lamar Alexander. "The late Alex Haley, the author of *Roots*, lived his life by these six words: 'Find the good and praise it.' Today we praise the American tradition of transferring or reaffirming immense power as we inaugurate the President of the United States."

Rachel Weiner of *The Washington Post* offered real-time commentary on the moment in her online piece, "Why Lamar Alexander Quoted Alex Haley" (2013). Weiner hypothesized that it was because Haley was a constituent and friend to the senator. Senator Alexander considered Haley "the greatest storyteller Tennessee has ever produced" (Legg 2012). A former aide to the senator remarked how "you can't work or even be around Sen. Alexander for very long without hearing him quote his friend Alex Haley" (Lefler 2008). Satisfied by this explanation, Weiner's rationale went to press as the last word on a significant moment.

Yet when we slow down and critically reflect upon what took place, we notice a discursive coup. Senator Alexander attempted to (mis)direct the nation's attention away from a sordid, racialized present onto his vision of a transcendent future. For all to see, the White, Republican Tennessean crossed the partisan aisle to rally the nation behind its first Black president. And he deputized perhaps the perfect person to assist.

In 1976, Haley's *Roots: The Saga of an American Family* and its 1977 television serial adaptation (*Roots: The Miniseries* 2012) ushered in a social media moment that pre-dated the tethering technologies of the twenty-first century. Even without Twitter and Facebook, *Roots* was the talk of the town. It was the book you had to read and the show you had to see. The novel received the National Book Award and a special citation from the Pulitzer Prize Board (H. Taylor 1995: 48). In its first eighteen months, it sold 1.5 million copies with millions to follow later in over twenty-eight countries and twenty-one languages (Moore 1996: 200). During an unseasonably cold week in January, meeting places from neighborhood sports bars to the Las Vegas Strip all but shut down as audiences stayed home and watched a predominantly Black cast premier on the golden screen. Nielsen Media Research reported that over 100 million viewers—roughly half the country—huddled around the television to watch the final episode of the miniseries (Bird 2017). *TIME* would herald the bi-genre blockbuster "Haley's Comet" (Marmon 1977: 14). And Alex Haley, "the *Roots* man," became a household name (Oakley Page 1995: 42).

Fostering the genealogical imagination of millions, the inspiring tale proved a viable source from which Americans, especially African Americans, could cull a socially-useful past. *Roots* took hold after Alex Haley's twelve-year odyssey to trace his ancestry back to Kunta Kinte, an enslaved Mandinka whose perseverance in Colonial America begat a New World bloodline. Memories of an enslaved African forefather were passed down orally through the generations, but Haley would traverse the Atlantic to graft legend to history. The result was a telling of America's bicentennial story through the eyes of Kunta Kinte's descendants—from slavery to acclaimed author, from segregation to integration. Audiences learned that anything is possible in the USA *if you know your roots*.

The theme was as timely as it is timeless. When the promises of the Civil Rights Era began to fade, *Roots* reinvigorated Americans' optimism for integration. An author with ample reason to hold a grudge against the country became its chief evangelist, providing a historical framework in which Black people could *identify* America as home. Between the 1979 follow-up miniseries (*Roots: The Next Generations* 2012), the 1988 sequel (*Roots: The Gift* 2012), and the 2016 remake (*Roots* 2016), Haley's culturally constructed lineage is all but assured to continue in the new century.

And this is to say nothing of Senator Lamar Alexander's aforementioned invocation. What better reference than *Roots* to restore "Faith in America's Future"? Despite the loss of Senator Alexander's choice for President, the man responsible for *Roots* could help him take the high ground and frame the defeat as of little negative consequence. The senior Republican Senator could save face and proclaim that the republic still stood for something worthwhile. The incredulous could identify with Alex Haley for themselves and "find the good and praise it."

But this was not universally the case. In the month prior to President Obama's second inauguration, director Quentin Tarantino's controversial slave-revenge film *Django Unchained* (2012) debuted in theaters nationwide as a sort of "counter-story" to *Roots* (Merriweather-Hunn, Guy, and Maglitz 2006: 244–50). An homage to Spaghetti Westerns and Blaxploitation, the film has Tarantino's Black protagonist visiting his White transgressors with a most violent vengeance. For some, like African American film director Spike Lee, *Django* represented a disrespectful gesture toward the memory of Black people's ancestors (Platon 2012). For others, such as *Ebony* magazine's Arts and Culture Editor Miles Marshall Lewis, there was something "satisfying" about Django's revenge (Lewis 2012).

Artists involved in the two films campaigned for their respective portrayals of slavery. Tarantino railed that sentiments like Lewis's are much more human and relatable than the brand of Americana sold by *Roots*. Riffing on a scene in the miniseries, Tarantino quipped: "We ain't gonna have that *Roots* bullshit, where Chicken George [Kunta Kinte's grandson] gets the whip and…says, 'To whip you would make me as bad as you.' I'm saying to myself, 'Whip his ass!' Django whips his ass!" (Lewis 2012). LeVar Burton, who played the young Kunta Kinte in the original miniseries, did not wholly dismiss *Django*, calling it an entertaining piece of comedy (Lewis 2012). But he stressed that viewers must recognize that "*Django* is not history. *Django* is not *Roots*... *Roots* is the story of a history of a country" (Obie 2013). In naming *Roots* as a definitive depiction of the nation's past, Burton expresses the extent of *Roots'* influence. And yet by way of critique, Tarantino expressed just some of the parameters within which *Roots* may (and may not) portray America's social realities.

In conversation with the scholarly working group, Culture on the Edge, this volume revisits the legacy of Alex Haley to investigate the nuances of cultural formation. It identifies the sign "roots" as a signifier not only of "cultural agreeability," but more poignantly the "masking and concealing of the competing interests and con-sensus-building that ultimately determine(s) what such a term will come to signify and be represented by" (Miller 2015: 10). At stake is our very understanding of the politics of "culturalism," the devel-opment, deployment, and enforcement of essentialized, social self-understandings (Bayart 2005: xii). This case study explores how and why post-civil-rights Americans have used *Roots* to position themselves in relation to historiography, origins, and race. In so doing, it aims to provide a language for articulating how human beings put identities to work.

A Culture of "Operational Acts of Identification"

Jean-François Bayart's understanding of identity is a useful point of departure. Rather than taking "identity" as a static symbol that intrin-sically links people together, he observes human beings engaged in "operational acts of identification" (Bayart 2005: 92). Each of us is an ever-changing tally of identificatory acts conducted by ourselves and others. We arrive at our cultural positionality by factoring our agency within the physics of other people's social moves. Triggered by the untempered power of some acts (i.e. "culturalism"), Bayart challenges theorists to examine the "processes of forming cultural or political identities whose crystallization is often recent, and can in any case be dated with relative precision" instead of falling prey to unsub-stantiated claims about "the existence of identity-related divinities, the primordial identities, that imperturbably traverse the centuries, each provided with its own core of authenticity" (Bayart 2005: 85). The scholarly study of *Roots* must be more than a hagiography that rehearses a multimedia seven-generation family history that spanned the Transatlantic Slave Trade. My analysis strives to determine what gave purchase to the roots discourse for Haley and his captivated audience. This critical difference distinguishes my efforts from the more cautious efforts found in some postmodern scholarship.

For instance, Cultural Studies thinkers have warned of the limitations of the roots discourse for discussing human meaning-making. In their introduction to *Mapping the Subject: Geographies of Cultural Transformation*, Steve Pile and Nigel Thrift suggest that "the ethnic absolutism of 'root' metaphors, fixed in place, [might be] replaced by mobile 'route' metaphors which lay down a challenge to the fixed identities of 'cultural insiderism,' [with] metaphors like diaspora" (1995: 10). They are concerned that the root metaphor may reify the very hegemonic regimes that the disenfranchised seek to critique. Thus "routing" offers a furtive reminder that the meaning-making of the colonized and colonizer are but variations on a theme. But literary critic Helen Taylor rightly rejoins that:

> this all makes sense, until one focuses on Haley's *Roots*, the post-war, postcolonial text that most successfully foregrounded the historical struggles and present dilemmas of African Americans and—by analogy—displaced and rootless Blacks everywhere.

She explains that *Roots* was not simply a description of "hybrid exchanges" but an explanation of "diasporic people's loss of and need for origins" founded in the "routes of one man and indeed one man," Haley himself (H. Taylor 2001: 67). Thus the critical study of *Roots* can and should contribute to theorizing about humans' audacious and conspicuous attempts to make meaning.

Bayart would add that the surrounding politics are not accidental but integral to our data set. Hybridity is a cultural default mode, not an exception to sociological rules. The rhetoric of rootedness is an example of "the complex relations between political action and cultural repertoires created precisely in the darkness of these muddy waters that all the ethnic cleansing in the world will never make clear" (Bayart 2005: 109). At the same time, such edgy cultural productions are what bring the politics of identity into view. Rather than commending certain expressions of Blackness, Americanness, or rootedness, this book will inventory the "maximalist" claims and discursive violence that result from these expressions (Lincoln 2006: 5). The challenge is working through both the nostalgia (e.g. Senator Alexander) and vitriol (e.g. Tarantino) that efface *Roots'* constructedness. When we do so, we will realize that identity politics is not just the rhetoric of minoritized groups, but rather an assertion of value in the face of those whose normalcy is, by comparison, usually discredited (The Combahee River Collective 1977). It is a contest over the difference that difference makes and thus the root of cultural formation.

The political history of religion provides a precedent for such deconstruction. Hence, Bayart frames the "cultural heterogeneity of political societies" as "'discursive genres' of politics, limited in number, but which are in theory irreducible to one another." For him, "a discursive genre corresponds to a relatively stable form of more or less homogenous utterances, for example, statements of the Islamic, Christian, Hindu, Confucian, nationalist, liberal, or Marxist-Leninist types" (Bayart 2005: 110). But these examples are not pure holistic structures that naturally exist as self-evident entities. They are complicated amalgamations of prior human engagements, scavenged to create something useful for knowing and being understood. The elite are those who can envelop their spheres of influence within mythologies that narrate their totalizing aspirations—all the while covering over the complexity of the hybrid pasts of which we are all products. They are the ones who communicate purpose and certainty in a mysterious world. Daunting as it may be to realize that "the irreducible diversity of discursive genres is the foundation of the heterology constitutive of every society," religious studies can offer the scholar reprieve (Bayart 2005: 110). In DuBoisian terms, we can "peer back…through the thickening veil of wish and after-thought" because cultural productions of this scale come with cargo—notably the tawdry mess that are their canons (Du Bois 2007 [1920]: 8). Alex Haley's *Roots: The Saga of an American Family* is best understood in this tradition.

Prolific cultures (i.e. world religions, nation-states, diasporic communities) employ a wide range of media to express their will across social strata, but canons make those attempts palpable. Canons, or what Bayart calls "cultural repertories...are not limited to explicit discourses, whether oral or written, but extend to the modes of communication, for example, gestures, music, and clothing" (Bayart 2005: 111). What unites their diversity is not some phenomenology or universally-recognized set of meanings, but participants' mutual use of them to recognize those within and outside of cultural boundaries. To some extent, these operationalized acts of identification limit, or at least prioritize, the "heterology" of social activity, but the meaning-making possibilities remain vast. Hence, Jonathan Z. Smith maintains that:

> ...it is possible to predict the *necessary* occurrence of a herme-neute, of an interpreter whose task it is continually to extend the domain of the closed canon over anything that is known or everything *without* altering the canon in the process. It is within the canon and its hemeneutes that we encounter the necessary obsession with exegetical totalization. (1982: 48)

This semiological maintenance gilds the "strategic syncretism" of identity formation with the aura of uniformity (Bayart 2005: 86). Where some have no problem working from the assumption of a single unmediated Africana "cultural identity," ethnographer Velma Love provokes theorists to survey a variegated "cultural landscape" that includes "African," "colored," "negro," "Black," Afro-American, and African American lives. In so doing, we might reveal the "diverse and intense efforts" behind each (per)mutation (Love 2013: 87). Guile cultural exegetes like Alex Haley see to it that to do so, we must tangle with their take on roots.

So beyond friendship and political intrigue, part of why Lamar Alexander quoted Alex Haley was because *Roots* is so enmeshed in the canonical narrative of America that its brazen exemplar is now commonplace. To borrow from philosopher Jacques Rancière, *Roots* distills America into a comprehensible "sentence-image" (2007: 45). It presents a convenient "montage" whose *"mimesis"* of integrationist ideals finds power not in its reproduction of what the nation has been, "but of a certain codification and distribution of resemblances" to the ways Americans identify with the nation (Rancière 2007: 104). To critically identify rootedness is to underscore the modalities of American cultural formation. I liken this endeavor to Rancière's description of art criticism:

> Erasing the genealogy that renders our "images" material and conceivable; erasing the characteristics that lead to something in our time being experienced by us as art, as to keep photography free of all art—such is the rather heavy price to be paid for the desire to liberate the pleasure of images from the sway of semiology. (2007: 80)

On this score, Alex Haley's *Roots* has held captive the American imagination in two elusive and interrelated ways.

First, beyond books sales, Nielsen ratings, and other metrics, *Roots* tapped into the core of certain principles about American identity. At the zenith of Haley's Comet, *TIME* journalist William Marmon asked readers "Why *Roots* hit home," answering the rhetorical question with Louis Armstrong's reply to those seeking a definition of Jazz, "If you have to ask, I can't tell you" (Marmon 1977: 69). Nevertheless, Marmon sought answers from a range of intellectuals to speak to the *je ne sais quoi* of America's *Roots*. S. Allen Counter, a Black neurophysiologist and founder of the Harvard Foundation for Intercultural and Race Relations, opined, "It sounded like us, it looked like us, it was us. We've always wanted Whites to understand how our backgrounds are different from theirs. Now they should understand a little better where we are coming from" (Marmon 1977: 71). John Callahan, an esteemed literary scholar at Lewis and Clark College, spoke for White people saying, "We now know our roots are inextricably bound with the roots of Blacks and cannot be separated" (Marmon 1977: 70). Such sentiments have led literary critic Helen Taylor and historian David Chioni Moore to respectively liken *Roots* to "a Black family Bible" and "a sacred text" (H. Taylor 1995: 45; Moore 1994: 198).

The scriptural analogy is evocative as it is mystifying and leads to my second concern. For despite *Roots'* massive popularity, it has conspicuously gone uninterrogated by academics. When Taylor began her research on *Roots* in 1995, "computer and library searches yielded a surprisingly small amount of published material on the subject" (1995: 54). Moore contends that this is not incidental. "The [scholarly] silence on *Roots* has resulted from a tangle of factors," notably the text's popular appeal, its blissfully integrationist themes and its dubious authorship, a complicated legacy to be further explored. He continues, stressing:

> These very factors, and *Roots'* situation on the "wrong end" of every one of them, makes *Roots* an important case study in American letters, on themes of fact and fiction, studies of the three "brows," and questions of originality, literary politics, the African American tradition, and to borrow Jane Thompson's influential phrase, the cultural work of American fiction. (Moore 1996: 198–99).

Robert J. Norrell's *Alex Haley and the Books That Changed a Nation* (2015) and Matthew F. Delmont's *Making Roots: A Nation Captivated* (2016) have since filled in much of the historical lacunae. *Reconsidering* Roots*: Race, Politics, and Memory* (2017), edited by Erica L. Ball and Kellie Carter Jackson, has also brought sophisticated reflections on the legacy it casts and is a part of. But what would it mean to theorize about the politics of *Roots* in light of the history of ideas, particularly the genealogy of privileged cultural texts? To scrutinize the fabrication of identity in the culturalist convention outlined by Bayart, we should similarly revisit the category of scriptures as an analytical root metaphor.

Before proceeding, a point of clarification is in order. Observing Alex Haley and scriptures should not be equated with a discussion of Alex Haley and texts. The latter, so far as it is focused on a medium of discourse, is but a facet of the former, which is interested in the very politics of discourse. For Wilfred Cantrell Smith, scriptures— or "scripturalizing," as he prefers—is "a human activity…a human propensity…a potentiality." Instead of an ontology of "scripture," he recommends that we perceive the phenomenon as "subsections of the ontology of our being persons" (W.C. Smith 1993: 237). That is to say, scriptures should be thought of anthropologically.

Scriptures in Process

The anthropology of scriptures is not limited to religion but takes interest more generally in identifiable products on the edge of cultural formation. During his 2008 presidential address to the Society of Biblical Literature (SBL), J.Z. Smith challenged the exceptionalism espoused—whether consciously or subconsciously—by professional biblical scholars (2009: 5). SBL and the American Academy of Religion (AAR) had ceased to hold cooperative and concurrent meetings—a fact he took as symptomatic of Western efforts to set apart biblical engagement from comparable phenomena associated with the "world's religions" and their texts. Having drawn upon W.C. Smith's concept of scripturalizing, a critical history of ethnography, and the occasion itself, J.Z. Smith advocated that "the trajectories of traditions, comparisons, [and] ethnographers [be] placed along more familiar aspects of biblical studies" (2009: 27). The theoretical framework of my project emerges from such a possibility.

The approach I am proposing here builds on what James A. Clifford calls the "cluster of disciplinary practices through which cultural worlds are represented" (1997: 8). The critical historian of anthropology is one among many who has taken issue with the "borders" that essentialist narratives erect, and calls for a study of "borderland[s]…zone[s] of contacts—blocked and permitted, policed and transgressive…highlight[ing] embodied activities in historically defined places" (1997: 8). The anthropology of scriptures is a commitment to map the very processes that efface their construction and advance their users' agendas. It asks us to call out what and why people are doing with their cultural master texts. Before us is the opportunity to assess what critical scriptures scholar Vincent L. Wimbush calls the "textures," gestures," and "power" being named (2008: 3). It is a challenge to inquire what Alex Haley can teach us about our operational acts of identification.

Gilles Deleuze and Felix Guattari's rhizome provides an instructive image for beginning to think about *Roots* as a sort of scripture and scriptures as roots. A rhizome is a system of ever-growing, underground branches that bud from the shoots of a tuber but is so dense that it appears to have no origin. The philosophers recognize that human meaning-making does not really look like the monolithic "root-book...[that] imitates the world, as art imitates nature: by procedures specific to it that accomplish what nature cannot or can no longer do" (1987 [1980]: 5). On the contrary, in scriptures, or the "root-book," we see a "radicals-system, or fascicular root... This time, the principal root has aborted, or its tip has been destroyed; an immediate, indefinite multiplicity of secondary roots grafts onto it and undergoes a flourishing development" (1987 [1980]: 5). Thus Deleuze and Guattari contend that signifying at-large resembles a dense, organic network of branches. "To be rhizomorphous is to produce stems and filaments that seem to be roots, or better yet connect with them by penetrating the trunk, but put them to strange new uses" (1987 [1980]: 15). While I am in agreement with Deleuze and Guattari about the rhizomorphic nature of meaning-making, the anthropology of scriptures can press the point even further.

Scriptures may indeed be yet another artifact of human signifying, but they reek of ambition and are far from benign. Pierre Bourdieu might have us recall that social practices like scripturalizing talk *around* social effects because to talk *about* them would appear unseemly, unnecessary, and even uncouth. But in going "undiscussed" and "undisputed," the practices become *routinized* (Bourdieu 1977: 168). Michel De Certeau highlights that "the scriptural enterprise" introduces a new sense of normal that disrupts previous notions of "everyday life" (1984: 135). My anthropology explores how and why some rhizomes grow so radically that they insist on their own centrality. Clifford discovered this for himself in his meditation on the ethnographic self in the Western socio-intellectual tradition:

> During the course of this work, *travel* emerged as an increasingly complex range of crossing and interaction that troubled the localism of many common assumptions about culture. In these assumptions authentic social existence is, or should be, centered in circumscribed places—like the gardens where the word "culture" derived its European meanings. Dwelling was understood to be the local ground of collective life, travel, a supplement; **roots always precede routes**. But what would happen, I began to ask, if travel were untethered, seen as a complex and pervasive spectrum of human experiences? Practices

of displacement might emerge as *constitutive* of cultural meanings rather than as their simple transfer or extension. The cultural effects of European expansionism, for example, could no longer be celebrated, or deplored, as a simple diffusion outward—of civilization, industry, science, or capital... And is not this interactive process relevant, in varying degrees, to any local, national, or regional domain? Virtually everywhere one looks, the processes of human involvement and encounter are long-established and complex. Cultural centers, discrete regions and territories, do not exist prior to contacts, but are sustained through them, appropriating and disciplining the restless movements of people and things (Clifford 1997: 3, emphasis added in bold).

For certain, a critical study of Alex Haley's *Roots* should observe the text as an expression of routing. It may even be argued to exemplify what Paul Gilroy describes as "the stereophonic, bilingual, or bifocal forms originated by, but no longer the exclusive property of, Blacks dispersed within the structures of feeling, producing, communicating, and remembering" (1993: 3). But more than this, it is an occasion to ask how and why roots seem to precede routes. What are the social "technologies" and "instruments" used to make knowing one's roots the dividing line between "the ruler" and "the unruly" (Sheth 2009: 26)? We must ask this question because, anthropologically speaking, well-worn routes appear to have a way of "seducing" readers into projecting primacy, ultimacy, and normalcy on cultural texts despite the evidence of the texts' constructedness (Cole 2005: 33). To identify *Roots* as a sort of scripture is to register the work that makes it not just another text. It is to understand how and why it is not simply a story people read, but a story that *seems* to read readers back.

Making Roots Work

Thus we can critically read American immigration history—or better put, the history of American assimilation—to better understand rootwork. In this cultural field we see roots rhetoric deployed to name facets of the process. For our purposes, they not only express the ramifications of identifying what roots do, but also prompt theorists to consider who is using roots to identify whom. Through a grounded theory approach, we can critically observe three operational acts of identification that happen around what some might call scriptures or roots: *uprooting, routing,* and *taking root.*

Uprooting entails one party's displacement of another. Emigration, according to Oscar Handlin, follows from the forced removal from a location where one was more firmly rooted (1973 [1951]: 34). The harrowing circumstances of the present are intrinsically linked not to home as it were but home as veiled in nostalgia. Most notably missing is the cultural trellis that made home at all tenable. In his classic, *The Uprooted*, Handlin describes the experience as:

> ...a history of alienation and its consequences...for emigration had stripped away the veneer that in more stable situations concealed the underlying nature of the social structure. Without the whole complex of institutions and social patterns which formerly guided their actions, these people became incapable of evading decisions.
>
> Under such circumstances, every act was crucial, the product of conscious weighing of alternatives, never simple conformity to an habitual pattern. No man could escape choices that involved, day after day, an evaluation of his goals, of the meaning of his existence, and of the purpose of the social forms and institutions that surrounded him. (5–6)

Writing in 1951, Handlin was comfortable arguing that the experience of nineteenth-century European émigrés "was more complex than that of eighteenth-century Negroes" (5). Rather than rehearsing expansive literature to the contrary or presenting a synthesizing qualification (Hahn 2005 [2003]; Long 2004 [1986]; Wilkerson 2010; Simmons 2014), it is more crucial for us to recognize how Haley might respond to such a claim.

Haley indicts White people—whom "the African" calls the *toubob* or White specter—for the uprooting of his ancestral patriarch (2007 [1976]: 27). It is the early modern West's emerging national appetites —and the "White men's magic" of Enlightenment erudition—that invites, incites, and energizes their election to identify another as free for the taking (Wimbush 2012). Under that gaze, "I think, therefore I am" is a privilege Black people have no time to enjoy. The disorientation has robbed them of everything but the forlorn hope that requires them to assess the very meaning of being. But Haley postulates that human beings are too resourceful for life to ever remain so dire. On this account, his family are virtuosi with the knowledge to find roots, ever ready to share their gift with those who would listen.

Routing underscores the meandering characteristic of those negotiating with the liminality of a scenario. As previously considered, the journey toward rootedness involves an inordinate amount of ambivalence. The very agency of the uprooted happens in tandem with those more firmly planted in a habitus (Bourdieu 1977: 72). Stuart Hall's discussion of *routes* appreciates the complexity of these negotiations. And yet, speaking to the African diaspora, he elaborates on the difficulty involved. "...Africa we must return to—but 'by another route': what Africa has *become* in the New World, what we have made of 'Africa': 'Africa'—as we re-tell it through politics, memory, and desire" (Hall 1990 [1979]: 232). For him, the desire for a place in the world appears integral to the human experience, hence the "symbolic journeys" toward rootedness.

Roots exemplifies routes so far as we recognize that the generational saga proffers an ethnic status in response to a racial void. It presents a vision of America into which Black people now wish to see themselves, often by negotiating a memory of Africa compatible with U.S. ideology. But the bi-part formation that is African American life should not be confused with a simplistic understanding of benign cultural acceptance. Crucial for Hall and Haley is the gravity of uprooting, for even the most articulate and impassioned Africana expressions (i.e. routing) take on a New World accent. "It was the uprooting of slavery and transportation and the insertion into the plantation economy (as well as the symbolic economy) of the Western world that 'unified' these peoples across their differences, in the same moment as it cut them off from direct access to their past" (Hall 1990 [1979]: 227). Put simply, the damage had already been done. Routing is the way in which one learns this and begins to deal with the consequences.

Taking root refers to the means by which the grief of uproot is overshadowed by the resolve to make a scenario work in one's favor. It is to actively engage in discourses whose net success brings a sense of being at home. Thus, in *The Transplanted*, John Bodnar contends that American emigrants did not simply assimilate by osmotic acculturation or parroting one particular politic. They endeavored to find themselves at sites exuding:

> ...the challenges of capitalism and modernity: the homeland, the neighborhood, the school, the workplace, the church, the family, and the fraternal hall. An array of leaders and orators offered solutions and life paths to deal with the overpowering reality of social changes. (Bodnar 1985: xvii)

After venerating or even becoming "gods of the metropolis" (Faucett 1944; Curtis and Sigler 2009), the rooted have made peace with otherwise disheartening and disorienting circumstances. Thus, Haley's story ends with the presumption that generational perseverance—as expressed through oral and written histories—enabled him to take root in America.

There are many questions to be asked about these all too familiar identity politics. It is unclear whether Haley ever entertained the notion that Kunta Kinte might not claim him back. Haley could be like the Antillean of Frantz Fanon's musing, whose time at the metropole makes him increasingly less interested in the culture of his birth, less intelligible to his kin, and less likely to relinquish his newfound status (Fanon 2008 [1952]: 185–97). The thought experiment is moot because Haley has the last word on naming what it means to have roots. So whereas *routing* expresses the *uprooted*'s search for these sites of validation, *taking root* signifies a feeling of control over them.

A Tone Poem and a Mood

Identifying Roots presents a cultural history of Alex Haley's work as a tone poem in operational acts of identification. More than a solitary narrative, Haley's *Roots* is an extrapolation of a modern mood, a riff on the need to be culturally relevant. My case study examines the strategies and tactics Haley employed in developing a family origin story into an acclaimed national history. This book reframes the concept of "roots" as a heuristic around which we can construct what I call an anthropology of scriptures—a vocabulary and grammar for elaborating the nuances of identity. Roots becomes a way of naming the living narratives through which humans know and in which humans are known. Ultimately their significance exceeds any one individual, including their authorities. And since they help us endure the human condition, we will do almost anything to protect them. For with roots we have a reason for being—a precedent with potential. Without them, our agency lies at the brink of erasure as some other person dares to write our history and our destiny for us.

Beyond naming the cultural developments that form and inform our social orders, we can parse the volatile politics subtending the operational acts of identification in terms of *uproot*, *routing*, and *taking root*. Rather than dismissing the analytical utility of rootedness, I present this vocabulary and grammar as first fruits borne of critically investigating identity formation in light of *Roots*. To be clear, the anthropology of scriptures is my attempt to articulate the dynamics of identity, especially around cultural texts, in a social setting.

My book intentionally uses a number of methods to further the literature on the social theorizing of identity. It is important to me that my arguments are intelligible and demonstrable to historians, literary critics, and students of society and culture. I aim to impress that one could theorize an anthropology of scriptures from any one of these intellectual field positions and that the academic study of religion has a contribution to make to the broader study of identity in the human sciences. Furthermore, I have penned this monograph such that readers need not read it in its entirety. When read with the introduction and conclusion, Chapters 1 and 2, Chapter 3, Chapter 4, and Chapter 5 can stand on their own as essays.

The first two chapters outline an intellectual biography of Alex Haley to highlight modernity's indenture to history and writing as meaning-making enterprises. Throughout his maturation and professional career, historiography becomes the primary avenue for navigating America's racialized terrain.

Chapter 1 situates Alex Haley within the modern West, and more specifically, the Black Atlantic. His formation in the tradition of Black uplift was reinforced by his family's relative wealth, education, and status. Specifically, Haley's interest in historiography—the writing of historical moments—aided his relative success with integration: first, as Chief Journalist for the United States Coast Guard during WWII; second, as a renowned reporter of iconic Black Americans during the Civil Rights Movement. Acclaim in these positions afforded him the opportunity to work collegially with White people in an era of high racial tensions.

This tension comes to the fore in his relationship with Malcolm X. While both Black men were striving to negotiate the legacy of Jim Crow, Haley's Southern, rural, and Christian integrationist sensibility stood in contrast to that of the urban, Muslim Black Nationalist's rhetoric. Nevertheless, their partnership was mutually beneficial. Haley's journalism connections and reputation gave Malcolm access to America's mainstream readership. In return, Haley witnessed the appeal of Malcolm's Afro-consciousness—a modern intellectual tendril that would be of later use in his own approach to racial politics. *The Autobiography of Malcolm X as Told to Alex Haley* (X and Haley 1999 [1965]) epitomized their agreement that a richer testament to Black life could improve race relations in America.

Even so, this collaboration is a site of inter- and intra-racial contest. Haley used his editorial privilege to characterize Malcolm as a cautionary tale for those White people who rejected integration and those Black persons tempted by Black Nationalism. The premeditated murder of Malcolm X only furthered Haley's case, making the slain figure's story the perfect preface for an integrationist apology. In a novel preliminarily titled *Before This Anger*, Haley planned to recount his family's ability to negotiate racism though hard work and faith in the American Dream—contra the critiques leveled by people like Malcolm X. The coup de grâce to Malcolm X's lingering appeal would be certitude about ancestral roots, the "X-factor" that so many Black people lacked. Haley's own genealogical odyssey became a search for *Roots*. It presented historical proof of why his family was better (off) than so many others. Haley's contest and collegiality with

Malcolm X illustrate how identity formation never happens in isolation but within larger systems of identification.

Chapter 2 follows Haley's experimentation with harnessing historiography for more interested ends. *Before This Anger* would morph into a deliberately constructed American scripture that would solidify his own rootedness in post-civil-rights America. Though the massive volume would take him twelve years to write, the real intellectual labor lay in the lengths Haley went to credential his story with institutional bona fides. He appealed to anthropologist Jan Vansina, U.S. and British museums, the Gambian foreign ministry, and a supposed Mandinka *griot*, or oral historian, to justify his ancestral claim to a historicized Kunta Kinte, a young Mandinka man who was taken from The Gambia to the New World in 1767. Although *Roots* showcases personal insights (here expressed as familial knowledge) as the *sine qua non* of a prodigious life and lineage, Haley's method belies recognition that rootedness is a socially negotiated and curatorial matter.

What set Haley's claims apart was their reach beyond the traditional barons of history. For Black people, *Roots* was a version of a myth that elders had long spoken of but could seldom prove. Haley touted the ability to verify it. For White people, it reconciled America's love of freedom with the conspicuous presence of slavery's progeny. The nation could rest assured—with Haley's testimony—that "life, liberty, and the pursuit of happiness" were available to people on both sides of the color line. The televised miniseries captivated Black people and White people with its rehearsal of star-spangled commonplaces in a new African American vernacular. The best-selling novel and record-breaking television program entered more homes than the literati had ever dreamed. And the ensuing media spectacle insisted that subsequent tellings of American history would be conspicuous without some consideration of the African American experience.

Yet Haley's fame was marred by extraordinary controversy. The research trips and promotional lectures used to curry interest came at the expense of his own familial life. A costly divorce, alimony payments, and back taxes raised the stakes of his project. And after *Roots* became a multimedia phenomenon, professional historians, journalists, literary critics, and lawyers scrutinized Haley's claims. The national hero fell into authorial obscurity. But *Roots* was too entwined with America's post-racial triumph to be untangled; his history, too pivotal to be troubled by facts. *Roots* became an inspiration for monuments across the United States. In the challenges to his historiographic authority, we see the distinction of scriptures from mere texts. "Scriptures" names both the ends (i.e. rootedness) and means (i.e. *Roots*) of a cultural production so significant that its importance no longer rests in the liminality of specific authorship or originary material but in their very definition of how identity politics are further mediated.

Chapters 3 and 4 move beyond "the historical Haley" to theorize *Roots* as a meta-reflection on scriptures as sites of identity politics. Although Haley "vectors" the concept of rootedness through his bloodline, his diction finds precedent in the history of the roots discourse in the Black Atlantic and the broader West. Because of this purchase, his ludics can voice the intricate demands of modern identity formation (Folkert 1989: 170–9). Furthermore, the gravitas of his historiographic appeals increases the reward for dutiful readership—deep American roots.

The third chapter uses Close Reading to show *Roots: The Saga of an American Family* as Haley's description and prescription of how identity works in America. Haley, I argue, constructs *Roots* as a frame story that presents his understanding of identity (i.e. rootedness) as a solution to America's racial problems. He acknowledges that in the year of the novel's publication, 1976, *de jure* integration has yet to take place. This provides him a fortuitous opportunity to present himself as a consummate American who managed to realize the nation's promise. In the preface to his novel, he offers his *Roots* as a "birthday gift" to the bicentennial nation.

Within the novel proper, Haley leads readers through two cycles of rootwork. The first half of the book follows Kunta Kinte's *uproot* from Africa, his futile *routing* through America as a defeated runaway, and his *taking root* as a New World patriarch who passes on African traditions to his daughter, Kizzy. The second half of the novel goes through this cycle again with each verbal inflection personified by a descendant of Kunta Kinte. Kizzy is *uprooted* from her nuclear family and raped by her new slave-master. Their son, George *routes* through a biracial struggle wherein trusting his father leads to the rent of his own family. But George's son, Tom helps the family *take root* in the old ways passed on by Kizzy and Kunta—and eventually in the Reconstruction South. All along the way, readers join the characters in a search for agency through family history, conjure roots, the Quran, the Bible, newspapers, and other meaning-filled cultural texts (i.e. scriptures). Haley makes clear that prosperity is the result of reconnecting with one's "source-place," a lesson he reveals to have mastered on his own by the book's end (2007 [1976]: 439).

The fourth chapter demonstrates how Haley's audience took ownership of this lesson in earnest. Defining national identity in terms of genealogy and roots became increasingly commonplace in the years following Haley's Comet. Through *Roots*, Americans came to not only better understand rootedness as a core American value, but also as a dynamic dramatization of the American experience of assimilation. I contrast how twenty-first century artists make use of Kunta Kinte-laden imagery to narrate their own American success stories to the way African American youth in the late 1970s and '80s would comically ostracize deviants within the community by calling people "Kunta Kinte." Locating these and other appeals within the theoretical frameworks of critical scripture studies, I argue that Kunta Kinte has become "rootinized" in post-civil-rights America. The power of such references is not simply in their frequency (i.e. *routine* appearance), but in their proven utility for expressing the American experience—sometimes in ways beyond Haley's own intent.

To this point, I deploy a discourse analysis of "Kunta Kinte" allusions in African American television and films made between 1977 and 2016. Each clip is coded according to the category of *uprooting*, *routing*, and *taking root* in order to determine how these films use the character to move story and audience. With the help of critical humor theory, these categories further underscore how we can elaborate on operational acts of identification—in this particular case, inter- and intra-racial performance as mediated through appeals to Kunta Kinte. Haley's protagonist has a semantic range wide enough to express identifiable experiences of America as both dream and nightmare. Though Haley would hardly approve of the negative inflection, even this communicates an investment made in *Roots* as a shared cultural text. In further charting the dynamics of rootedness, the chapter provides a theoretical language for further parsing who is *uprooting* whom, among what concerns are people *routing*, and on what terms may people *take root*.

The final chapter of the book addresses scholarly resistance to theorizing about scriptures in terms of roots. Like Wilfred Cantwell Smith, many in religious studies appeal to rhetorics of transcendence as a quality that distinguishes scriptures from other influential cultural texts. This proves unsatisfying when transcendence is deconstructed or *deracinated* as the deep-seated resolve of people attempting to transcend perceived problems. And in post-civil-rights America, the limits of the sacred are perhaps no more apparent than in the visceral ramifications of racial discourse around religion.

In Chapter 5, I revisit how late twentieth and early twenty-first century minoritized theologians appealed to *Roots* to legitimate themselves and their intellectual production within guilds such as the American Academy of Religion and the Society of Biblical Literature. When they needed assistance in identifying themselves within the canonical texts, traditions, and thinkers in their field, they appealed to *Roots* to launch their critiques. I find parallels in the various American memorials that orient visitors around Haley's saga for a vision that transcends America's racial—and biblically-infused—realities. This ironic turn to the secular should remind scholars why—critically speaking—scriptures refer to rootwork rather than "holier than thou" cultural forms.

Moreover, I contend that were we to predicate "scriptures" on naturalistic understandings—rather than the "sui generis religion" predilections critiqued by Russell McCutcheon (1997)—we would better observe the ways marginalized communities read, write, and redact themselves within the tradition of their dominators to express agency. Refusal to examine "non-religious" examples only effaces the very rootwork (e.g. techniques, politics, contexts) that make a text into scripture. In separating scriptures from the notion of sacredness, critical scholars can better identify the moves people make with their texts.

Identifying Roots concludes with consideration of the Black Lives Matter debate at hand during the penning of the monograph. In a land where the phrase "All men are created equal" is written in its foundational documents, some Americans still find street protests, teach-ins, and balloted elections necessary to insist on their own worth. At the risk of dating my own theorizing, I hope that it gives you, the reader, some understanding of why I think an anthropology of scriptures can be of use.

Throughout the book, I employ "ethnographic autobiography" or a discretionary inventory of how my positionality colors the development of an argument, "turn[ing] the question" to issues of "know-how" (Wolcott 2005: 237). This should not be confused with autoethnography, where the "research not only has a role but is often the principal figure" in authorizing insights. Rather, I intend for my experiences to pique your curiosity about what might be at stake in the examples of *Roots* and the scriptures operating in your own personal history.

Insightful people have spilled blood and ink demonstrating the relative significance of cultural texts. This monograph is driven by the more foundational question of why human beings cannot help but follow specific cultural scripts. Even if rhizomes are the most accurate way to illustrate knowledge production, scholars must also grant that roots also signify liberties humans take to identify the value of constructs like order, difference, and meaning. But before we haphazardly champion some ideologies over others, we must first recognize that the language-games that irrigate our cultural fields also wet the slippery slope of our hellish potential. The anthropology of scriptures challenges us to question those things which seem to insist on their self-importance. With this critical discourse, I invite students of the human to identify people's unexamined grasping for roots in a rhizomatic world.

1 Identifying with Alex Haley "Before This Anger"

Scriptures are not intrinsically interesting. My own fascination with Alex Haley's *Roots* was born out of an ongoing realization about the importance of rootedness in modern America. Like Haley, I am a descendant of enslaved Africans, yet I came of age in a post-*Roots* world. Seemingly all my living elders had watched the miniseries in January 1977 and could tell me a tale about their journey to and around the screen. I saw the book on relatives' shelves. And though I am unsure of how many of my family members actually read the text, I knew its allure came not from it being beheld but for it being ever-present. Grade school taught me that Haley's story was my story—whether I wanted it to be or not. Entangled in all of this was a tacit agreement by nearly everyone I have known—especially those calling themselves African Americans—that few things are more meaningful than knowing one's roots. The absence of this knowledge was too dangerous to chance, for there might be a bewildering day when you need to be reminded of who you are and where you come from.

In 2010, the importance of knowing one's roots again made news when the state of Texas reissued birth certificates to African Americans dismayed by the classification, "Negroid." The state's decision followed the 15-year-long protest of Kathryn and Lloyd Patterson, whose son "was teased mercilessly" after "word got out to neighborhood kids that the race listed on the son's 1980 birth certificate was Negroid" ("Texas Birth Certificate" 2010). A spokesperson for the Texas Department of State Health Services had defended that "Negroid" was a bona fide classification until 1977, when federal standards mandated it be discontinued.[1] Texas agencies slowly complied, but birth records could not legally be changed. When the evening news featured the Pattersons' story, African American Houstonians took a second look at their birth certificates and took umbrage with the label. Their political mobilization pressured the state to revisit the policy, now amended to allow certificate revisions upon request.

The Pattersons won a battle in an epic war that shook Americans into consciousness. This conflict over a certifiable identity is about more than the Pattersons' frustration with state-sponsored racism. It is a birthpang of American integration. The nation's "mis-education" about the persistence of racism is not a matter of ignorance but an induced, erudite amnesia (Woodson 1990 [1933]). It is an addiction to a learned anesthetic that dulls the senses to the suffering of a designated other. Racism is taught, studied…mastered in America. And to learn anything contrary is an attack on the body politic. Robert Wald Sussman outlines the war's many theaters in *The Myth of Race: The Troubling Persistence of an Unscientific Idea* (2014):

> …[O]ver the past 500 years, we have been taught by an informal, mutually reinforcing consortium of intellectuals, politicians, statesman, business and economic leaders, and their books that human racial biology is real and that certain races are biologically better than others. "Negroid" was an Enlightenment-era taxonomy that provided the West the intellectual grounds for restricting inalienable rights according to racial qualifications and quantifications of humanity. (2–3)

Not until the twentieth century did the comparative project begin to recede from the scientific literature. For example, physical

---

1   In 1977, the Office of Management and Budget directed federal agencies to transition to the use of "<u>Black.</u> A person having origins in any of the Black racial groups of Africa" (Office of Management and Budget 1977). This is also the year when *Roots: The Miniseries* aired. Whether Haley's story was the root cause of the change in precedent is unclear. More importantly, *Roots* provided a post-facto rationale for the obsolescence of the label "Negroid" and the salience of African-interested identifiers, especially later preferred terms such as "Afro-American" and "African American."

anthropologist L.H. Dudley Buxton compared the cranial measurements of Australian Aborigines ("Australoid") and Africa's indigenous southern population (Negroid) to make sense of the diversity of the human species (1935). Even though his article in the journal *Anthropos* attempts objectivity in regard to social differences, his final comments nevertheless betray an optimism in the ethnocentric correlation between physical and cultural anthropologies.

> It is not within my province to attempt to correlate cultures, whether advanced or archaic, with physique. Naturally under most circumstances, especially where various forms of exogamy are practised (which actually means physical endogamy within the group) people of the same culture will tend to be of the same race. On the other hand culture can be transmitted independently of race, and race independently of culture, especially since the expansion of race usually consists of the gradual spreading of the dominant type over possibly a long period. (Buxton 1935: 350)

It is out of these nuanced and racialized potentialities that Buxton finds justification for his curiosity. "The light which the examination of man's physical form can throw on the ethnological problem is a debatable one. It is, however, of great importance to study every possible form of evidence in the hope that even data which at first seem remote, may eventually prove of value in the elucidation of ethnological problems" (Buxton 1935: 343). This is the modern science with which the West meaningfully and purposefully forgot Africa's humanity.

As of late, the American Anthropological Association (AAA) has worked to right this understanding of human origins. In 1997, the Executive Board of the AAA challenged the U.S. Office of Management and Budget to amend the race-based census categories to self-reported ethnic identity markers. "Historical research," they wrote, "has shown that the idea of 'race' has always carried more meanings than mere physical differences; indeed, physical variations in the human species have no meaning except the social ones that humans put on them" (American Anthropological Association 1997). State and local governments have similarly begun to untether themselves from antiquated nomenclature in an attempt to escape damning labels of prejudice.

Cultural critic Ta-Nehesi Coates pushes for a distinction between such deceptive placation and substantive social change. In the former:

> ...racism is rendered as the innocent daughter of Mother Nature, and one is left to deplore the Middle Passage or the Trail of Tears the way one deplores an earthquake, a tornado or any other phenomenon that can be cast as beyond the handiwork of men. But race is the child of racism, not the father. And the process of naming "the people" has never been a matter of genealogy or physiognomy so much as one of hierarchy. (2015: 7)

I came to a similar conclusion about "the ethnological problem" in pondering the word "Negroid" on my own birth certificate. I was haunted by the ease with which humans claim to know the world, the self, and the other. Upon seeing that word, I realized that my existence was ultimately defined by what people could most convincingly write about it. I now understood that I was connected to "the machinery of representation"; my identity, a "cybernetic" enterprise, the product of forces organic, material, and conceptual (De Certeau 1984: 146). I was not just situated in a hermeneutical circle whose dizzying effects could be ameliorated by private or personal rehearsal of my social location (Shklar 2004 [1986]: 657–8).[2] I found myself within a scriptural circle, and I would have to read and write my way out of it.

2   Judith N. Shklar questions the analytical utility of the hermeneutical circle concept on account that it assumes a chief "interpreter" or "an organizing and illuminating principle apart from him there at the core to be discovered" within the variety and creativity of human meaning-making (2004 [1986]: 657). It also presents a sense of arbitrary closure around that very meaning-making, contrary to the people's observable rhizomatic expressions. Shklar goes on to qualify that "[o]nly the Bible meets these conditions. It is the only possibly wholly self-sufficient text" (2004 [1986]: 658). She concludes that the hermeneutical circle may provide an unsettling "theory of explanation" for how scriptures (i.e. the Bible), the social sciences, and the natural sciences operate (2004 [1986]: 673). The anthropology of scriptures should be understood as a preliminary step in helping others accept that particular analytical challenge and how it extends to cultural phenomena like and beyond the Bible.

More honestly, this would be impossible. At most, I could only ever root around within its circumference because its originary roots, the rules of its radii were premised on "the credibility of discourse... To make people believe is to make them act. But by a curious circularity, the ability to make them act—to write and to machine bodies—is precisely what makes people believe" (De Certeau 1984: 148). Perhaps this is why the Pattersons were not satisfied with knowing their roots for themselves. They needed the neighborhood bullies, Houston's African American community, and the State of Texas to recognize them. The new birth certificates represent the Pattersons' relative success at making their own roots known while revealing their need to have that knowledge authorized by committee. Even still, the irony signals a scriptural "revolution," an "inversion" wherein the subjects of "the writing machine" become, on some level, operators (De Certeau 1984: 135).

Roots became of interest to me because it, too, brashly attempted to upheave America's ability to legislate cultural assumptions in terms of racism. Its pages convey Alex Haley's discovery of his situation within a scriptural economy and his identification of the discursive coin of the realm—historiography. Like those Texans identified as Negroid on their birth certificates, Haley came to regret his own mis-education about his identity. He repeatedly expresses his shame—before and after *Roots'* publication—of the defeating ideas he once took to be true. "It embarrasses me to say that up to that time [his trips to Africa] I really hadn't thought all that much about Africa. I knew where it was and I had the standard cliché images of it, the Tarzan Africa and stuff like that" (Haley 1973: 13). Shortly afterward in 1977, he elaborated:

> It embarrasses me to think how ignorant I was about the people and the culture of the earth's second-largest continent. Like most of us, Black and White, I formed my impressions of Africa and of Africans mostly from Tarzan movies, Jungle Jim comics and occasional gleanings through old copies of *National Geographic*. (Fisher: 1993 [1977]: 405)

Haley's juxtaposition of pulp fiction (i.e. Tarzan, Jungle Jim comics) and popular scholarship (i.e. *National Geographic*) highlights racism's link to a fetishizing of the primitive. Haley, too, experienced how printing certified the past and how "telling the origin of something often acts as a natural authorizing statement" (L.D. Smith 2013). By the same token, Haley believed he could craft a convincing historical narrative that would overturn one that had effectively drawn only a "fine line between Black people and anthropoid apes" (Blayney 1986). His iconic presentation of his ancestors' journey from slavery to emancipation would insist that the nation render the meaning of Black identity as rooted in a "civilized" Africa. If done successfully, his present and future would be altered in his favor. Haley could tell his story seemingly on his own terms. And as we will see in Chapter 2, he would nod to the genres of pulp fiction and popular scholarship to do so.

Haley's example helps us extend, if not sharpen, the conventional wisdom regarding oppositional identity formation. In 1984, theorist and activist Audre Lorde challenged second-wave feminists to consider how thoroughly their agenda had been enveloped within the definitively patriarchal assumptions of White supremacy and heteronormativity. In turn she recommended a broadening of consciousness-raising circles to include women of color and lesbian voices, for:

> within the interdependence of mutual (nondominant) differences lies that security which enables us to descend into the chaos of knowledge and return with true visions of our future, along with the concomitant power to effect those changes which can bring that future into being. (Lorde 2007 [1979]: 112)

Liberation could not happen by reliance on the status quo.

> Those of us who stand outside the circle of this society's definition of acceptable women; those of us who have been forged in the crucibles of difference—those of us who are poor, who are lesbians, who are Black, who are older—know that survival is not an academic skill. It is learning how to take our differences and make them strengths. *For the master's tools will never dismantle the master's house.* They may allow us temporarily to beat him at his own game but they will never enable us to bring about genuine change. And this fact is one threatening to those

women who still define the master's house as their only source
of support. (2007 [1979]: 112)

Lorde's admonition foregrounds how alternative attempts at identification are frequently indebted to normative tools and techniques. But
to more fully engage what she hints at here, we should also acknowledge the caveats to her description of being "outside the circle" of
acceptability. Bourdieu reminds us that those beyond the margins of
"orthodoxy" appear (cf. Gk. *doxa*, "to seem or appear") especially
marked by its sphere of influence. In effect, the heterodox covet at
least some of the orthodox's privileges and vie for it by audaciously
participating in comparison themselves (1977: 164).

Lorde's unashamed politics of "define and empower" do not
require her to tease out the replicative aspects of the master-slave dia-
lectic, but we must do so if we are to understand the roots of identity
formation. Rhizomatic operational acts of identification may be the
actuality, but those enveloped by the scriptural circle are moored in a
reality of roots, an economy of ineffable naming too costly to wholly
question. Wholesale investment in a roots discourse does not discount
one's appreciation of what came before. Monica Miller (2013) details
this in respect to origins:

> Seems to me that claims of origins always begets new discourses
> of origins on prior origins of which such origins are used in the
> present to create new claims of beginnings which in the future
> will be posited as "The" origin point for a new discourse on
> authenticity. Only until…a new (origin) narrative takes its place
> and the cycle begins again.

Human innovation is always indebted to the past, even the past of our
oppressors. That relationship and the obfuscations surrounding it are
our data.

The anthropologist of scriptures calls out the persons, productions,
and processes that cultivate certitude to the contrary. Given that this
is the site wherein agency is expressed, the scholar can never identify
people for who they are, but for whom they are being made out to
be. This first chapter chronicles Alex Haley's discovery of his place
within twentieth century America's scriptural circle. It introduces the

familial, socio-political, and economic institutions with which he bar-
ters to realize and revise his own self-understanding as Alex Haley. In
following his journey, we will observe his increasing recognition of
historiography as the genre of rootedness in his context and how he
used it to draft Malcolm X's biography into the prelude of a promised
personal and national salvation. Keyed into the optimism of the Black
uplift tradition and the desires subtending Black Nationalism, Haley
prophesied a way toward an integrated America life in a trip back to a
novel time that he initially titled *Before This Anger*, when Black people had the roots to withstand even the most horrific strife. This is the
story of a man who dared to identify roots on his own terms because
he knew all too well the terms with which he was being defined.

Palmer (1921–1939)

> Down at the W.E. Palmer Lumber Company, [Grandpa] would
> let me play around the big stacks of oak, cedar, pine, and hick-
> ory, all in planks of different lengths and widths, and with their
> mingling of good smells, and I would imagine myself involved
> in all kinds of exciting adventures, almost always in faraway
> times or places. (Haley 2007 [1976]: 855)

Family names make genealogies into pantheons. They bestow children a birthright to the accolades of heroic progenitors. However, the
inheritance is not simply received. It is to be lived, a next chapter
or further adventure already begun. In the starkest terms, the beneficence is a burden. The name is a reminder of one's indebtedness to
those before. A family name makes clear what is true for all persons:
one's story is never one's own.

Alexander Murray Palmer Haley was born on August 11, 1921 in
Ithaca, New York. His father, Simon Alexander Haley, was a Master's
student in the agriculture program at Cornell University. His mother,
Bertha George Haley (née Palmer), had studied piano at the Ithaca
Conservatory of Music (Haley 2007 [1976]: 852). In September of
1921, the young family traveled to Henning, Tennessee, Bertha's
hometown. Mother and son would remain with her parents while
Simon returned to Ithaca, NY to finish his studies. After receiving

his degree in 1922, Simon accepted a teaching post in Tennessee at nearby Lane College, a historically Black institution founded by the Christian Methodist Episcopal church where Simon and Bertha first met as undergraduates. The Haleys lived together until 1925 when Simon would continue his work, and Bertha and the baby would return to live with her parents (Haley 2007 [1976]: 854).

The extent to which these transitions affected the young Haley is unknown, but Henning provided the definitive comfort and stability of home. His maternal grandfather, Will, was the proprietor of the W.E. Palmer Lumber Company, the first Black-owned business in Lauderdale County (Haley 2007 [1976]: 847, 854; Norrell 2015: 2). His two-story, early twentieth century bungalow, known as "Palmer House," sheltered one of the most prominent Black families in West Tennessee. Simon and Bertha's wedding reception at Palmer House

Figure 1 Palmer House.
Source: Thomas R. Machnitzki, "Alex Haley House and Museum," *Wikipedia.* December 2007. https://en.wikipedia.org/wiki/Alex_Haley_House_and_Museum#/media/File:Henning_Alex_Haley_Home_and_Memorial.jpg, CC BY-SA 3.0.

had the distinction of having White people in attendance—a rare event given Tennessee's racial climate (Haley 2007 [1976]: 851). And Will treated his grandson as the son he never had, letting the boy have free reign playing in the lumberyard. Although Alex was named for Simon's father Alec, a sharecropper tilling the tortured fields left behind by Reconstruction, he was affectionately called "Palmer" by the Henning clan.

Will Palmer was one among an emerging Black professional class "that believed strongly in the importance of creating their own institutions. Foremost among these, of course, were churches and the Black-controlled denominations that linked them together" (Glenn 2011: 128). Bertha taught at the Palmer-Turner School, an all-Black grade school named in honor of Will Palmer and Carrier White Turner, a Fisk University graduate who began the first formal schooling program for Henning's Black community (Norrell 2015: 4–5).[3]

3   The Palmer-Turner School was founded in 1873 when Carrie White Turner came from Fisk to begin the school. It initially met at New Hope CME. In 1915, the Rosenwald Foundation provided a matching grant to raise funds for the construction of its own building for the Black school, an effort to which Will Palmer provided the first one hundred dollars. Chicken George was also instrumental in lauding education to Lauderdale County's Black youth ("Chicken George" 1977: 22). In 1950, a new and larger school was built (Staff Writer 1950). In 1974, the school was integrated and renamed Henning Elementary School ("Chicken George" 1977: 22).

In *Roots: The Next Generations*, viewers are introduced to Carrie Barden, who comes to Henning from Fisk at the behest of Haley's great-grandfather, Tom Murray. Carrie Barden marries a White man named Jim Warner, whose father was a Confederate colonel during the Civil War.

I am uncertain how true to life this portrayal is, but the narrative clearly pays homage to Carrie White Turner and plays into the larger integrationist theme of Haley's *Roots* agenda.

On the Tennessee genealogy website, *TNGenWeb*, a user by the screen name "Taneya," confirms that the show's Carrie Barden is based on Carrie White Turner and provides a family photograph of Jim and Carrie Turner along with an image from a 1940 census ledger with entries for Jim and Carrie Turner, Cynthia Palmer and Elizabeth Murray (both born in North Carolina). The information was shared by a descendant of the Turners named "Sharon," who confirms that Jim was indeed a White man (Taneya 2012).

The three-year-old Palmer accompanied his mother, "a common practice of Black teachers in West Tennessee." He was primed to take his place among the classically educated paragons that W.E.B. Du Bois called "the talented tenth" (Du Bois [1903] 2007). These were the "favored sons of the freedman" who would lead Black people to prosperity beyond the debilitating mapping of the color line. Their resolve came from:

> the very bottom of knowledge, down in the very depths of knowledge there where the roots of justice strike into the lowest soil of Truth. And so they did begin; they founded colleges, and up from the colleges shot normal schools, and out from the normal schools went teachers, and around the normal teachers clustered other teachers to teach the public schools. (Du Bois 2007 [1903]: 21)

Palmer (whom the country would later come to know as Alex Haley), was being groomed to cherish the university, that "human invention for the transmission of knowledge and culture from generation to generation through the training of quick minds and pure hearts" (Du Bois 2007 [1903]: 20). He was the beneficiary of those who had studied in its halls, fed its students, and chartered its development.

Life at Palmer House also marked the beginning of the young Haley's co-curricular education, a dichotomous experience divided between book learning and oral tradition. He listened eagerly to his Grandma Cynthia's (née Murray) recollections of days stretching back before emancipation (Shirley 2005: 20). Bertha did not share Palmer's love of these "colorful stories." In childhood, she reluctantly endured them (Norrell 2015: 8). But as she matured, she developed an aversion to her parents' talk of slavery days and, what she considered to be, the droning sounds of their folk dialect. Haley recalled his mother exclaiming, "I'm sick of all that old-timey stuff!" whenever Cynthia's stories would begin (Haley 2007 [1976]: 856). In adulthood, Haley would opine:

> She was the first person in our family who ever went to college. You see it in every poor immigrant group that's come to this country; the first thing its members want to do as they begin to make it is to forget their homeland—its traditions and its

culture—and to fit in with the new one. Momma wanted nothin'
to do with no Africans, and even less with slaves; she was
embarrassed by all that. (Fisher 1993 [1977]: 396–7)

Haley's parents championed college as a primary means of "Black
uplift," particularly a twentieth century version of the ideology that
correlated Black people's social status in America with a rise in class
and the amassing of cultured prestige (e.g. education, professional
titles, "proper speech"). This "higher education," it seemed, had
tutored Bertha to privilege book learning, even if at the expense of
other manners of knowing and expressing agency.

Despite Bertha's apologetics, her parents should be recognized as
subscribing to the same underlying politics. After all, they owned and
operated one of Henning's central businesses, helped start a school for
local Black children, and sent their daughter to college. The infight-
ing represents differences in the sites where Bertha and her parents
developed their understanding of Black uplift. Historian Kevin M.
Gaines explains:

> Popular meanings of uplift, *rooted* in public education, eco-
> nomic rights, group resistance and struggle, and democracy tend
> to be absent in those records in which Black elites espoused
> bourgeois values of race progress in several settings: in the pul-
> pit, at academic "Negro" conferences held at Black colleges…
> (1996: 3, emphasis added)

Bertha's historical memory developed in the latter settings that
Gaines outlines. Her parents, however, were of the generation whose
efforts erected those spaces—efforts inspired by their parents' first-
hand accounts of slavery. This is not to say that Bertha was unaware
of this history. Rather, Bertha believed that in moving on, Black people could move forward.

Alex Haley recollects having a long-standing appreciation for both
knowledge bound in books and found beyond them. For his fourth
birthday, his parents and grandparents gave him a slice of a redwood
tree. His father explained how its concentric tree rings marked a
year's time. Already on the tree stood pins to mark events like the
Emancipation Proclamation, the Civil War, the birth dates of famous

Black Americans as well as those of various relatives. The family encouraged Palmer to mark other events he deemed important. "From then on," he later said, "I read every book I could handle" in search of significant moments (Haley 1983: 64). Immersing himself in others' stories would become one of the primary ways he tackled the drama in his own life. In 1926, Will Palmer died from a heart attack. Traumatized by the sight of his grandfather's death, Palmer required medication. He would later recall, "I was so hysterical that Dr. Dillard had to give me a glass of something milky to make me sleep that night" (Haley 2007 [1976]: 855). Simon returned to Henning to handle Will Palmer's debts, eventually selling the lumberyard where Alex had often played. When Simon resumed teaching, he took the Haley family on an odyssey from a teaching post in Langston, OK, back to Cornell for a master's degree, and on to a professorship at A&M College in Normal, AL (Norrell 2015: 10).[4]

All along the way, intermittent ailments took their toll on Alex's mother. In 1931 and at the young age of 36, Bertha Haley died of tuberculosis. (Haley 2007 [1976]: 849, 860) She was buried in Henning and survived by Simon, a ten-year-old Alex, and his younger brothers, George (b. 1925) and Julius (b. 1929 or 1930).[5] Simon's mother, Queen, would move to Normal, to help care for the children. Biographer Anne Romaine remarked:

> ...on those occasions later in life when [Haley] reflected on his childhood, his memory always seemed to be more sharply focused on the events in the lives of those around him than on his own youthful adventures. About his own immediate family, Haley, rarely short of words, dislikes to talk about this period.[6] (Romaine 1.56—Alex Haley Book Draft: 25)

4   Norrell notes that local White people referred to Normal, AL's A&M College as "Nigger Normal," adjoining the racial slur to the name of the town and the designation for a teaching college (2015: 10).

5   Haley lists Julius's birth year as 1929 (Haley *Roots* 2007 [1976]: 860). But Julius's obituary records the date of birth as December 5, 1930 ("Julius Haley Obituary" 2010).

6   Haley's reserve is intimated in a variety of accounts (Haley 2007 [1976]: 860; Norrell 2015: 14).

As an adult, Haley would refer to Palmer House as his "boyhood home." As he went into adolescence and away from Henning, the propriety of university-informed Black uplift remained a constant in Haley's otherwise tumultuous life.

In 1933, Simon married his colleague, Zeona Hatcher (Haley 2007 [1976]: 860). She was a harsh taskmaster according to Palmer's brother George—punishing the children by sending them to their rooms and having them memorize chapters from the Bible (Romaine 1.53—Book Proposal for Alex Haley's Biography: 16). Zeona and Simon had a daughter, Lois, within a year of their marriage. In 1936, the family followed Simon to A&M College in Larmon, MS, and then to Elizabeth City Teacher's College in North Carolina. The Haleys would frequently provide board to Simon's young, Black mentees. Still, the presence of family members and students did little to fill the void Bertha left in Alex's home life. Doreen Gonzales adds that "[t]hough Alex never spoke of it publicly, Julius recalled times when Zeona taught at one school and Simon at another. During these periods the family would be broken apart" (1994: 27).

Palmer House took on even more importance in these difficult formative years. After Will Palmer died in 1926, Grandma Cynthia's older sisters made a tradition of gathering at Palmer House and swapping stories on the porch (Haley 2007: 856). Their corporate memory of family history, Haley later recalled, was much more vivid than what the youngest Cynthia could remember on her own. When Palmer would visit Henning on vacations, he heard about his great-grandfather, the hardworking Tom Murray and Tom's father, a cockfighter and yarn-spinner named Chicken George.

What other memories the matriarchs were able to summon is unclear. Hagiography on Haley places great confidence in the author's later dramatized account of his origins. *Roots* and published accounts following its publication have the women recalling his forebears with stunning detail (Haley 1972: 13; 2007 [1974]: 86–8; 2007 [1976]: 859–60). Chicken George's mother was named Kizzy.[7] And her father

---

7   In Anne Romaine's biographical notes on Alex Haley, she explains that not only did Bertha "discourage Alex from listening to their stories," the stories were not all positive. Tom Murray was commended. Their mother,

was the family's "furthest-back person," an ancestor they called "the African."[8] He had landed at the American port of "Naplis," and though his slave name was "Toby," generations remembered his true name as "Kin-tay." As will be discussed in Chapter 2, Haley used these clues to rediscover Kunta Kinte's provenance in a mid-eighteenth century Mandinka village in The Gambia. All of these ancestors seemed mythic to Haley, he wrote, like characters from the Sunday School stories he heard at Henning's New Hope CME Church (Haley 1972: 13; Fisher 1993 [1977]: 397). Historical critics have questioned the precision of this account. In other pre-*Roots* dispatches, he said that the women referred to their furthest-back person as "the Mandingo," indicative of tribal roots that would not need to be discovered (Haley 1965, cited in Delmont 2016: 25).

    The mark of fabrication we call consistency is a curious technique for impressing the notion of a stable sense of identity.[9] The question is what did "the African" enable Haley to do that "the Mandingo" could not. Contextually, "Mandingo" already had a loaded place in the mid-twentieth century zeitgeist, thanks to popular antebellum adventures like Kyle Onstott's 1957 *The Mandingo* (which gave way to the titular figure's afterlives in the genre of Blaxploitation). It also had lexical usage in the cataloguing of African peoples by Western scholars. The 1911 *Encyclopedia Britannica* contributor Frank Richardson Cana derides the term as a "corruption" of the word used by West African Mande people whom he has heard refer to themselves as "Mandiña," or even "Madiña" (Cana 1911). Maybe Haley simply

---

whom she lists as "Arrena," was spoken of in "glowing terms." Chicken George, however was derided as "just scandalous" (Romaine, 1.53—Book Proposal for Alex Haley's Biography: 16).

    8 In *Roots*, Haley actually refers to the ancestor as the "farthest-back person" (2007 [1976]: 857). However in an earlier article, he describes Kunta Kinte as his "furthest-back person" (Haley 1972: 12). The difference may be a conflation of the near-homophones, the prior dealing with distance and then after with time. Or it may indicate a conceptual change in traversing geography versus history.

    9 For theorizing on the concept of fabrication and social construction, see Russell T. McCutcheon's edited volume *Fabricating Identities* (2017).

forgot the matriarchs' favored designation or maybe he scaled back the specificity of his matriarchs' memory in order to soften the ground for his own journey to find Kunta Kinte.

The shift is significant in what it discursively achieves. In eventually distancing his perfected knowledge (i.e. "the African," the Mandinka, Kunta Kinte) from the matriarchs' (i.e. "the Mandingo"), Haley established an "aura" around this knowledge that attaches rather than "detaches the reproduced object from the domain of tradition" (Benjamin 1936). Whatever was recovered on the porch symbolized an authentic intelligence—worn by a historical distress and imperfect memory. The elder women embodied this in a manner made all the more clear when contrasted with the smoothness of the emerging class of elite Black intellectuals in whose literature and institutions Palmer was being tutored.

Whether Palmer was at home on vacation in Henning or in itinerant residence at one of the historically Black colleges where Simon taught, the family was grooming him to make good on the investment of heroes from bygone eras. Simon hoped at least one of his sons might take a PhD and become a college president (McGuire and Clayton 1977: 47). Palmer undertook the standard battery of math, English, history, and geography, but Simon also insisted he learned to type—a skill the professor insisted would be of future importance (Haley 2007 [1976]: 860). According to biographer Anne Romaine, he cut his teeth on the works of Paul Lawrence Dunbar, W.E.B. Du Bois, and Booker T. Washington (Romaine 1.53—Book Proposal for Alex Haley's Biography: 14). His father had introduced him and his brothers to the prolific George Washington Carver in hopes that the scientist might enkindle their own prodigy (Haley 2007 [1976]: 886; Norrell 2015: 12).[10] Simon preached that education was "the key to improving the circumstances of the race" (Glenn 2011: 137).[11] In

10 In *Roots,* Haley recalls meeting George Washington Carver. Norrell indicates that Simon drove Palmer to Tuskegee to meet him, but it is unclear that a connection was indeed made.

11 Haley commends education to African Americans as a way to honor the ancestors (Haley 1990 [1986]: 134, 138, 140). Norrell's biography of Palmer's early years presents education as a central theme in his upbringing (2015: 1–16).

Haley's autobiographic reconstruction, we witness him building up a canon of inspiration. For the student of scriptures its importance is less in whether his reporting is an accurate inventory of what he actually read and more as an account of how he perceived the world would read him. He needed a useable past, and these are the works he was supposed to be reading. The stories from the porch were about "car[ing] where you come from," as Cynthia would say (Fisher 1993 [1977]: 396). But Simon's teaching was about progress, and he wanted to be duly certain that Alex would have the credentials to join the Black professional class.

Palmer may have been more taken with the stories from the porch, but he could not escape the crucible of a more formalized approach to Black uplift. Simon's firstborn was not without aptitude, but his ambivalence toward institutional education led him elsewhere. In 1936, Palmer finished high school at A&M Normal College two years early, though he did so with a "C" average (Haley 1990 [1986]: 154, 156; Romaine 1.53—Book Proposal for Alex Haley's Biography: 17). He entered college at the age of 15, but, to the chagrin of his father, dropped out two years later. In a 1976 interview with *The Black Scholar*, he admitted to coasting through classes, "generally sitting up there seeing my own little fantasies in my mind's eye. I was 15 when I went into college and this was simply because my father's life and soul was education" (Allen 1976: 33). Hoping the military would ground him, Simon required his adventure-minded "daydreamer" to enlist (Allen 1976: 33). A veteran of the First World War, Simon knew the demands of the service and its proclivity to dispense a concentrated dose of reality to early twentieth century Black youth.

To be sure, the armed forces were enticing. They enabled many to travel and see other social worlds with different (sometimes, more amenable) rules than home. Their fraternity lent servicemen a surrogate family in lieu of the ones from which they were separated, whether because of the call of duty, or some other post-Emancipation sojourn. And they promised the opportunity for meritorious advancement. Simon figured that the segregated organizational structure, the stark command hierarchy, and the arduous tasks would teach Palmer that life's benefits are hard fought, perhaps even more so than in civilian life. In 1939, Palmer joined the United States Coast Guard, whose major selling point was its abbreviated enlistment contract. Whereas the other branches demanded four years of service from their recruits, the Coast Guard required a shorter, three-year stint (Allen 1976: 35). In total, he would spend twenty years in the United States Coast Guard (USCG) and never return to college. He would also take key steps to becoming the Alex Haley the nation would identify as their own.

This was the story of a boy obliged to family, education, and Black uplift. To borrow from Foucault, Palmer was "doomed historically to history, to the patient construction of discourses about discourses, and to the task of hearing what has already been said" (Foucault 1994 [1963]: xvi). Like his father Simon, he could devote himself to the halls of Black academe, even eschewing the folksy ways of his elders as Bertha did. He could lose himself in the tales of his grandmother Cynthia Palmer Murray, just as he let fly his imagination within the lumberyard of his grandfather Will Palmer. Even in his escape to a new world, that of the military, he was following in the footsteps of his veteran father. These roots defined his reality. For all of Palmer's recalcitrance, his formation reflected an ambivalence between a set of bound terms: becoming a man of letters or a man with a story to tell.

Chief Journalist Alex Haley, USCG (1939–1959)

Informed by a Black folk-aristocratic family's mores and a racialized set of great expectations, Alex Haley struggled to find a sense of freedom. That the adolescent sought liberation within the strictures of military life brings his wanderlust into relief. However, later in life, Haley spoke fondly of his time in the U.S. Coast Guard saying, "You don't spend twenty years of your life in the service and not have a warm, nostalgic feeling left in you… It's a small service, and there's a lot of esprit de corps" (United States Coast Guard 2016). In 1999, the Coast Guard would posthumously christen a ship in his honor, the *USCGC Alex Haley*. One personal effect made all the difference in his maritime service: his typewriter. Haley used writing to advance his station in ways that race otherwise hindered.

Despite the uniformity demanded in military service, racial stratification shaded the ranks from enlistment to leadership. As WWII historian Andrew E. Kernstein observes:

> [a]lthough Blacks had served valiantly in all American conflicts from the Revolution to the First World War, the War Department systematically discriminated against them. In 1939, African American participation in the army was at a nadir.... The navy was even worse. African Americans could only enlist to work in the galleys. The Coast Guard's racial policies were slightly more enlightened and were far more liberal than the Marines and the Army Air Corps, which prior to the Second World War did not allow any Blacks to serve. (2002: 15)

Like the majority of Black sailors and Coast Guardsmen of the time, Haley would have to start in menial service positions, holding the rating of Mess Attendant, Third Class. Yet hardship did not deter him. Haley established himself as a valued comrade.

Ironically, Haley's success came in large part from the writing and typing skills that he fostered at the behest of his father. Regarding his early tours, Haley would say that his most cunning enemy was "boredom," which he combatted by reading all the books available at his post (Allen 1976: 35–6). To the annoyance of his sleeping shipmates, he would spend nights typing letters to family, friends, and women they met while in port. Derision turned to envy as Haley received more and more mail.

With some of his letters, he courted a young woman named Nannie Branch, whom he had met at a church dance while at a North Carolina port. They met and married in 1941 while Haley was on shore leave (McCauley 1983: 28; Delmont 2016: 13). Crewmates solicited him to ghostwrite in hopes that Haley's good fortune would rub off. His social and financial success as a "Cyrano De Bergerac" tempted him to try his hand at writing stories for pulp magazines such as *True Confessions* and *Modern Romances* (Allen 1976: 35–6). These were the first in a long line of rejections he would receive from popular press outlets. But Haley would remain enchanted with the typewriter. In *Roots*, he reminisces, "the idea that one could roll a blank sheet of paper into a typewriter and write something on it that other people would care to read challenged, intrigued, exhilarated me—and does to this day" (Haley 2007 [1976]: 861).

Japan's December 7, 1941 attack on Pearl Harbor thrust Haley into World War II and deeper into the throes of writing. He spent 1941–1942 patrolling the Atlantic seaboard. In 1943, he was assigned to the *USS Murzim*, a cutter with the dangerous task of transporting munitions throughout the Pacific Theater (Norrell 2015: 20). On January 29, 1945, its sister ship, the *USS Serpens*, had exploded at Guadalcanal after a cargo loading mishap (United States Coast Guard 2016). Maritime tragedies like these enthralled Americans, both at home and on the front, who struggled to understand how their world was changing. This gave Haley a captive audience. In addition to starting an on-ship newsletter called the *Seafarer*, Haley wrote for numerous official Coast Guard publications. One of his editorials, entitled "Mail Call," discussed the low morale among servicemen who had yet to receive mail from their loved ones. Newspapers across the country reprinted the article as part of the war effort (McCauley 1983: 33; Norrell 2015: 23–4). Haley's ability to convey the Coast Guardsmen's experience and desires made him a relatable figure to his crewmates, Black and White.

Although Haley was conscious of race's imbrication in the US military, he identified it as second to the interracial Americanism he had seen aboard the *Murzim*. WWII had redrawn the lines between friend and foe in broad, international strokes. The nation was united in seeking the welfare of its government-issue protectors. Civil rights organization the National Association for the Advancement of Colored People (NAACP) had sincere doubts that jingoism could overwrite an insurmountable culture of segregation. Haley disagreed, sending his perspective to Walter White, the Executive Secretary of the NAACP in 1943. Steward, First Class Haley postulated that prejudice could not be overcome by the "the new colored man" unwilling to work his way up from the lowliest of jobs, nor by the "colored personnel" who were satisfied "wash[ing] tables" and "serv[ing] dishes" (Haley 1943). It required a willingness to showcase a dedication to hard work and skill that exceeded the expectations of others. He offered himself as an example. At an earlier post, the *Pamlico*, Haley took volunteer courses in signal operation after completing his work in the galley, eventually leading his supervisors to assign him signal watch duties. Later on the *Murzim*, he managed a ship newspaper out of "an office of [his] own" (Haley 1943). On account of his success he had no problem boasting to Secretary White:

> I can safely say that I believe I am one of the most respected men on board this ship in spite of the fact that a very large majority of our crew is composed of southerners. Not long ago, I was voted the best shipmate, the most popular and most versatile man aboard. (1943)

The biggest honor, he claimed, was a letter of recommendation for officer training school at the Coast Guard Headquarters from the ship's Captain.

Haley's qualification of the "so-called 'race problem,'" as he put it to White, is revealing of his own upbringing (1943). In explaining the reason for his ascendance, Haley cited "excellent family training and background and a fair education." He went on to say that his real ambition was to be assigned a post where he could be in contact with other "colored serviceman"—enlisted or soon to enlist—whom he could mentor:

> to apply themselves wholeheartedly in order to achieve the numerous ends open to them. I believe, honestly, that there is not man in service [sic] better fitted for this sort of job better than I and certainly know that there are none who could possibly appreciate the opportunity more so. (1943)

Haley was not only a product of Black uplift; he was seeking to replicate it in a fashion similar to his father, tutoring the next generation. His object could not have been more timely. Many servicemen struggled with the return to life at home. The Serviceman's Readjustment Act of 1944, or G.I. Bill, offered low-interest loans, low-cost mortgages, and scholarships for many veterans looking to start anew, but the country's systemic racism hindered many Black veterans from cashing in on these benefits (Humes 2006: 92–104). Navigating the military in a Black body remained a difficult feat.

While Haley's letter of recommendation failed to result in a postwar officer's commission, his prowess with letters brought him advancement and distinction. Haley had found a purpose, or at least a path to find it. Stationed in New York in 1944, he continued his service in the Coast Guard's public relations outfit. He and Nan made a home in the burgeoning African American community of Harlem, giving birth to children, Lydia (b. 1944) and William (b. 1946) (Gonzales 1994: 33). In 1943, shortly before the Haleys' move, the fire of the Harlem riots shed a light on the racial animus present in the postwar period (Aberjhani 2003: 145). Haley was optimistic of the possibilities ahead, diving into his journalism assignment with exceptional seriousness.[12] In addition to disseminating information on Coast Guard

12   In the June 1954 issue of *Reader's Digest*, Haley wrote an article entitled "The Harlem Nobody Knows." The "nobody" refers to those "critics" who see "the six-square-mile section of New York City [with] the largest concentration of Negroes in the world—375,000—...as the sinkhole of U.S. capitalism." Haley's article argues that although the area may "symbol[ize]... American discrimination against the Negro," it also represents astounding progress, opining that "No other community on earth has come so far so fast" (Haley 2007 [1994]: 37). Haley takes umbrage that the entrepreneurial achievements that abound in Harlem "went unnoticed by the general public" and that "[i]nstead, Harlem was gaining prominence as a Mecca of Jazz... [and how in] the Roaring Twenties its cabarets and dance halls swarmed with revelers" (37–8).

Haley is more optimistic than descriptive. Unmentioned in the piece, for instance, is the riot of 1943. On June 20, a White patrolman named James Collins had tried to settle a dispute between hotel staff and a dissatisfied Black guest. Collins had arrested the guest for disturbing the peace when another Black guest, named Robert Bandy, and his mother intervened. Bandy was on leave from Army duty, and after physically confronting Collins, Bandy and his mother ran. Collins responded by shooting and wounding Bandy in the shoulder. A riot ensued after word spread that Bandy had died in the altercation (Aberjhani 2003: 145–6).

Haley's article reflects nostalgia for the economic boom that the "Negro Mecca" experienced prior to WWII and is indicative of his belief that Black uplift can redeem the ghetto, just as it did the rural South. Historian Jonathan Gill helps underscore how this was part of Haley's dreaming (2011: 344). And it is crucial to recognize Harlem's cracks as a niche through which Malcolm X would later route and take root.

activities, he answered inquiries from civilian news agencies. His dutifulness did not go unnoticed, as detailed in a 1949 Coast Guard press release entitled "New York Newsmen Pay Glowing Tribute to Coast Guard's Only Chief Journalist."

> …You can call him "chief" now—the amiable, industrious and ever helpful Alex Haley, the man behind the public information phone at New York City's Coast Guard Headquarters, who has just about become "Mr. Coast Guard" to the working press of the metropolis. When there's a ship in distress along the Atlantic coast, a plane down at sea, a fishing party marooned or on any one of a hundred other mishaps, Haley's the guy who feeds the newspapers and wire services the latest information. If he's got it, you have it. If he hasn't got it, he'll get it—that's Haley. This amazing, 28 year-old dynamo, who has two phones in his home so his pretty wife can take information from the C.G. Headquarters while he passes it on to the papers, has just been notified that he has received the rating of chief journalist, the only such title in the service. (United States Coast Guard 2016)

By this point, Haley had modified his ambitions, setting his sights at freelance writing for popular press outlets. After a day's work at his station, he would spend evenings drafting magazine articles. Most of these revolved around adventures at sea. Editors rejected his proposals until 1950, when *This Week* printed a "short piece called 'They Drive You Crazy,'" a Coast Guard tale for which he received one hundred dollars. The printed version retained very few of his own words. Haley later opined that editors were more interested in his content than his prose and that he was happy just to see his name on paper (McCauley 1983: 38). Anxious to support his growing family, Haley frequently ghostwrote for publications like the *Coronet* which paid twenty-five dollars per successful pitch plus an additional seventy-five dollars to authors willing to cede bylines to "famous people like Kate Smith, Robert Q. Lewis and so forth" (McCauley 1983: 32).

Haley used his New York journalism connections to track down potential publishers, but publications came slowly. In 1951, the Coast Guard relocated his family to San Francisco. There he continued his public relations duties and developing his personal portfolio. In 1954, he was transferred back to New York City, where he served until his retirement in 1959 (United States Coast Guard 2016). By then, one in five pitches, he estimates, began finding themselves in print with greater regularity (McCauley 1983: 42, 44–5).

This was the story of a man who identified writing as a discursive conduit. Author Chinua Achebe understood that "[o]nce you realize how the world is organized, you must then, as a writer, ask: What am I doing writing stories in this kind of situation? Who is going to read them? What use is all this going to be?" (Appiah 1992: xi). Haley pondered similar questions and stumbled upon answers after leaving home. His military career advanced in tandem with his desire and ability to communicate his intentions. Personal correspondence helped the young Haley stay connected and even maintain a relationship in the States, all the while increasing his status with his crewmates. He represented the will of the U.S. Coast Guard through signal watch duty and his journalistic projects. He answered the needs of his country and race with writings that sustained them through troubled times. In return for these efforts, he rose in rank and began a family in what could have been a defeating epoch. "The skills of a great writer are measured by their effects: it is not merely our understanding of the possibilities of human culture are enlarged, but that our passions are engaged," theorizes Kwame Anthony Appiah (1992: xvii). By this measure, Haley was becoming one.

Alex Haley, Member of the Society of Magazine Writers (1959–1964)

Alex Haley's professional rise came at great costs. In the Coast Guard, he experienced writing's potential for bringing about change. But mastering the dynamics of writing would demand a self-centered devotion. The Haleys' return to New York became less of a homecoming and more of a parting of ways. Nannie Branch may have initially been wooed by Haley's letters from sea, but by 1956, his writing career had become a point of consternation (Norrell 2015: 37–8). In a later interview, Haley recalled that Branch ended the relationship with the ultimatum, "It's me or the typewriter," to which he replied, "I wish you hadn't phrased it like that" (Associated Press 1985: 27). Branch and Haley would not formally divorce until 1964, but the couple amicably separated in 1959, the year of his discharge from the Coast Guard (McCauley 1983: 45).

Haley saw retirement and his separation as an opportunity to join the Black bohème in Greenwich Village. Lydia, William, and Alex's retirement checks went with Branch while Alex set out to pursue his freelance journalism career (McCauley 1983: 46). He took up residence with George Sims, a childhood friend from Henning who lived and worked in an apartment building on Grove Street (Gonzales 1994: 38; Blackstone 2017).[13] Neighbors like artist Joe Delaney and singer Harry Belafonte tutored him in the starving artist lifestyle (Haley 2007 [1991a]: 77). Author James Baldwin encouraged him to keep at his craft (Gonzales 1994: 38–9; Shirley 2005: 31; Norrell 2015: 38). He bonded with religion scholar C. Eric Lincoln over heated debates and jocular conversation (Shirley 2005: 31; Liukkonen 2008). (Haley would even name a character after Lincoln in *A Different Kind of Christmas* [1988: 12].) With occasional publications in *Reader's Digest* and other outlets, Haley was living paycheck to paycheck. But between child support and his living costs, he would at times have as little as "18 cents and two cans of sardines"[14] (Haley 2007 [1991a]: 76).

Haley understood the Spartan demands of his craft. But, familiar with the works of Richard Wright, James Baldwin, and Ralph Ellison, he knew how to register his feelings of invisibility (Norrell 2015: 30). White people, he recalled, "dealt with me as if they didn't even see me—I was just a cipher" (Haley 1978: 18, cited in Delmont 2016: 17). At the same time the country's swelling civil rights fervor opened new opportunities for Haley to showcase his journalistic mettle. In the mid-1950s and into the '60s, Black Americans were contesting

13 Haley rented a room in the basement of the apartment building due to his relatively limited finances. For more information on Haley's experience on Grove Street, see the "Grove Street" page at the Alex Haley Roots Foundation Website, http://www.alexhaley.com/grove_street.htm.

14 The Alex Haley Museum and Interpretive Center has the "18 cents and two cans of sardines" on display.

their second-class treatment in a range of domains. Historian Joseph E. Luders frames the period as an "ensemble of distinct struggles involving, among other things, the desegregation of public schools and accommodations, voting rights, and an end to employment discrimination" (2010: 8). The sites of contest (local, regional, national, and international) were as diverse as the opinions about how to manifest such change. And although these efforts are remembered today as a monolithic attempt at changing a nation's ethics, the era was a discursive battle over "public opinion, mass attentiveness, and electoral significance" (Luders 2010: 199). "The escalation of civil rights agitation," Luders explains:

> ...put pressure on the federal government to redress these grievances...the developing commitment of the national state to African American civil rights came about more because of political calculation and national security interests than from a shift in moral conviction. (2010: 152–3)

Activists, politicians, entertainers, and scores of lesser-known persons were drawing national attention to the problem of the color line. And media coverage was a crucial tool for leveraging socio-political pressure (Luders 2010: 198).

In Alex Haley—a proven communicator and ideological integrationist—they had a medium who could describe the shades of "Blackness" for inquisitive White readers.[15] In 1959, *Reader's Digest* tapped Haley to write features on prominent figures in the Black community, a list including singer Mahalia Jackson in 1956, and in 1960 Olympian Wilma Rudolph, and even his own brother, George Haley, the second Black graduate of the University of Arkansas' School of Law.[16] For the next two decades, the widely-read, conservative-leaning magazine hired Haley to guide its international readership on

15 On the significance of "mediums" in African American cultural history and their role in integration, see Emily Suzanne Clark's *A Luminous Brotherhood: Afro-Creole Spiritualism in Nineteenth-Century New Orleans* (2016).

16 *Reader's Digest* has collected the essays Haley wrote for the magazine in *Alex Haley: The Man Who Traced America's* Roots (Haley 2007).

a tour of Black America. Alex Haley entered the 1960s as a journalist in-demand with bylines in typically-American publications, including *Boys' Life* (the magazine of the Boy Scouts of America) and *The Saturday Evening Post*.[17]

In 1962, the adult magazine *Playboy* approached him for the launch of a monthly column called *The Playboy Interviews*. The feature aimed to give an in-depth look into the psyche of America's movers and shakers. Searching through a subsidiary's archive, magazine editor Murray Fisher stumbled upon a verbatim transcript of a Q&A that Alex Haley had begun with jazzman Miles Davis (Oliver 2002). Fisher found a raw richness in its pointed presentation, a remarkable format in a time when summary and gloss were the gold standard for human-interest stories. Davis's candor about the country's racial climate stood in stark contrast to the placatory pieces in the mainstream press. Fisher invited Haley to complete the interview and submit the transcript for publication. The resulting piece inaugurated the successful series and the popularizing of the Q&A interview adopted by many American magazines since (Fisher 1993: ix). Haley talked to the likes of activist Martin Luther King Jr. (in 1965), champion boxer Cassius Clay (later named Muhammad Ali, 1964), American Nazi Party leader George Lincoln Rockwell (1966), and late-night television host Johnny Carson (1967).[18] With a steady stream of human-interest stories, he had come a long way from his days as an aspiring writer. His publications brought him entry into the Society of Magazine Writers, a credential he proudly displayed on business cards and letterhead (Haley 1963).

But Alex Haley wanted to live the American Dream. While education and literacy had brought him opportunities unknown to many of his contemporaries, the veteran journalist's climb up the social ladder was not without its challenges. Although Haley wrote numerous

17 Darren Despoli has collected digital editions of these pieces and other articles at his Alex Haley Tribute Site, all licensed under Creative Commons use or with copyright permissions (Despoli 2007a). This is the most comprehensive collection of Haley's published works.

18 *Alex Haley: The Playboy Interviews* features all of Haley's interviews and essays for the magazine (Fisher 1993).

articles chronicling the institutional disparities among Black and White Americans, he rarely discussed his own personal encounters with racism. When his young family drove from New York to San Francisco in 1954, motels repeatedly denied the uniformed Haley lodging on account of race. He later identified this incident and the rocky search for freelance writing employment as "the two times [he] was furious about race prejudice directed at me" (Frankel 1966: 37). Racial prejudice kept Haley from the uplift for which he had been working. "By the time I got to San Francisco," he said in an interview, "I was ready to join the Black Muslims only I hadn't heard about them then" (Frankel 1966: 37). But he resented that White animus should be grounds for Black Nationalist causes such as the burgeoning Nation of Islam (NOI).

Haley had first heard about the NOI while living in San Francisco. In 1959, a friend told him about her family's conversion to NOI (McCauley 1983: 86). He could relate to the disaffected crowds amassing around the prophet, the Honorable Elijah Muhammad. However, the Nation of Islam stood at odds with Haley's sense of American identity.[19] On the one hand, he found incontrovertible their fundamental grievances against their White oppressors. Haley's *Reader's Digest* essays showed the lingering effects of the slave trade on his contemporaries. At the same time, these stories turned around a triumphal optimism about Black resilience and American potential. He had seen too many of his kind confound the worst of America by proudly donning *their* nation's Olympic jersey, saluting *their* country's flag, and contributing *their* compositions to the Great American Songbook. Haley could not and would not excuse what he interpreted as the NOI's perverse reading of America.

19 In regard to Haley's characterizations of the Nation of Islam, one should be careful for the ways in which the group is set up as a strawman. As Edward E. Curtis IV has shown (2006), the Nation of Islam is a tradition that subsumes a host of Black people's grasps and attempts to work out their lives in, through, and around Muslim identity. That is to say that we must not unconscientiously elide Haley's characterizations into scholarly redescription.

In March 1960, Haley wrote an exposé called "Mr. Muhammad Speaks" (2007 [1960]). The piece placed Elijah Muhammad and the NOI in opposition to what Haley believed to be the laudable aspirations of America's Black faithful.

> Among every 300 Negroes there is one registered Muslim— anti-White, anti-Christian, resentful, militant, disciplined—and sworn to follow Elijah Muhammad to the death. How far can he go?
>
> In Chicago, Detroit, Washington, Philadelphia and New York, I talked with top-caliber Negro professional men, with scholars and executives to whom the mere thought of cult membership is repugnant. I heard unanimous denunciation of the anti-White, anti-Christian aspects of the Muslim program. Yet all these people felt that beyond doubt Muhammad is a figure to be reckoned with—because there is so much truth in his charges.
>
> As long as inequity persists in *our* democratic system, Elijah Muhammad—or some variation of him—will be able to solicit among the Negro population enough followers to justify the title, "the most powerful Black man in America." It is important for Christianity and democracy to help remove the Negroes' honest grievances and thus eliminate the appeal of such a potent racist cult. (Haley [1960] 2007: 57, emphasis added)

Haley was forthright in his disapproval of the NOI's agenda. By contrasting the "anti-White," "Muslim program" with "Christian… democracy," he hoped his readers would look more favorably upon integrationist efforts.

Haley continued this strategy by collaborating with a White journalist named Alfred Balk. Their 1963 article, "Black Merchants of Hate," further exploited the tension between the Black separatist and integrationist camps in favor of the latter's strategy (Haley and Balk 1963). The article begins with a chilling scene that "not only shocked the police of New York City but left a deep and lasting impression on law-enforcement officers throughout the country." A White police officer had used excessive force against one of two Black Harlemites who had been embroiled in an argument. The victim was a "Black Muslim," and as he was hauled to the police station, a hundred of the movement's men quickly stood at the station's doors—in line, uniformly clad in dark clothing, "intense," and "silent." When their wounded brother was brought to the hospital, some of the vigilant followed. They were soon joined by their brothers and others from the neighborhood until their numbers swelled to some eight hundred persons. Fearing a riot, the police tried to broker a deal with a local NOI spokesperson named Malcolm X, who was demanding medical treatment for his brother and the punishment of the offending officer. The police obliged, and "then…Malcolm did something which witnesses still recall with disbelief. He strode to the head of the angry, impatient mob, stood silently, and then flicked his hands. Within seconds the street was empty." Stunned, a policeman is said to have remarked, "No man should have that much power." Haley and Balk went on to assure readers that this was no isolated incident, but representative of "the awesome discipline and power of this militant, semisecret, anti-White, anti-Christian sect."

Haley and Balk concluded their assessment with quotations from integration proponents and an ultimatum to the American people. Contrary to separatist rhetoric, they explain, White and Black militant groups increase the chances of antagonistic meetings between the races, so "churches, community leaders and public officials had better pay heed." The authors lead readers, especially White readers, to believe that they could choose to work with "moderate, responsible organizations like the N.A.A.C.P. and the Urban League," or see their fears realized by "extremists [like]…[the] Black Muslims and White Citizens" (Haley and Balk 1963).

With his earliest Coast Guard and freelance pieces, Haley had earned the right to comment on America. Readers trusted him to glorify national heroes, Black and White alike. By 1963, he was building on that goodwill and instructing readers to make choices about the America in which he wanted to live. His early coverage of the NOI showed a thorough interest in shaping public opinion and the nation's racial landscape.

Despite Haley's bias-laden reporting, Elijah Muhammad appreciated his coverage of the movement and its grievances. The prophet believed that his truths would outshine the tarnish of Haley's opinion.

Thus Haley continued to receive access in exchange for exposure.[20] Haley found an angle in the relationship between the movement's leader and spokesperson. His characterization of the brewing tension complemented his own integrationist goals.

The initial 1960 piece for *Reader's Digest* casts Malcolm and Muhammad as an ironic pairing (Haley 2007 [1960]: 52–3). It quotes Malcolm's insistence that the Honorable Elijah Muhammad is "the *boldest* Black man in America...the most *powerful* Black man in America...the *smartest* Black man in America." But Malcolm's doxology reads hollow against Haley's description of the two. Malcolm was a "tall," "whip-smart," "aide-de-camp" whose calm, cool demeanor enraptured audiences. Elijah Muhammad was "a meek-looking man," a "shy-looking little man," who "shouted" at the audience. The Haley and Balk essay adds that Elijah Muhammad "was a short, rather unimpressive-looking man, slight and light-skinned... His face showing no expression, he moved quickly to the speaker's platform," while Malcolm was "a lanky, energetic, good-looking man named Malcolm Little... Articulate, single-minded, the fire of bitterness still burning his soul" (Haley and Balk 1963).

In contrast to the single-minded precision described in the 1960 article, the 1963 essay suggested that the NOI was at risk of an internal power struggle. Haley and Balk hint that "[w]hile Muhammad appears to be training his son Wallace to succeed him when he retires or dies, many Muslims feel that Malcolm is too powerful to be denied the leadership if he wants it." Rather than portraying Malcolm and Wallace D. Muhammad as torchbearers of the movement, Haley characterized the leadership structure as volatile.

Haley set his literary focus on Malcolm X—the rising, outspoken, public face of the movement. The NOI, Haley believed, would live or

---

20 Haley's self-assurance extends from the relationship he cultivated with the NOI. As a possible follow up to the *Autobiography*, he pitched a book on Elijah Muhammad, saying "...I know that it can be said authentically that though some other writers might presently have bigger 'names' ([James] Baldwin, [Louis] Lomax, [C. Eric] Lincoln), that actually I have the very best inside track to the Muslims' confidence" (3.24—Alex Haley to Paul Reynolds, February 27, 1965, Anne Romaine Collection).

die around the spokesperson's charisma. Not wanting to overshadow his mentor, Malcolm resisted Haley's request for a *Playboy* interview until blessed by Elijah Muhammad. Furthermore, Malcolm doubted that the "White press" would relay his own raw, scathing remarks about "the White devil," but *Playboy* surprised him with the verbatim inclusion of each and every word, no matter how scandalous (X and Haley 1999 [1965]: 392). Haley played interlocutor on behalf of the integrationist cause, and the shocking article became one of the magazine's most controversial. With this and Haley's other essays, readers' hungered for more of Malcolm. Book publisher Doubleday signed Malcolm, Haley, and an uncredited Murray Fisher to develop *The Autobiography of Malcolm X as Told to Alex Haley* (Fisher 1993: x).

This was the story of a man increasingly identified by his words. Haley's writing skills raised his capital in a Bourdieusian sense (Bourdieu 1997 [1986]). He may have spent time as a starving artist, but he was able to carve out a living (i.e. economic capital) with what he put on the page. Each byline (i.e. cultural capital) proved his worth to readers, colleagues, and employers, earning him purchase with substantial credentialed institutions like the Society of Magazine Writers and Doubleday (i.e. social capital). Haley's professional rise was the payoff of his dutiful—though wayward—obeisance to the values of Black uplift, Protestant American ideals, and the integrationist vision of his forebears. It verified his rootedness in the nation and the written means through which it was demonstrated.

While Bourdieu's understanding of capital helps us in identifying the appearance or "doxa" of roots in a habitus (Bourdieu 1977: 166), Haley's growth in status cannot be reduced to a simple accumulation of social, cultural, and economic capital. As we have already seen, the course of his career was shaped by a lack of means as much as his childhood upbringing was relatively posh in intellectual accoutrements and financial trappings. Alex Haley was not definitively rich, nor was he unequivocally poor. He was neither a savant, nor daft. And though he frequently rose above his station, his sense of belonging anywhere was never certain. To understand Haley as an exemplar of a scriptural economy, as a man worthwhile on account of the word, we must shift our data to a more dynamic understanding of identity.

Should we want to consider Haley in terms of Bayart's "operational acts of identification," we should turn to Bourdieu's under-appreciated contribution of "liquidity"—the exchange of capital within a social system and its results on the persons and institutions within (Bourdieu 1997 [1986]: 55). Bourdieu argues that the fluid exchange of capital ultimately contributes to the maintenance of the social system itself and that the participating persons and institutions may shift positions within it, but "every reproduction strategy is at the same time a legitimation strategy aimed at consecrating both an exclusive appropriation and its reproduction" (Bourdieu 1997 [1986]: 55). Hence, Haley occupies America as a wordsmith, offering occasionally profitable words in return for a sense of place. The correlation between Haley's rootedness and his words' worth should prompt us to probe Bourdieu's rhetorical questions.

> How can this capital, so closely linked to the person, be bought without buying the person and so losing the very effect of legitimation which presupposes the dissimulation of dependence? How can this capital be concentrated—as some undertakings demand—without concentrating the possessors of the capital, which can have all sorts of unwanted consequences? (Bourdieu 1997 [1986]: 48)

In fact, it is his "subversive critique" where we can most clearly identify beholdeness or paid interest (Bourdieu 1997 [1986]: 55). Haley put up his marriage to Nanny Branch as collateral against an investment in the writing craft. His authorial rise could be measured in child-support payments and time away. Along with Haley's submission to editorial opinions and the formative lessons of his upbringing, these were the costs of identifying with roots.

"As Told to Alex Haley," 1963–1966

One might ask if Haley's entanglements were so problematic, why would he continue to seek roots? Assuming he even had a choice in the matter, we will see that the rootedness for which Haley pined was more than possession of the American Dream. It was participation in a culture and the means of defining it. Contrary to its appearance as an ideal, rootedness is a game of comparison, of having and being more than an other person. Such a contest is most visible in the competition between two Black American subversives—Haley and Malcolm X— and the book upon which they would collaborate.

While they work out their relationship to America and to each other on paper, the historical place of "Africa" in their autobiographical renderings becomes crucial. But before honing in on the role of origins in their identificatory acts, we should think further about the context where their overtures to the past played out. The occasion of the *Autobiography* was of timely significance for Malcolm X and Alex Haley. Both men were in the midst of reinventing themselves and the book served as an effective vehicle for their particular aims. By many accounts, the two-year (1963–1965) collaborative project resulted in one of the great American books of the twentieth century.[21]

It is the tale of a man who knew strife from birth and rose to voice a fierce civil rights message. It showed a man on a pilgrimage to find himself. His father was "an itinerant Baptist preacher" and "president of the Omaha branch of [Marcus Garvey's Universal Negro Improvement Association (UNIA)];" his mother "served as reporter of the Omaha UNIA" (Dyson 1995: 4).[22] Both in the church pew and at home, Malcolm heard the importance of Black self-reliance and unity (James 2009: 293).[23] But his parents' Midwest activism

21 Historian of religion in America, Stephen Prothero includes Malcolm and the *Autobiography* in the "Prophets" section of *The American Bible: Whose America Is This? How Our Words Unite and Divide a Nation*, but does not include Haley's *Roots* (Prothero 2012). I argue that *Roots* would make a worthy addition to this canon.

22 Dyson offers a critical reading of Malcolm, *The Autobiography*, and what he calls, "Malcolm's readers."

23 Drawing upon Booker T. Washington's "Tuskegee economic philosophy...Garvey's political problematic was that of identifying an economic theory and practice (*praxis*) that would support the superstructure of the Black man's political objective," James writes (2009: 293). Earl Little's leadership in the church and the local UNIA chapter were part of wider attempts at creating Black, self-sufficient, socio-economic networks.

incited the vigilantism of the Ku Klux Klan and other White supremacist organizations—first in Omaha, then Milwaukee, and finally
in Lansing (Marable 2011: 22–5, 30).[24] When his father was killed
under a Lansing streetcar in 1931, Malcolm's mother was left to
raise eight children during the Great Depression (Dyson 1995: 4; X
and Haley 1999 [1965]: 10; Marable 2011: 31–8).[25] The economic
and psychological burden led to her institutionalization, leaving the
children to cycle through the foster care system until adulthood. The
Autobiography recounts Malcolm's childhood and describes his
sojourn from street hustling, to the NOI, and into the wider Muslim
ummah.

As news outlets increasingly placed Malcolm X as the NOI's
standard-bearer, Elijah Muhammad showed little tolerance for the
unwanted attention his spokesperson brought to the organization.
On May 5, 1962, the Los Angeles Police Department shot and killed
an unarmed, NOI member named Ronald Stokes. When Malcolm
was dispatched to Los Angles, he was primed to call for vengeance
against a police officer, but Elijah Muhammad ordered him to "play
dead on everything...cool [his] heels" (Branch 2007: 13). Malcolm
reluctantly obliged, but this did not quench his penchant for voicing incendiary commentary. In June 1962, a month after the Stokes
incident, Malcolm labeled the tragic crash of Atlanta-bound Air
France Flight 007 as an act of God, and the death of a hundred of
the city's leading White citizens as retribution for racial injustice

24 The Littles moved throughout the Midwest in an attempt to develop
local UNIA chapters. They moved from Omaha to Milwaukee in 1926, on to
East Chicago, IN in 1927, and finally to Lansing, MI in 1928. Save for their
time in East Chicago, Manning Marable notes, the Littles were forced to move
because of difficulties with White supremacist groups—the KKK in Omaha
and Milwaukee and the Black Legionnaires in Lansing (Marable 2011:
22–5, 30).

25 The *Autobiography* says that the local Black community believed that
the streetcar accident resulted from the actions of a White supremacist group
called the Black Legionnaires. Manning Marable adds that "a forensic reconstruction of Earl Little's death suggests that the story...may have been true"
(Marable 2011: 31–8).

(Branch 2007: 14). Malcolm's escalating rhetoric had also brought unwanted scrutiny from the FBI, who were investigating the NOI as a potentially "subversive" group (Federal Bureau of Investigation 1962). Elijah Muhammad suspended Malcolm from duty after the spokesperson called the November 1963 assassination of President John F. Kennedy a case of "chickens coming home to roost" (Dyson 1995: 11–12; Tyler 2006: 29). The ninety-day silence was to remind Malcolm and Americans that the prophet was the true voice of the movement.

By this time, Malcolm had already begun to question Elijah Muhammad's passive leadership and had further reason to speak out against the prophet's indiscretion. In 1963, rumor had spread that Elijah Muhammad had fathered children with various women from his secretarial staff—actions that went against the NOI's strict protocols on monogamy (Tyler 2006: 29). By silencing Malcolm, Elijah Muhammad had preemptively softened the critique that the discredited spokesperson could make from within the movement (Marable 2011: 278).

Malcolm turned his attention beyond the movement. In 1964, he a launched a Black Nationalist organization called the Organization of Afro-American Unity (OAAU) and the Sunni-endorsed Muslim Mosque, Inc. (MMI) (Marable 2011: 319, 334). Through the secular OAAU, Malcolm would present the plight of Black Americans at every forum from college campuses to the United Nations. Contrary to Elijah Muhammad's NOI, MMI enabled Malcolm to theologize an agenda in terms concordant with an "orthodox" world religion. The OAAU and the MMI acted as institutional evidence of Malcolm's charisma and independence from the NOI.

The *Autobiography* transitioned from being an evangelistic tool for Elijah Muhammad into Malcolm's chance to reinvent himself. The inflammatory statements that brought him notoriety severely limited his pool of potential alliances, White and Black (X and Haley 1999 [1965]: 382).[26] But the *Autobiography* provided a narrative justification

---

26 Malcolm was forthcoming about the challenges of interpolation.

In trying to create "an all-Black organization whose ultimate objective was to help create a society in which there could exist honest

for the less palatable aspects of his career. Haley prompted Malcolm to divulge moments from his harrowing childhood in Michigan, a tragic trajectory beginning with the racially-motivated murder of his father, the mental ailments plaguing his mother, and the subsequent dispersion of him and his siblings (Gonzales 1994: 44). These, Haley believed, would help readers rationalize Malcolm's criminal record and conversion to the NOI. They would also keep otherwise skeptical readers engaged enough to see Malcolm's increasingly inclusive viewpoint, and ultimately the beauty of Haley's integrationist perspective.

The *Autobiography* also provided Malcolm room to embellish his past in light of his emerging goals. Malcolm reminisced about his days as the streetwise Detroit Red—now immortalized in the bravado of Black culture—instead of the fewer, lesser, haphazard capers recorded in Malcolm Little's police record (Marable 2011: 39–69, esp. 51).[27] This negative autobiographical reconstruction offered readers an anti-hero whom they could shamefully admire, and it made his conversion seem all the more vivid. Regardless of the NOI's

---

White-Black brotherhood" his previous persona as a "so-called Black Muslim"…kept blocking me. I was trying to gradually reshape that image.

Though fueled by the same passion as he had when working for the NOI, I made a concerted effort to explain that "True Islam taught me that it takes *all* of the religious, political, economic, psychological, and racial ingredients, or characteristics, to make the Human Family and the Human Society complete."

He marked his visit to Mecca as a pivotal moment for himself in hopes that it would become a turning point in the role of public opinion.

27 Without a doubt, police records indicate that Malcolm X had engaged in criminal behavior, but Manning Marable provides substantial evidence to show that the Detroit Red of the *Autobiography*—"a young Black man almost completely uninterested in, even alienated from, politics"—is a post-facto caricature (Marable 2011: 52). Marable documents how Malcolm took on numerous jobs, depended on the generosity of family members, and "spoke frequently about Black Nationalist ideas," counter to the independent, career criminal image provided in the *Autobiography*. Malcolm was not as "bad" as he thought he was, according to Marable.

controversial beliefs, the discipline demanded by the movement provided the boundaries Malcolm lacked as an adolescent and young
adult. Readers could appreciate Malcolm's everyman-struggle to
come of age. The *Autobiography* gave Malcolm a chance to convince
the world that his time with Elijah Muhammad and "the hate that hate
produced" were just the unfortunate prelude to the start of something
new—namely, the OAAU, the MMI, and a promising future for race
relations.[28]

Alex Haley similarly used the *Autobiography* to confound expectations about his potential (or lack thereof) as a writer. As much as he
was telling a story, he was writing his way toward increased professional stability. Haley increasingly resented the rejection, censorship,
and micromanaging that came from pitching freelance essays. His
profiles on Black people and Black life filled a particular niche, and
now he was represented by Paul Reynolds, a top-tier literary agent.
Haley believed that the *Autobiography*, if done correctly, would bring
him more creative independence and publishing contracts.

Haley's wish to be identifed as a serious writer by his peers also
had ramifications at home, where he was under major socio-economic
pressures to succeed. In 1964, Haley had officially divorced Nannie
Branch and married fellow journalist, Juliette Collins, with whom he
welcomed a daughter, Cynthia (b. 1964; Romaine 1.31—Alex Haley
Book Outlines and Book Draft: 58–9).[29] Their young family rented a
house in Rome, New York and struggled to meet their bills. To make

28 The phrase comes from a *Newsbeat* documentary series titled *The
Hate That Hate Produced*, a five-part series produced by Mike Wallace and
Louis Lomax, July 13–17, 1959. The news magazine exposé introduced the
NOI to America's television-viewing public. Lomax, a Black television journalist, had told his White colleague, Wallace, about the movement's fiery
rhetoric and militant features. The two reporters presented the NOI as an
equal and opposite response to segregationist policies and White supremacist
ideologies. The documentary is an antecedent to "Black Merchants of Hate"
(Haley and Balk 1963).

29 In an interview, Haley's son, William "Fella" Haley, told Anne
Romaine that there is no documentation of Alex's divorce from Nan. He
believes his father's second marriage was, in Romaine's words, "Alex trying
to do the right thing in light of Juliette's unplanned pregnancy."

ends meet, Haley tried to line up a steady stream of small writing projects and took several advances from Doubleday.[30] His fortune (or lack thereof) depended on the book's reception.

Casting his lot with Malcolm was a risky endeavor. Haley did not want readers to mistake the collaboration as an ideological alliance. As he explained to his agent, "'Co-authoring' with Malcolm X, would, to me, imply sharing his views, when mine are almost a complete antithesis to his." Instead Haley insisted that Doubleday publish *The Autobiography of Malcolm X as Told to Alex Haley*, denoting his role as "a purely clinical job of shaping a great volume of Malcolm X's printed and taped material into the form of a book" (3.24—Alex Haley to Oliver G. Swan, Paul Reynolds & Son, August 5, 1963, Anne Romaine Collection). Paul Reynolds shared Haley's concerns and advocated that his client emphasize "somewhere that [you] are not a Black Muslim," continuing, "I'm just thinking of your future career. You are not a Black Muslim, so I'd rather people didn't think you was" (3.26—Paul Reynolds to Alex Haley, October 1, 1963, Anne Romaine Collection). Haley, nevertheless, was under FBI surveillance as a result of the project, so to impress the point, he

30 Haley's financial desperation comes through in his correspondence with his literary agent, Paul Reynolds. There Haley reports on a potential deal with Scribner & Co. to write the inaugural volume of a children's book series on "historic Negroes" (3.24—Alex Haley to Paul Reynolds, October 24, 1963, Anne Romaine Collection). Haley shows excitement at the additional employment, though nothing comes of this particular project (3.24—Alex Haley to Paul Reynolds, July 9, 1965, Anne Romaine Collection).

Alex becomes enthused about other profitable writing projects, including a book-length interview on celebrity attorney, Melvin Belli. Haley promises that he could write the Belli biography while finishing *Before This Anger*. Between the success of the *Autobiography*, the proposed book on Belli, and *Before This Anger*, Haley believes that his finances will be settled, exclaiming, "Two more years, according to my schedule, I figure to 'have it made.'" The "it," to which Haley is referring, is spelled out in another letter (3.24— Alex Haley to Mr. William D. Cabell, September 20, 1965, Anne Romaine Collection). Haley explains to his attorney that he is unable to pay the IRS $4,232.91 in back taxes and that he has been borrowing money from his brother, George, for living expenses.

sent the Bureau an informal resume detailing his previous coverage of the NOI, his "as told to" credit in the *Autobiography*, and his services as a Coast Guardsmen (3.24—Alex Haley to the Director of the FBI, November 19, 1963, Anne Romaine Collection). In a show of diplomatic transparency, he carbon copied Doubleday, his literary agent, and Malcolm.

Not only was Haley's literary future in question, but the book's viability was far from assured. The *Autobiography* needed to counterbalance the rawness of Malcolm's social vision with the potential for interracial marketability. Haley had to frame Malcolm's most "shocking" sentiments in such a way that Malcolm would approve and that readers would suspend some of their offense. For example, in early drafts Haley recorded Malcolm blaming the "Jews" for the socio-economic oppression of Black people. Paul Reynolds feared that this sort of rhetoric would alienate a "very sensitive and also of course very powerful" demographic heavily invested in the media and entertainment industry (3.26—Paul Reynolds to Alex Haley, October 1, 1963, Anne Romaine Collection). In response to Reynolds' concerns, Haley collapses Malcolm's anti-semitism into a broader racism, replacing "Jews" with "Whites" (3.26—Alex Haley to Paul Reynolds, October 3, 1963, Anne Romaine Collection). While this sort of language was still inflammatory in the eyes of Reynolds and White readership, it was preceded by Malcolm's reputation and thus expected. Jewishness, economics, and anti-semitism however were too sensitive of topics, perhaps because they drew too much attention to the artifice of whiteness.[31] Whatever critique was to end up in print, its words had to keep the attention of those being critiqued.

31 Haley's discussions with Reynolds also highlight the difficulty between the world Haley described in his writings and the comfort zone and assumptions of people like Reynolds. For instance, Reynolds struggled to comprehend Malcolm's Harlemite "slang" and questioned its utility in the *Autobiography*. Haley defended its inclusion on the grounds of authentic representation (3.24—Alex Haley to Paul Reynolds, December 11, 1963, Anne Romaine Collection).

Near the end of the project, the task of interpreting Black and White people to each other vexed Haley to the point that he mused about writing a cross-cultural etiquette guide called, "How to Co-Exist with Negroes"

Committed to a readable and profitable story, the two men established a rapport. Between 1963 and 1965, Haley would earn a reticent Malcolm's trust. They worked late into the evening; sometimes in Haley's home, other times in Malcolm's. When Malcolm reconnected with his mother after her institutional release, Haley vicariously celebrated their reconnection while coming to terms with his own father's deteriorating bodily and mental health.[32] By 1964, Malcolm suspected he would not live much longer—either because of an NOI reprisal or because of White aggression—and became mindful of his family's future. Originally, Malcolm had stated that the NOI should receive his portions of the profits were he to die, but he had Haley revise the agreement to instead list his wife, Betty, as the sole beneficiary (3.26—Malcolm X to Paul Reynolds, March 21, 1964, Anne Romaine Collection). Malcolm and Betty would also name Haley the godfather of their daughter, Attallah (X and Haley 1999 [1965]: x).[33] In this two-year span, Malcolm came to see Haley not only as a writer, but as a friend.

Scholarship tends to name the differences between Malcolm and Haley, but equally profound are the places where they found common ground. Sociologist Michael Eric Dyson scores the *Autobiography* as a reflection of "Malcolm's need to shape his personal history for public racial edification while bringing coherence to a radically conflicting set of life experiences and coauthor Alex Haley's political biases

---

(3.24—Alex Haley to Paul Reynolds, January 28, 1964, Anne Romaine Collection).

32 In a 1958 request to remain at his duty station in San Francisco, Haley describes his father as suffering from "serious," "non-socially-harmful but psychosomatically debilitating" illness. Simon lived until 1973, but the letter intimates that his condition would worsen with time (3.23—Alex Haley to Commandant (PE) Via Commander, 12th Coast Guard District (P), April 21, 1958, Anne Romaine Collection).

33 Attallah Shabazz speaks of this in the foreword to the *Autobiography*. In interviews, Haley discussed being Attallah's godfather and his closeness to Malcolm's family (Blackside, Inc. 1988). His friendship with Betty included amicable phone conversations and the swapping of recipes (Allen 1976: 37). And in the "Epilogue" to the *Autobiography*, Haley recalls giving Attallah and her sister, Qubilah, dolls for Christmas (X and Haley 1999 [1965]: 430).

and ideological purposes" (Dyson 1995: 23). Historian Manning Marable elaborates on the conflict, going to great lengths to establish Alex Haley as "a retired twenty-year veteran of the U.S. Coast Guard [with] an agenda of his own...[a] liberal Republican...[who] frames [Malcolm] firmly within mainstream civil rights respectability at the end of his life" (Marable 2011: 9–10).

Certainly, Haley's Malcolm should not be taken as the "historical" Malcolm or some unassuming biographical portrait (Gopnik 2010). Neither should we oversimplify Haley to be unsympathetic to Malcolm's concerns. By Haley's own admission, his views were *"almost* a complete antithesis," but not absolutely counter (3.24—Alex Haley to Oliver G. Swan, Paul Reynolds & Son, August 5, 1963, Anne Romaine Collection, emphasis added). The scholar should read the *Autobiography* as data for not only understanding Malcolm X, but also (and perhaps, more so) Alex Haley.

As written in the 1960 "Mr. Muhammad Speaks," Haley, too, perceived the "inequity" Black people experienced in cities such as "Chicago, Detroit, Washington, Philadelphia and New York." Haley and Malcolm were part of the Great Migration of Blacks, who from 1910 to 1970 left the rural South for America's urban centers in search of socio-economic opportunity and shelter from racial discrimination. Haley, a Tennessee native, arrived in New York and San Francisco by way of his journalism career. The Nebraska-born Malcolm had lived in Midwestern cities and Boston before settling in New York. In her book, *The Warmth of Other Suns: The Epic Story of America's Great Migration*, journalist Isabel Wilkerson describes what migrants such as Haley and Malcolm saw in these cities—"the social geography of Black and White neighborhoods, the spread of the housing projects, as well as the rise of a well-scrubbed Black middle class, [and] alternative waves of White flight and suburbanization" (2010: 10). In the city, Haley and Malcolm both identified a need for Black uplift, and it was this mutuality that also challenged Haley to distinguish himself and his vision for Blacks in America.[34]

---

34 This need was one felt widely among Black peoples of the period and was met through a variety of "religio-racial" identity formations. See Judith Weisenfeld's *New World A-Coming* (2016: 127).

Haley had every intention of critiquing Malcolm's position with a follow-up work. America, Haley thought, deserved a constructive way forward that conserved the best of the past and moved toward a felicitous future for those peoples who had not been part of it. In the two years (1963–1965) that they collaborated, Malcolm kept a full schedule of traveling and lecturing. The disruption left Haley annoyed but also with time to gather his own thoughts (3.24— Alex Haley to Paul Reynolds, October 15, 1964, Anne Romaine Collection). Two projects give a sense of Haley's thinking. One was a draft for a Broadway play (with potential for adaptation as a novel and film) to be called *Booker*. It would follow a fictitious Henning man carried by "the siren song to 'Go Nawth'" only to become lost in the trappings of urban life (2.25—Alex Haley to Paul Reynolds, October 24, 1973, Anne Romaine Collection). Another was a collection of short stories about small town life in *Henning*. Neither came to fruition, but they afford a glimpse to his reflective posture. At this time, Haley was beginning to view his own Henning upbringing in contrast to the urban streets where Malcolm's movement was most appealing. *Booker* would be a stand-in for Malcolm and other Black people carried away by city life while *Henning* would remind readers of better, simpler times in the rural South.[35] While White authors like *Gone with the Wind*'s (1936) Margaret Mitchell also tried to fill the literary niche of an amicable South, Haley's nostalgia was markedly different in that it reckoned a place for Black people. This would help a multiracial American readership identify with Haley over his predecessors.

Though these two planned works did not manifest as intended, the contrast Haley was trying to strike would be present within the

---

35 In 1973, Haley understood *Roots*, *Booker*, and *Henning* as something of a "trilogy" (2.25—Alex Haley to Paul Reynolds, October 24, 1973, Anne Romaine Collection). As will be discussed later, neither *Booker* nor *Henning* came to fruition, but Haley and Norman Lear co-produced a short-lived 1980–1981 television show called *Palmerstown U.S.A.* It revolved round two young boys—one Black and one White—who develop a friendship in a rural Southern town after the Depression. The show was loosely based on a friendship Haley had as a boy in Henning (Cannon 2014).

novel he would eventually call *Roots*. Its original title, *Before This Anger*, referred to the broken promises of the Great Migration, but also to the contempt with which Malcolm and other Blacks held for White people (2.25—Alex Haley to Paul Reynolds, October 24, 1973, Anne Romaine Collection). Haley believed this indignation to be unrighteous and unfruitful. It would "portr[ay] the pastoral simplicity and the *root* Christian culture of the 1930s Southern Negro" (3.24—Alex Haley to Paul Reynolds, September 3, 1963, Anne Romaine Collection, emphasis added). The memoir would recount how Haley's great-grandfather, the blacksmith Tom Lea, and eventually his grandfather, the lumberyard owner Will Palmer, built Henning into the integrated town where Haley grew up. *Before This Anger* would end with Haley realizing that he could not have become a relatively successful Black professional without his upbringing in Henning, where his family had lived amicably with White people since Reconstruction (3.24—Alex Haley to Paul Reynolds, October 15, 1964, Anne Romaine Collection).

Malcolm, at least as Haley presents him, would not reject this premise so much as qualify it. In *The Autobiography*, Malcolm recalls how his childhood ambition to become a lawyer was rejected by his White, eighth-grade English teacher, Mr. Ostrowski, who called it "no realistic goal for a nigger" (X and Haley 1999 [1965]: 38). Malcolm elaborates:

> I've often thought that if Mr. Ostrowski had encouraged me to become a lawyer, I would today probably be among some city's professional Black bourgeoisie, sipping cocktails and palming myself off as a community spokesman for and leader of the suffering Black masses, while my primary concern would be to grab a few more crumbs from the groaning board of the two-faced Whites with whom they're begging to "integrate." (1999 [1965]: 40)

This statement stands in stunning contrast to the life of George Haley, Alex's brother and subject of the *Reader's Digest* article, "The Man Who Wouldn't Quit" (2007 [1963]). The biographical essay describes George as having strategically entered the University of Arkansas

School of Law to pave the way for further integration (44).[36] Enduring enormous harassment, George overcame prejudice to become the *Law Review*'s editor. Following graduation, George served as a deputy city attorney in Kansas City, Kansas, and the vice president of the state's Young Republicans (49). For Alex Haley and his family, successful Black uplift required a steadfast commitment to integration. When George was elected to the Kansas State Senate in January 1965, Malcolm had Alex "tell [George] that he and all the other moderate Negroes who are getting somewhere need to always remember that it was us extremists who made it possible" (X and Haley 1999 [1965]: 430). In George Haley, Malcolm identified a potential, never-realized version of himself.

By 1964, the collaborators held more in common ideologically than when Haley had first covered Malcolm. Malcolm's travels abroad—especially his April 1964 pilgrimage to Mecca—convinced the former NOI spokesperson of the possibility of racial reconciliation (X and Haley 1999 [1965]: 369).[37] But "Afro-American unity," as his new organization was named, remained the priority (X and Haley [1965] 1999: 382). In a 1965 interview session recorded in the *Autobiography*, Malcolm tells Haley:

> I kept having all kinds of troubles trying to develop the kind
> of Black Nationalist organization I wanted to build for the

36 Alex contextualizes George's decision, placing it in relation to a 1948 federal court ruling that forced the University of Oklahoma to accept "George McLaurin," a retired Black professor (Haley 2007 [1963]: 46).

37 While on Hajj, Malcolm wrote to his MMI associates with instructions for the "Letter from Mecca" to be forwarded to the press. Upon completion of his pilgrimage, Malcolm was ready to meet the press with prepared remarks about the letter. Haley quotes Malcolm:

> In the past, yes, I have made sweeping indictments of *all* White people.
> I never will be guilty of that again—as I know now that some White
> people *are* truly sincere, that some truly are capable of being brotherly
> toward a Black man. The true Islam has shown me that a blanket indict-
> ment of all White people is as wrong as when Whites make blanket
> indictments against Blacks… It was in the Holy World that my attitude
> was changed.

> American Negro. Why Black Nationalism? Well, in the com-
> petitive American society, how can there ever be any White-
> Black solidarity before there is first some Black solidarity? If
> you will remember, in my childhood I had been exposed to the
> Black Nationalist teachings of Marcus Garvey—which, in fact,
> I had been told had led to my father's murder. Even when I was
> a follower of Elijah Muhammad, I had been strongly aware of
> how the Black Nationalist political, economic and social philos-
> ophies had the ability to instill within Black men the racial dig-
> nity, the incentive, and the confidence that the Black race needs
> today to get up off its knees, and to get on its feet, and get rid of
> its scars and to take a stand for itself. (382)

Haley was encouraged by Malcolm's new-found optimism, but it was
not the integrated America for which Haley hoped. Haley had seen
the possibilities in Henning and in his own career path. The writer
was far more interested in racial reconciliation than a racial reckoning. Creating a place befitting Black people alone would leave no
room for White people to make the about-face necessary to see him
as truly American.

An appreciation for history served as common ground for
Malcolm and Haley, though they disagreed on how to respond to it.
For Malcolm, the appellation "X" signified the rejection of a Western
meta-narrative in which he was to be known by the name of his
enslavers. In the *Autobiography*, he declares:

> Human history's greatest crime was the traffic in Black flesh
> when the devil White man went into Africa and murdered
> and kidnapped…millions of Black men, women, and children
> who were worked and beaten and tortured as slaves. The devil
> White man cut these Black people off from all knowledge of
> their own kind, and cut them off from any knowledge of their
> own language, religion, and past culture, until the Black man in
> America was the earth's only race of people who had absolutely
> no knowledge of his true identity. (X and Haley 1999 [1965]:
> 165)[38]

38 The quotation comes from Malcolm's distillation of the Nation of
Islam's cosmological myth in which the "original man" was Black (Curtis
2006: 31–4).

While on the Hajj and "trying to internationalize our problem," Malcolm told Haley, he wanted "to make the Africans feel their *kinship* with us Afro-Americans...[to] think about it, that they are our blood brothers, and we all came from the same foreparents" (X and Malcolm 1999 [1965]: 426–7). Malcolm believed that a renewed historical connection between Black Americans and Black Africans could turn the tide in the civil rights struggle. Haley, too, believed there was hope in making history work for the integrationist movement. Despite their different intentions, both identified the past with fertile, common ground.

As connoted by the first word in the title *Before This Anger*, the past would play a central role in Haley's riposte to Malcolm, but Haley was slower to recognize the symbolic power of an African heritage for his own purposes. For certain, he wanted to write an origin story to explain his own success as a Black man in a White world. It would be informative for those Americans on both sides of the color line who were seeking a way forward—together. We see glimpses of this narrative in his underdeveloped projects like *Henning* and *Booker* as well as his feel-good profiles of successful African Americans in *Reader's Digest*. But at this point in his struggle with Malcolm and America, Haley identified more potential in the British Isles than in the African continent.

Haley had initially planned to originate his family narrative in Ireland. In 1966, he intended to account for his own success by recounting not only his maternal (i.e. Palmer clan) but also his paternal (i.e. Haley) genealogy. *Before This Anger* would follow the mold of the typical (and clearly typifying) European origin story. Historian Matthew F. Delmont explains that before Haley looked to Africa for roots, his ancestral search took him to Ireland (Delmont 2016: 41). Haley's paternal grandmother, Queen Jackson Haley, was the daughter of the enslaved Easter Jackson and slave owner James Jackson, whose father hailed from Carrickmacross, Ireland (Haley 1966, cited in Delmont 2016: 41). The distressing twist on the immigrant story would set the stage for Haley's rags-to-riches tale. He would narrate how his American family went from the receiving end of the overseer's boot and strap to working alongside White, salt-of-the-earth, Southerners. Next to Haley's history, readers would identify

Malcolm's anger as foreign to the immigrant nation's roots. Africa would only later become of interest for Haley, and the story of Queen would be revisited in an ancillary way after the *Roots* moment.

Today's cultural critics may be tempted to identify Haley as playing a game of racial minstrelsy at worst or respectability politics at best. And such evaluations should not be confused as analysis in the anthropology of scriptures so far as both descriptions miss what Haley read about America as an immigrant nation. Respect does not seem to be gained by simple possession of a pristinely staged past. It is the reward for performing a particularly dramatic narration of the state of the nation in respect to a messy past. Thus, I do not see Haley's interest in Europe as a product of White envy as much as an entrepreneurial attempt at fixing the national problem of White guilt.

Haley turns his gaze toward Africa when he realizes that the root of the problem is in the overlap of the Black Atlantic scenario and the social economics of the Transatlantic Slave Trade. The possession of an origin myth could almost certainly make a difference for Black people. And it would be an overstatement to suggest that White people could not live with a history of slavery—they can, they have, and many quite easily still do. But Haley saw possibilities in cultivating a mutuality between the ends of Black Power and the means of White empathy. Haley could be the bearer of redemption. And historically, there is nothing natural or unconstructed about this claim.

For the social theorist, it is telling that Haley did not intrinsically identify rootedness with Africa. Rather, rootedness or "the before" signified "power," the ability to overwrite another's narrative. In fact, rather than identifying Haley as someone in possession of African roots, it is more appropriate to read him as one among many Black persons who came to identify the potential of laying claim to Africa. During and after the development of *Roots*, Haley himself offers different accounts of how Africa came to be of importance to him toward the end of his collaboration with Malcolm X.

The first account, attested toward the end of *Roots* and in a 1973 issue of *Oral History Review*, has Haley relegate the British Isles from *root* to *route*. While Malcolm was advancing his case abroad and making international alliances, Haley was growing frustrated with the source of the *Autobiography* (and his future earnings) (3.24—Alex Haley to

Paul Reynolds, October 15, 1964, Anne Romaine Collection). Haley fortunately had steady work with *Playboy*. In the early part of 1964, *Playboy* sent Haley on assignment to interview British actress Julie Christie (McCauley 1983: 104). When arrangements for the press junket fell through, Haley was left to bide his time in London.

> And that was how I, who always innately had loved history and had been steeped in history by Grandma and others from the time I was a little boy, found myself plunked in one of the places on earth that had probably more history per square foot than anywhere I know—London. (Haley 1973: 9)

There across the pond, Haley had an exotic place to imagine the past he so desperately needed. Haley would make his way into the British Museum and see a haunting image of the Rosetta Stone. He beheld the Greek, demotic script, and hieroglyphs with which historians had unearthed antiquity. The exhibit triggered Haley's memory of the African utterances of his grandmother, and he envisioned himself as a Black Jean-François Champollion. If he could trace the sounds' origin, he could discover from where in Africa his "furthest-back person" came. If he could document his family back to Africa, he could begin to fill in the excised history for which he and so many Black Americans longed.

In another account, a 1981 interview with biographer Mary Seibert McCauley, Haley roots his interest in Africa, albeit by a different historical route. Rather than being inspired by an eighteenth century orientalist translator, he was taken with the discourse of Afrocentrism (Moses 1998).[39]

39 Although the term Afrocentrism "became fashionable as a result of the efforts of its repackager, Professor Molefi Asante, during the 1980s, [i]t is important to note that the term was used at least as early as 1962 in connection with the Encyclopedia Africana project under the sponsorship of Kwame Nkrumah and W.E. Burghardt Du Bois..." (Moses 1998: 226). This earlier usage of the term focused on the geographic parameters of the encyclopedia, but the intellectual project, Moses notes, is part of an ongoing eighteenth and nineteenth century historiographic tradition to constitute Africa as a locus for working out diaspsoric, especially African American, racial realities (Moses 1998: 17).

It was in the early sixties. It was at the time when what came to be known as the Civil Rights Thrust began everywhere, and the social order among us Black people was such that suddenly there was a lot of talk about Blackness. The phrase "Black is beautiful" came into vogue. Another thing was that Africa began to be spoken of as the motherland. Phrases like those were spoken among us, at least as I recall, we who hadn't previously really thought that way about Africa nor Africans [sic]. I can remember when the few Africans who were in this country, if they came in contact with most of us Black people here, were almost obsequious in trying to be liked, accepted at all. I remember when most Black people here didn't pay Africans any particular attention, when we maybe saw them as curiosities or something like that. But when the Civil Rights Thrust began to come along, we began to take pride in Africa as the motherland. And all of this was right in the period when I had just finished *The Autobiography of Malcolm X.* That put me into the world of books whereas previously I had been writing magazine articles. Then I began to hear this whole exotic Africa thing and Africa as the motherland which had that sense about it, a sense of ancestry really in the sense of being the symbol source of Black people. Then what particularly moved me was that now or then, traveling as I did at the time and living in New York City, I saw a lot of these kind of things. I began to perceive this. Now or then I would see some African person look at some Black American who had a strong physiognomy, strong facial features, and would say to that person something like "you have the features of a Walach or some other tribe!" I began to notice that the Black person when told this would almost hug the statement in mystical delight. And these were the same people whose fathers probably would have fought an African for claiming they looked like Africans. I remember, I thought myself. I wondered. I wondered what tribe we were—my family. Then that linked directly into the stories I had earlier heard about the "African" in our family. I wondered what tribe he was. Not only did I remember the story but I remembered the fact that the story had contained phonetic things he had said to his daughter. So now came the thing—what was that he spoke? That was a clue perhaps to his tribe. All of these were just little parts of what led into the search. I would say that, other than the stories told on the front porch, this is the only specific thing I can think about. (McCauley 1983: 110–11)

Without question Haley belongs within an Afrocentric setting. However his relationship with the movement was more conspicuously American than many other African Americans would care to admit. His endgame was to restore Black people's full historical knowledge that they might move past their anger and live the American Dream—as his family had. Whether Malcolm's emerging cosmopolitan and pan-African leanings inspired the writer is a matter of debate (Delmont 2016: 23).[40] But in Malcolm, Haley had witnessed the power of identifying rootedness with Africa. Radical or reformed, Malcolm was increasingly becoming a mainstream figure, and Haley would need to work out an answer to the leader's agenda.

Haley saw Malcolm for the last time in early January 1965. They met in Malcolm's car in the parking lot of Kennedy Airport. Malcolm was on his way to a speaking engagement. Haley had just come from Kansas City where his brother, George, was sworn into the Kansas State Senate. Haley had a layover before flying upstate, giving him just enough time to visit with Malcolm. Malcolm was frustrated with his own failed attempts at building a coalition among the various civil rights groups. They believed his stance "too moderate" for the "so-called militants" but "too militant" for the "so-called moderate" organizations (X and Haley 1999 [1965]: 431). Haley remembers Malcolm complaining how "his old 'hate' and 'violence' image" was all people wanted to engage, either as a foil or for inspiration. The conversation was joyous as well, for Malcolm and his wife Betty were expecting their fifth child.

But by February 18, 1965, Malcolm was under extreme duress. The NOI had stalked Malcolm after he had assisted two former secretaries of Elijah Muhammad in filing paternity suits (X and Haley 1999 [1965]: 432–3). On February 18, Malcolm called Haley from a

---

40 As Delmont points out, popular accounts suggest Haley learned from Malcolm the importance of Africa despite the lack of evidence in Haley-penned primary source materials. I agree with his assessment, but it is undeniable that Malcolm was doing rootwork before Haley's eyes.

Mississippi speaking engagement with plans to read the latest draft of the *Autobiography*, which was nearing completion. The two scheduled to meet in New York City sometime during the February 20–21 weekend (X and Haley 1999 [1965]: 433).

On February 21, 1965, members of the NOI assassinated Malcolm X. Malcolm was on the stage of New York City's Audubon Ballroom where he was delivering a speech before members of the OAAU (X and Haley 1999 [1965]: 442–3). As he had done so many times before, he extended the Muslim greeting, "*As-salaam alaikum*," and was met with an enthusiastic response from the crowd, "*Walaikum salaam*." Before he could begin his remarks, a staged altercation between two NOI members distracted everyone while three NOI members rose from the front row and fired gunshots at Malcolm (Marable 2011: 435–41).

Malcolm's death placed Haley in a bind. The author had lost his "friend" and his subject matter—difficulties that were inextricably linked (2.25—Alex Haley to Dick Seaver, Editor at Grove Press, Anne Romaine Collection).[41] On the same day as Malcolm's death, Haley pleaded with his agent, Paul Reynolds, to help Betty receive financial assistance, including an advance on the *Autobiography*.[42] Haley noted in the same letter that the success of the book was assured given the

41 In this letter, Haley contrasts his "good friend[ship]" with celebrity lawyer Mel Belli (a potential subject for another biography) with that of his "warm relationship" with Malcolm. Haley resists calling Malcolm a friend because of their ideological differences. But given the more intimate aspect of Haley and Malcolm's relationship, I am inclined to believe that Haley compartmentalized the social, professional, and political aspects of their relationship.

42 Haley anticipates Betty's needs for funds after the death of Malcolm X. Malcolm had recently informed him that their family's funds totaled "two or three hundred dollars" after having moved out of their NOI-owned house. Haley shows great concern that the book's assured success would give the family some much-needed income (Romaine n.d. 3.24: Alex Haley's Letter to Paul Reynolds, February 21, 1965). The relationship was not without tension. Haley also notes the difficult time he had in working out the financial details of an aborted Malcolm X film (2.25—Alex Haley's Letter to Paul Reynolds, March 10, 1974, Anne Romaine Collection).

intrigue surrounding Malcolm's life and death in the minds of the public. But in the weeks following the murder, Doubleday wanted to distance itself and its employees from the violent events. On April 21, 1965, Doubleday sold the *Autobiography*'s publishing rights to Grove Press.[43] Published that same year, the book was an instant bestseller and has been since heralded as a "classic" (Dyson 1995: 23).

The *Autobiography*'s success is in no small part due to Haley's framing of Malcolm's life. The 1999 edition of the work coincides with the U.S. Postal Service's commemoration of his life with a "Black Heritage stamp," enshrining Malcolm's story as worthy of national remembrance and as "a testament of great emotional power from which every American can learn much" (X and Haley 1999 [1965]: inside cover). In his final days, Malcolm felt unheard among the other voices in the Civil Rights Movement, but the *Autobiography* made him an unignorable martyr.

Left to finish the book without Malcolm's approval, Haley had the authorial freedom to craft Malcolm's story into, what Marable calls, "a cautionary tale about human waste and the tragedies produced by segregation" (Marable 2011: 9). Likewise, literary critic Barrett John Mandel likens the work to a conversion narrative (Mandel 1972: 269).[44] Compelling cases have been made in both regards, but it is

---

43 Haley's lawyer at the time, Malcolm Reiss, finalized the transfer of contract from Doubleday to Grove Press in 3.26—Malcolm Reiss's Letter to Ken McCormick, Esq. Doubleday & Co., April 21, 1965, Anne Romaine Collection. Reiss details the occasion of the transfer to Percy E. Sutton of Sutton & Sutton in 3.26—Malcolm Reiss's Letter to Percy E. Sutton, Esq. April 14, 1965, Anne Romaine Collection.

44 Mandel writes:

> Like St. Augustine, John Bunyan, Jonathan Edwards, and Vavasor Powell, Malcolm has written a spiritual conversion autobiography. The *Autobiography* is that of a sinner who becomes a saint, and the saint, like his Christian parallels, is a preacher. One notices the parallels especially to John Bunyan, who as he became a "saint"—the word was commonly used for Puritan Brethren in the seventeenth century and was still used by the Plymouth Brethren in the nineteenth century—became increasingly repugnant to the established authorities, who went to great lengths to stop his preaching. (1972: 269)

important to note that Haley saw himself as presenting a true portrait of his friend. Haley ends the *Autobiography*'s "Epilogue" with these words:

> After signing the contract for this book, Malcolm X looked at me hard. "A writer is what I want, not an interpreter." I tried to be a dispassionate chronicler. But he was the most electric personality I have ever met, and I still can't conceive him dead. It still feels to me as if he was just gone into some next chapter, to be written by historians. (X and Haley 1999 [1965]: 463)

By the book's publication in 1965, Haley was no longer trying to show a change in Malcolm as much as he was outlining the possibilities for an integrated America—a nation that, with historical knowledge, could move past "the hate that hate produced" and change for the better. Haley's association with the *Autobiography* made him a sought-after authority on the life of Malcolm X with "the capacity to earn a minimum of $100,000 a year by writing articles and lecturing" (Bell 1977: 51, cited in McCauley 1983: 112). Yet Haley was more committed to articulating his own view on America with *Before This Anger*. Although Doubleday had ceded the *Autobiography* to Grove Press, the publisher had retained a separate contract for Haley's proposed novel. The original terms of the August 1964 agreement stipulated that Haley would complete a manuscript in a year's time. By August 1965, however, Haley had yet to begin his first draft (McCauley 1983: 112). What he did have was a strategy for writing another bestseller, and this would be enough to pacify the publishing house until the book's 1976 release.

Conclusion

As of 1966, Haley had mentioned little about his novel idea except to family, his agent, and Doubleday. It was around this time that he connected the idea of *Before This Anger* with his personal search for his African ancestry (McCauley 1983: 114). He realized that if he could begin his story in Africa, then Americans would better understand the tragedy of slavery and the necessity for an integrated nation. Before him was the challenge of an expensive and daunting historical quest, but Haley would draw on his journalism and public-relations skills to rise to the occasion. After all, this was the story of not just a man, but a world rooted in scriptures.

The Civil Rights Movement showcased the power of language and national memory to stimulate the political imagination. But as much as we may notice this as a sort of first principle, our critical understanding of social change should be attuned to how actors accomplished this in local settings. Alex Haley had done the work of identifying some of the central media of social interaction in the modern world—history and writing —in hopes that he could deploy them for his own purposes. He operationalized the past by writing profiles of Black "firsts," bolstering efforts to make sure that they were not Black "onlies" on the ladder of success. Haley himself wanted to climb that ladder. And the most effective way for him to appeared to be writing the world and his story his way.

His interlocutor Malcolm X had a similar idea as made evident in the *Autobiography of Malcolm X as Told to Alex Haley*. In it, readers see who Malcolm was and came to be, presumably in his own words. That idea of authentic expression however fails to recall the ways Haley edited the final product and the way Haley's agent Paul Reynolds pushed Haley and Malcolm to write with a reading audience (read: White book buyers) in mind. This serves as a reminder that the idea of the self-made person or the author is an illusion of culture. The histories and the writings that seem to make the world turn result from the push and pull of identity claims, of reading and being read.

Hence in this chapter the idea of "scriptures" has been considered not in terms of a monolithic root-book but more poignantly as the discursive forms through which operational acts of identification are often and effectively mediated in a domain. Thus I offered an intellectual biography of Haley's formation and early career that was predicated on genre or customary pivotal social expression rather than so-called great books that may have influenced him. In broader terms, the anthropology of scriptures investigates the modalities of meaning-making and identification that make our wants and desires legible.

The next chapter will focus on how such modalities can become wholly associated in a text, and on the cultural factors that make scriptural development a complicated yet tantalizing enterprise. As much as people associate scriptures with life-giving rootedness, we will see that revolutionary or counter-cultural scriptural engagement can also lead to dangerous results. Alex Haley authored *Roots* within this tension, and we will follow his missteps and success to identify the power dynamics of scriptures as a tool for cultural formation.

2 "The Book That Changed America"

Scriptures are not safe. A sureness accompanies the mastery of them, but the situations in which they become significant belie the antithesis of certainty. People turn to scriptures in times when change is needed and when change is feared. They are the means through which we relate to the people and events near us. Thus, if scriptures are to be understood as emblematic of the very "credibility of discourse" in a social context—that is, the convincing display of rootedness—then we can begin to see their dynamic relationship with identity formation (De Certeau 1984: 148).

People work out who they are—their rootedness—through scriptures. The "classical" Western etymology of roots (cf. Latin *radix*) claims access to a non-derivative foundation just as vernacular usage of "radical" denotes an other's place at the edge of a cultural field (Blyth 2011: 300). This is more than the latent irony of ambivalent connotations. It is an omen portending the stratification of all who dare to take hold of roots. The rooted status of belonging only makes sense in contrast to a reality in which some "other" in some way is out of place. Identity is a process of policing by definition (Newton 2017b).

Following the lead of Vincent L. Wimbush, social theorists would do well to heed the critical importance of surfacing vernacular (cf. Latin, "home-born slave") significations of scriptures to "refract" the "transgressions" covered by the category. "For what we are confronted with in 'scriptures' is about nothing less than how human beings are determined and how they shape and reshape themselves in relationship to the politics of language and knowledge as centering forces" (Wimbush 2016: 10). An anthropology of scriptures, therefore, calls for an interrogation of who arbitrates the rules of their use along with the costs and benefits of being identified with them. What price did Haley pay for daring to rewrite the nation's history?

To review, in Chapter 1, we identified Alex Haley's formation within a scriptural economy. His very existence seemed bound by the power of the word and the arc of history. Haley's first lessons in rootedness emanated from his exposure to the Black uplift tradition and his parents' insistence on formal education as the key to societal integration. Even when Haley rendered the American dreaming of his father academic, he nevertheless followed his father's footsteps into the U.S. military. His writing skills advanced his station in and out of the service, enabling him to pursue a career in journalism. And in the eyes of a majority-White readership and publishing industry, his best-received pieces featured successful Black persons within America's larger racial struggle. Contextualizing them further solidified his standing in professional spaces otherwise precarious for a Black body.

Haley's maneuvering into high society was by no means an easy endeavor. His commitment to acquiring bylines forced the hand of his first wife. He simply could not chase a writing career and raise a young family, so instead he chose divorce and child-support payments. Similarly, Haley's journalistic ties to the Nation of Islam put him in the crosshairs of the FBI. Though his own conservative politics proved amenable to their cause and assuaged their fears, his collaboration with Malcolm X was no less controversial. Haley's editor, Paul Reynolds, worried that the relationship would open his client to guilt by association. Haley, though, sensed its potential.

Chronicling Malcolm's journey, Haley saw how "there but for the grace of God go I."[1] America's racial landscape painted Black people with too broad a brush for their differing theologies alone to distinguish them. Furthermore, their eventual friendship would not be held back by Christian or Muslim confessions. What differentiated them was the way in which they identified America at its root and what it could become for them. For Haley, America meant home. And though the country had not always welcomed his kin, he

---

1   The colloquialism I have used here is an interpellation of 1 Corinthians 15:8–10 with various English renderings beginning in the late modern period.

boasted a foresight to envision the coming of liberty and integration for Black people. Malcolm read America differently. America had not just maligned Black people, it had systematically disenfranchised them. He was impassioned with a righteous anger that insisted there could be no liberation, reconciliation, let alone integration, without "Afro-American unity" first. Haley and Malcolm had contrasting visions about how Black bodies should be identified within America, but they were united in their recognition that a new historiography could bring forth their dreams. In this way, *The Autobiography of Malcolm X as Told to Alex Haley* reflects—and "refracts"—a rootedness in America.

Readers may have a hard time appreciating the transformational and transgressive power of the *Autobiography* in America—an accidental consequence of its scriptural success. The controversial book that Haley had every reason not to write was one of ten nonfiction books listed as "required reading" by *TIME* (P. Gray 1988). Paul Gray, the magazine's literary critic, observed: "at once an unsparing confession and spiritual quest, the book tells a haunting tale of racial persecution and rebirth." Religious studies scholar Stephen Prothero included it among the "Prophets" in his anthology, *The American Bible* (2012), originally subtitled: *How Our Words Unite, Divide, and Define a Nation. The New Yorker*'s Adam Gopnik opined that if the book revealed anything salvific for American self-understanding, then Alex Haley was Malcolm's Apostle Paul (2010). Even after death, Malcolm's words demanded a hearing, insisting on national recognition in spite of their critique of the American project.

Alex Haley wanted to tap into this scriptural potential, but for his own ends and his own story. His project would reach *before* the anger that typified Malcolm's discontent and move readers to a more radical, post-civil-rights vision of America—integration. Like the *Autobiography*, history provided the site of contest, but Haley would counter signs of "Black" "melancholy" with a steady regimen of "hope" and "progress" (Winters 2016). His family's patriotic optimism, narrated in literary form, had the makings of a baptismal catechism, a "re-birth of a nation," and a recreating of Americanness in his own image.[2] What Mecca appeared to do for Malcolm and his public image, Haley set out to do for America and its conscience. Michael Eric Dyson judges *Roots* a success on this score: "If the Black freedom struggle of the '60s had liberated our bodies from the haunting imperatives of White supremacy, Haley's book helped free our minds and spirits from that same force" (Dyson 2007: x). When we suspend unexamined agreement with nationalist triumphalism, we can more clearly identify the revolutionary and treasonous act that brokered this freedom. Always and already suspicious of America, Malcolm relished the tensions with the status quo in his *Autobiography*. Haley believed such tensions to be part and parcel of the American experiment. The difference between the two men was not whether but how they made that tension work in their favor.

Haley took roughly twelve years to mount a fully-formed, published response to the anger recorded in the *Autobiography*. As will be discussed in this chapter, a lot happened within his personal life during this period. Especially important were the wider discursive changes that took place in America. The growing influence of "African" consciousness along with Haley's interest in the furthest reaches of his own family history prepared him for a conceptual shift about the nature of his place in America. Figuratively speaking, he was among the throng of people still reeling from a barb in Malcolm's 1963 speech to the Northern Negro Grass Roots Leadership Conference, "You didn't come over on the *Mayflower*" (Bauer 2005). Malcolm had derived his solution to the Black American paradox from Nation of Islam prophet Elijah Muhammad. Expressive movements from Black Aesthetics to Blaxploitation experimented with rationalizations of the radical realities imposed by the notion of Blackness. Though Haley's allegiance

---

2   The word-play is intentional here. I am placing Alex Haley's *Roots* in comparison with other national myths that revolve around the color line. This would include D.W. Griffith's 1915 film adaptation of Thomas Dixon's *The Clansman: A Historical Romance of the Ku Klux Klan* (1905) and Nate Parker's 2016 film adaptation of Thomas Ruffin Gray's *The Confessions of Nat Turner: The Leader of the Late Insurrection in Southhampton, VA* (1831). Both films share the title *The Birth of a Nation*, signifying their contest for the origins and root of national imagining.

to the Black uplift tradition would disqualify him from fully aligning with either identifier, his own journey meanders squarely between both. The *Autobiography* became iconic for many of the intellectuals and artists experimenting with Black aesthetics (Marable 2011: 7–9). And in 1973, Haley earned a screenwriting credit for the *Super Fly* sequel, *Super Fly T.N.T.*, wherein the eponymous reformed Harlem drug dealer joins an African revolution against European occupiers. The poster's tagline, "Same dude with a different plan…in another country with a different man," aptly describes the strategy of identification that Haley would adopt. In 1972, Haley retitled *Before This Anger* as *Roots: The Saga of an American Family*.

In thinking about scriptures anthropologically, the title change designates the people Haley intended to impact. Matthew F. Delmont's archival study isolates one of the earliest glimpses into Haley's thought process. In a letter to friends, Haley unpacks his rationale, which seems to meet the approval of "nearly everyone." There are:

> …[n]umerous good reasons. One, primarily, the more I have written, the more it has impressed itself upon me that there is so much more to the Black saga than the topical "Anger." And that new title, "Roots," is more generic among mankind, and I see this book, really, as kind of the Black slice of the human saga. (3.1—Alex Haley to Elaine and Wally Wiser, March 4, 1972, Alex Haley Collection, Goodwin College, CT, cited in Delmont 2016: 67)

Malcolm's metonymic anger would appear almost petty next to Haley's more robust exploration of Black pathos.

Haley's diction is especially telling. In arrogating the generic nature of his *Roots*, Haley reconfigures America's anthropology. The genre, as it were, concerns "Black" people as "mankind," as "human," a syllogism of identification that Black people could not take for granted. *Roots* would advance on Malcolm's appeal to "the Black slice" of the demography while also winning over an even more integrated audience. In a 1978 interview with Mary Seibert McCauley, Haley shows no reserve in outlining the formation or execution of his *Roots* agenda.

> Writing *The Autobiography of Malcolm X* taught me that I could
> write about an unpopular subject and have it received emphat-
> ically and sympathetically. I did not editorialize but simply
> started with the subject as a child—as a fetus, actually—and
> related in a very low-key way, successively what happened to
> him, from childhood to adulthood. And I used that same tech-
> nique with Kunta Kinte [*Roots*]. It taught me to let the read-
> ers write their own editorial. I don't do it for them. (McCauley
> 1983: 99–100)

Though in casting the book as *his story* (that is, Haley's) and history
(that is, America's), the limits of editorial license were largely set.
Those readers who completed the book would have already entertained Haley's anthropology for nearly 700 pages; viewers of the
original miniseries, nearly ten hours. Haley's own self-promotion,
the public's excitement, and scholars' debates would further *Roots*'
relevance. As long as people kept Haley's Comet in sight, they might
come to understand what "roots" meant to him—namely, that he
was writing his family's right to lay claim to America's history and
promise:

> Why have I called it *Roots*? Because it not only tells the story
> of a family, my own, but also symbolizes the history of millions
> of American Blacks of African descent. I intend my book to be
> a buoy for Black self-esteem and a reminder of the universal
> truth that we are all descendants of the same creator. (Haley
> 2007 [1974]: 93)

While it is informative to understand what "roots" meant to Haley
in his own words, the anthropologist of scriptures is as much, if not
more, concerned with identifying what he stood to gain by identifying
with that particular discourse. Why might he have elected to alter his
and his audience's circumstances through "rootwork"? The specific
answer to the question might be lost to Bourdieu's "universe of the
undiscussed" (1977: 168–70), but artifacts to the discourse may be
discovered in the wake of the "Black Atlantic" (Gilroy 1993: 4).

Roots in the Black Atlantic

"Rootworking" is among the most common native terms for what scholars broadly categorize as Black folk religions.[3] Specifically, the name underlines the use of ground "roots" among other "natural and organic substances for physical deliverance" (Chireau 2008: 124).[4] Yvonne Chireau, a scholar of African American religions, summarizes that natural elements like ground roots have given Black people the raw materials for conjuration at least since the eighteenth century. Whether this rootwork is more rightfully "full blooded African" or a diasporic innovation is less important than the enticing idea that such items could heal and harm in precarious circumstances (Chireau 2003: 33).

Rootwork is well-attested in Black literature dealing with the legacy of slavery. The *Narrative of the Life of Frederick Douglass, an American Slave* (1845) presents one of the most illustrative instances of rootwork in the Black literary tradition. The eponymous author describes his impasse with an especially overbearing master named Edward Covey. Douglass manages to withstand the slavebreaker's beatings with the help of a charmed root (Douglass 2003 [1845]: 59–87). Similarly, in Zora Neale Hurston's novel, *Their Eyes Were Watching God* (1937), the grandmother of the protagonist, Janie,

3   In anthropology, "native terms" refers to the argot or vocabulary of the community being studied. In regards to scripturalizing, Grey Gundaker suggests that the unpacking of "native terms can yield nuanced, locally significant information about how scripturalizing informs participants' lives" (Gundaker 2008: iii).

4   Chireau explains that although the knowledge to manipulate these "natural and organic substances" has primarily been transmitted through oral means, in the 1920s, print instructions and advertisements began a popular means of continuing the tradition in Black urban enclaves (Chireau 2003: 143).

Grey Gundaker offers an evocative look at African American landscaping, from the eighteenth century through the beginning of the twenty-first century, as a noteworthy site of naturalistic expression (Gundaker 1998: 2005).

tells how the "hardness" that Blacks have experienced exists in part because of their being without roots:

> You know, honey, us colored folks is branches without roots and that makes things come round in queer ways. You in particular. Ah was born back due in slavery so it wasn't for me to fulfill my dreams of whut a woman oughta be and to do. Dat's one of de hold-backs of slavery. But nothing can't stop you from wishin'. You can't beat nobody down so low till you can rob 'em of they will. Ah didn't want to be used for a work-ox and a brood-sow and Ah didn't want mah daughter used dat way neither. It sho wasn't mah will for things to happen lak they did. Ah even hated de way you was born. But, all de same Ah said thank God, Ah got another chance. Ah wanted to preach a great sermon about colored women sittin' on high, but they wasn't no pulpit for me. Freedom found me wid a baby daughter in mah arms, so Ah said Ah'd take a broom and a cook-pot and throw up a highway through de wilderness for her. She would expound what Ah felt. But somehow she got lost offa de highway and next thing Ah knowed here you was in de world. So whilst Ah was tendin' you of nights Ah said Ah'd save de text for you. Ah been waitin' a long time, Janie, but nothin' Ah been through ain't too much if you just take a stand on high ground lak Ah dreamed. (Hurston 1998 [1937]: 16)[5]

The selections above draw attention to an important elision between two valences of the root metaphor. The transformative or conjuring power in Douglass's *Narrative* finds expression in the arboreal or family tree symbolism in Hurston's novel. According to author Toni Morrison, "rootedness" conceives of "the ancestor as foundation," the source of orientation. In the Black literary tradition, "the absence of the ancestor" is "frightening...and threatening." Similarly, in the world of the text, a lack of rootedness is the cause of "huge destruction and disarray" (Morrison 1984: 343). Rootedness "suggests what the conflicts are, what the problems are. But it need not solve the problems because it is not a case study, it is a recipe" (Morrison 1984:

---

5   Theophus H. Smith connects the idea of conjure and rootwork to African American biblical interpretation in *Conjuring Culture: Biblical Formations of Black America* (1995).

341). It is the task of the present generation to receive the roots of the old world and find ways of making them work in the new.

With *Roots*, Haley is presenting his family's history as a source from which Americans, especially Black Americans, can draw strength to move beyond the anger wrought by slavery. In an *Ebony* magazine article titled "We Must Honor Our Ancestors" (1986), Haley declared:

> We need to remind ourselves that, except for the endurance of our historic ancestors beneath those rock markers, we surely wouldn't be enjoying today's positive potentials and opportunities—a relative plethora of them which, in fact, our ancestral Blacks couldn't even have conceived. (1990 [1986]: 152)

Haley's understanding of roots is characteristic of what African American religions scholar and cultural critic William D. Hart refers to as an "Afro-Eccentric" perspective of American history (Hart 2008: x). The neologism is "a critical pun and trope [a burlesque of the Afrocentric idea] that mimics, underscores, and reminds us of the difference within the same, the manifold within the apparent uniformity of American Black people" (Hart 2011: 2).[6] It flourishes by making "a very bad situation, a chronic violence, dishonor, and social death appear to be better than it was" (2011: 3). Through Hart's lens we begin to see that the therapeutic benefits imprinted in the roots discourse are not necessarily a means of resolution but of coping with a contextual struggle.

I was recently reminded of the strangeness of it all when I was looking at my father's first edition of the 1976 book. The book jacket

6   In his 2008 book, Hart is especially interested in the genre of autobiography in Black religion. Two of his subjects, Malcolm X and a twentieth century African American Baptist-Buddhist named Jan Willis, are noted as having ties to Alex Haley (Hart 2008: 186). According to Willis's autobiography, she was a friend of Alex Haley. She credits him with inspiring her own genealogical search. In the midst of that search, she grew frustrated with the realities of slave history, an event that led to her eventual conversion to Buddhism. Willis also notes that sometime after *Roots*, Haley had been begun a comparative history of oral storytellers, but this work was never published (Willis 2008 [2001]: 217–18, 274, 361).

has the author's name, picture, and the book's full title, *Roots: The Saga of an American Family*. But in the full height of the text block, my father had inscribed "NEWTON FAMILY" with permanent marker. This could be seen as a pedestrian gesture demarcating ownership, though no other books in his library wear those letters. He could have simply written his first and last name, but instead this was the book of his brood—except it was not. It was the story of an American family—except when it was not. In those moments of bewilderment, Alex Haley convinced us of an alternative or otherwise way of viewing the world. His rootwork convinced a nation that the "dreadful fruitfulness of the original sin of the African trade" (Madison 1820)—and the bodies still scarred by it—could be transfigured into a glorious testament of national virtue. Hence, the thirtieth anniversary edition of the book arrogated a new superlative, "The book that changed America."

The anthropologist of scriptures observes the risks and gains of identifying with roots. This second chapter continues with an intellectual biography of Haley's deliberate construction of an American scripture. And it examines why Haley's rootwork remains a popular formula for the creative work of identifying oneself within the nation. This is the story of how Alex Haley, and his *Roots*, became America's history.

"A Master Storyteller"

For those who experienced the craze first hand or those studying it with the benefit of hindsight, what made Haley's work stand out from comparable slave and national narratives was the centrality of his grasping for roots. The author's biography was central to the story. It was also central to the story's marketing. Haley had lectured and written widely about his search in the decade before its publication in the winter of 1976. In 1977, Warner Bros. Records also released *Alex Haley Tells the Story of His Search for Roots*, a two-hour, double LP of Haley narrating how he found his *Roots*. Described by many as a "master storyteller," Haley recounted his search in such a way that it became as memorable as *Roots*' plot.

The miniseries adaptation gestures toward its magnificence in the opening to the first episode. The earth-tone logo flashes atop an ebony title card. A trumpet fanfare regales a voiceover, introducing a brief montage of Black-and-White stills of Alex Haley at work, in the thick of it, searching, finding, and now presenting his *Roots*.

> Tonight we present a landmark in television entertainment. *Roots*, the true story Alex Haley uncovered across a twelve-year search across the seven generations of his ancestry. After two years in production, we present this incredible saga in an epic motion picture. *Roots*, the current, number-one bestselling novel is the television event of the year. From primitive Africa to the ol' South, *Roots* sweeps across the panorama of a young America bursting with all the dreams, all the joys, and all the hardships of a vibrant country and its people through the years of slavery, the Civil War, Reconstruction and the struggle to survive. A film spanning more than a hundred years, generation to generation, continent to continent, slavery to freedom. (*Roots: The Miniseries* 2012, first broadcast January 23, 1977)

After a display of highlights from the coming series and an introduction of the cast, a timpani roll swells underneath the narrator's concluding crescendo, "Now we are proud to present the triumph of an American family, *Roots*." The hype makes explicit the stakes of the work and the difficulty of the task. Americans who stayed tuned would receive Haley's story as their story and as history because Haley completed the task of surfacing the roots of the rootless. His ancestral patriarch's perseverance saw to it that the old ways were passed on so that the begotten would never forget from where they—and their identity—came. And whether readers and viewers knew it at the story's beginning, Haley's charisma, eloquence, and success would convince them that their roots and his *Roots* were what they had been missing. In Haley's words:

> In all of us there is a hunger, marrow-deep, to know our heritage—to know who we are and where we have come from. Without this enriching knowledge, there is a hollow yearning. No matter what our attainments in life, there is still a vacuum, an emptiness, and the most disquieting loneliness. (Haley 2007 [1977]: 159)

Haley believed he could provide this sustaining knowledge in his own words.

The key rests with Kunta Kinte, the enslaved Mandinka who secretly taught his daughter native phrases, such as *Kamby Bolongo* (Gambia River) and *ko* (guitar), and his true name "Kinte" (Fisher 1993 [1977]: 403). These were passed on through the generations to Haley's Grandmother Cynthia and her sisters, who eventually relayed the words to Haley along with fleeting memories of "the African." Haley would cross-reference these details with historical surveys, archival findings, genealogical records, and Gambian oral histories to reconstruct his roots, unbroken by the machinations of the modern West. Black people—representative of all peoples—could have a place in a world that demanded a history of rootedness. And feeding the mystique of Haley were his consistent reminders that his root-work was not easy.

Scholarship on Alex Haley does not doubt the difficulty that lay before the task. Academics have all but sided with E. Franklin Frazier's skepticism of African cultural retentions in the modern African American community (Frazier 1974 [1964]: 13–14). As mentioned in my introduction, early work—from the late 1970s to about 2010—has focused on shortcomings in Haley's historiographic technique. Haley classified *Roots* as "faction," a neologism of fiction and fact whose hybridity articulates more truth than its disassembled root words (Huntzicker 2007: 75–6; Fisher 1993 [1977]: 431). *Roots'* genealogical, cultural, and historical presuppositions have not entirely held up under the conventions of scholarly value. But rather than looking for methodological flaws, more recent studies of Alex Haley have focused on detailing how Haley arrived at *Roots.* Instead of harping on the implausibility of Haley's myth, this chapter advances an explanation of how and why he told the tale that he did.

Haley's deconstructed search was a story about a man who had deciphered the strange markers of modern identity—history and writing—and tried to develop his own life-altering biography in its puzzling script. In the wooden nature of his translation efforts, the critic can see the cracks in the era's facade, the flaws of an intellectual artifice built on rooting one's ideas in the authority of an other. Haley's obsession with Africa may have originated with his 1964 viewing of the Rosetta Stone (Haley 2007 [1976]: 862), but whatever he saw in the British Museum was also a blatant example of history as a self-referential modality. In writing *Roots*, Haley simply exploited this approach by inductively proof-texting the narrative he needed to be true. What separates him from the professional historian are the rough edges apparent in his technique.

Figure 2 The Rosetta Stone in the British Museum, London.
Source: Hans Hillewaert. CC BY-SA 4.0
https://commons.wikimedia.org/wiki/File:Rosetta_Stone.JPG

Following his trip to London in 1964, Haley attended a family reunion in Kansas City. Cousin Georgia was present and expressed her pride in what the Haley boys had become (Norrell 2015: 97). George had worked with Thurgood Marshall on the landmark *Brown v. Board of Education, Topeka, Kansas* case and was an up-and-coming public servant (Valentine 2015). Alex had come to assist George on his campaign for the Kansas State Senate while also musing about his next writing project that would begin with Georgia's father, an industrious blacksmith named Tom Murray. She was most pleased with his desire to tell the family's story, still at this time called *Before This Anger* and reaching only as far back as the late nineteenth and early twentieth centuries (Haley 2007 [1976]: 864–5).

Satisfied with locating his roots in the recent past, Haley plumbed for memories of the hardworking elders who made a life for a Black family in Henning, TN, during and after Reconstruction. He recollected this legacy shortly after a 1965 trip to the National Archives where he located an 1880 census record that corresponded with Georgia's recollection of the Murray clan, who originated in Alamance County, North Carolina and later moved to Henning (Haley 2007 [1974]: 89; Haley 2007 [1976]: 866; Norrell 2015: 98). As excited as Haley was about the oral account, he took relief in having documentary evidence to support his forebear's claim. As he qualified in *Roots*, "It wasn't that I hadn't believed the stories of Grandma and the rest of them. You *didn't* just not believe my grandma" (Haley 2007: 866). But having documentary evidence to support the porch stories made a legitimate difference to him.

As mentioned in Chapter 1, 1965 was a watershed year for Alex Haley's search. George Haley's election to the Kansas State Senate precipitated another Kansas City family celebration wherein Haley could collect stories from his elders. In a letter to agent Paul Reynolds just after this trip, Alex is excited to report that he will be able to go back even farther than he had planned with *Before This Anger*, all the way back to an enslaved African ancestor:

> Two lucky facts make this possible: He happened to be one of the later slaves taken—one of the Mandingo tribe. Secondly, the family, all the way back, had been blessed with story-tellers,

who passed the stories down. (3.10—Alex Haley to Paul Reynolds, January 30, 1965, Alex Haley Collection, Goodwin College, CT, cited in Delmont 2016: 25)

In *Roots* and post-*Roots* accounts, Haley tends to conflate the two trips to Kansas City, creating the impression that he had always set his sights on historically identifying his "furthest-back person" after seeing the Rosetta Stone. However, his letter to Paul Reynolds immediately after the second reunion indicates that his interest in an African ancestor was a new development. Matthew Delmont also explains that this preliminary origin story departs from the final form of Haley's legendary search. The patriarch eventually remembered as "The African" is first called "The Mandingo," about which in an aside Haley rhetorically asks, "Isn't that an odd way to have to refer to your great-great-great-great grandfather?" Secondly, Haley tells Paul Reynolds that the family described the Mandingo as "a mean critter" who was sent to the West Indies to be "broken" before arriving in the United States (3.10—Alex Haley to Paul Reynolds, January 30, 1965, Alex Haley Collection, Goodwin College, CT, cited in Delmont 2016: 25). Yet *Roots* not only records Kunta Kinte making a direct trip to America, but also that "*Always*, Grandma and the other old ladies had said that a ship brought the African to 'somewhere called 'Naplis.' I knew they had to have been referring to Annapolis, Maryland [as the port of arrival]" (Haley 2007 [1976]: 880, emphasis added). And lastly, rather than working for Virginia slave-masters as depicted in *Roots* (2007 [1976]: 883), Haley is initially under the impression that "The Mandingo" was captive in South Carolina (Hogan 1966, cited in Delmont 2016: 38).

The inconsistencies between the diachronic and the ultimate synchronic search accounts merit skepticism about what knowledge Haley's family had passed on through the generations. To be certain, Haley's family had a history that had been passed on—a revolutionary stance that countered those who would equate Blackness with a void. But what that history comprised was still being determined. What is clear is that Haley consistently believed that he could profit from writing his family story (Delmont 2016: 44). He was steadfast in his belief that his family had experienced, struggled, and achieved in ways with which Americans could identify—far more than Malcolm (3.25—Alex Haley to Paul Reynolds, October 24, 1966, Anne Romaine Collection).

The *Autobiography* may have persuaded White Americans that, in the end, Malcolm was not all that different from them. *Roots* convicted them that Haley was at least as American (if not more) than them. That we remember Malcolm as the more militant figure is a product of Haley's way with words. *Roots* is a nationalist intervention couched in palatable terms.

It is in the evolution—rather than the stability—of the search account, that we can distill the orders of change Haley seeks with *Roots*. Stephen Sharot's sociology of religious action allows us to spell out Haley's early rootworking (Sharot 2001), or in Bayart's terms, "operational acts of identification." Sharot adopts the adjective "religious" to identify the social phenomena around which human beings persistently gather and then manage themselves through elite and popular groupings. Emile Durkheim's functionalism and Karl Marx's class structures augment Sharot's Weberian focus on action. The typifying qualities of these "axial" (Sharot 2001: 3–4; Eisenstadt 1986) or what Bayart more poignantly labels "culturalist" (Bayart 2005: 33–35) formations are in their effect and prohibition of change.[7] Though we are accustomed to understanding scriptures via their association with *a priori* forms typically classified as "religion," scriptures are better understood as formative tools to combat the otherwise volatile dynamics of our *a posteriori* realities. Scriptures as roots are the textbooks that insist on particular ways of knowing over and against competing epistemologies. Hence Haley's self-ascribed "Olympian chronicle" conjures more than a specific "classical"

---

7   Bayart argues that Weber himself was not a culturalist precisely because the sociologist was so interested in the fluctuations, appropriations, and inventions that are part and parcel to the invention of cultural stability. At the same time, Bayart acknowledges Weber's penchant for essentialist interpretations of what the Department of Religious Studies at the University of Alabama explain as "religion in culture" (Department of Religious Studies n.d.), yet he qualifies Weber's search for ideal types as a preliminary step in his exploration of the historical matrices and contingencies in which culture is formed (Bayart 2005: 33).

mythology (3.25—Alex Haley to Paul Reynolds, March 9, 1967, Anne Romaine Collection). It siphons the power of such epic orientations in order to mount the herculean task of turning America toward his worldview. Fantastic as it may seem, Haley is crafting a mythology that makes the Black Atlantic define the Transatlantic Slave Trade rather than the other way around.

As early as 1965, Haley was making sense of the post-civil-rights situation in terms of "rootedness." In this period he had viewed the 1963 film adaptation of Greek-American author/filmmaker Elia Kazan's *America America*. The story follows a young Greek man at the turn of the century with aspirations of leaving behind his country for America. By film's end, the protagonist endures the struggles of his homeland and arrives on the shores of New York City. According to Kazan's closing narration the young man works his way up from menial labor to a place where he can not only bring many of his family members over from Greece, but also start a new line that includes Kazan, the protagonist's nephew. After seeing the film, Haley further esteemed how his own people had "been in the bark, trunk, roots, leaves—throughout the family tree to America" (6.10—Notes on "America, America," n.d. [c. 1965], Alex Haley Collection, Goodwin College, CT, cited in Delmont 2016: 32).

But Haley did not long for assimilation. He departed from the nomic goals and principled assumptions of a White nation by seeing Black people's persistence as a salve for America's unrelenting racial shortcomings (Sharot 2001: 36). In a letter to Paul Reynolds, Haley outlined his intention of "'Rooting' a Negro family, all the way back, telling the chronicle, through us, of how the Negro is part and parcel of the American saga." And though Haley had in mind his "Mandingo" progenitor, he verbalized his commitment and faith in the potential of the American experiment. He continued:

> …without rancor, which I do not feel, which has not been my experience in any influencing way…[i]t is a book which I so deeply feel that America, the world, *needs* to read. For its drama, for its authentic image, for other reasons…I shall write it, when I get to the writing, with love. (3.10—Paul Reynolds to Alex Haley, February 8, 1965, Alex Haley Collection, University of Tennessee, cited in Delmont 2016: 26–7)

With his interest in history and the time he spent working in New York City, it is difficult to imagine Haley being unaware of the sentiment inscribed on the Statue of Liberty.[8] Mounted on the statue's base is Emma Lazarus's sonnet, "The New Colossus" (1883). The poem's second half reads:

> "Keep, ancient lands, your storied pomp!" cries she
> With silent lips. "Give me your tired, your poor,
> Your huddled masses yearning to breathe free,
> The wretched refuse of your teeming shore.
> Send these, the homeless, tempest-tost to me,
> I lift my lamp beside the golden door!" (Shapiro 2006)[9]

Lazarus made the case that America is a country for the rootless, for those looking ahead to new opportunities in spite of the histories of their homelands (Sollors 1994: 115).[10] Haley also conceived

8   I have found no conclusive mention of Alex Haley visiting the Statue of Liberty, but his living and working in and around New York City makes the idea of him not ever seeing the monument implausible. *Reader's Digest* pairs Haley's essay "What *Roots* Means to Me" with an image of a man, woman, and child looking out to Ellis Island (Haley 2007 [1977]: 158).

9   In an 1866 original manuscript edition of Lazarus's sonnet, "Keep" is followed by a comma. Although the 1903 Statue of Liberty plaque does not retain the comma, Gary Shapiro quotes Lazarus's biographer and English scholar Esther Schor saying, "ancient lands" are being addressed, not kept. The lack of a comma "doesn't seem like it demands a new interpretation" (Shapiro 2006). Haley, I am arguing, offers a different interpretation: immigrants should keep the "storied pomp" of their "ancient lands" and use it to build America.

10   According to historian Werner Sollors, the meaning of America became increasingly mediated by the immigrant narrative, following relaxed immigration policies after World War II, and the "civil rights bills of the 1950s and 1960s." After this period, "the metaphor of the 'invading hordes' had fallen into disfavor" and "the term 'American' actually became intertwined with ethnicity and flexible enough to include—in widely accepted public usage—such groups as immigrants, African Americans, and American Indians." Sollors does not go into detail about how *Roots* helped this accommodation except for a reference to Haley's posthumous receipt of the Ellis Island Medal of Honor by The Statue of Liberty-Ellis Island Foundation (Sollors 1994: 115).

of American identity as a commitment to making the nation home, but he was reticent about dismissing "the storied pomp" of "ancient lands." In his experience, those credentials were integral to the development of American roots.

Within the scriptural economy of the Afrocentric, post-civil-rights era, Haley rooted his argument in both Africa, an Edenic homeland that suffered a fall at the hand of Western imperialism, and America, a fraught frontier that became a Promised Land. This established a "textual field" concomitant with the DuBoisian twoness of African American life in which Haley expressed his search (Kort 2008: 220; Du Bois 2014 [1903]: 2). Haley remained resolute because these ideological spaces afforded him two forms of cultural capital that would legitimate his sojourn and orient his rooting. The first Sharot calls the "elite," the official, bureaucratic, globally-minded representatives of cultural institutions. The second Sharot calls the "popular," unofficial, folk sages whose locally-concerned directions give insight into the shortcomings and failures of the ruling entities (Sharot 2001: 64–6). In drawing upon both elite and popular human resources from Africa and America alike, Haley could make dually certain that his program would usher in the changes he desired. Ideally, the folk sages would endow their "thaumaturgical" benedictions upon Haley's search, while historiographic bureaucrats would approve Haley's due diligence (Sharot 2001: 36).

While the cultural production that is *Roots* gives the appearance of congruence, once we look more closely at how Haley made himself identifiable, we can begin to recognize how his efforts were far from seamless. His technique reflected what biblical scholar Shanell T. Smith calls a "hermeneutic of ambi-veil-ance," a "simultaneous attraction and repulsion to the powers" that be (cf. the notion of "ambivalence" as articulated by Homi Bhaba [1984: 126]), sewn together into a distortive veil that Black bodies don to obscure a persistent and probing panoptical White gaze (S.T. Smith 2014: 70). Well aware that his Blackness made him out of place in America, Haley embraced his conspicuousness to do the most unexpected thing—that which would be normal for White people. His Afrocentric rootedness empowers and distracts from his otherwise suspicious engagement with textual history—which of course is only strange because

Americans so quickly assume that Black people have no history, at least no history worth writing down. But there is a complementary synthesis, a sublimation happening under the cloak of research. Haley is preparing to make clear to America that rootwork here is not so different from rootwork there. The gap to overcome is not in oral history failing to be written, but American history writers (and readers) failing to listen. Haley's difference—that is, his rootedness in the oral traditions—allows him to rectify this on America's behalf.

His quest to do so was made possible, as he made it known, because he had been blessed by his ancestors. According to Haley's post-*Roots* recollections, when Haley's relatives shared with him the scattered legend of "the Mandingo," he also had received "something that galvanized…driven and sustained" him ever since. His Cousin Georgia, the lone-remaining sister of his Grandma Cynthia Palmer, had affirmed his search saying, "Boy, yo' sweet granma and all of 'em—dey up dere, watchin'. So you go do what you got do" (Fisher 1993 [1977]: 399). The monumental task of traversing a transatlantic genealogical gap would be made possible because of his family's insistence. In Haley's synchronic reimagining of his discoveries, this all happened after he had seen the Rosetta Stone and recalled his family's preservation of the mysterious African words. In regard to the diachronic accounts—informed by documentation from the time—Georgia christened his efforts at both family reunions, irrespective of Haley's focus on the African words. Her support was unconditional and not burdened by historical criticism.

In the case that Haley's African American cipher did not come solely from his matriarchs, what gave life to this part of the tale? These words likely came by way of more mundane though fortuitous means. Despite various alterations in the origin story, Haley consistently located the Mandingo's roots in the newly independent West African nation called The Gambia. In 1965, the former British colony made international news for its embrace of democratic elections and aspirations. According to Matthew Delmont, Haley was especially interested in the burgeoning nation-state, particular for research purposes (Delmont 2016: 37–8). The Gambia was home to Fort James Island, an imperial era trading outpost and military garrison. It was held by a number of European entities—initially the Dutch, mostly the British, and intermittently the French. Among its most valuable commodities were enslaved Africans, and Haley had plotted to visit the newly freed site along his way. At this point, however, its import was nothing more than symbolic for him. He even went so far as to admit his complacency with just the mere possibility of acquiring some memento from the visit (3.10—Alex Haley to Maurice Ragsdale, December 14, 1966, Alex Haley Collection, University of Tennessee, cited in Delmont 2016: 42).

And yet, symbols are powerful. After all, it was symbols—be it the Rosetta Stone and/or his great cousin's stories—that got him this far. *Roots'* symbolic reclaiming of Africa for Black Americans would become so palpable that in 2011, African American Chaz Guest and Gambian President Yahya Jammeh would work together to rename Fort James Island, "Kunta Kinteh Island," protected as a UNESCO World Heritage Site (United Nations Educational, Scientific, and Cultural Organization: World Heritage Convention 2017).[11] Symbols are as powerful as those who identify with them. And once substantiated, those who root themselves in them can take ownership of their importance.

The Throes of Research

As I have underscored previously (and outlined more fully in Chapter 1), Haley seems to operate under the thesis that he could write himself into significance. And yet, he was pragmatic enough to recognize that he could not do so without assistance. In that there is a fundamental lesson in identity formation: it is a communal activity in spite of the rhetorical flourishes about the authentic, homesprung, self-made person. Thus, once Haley had the idea of a much larger saga, he enlisted the help of people who could bring credibility to his musings. Haley employed George Sims, the childhood friend who helped him secure a room in the Grove Street apartment building, to serve as a researcher. Sims cached histories, novels, articles, and newspaper

11   See also the independent documentary film, *Kunta Kinteh Island* (dir. Elvin Ross, 2012).

clippings of interest for Haley to consult throughout the writing process. Beyond informing Haley's understanding, the amassed materials fed his authorial ambitions. The more he had, the more he insisted that his story could be history. But until 1966, word of Haley's ambitious search was limited to his family, his agent, and the Doubleday publishing company.

That same year Haley attended a lawn party where he met Lisa Acheson Wallace, the co-founder of *Reader's Digest* (McCauley 1983: 114; Haley 2007: 3–4). He regaled her with word of his genealogical search for his "furthest-back person." Riveted by his enthusiasm, she and *Digest* editors purchased serialization rights to the book and signed on for a three-hundred dollar monthly stipend, until the book's now-1967 release (McCauley 1983: 137).[12] More importantly he negotiated the *Digest* to cover research-related travel expenses for the year (McCauley 1983: 111). The possibility of reaching The Gambia was becoming a reality.

Haley further identified with The Gambia as a result of elite verification of his roots. He recollects loitering around the United Nations in hopes of liaising with West African foreign nationals to no avail (Haley 1973: 10); Norrell 2015: 106). At the time Haley had also been drawing much of his income from lecturing on Malcolm X at colleges and universities. This brought him into proximity with various books, academic specialists, and international students. Once he had trained his interest on The Gambia, he was primed for fortune to fall upon him again.

In a pre-*Roots* account, Haley shows off his sleuthing. He relays that there were very few Gambian students in the country (Haley 1973: 11), and that the closest was in residence at Hamilton College in Clinton, New York. In *Roots* and subsequent accounts, Haley emphasizes the happenstance of the encounter. During a 1966 visit to Ithaca's Utica College, Haley made known his desire to identify and translate the presumed Mandinka terms. A professor pointed

12 McCauley explains that Haley's agreement with *Reader's Digest* was in effect until 1967. The *Digest* would still publish an essay on Haley's search in 1974 and the book's serialization in 1977, but Haley would no longer receive a stipend or travel expenses from the company.

Haley thirty miles away to Hamilton College, where a bright young Gambian student named Ebou Manga resided (Haley 2007 [1976]: 869). In both accounts, Ebou Manga opened Haley's historical imagination to a new vista.

Haley was struck by Manga's calm and guileless demeanor, eventually adopting him as the model for "the African" Kunta Kinte—even more than the belligerent, polygamous portrayal of the Mandingo that had been spoken of by Haley's elders (Delmont 2016: 40). Manga was of the Wolof tribe and, according to *Roots* lore, "tentatively confirmed the sounds" that his family had remembered as the African's tribal name of "Kin-tay" and words from his native tongue (Haley 2007 [1976]: 869). What is most important is that Manga's family was well connected to The Gambia's governing class (Delmont 2016: 40). Soon after their first meeting in 1967, Haley and Manga flew to Banjul (née Bathurst), Gambia where they met with a group of esteemed men familiar with the country's various customs.[13] The setting was the appropriately named, "Atlantic Hotel," a popular watering hole for diplomats, government leaders, and other VIPs. The men proceeded to tell Haley that the clan name "Kin-tay" might refer to the Kinte clan, one of the oldest in The Gambia and shared by many villages. They left the meeting saying they would search for a *griot*,

---

13 In *Roots* (869), Haley explains that Ebou Manga's father, Alhaji Manga, organized the gathering. Haley adds that most Gambians are "Moslems." Haley does not mention that "Alhaji," is an honorific that many Muslims use to signify their having competed the Hajj, but he likely knows this from his research, if not from the variation Malcolm adopted after his trip to Mecca, *El-Hajj* Malik El-Shabazz.

McCauley, citing the album lecture *Alex Haley Tells the Story of His Search for Roots* (Warner Bros. Records 1977), elaborates that the meeting, on the patio of the Atlantic Hotel, was with government officials (McCauley 1983: 121). In 1994, Anne Romaine made contact with one of the men present, a politician and self-proclaimed "Expert on Senegambian Culture" named A.E. Cham Joof (1.59—Anne Romaine to A.E. Cham Joof, August 3, 1994, Anne Romaine Collection). Cham Joof discusses that he received neither credit (in *Roots*) nor payment for assisting in Haley's search (1.59—A.E. Cham Joof to Anne Romaine, [n.d., c. 1994], Anne Romaine Collection).

or oral historian, who could assist Haley in his search (Haley 2007 [1976]: 870). The heft of his story was just beginning to come into view. Haley returned to the States studying African history in greater earnest, though "investing very little of [his] time in writing" (Haley 2007 [1976]: 872). With the help of George Sims, he had amassed towers of books to consult. Among them was anthropologist Jan Vansina's groundbreaking work, *Oral Tradition: A Study in Historical Method* (Vansina 1965 [1961]). It presented historical and methodological considerations for taking seriously the role of orality in the study of African cultures.

In spring of 1965, Haley received word that a griot with knowledge of the Kinte clan had been found (Haley 2007 [1976]: 871). By May, Haley organized, what he described as, a "minisafari" to a village called Juffure to meet with a griot named Kebba Kanji Fofana (Norrell 2015: 112–15). For "nearly two hours," Haley listened to the griot recount in great detail the history of the Kinte clan. Then, Fofana spoke the words that Haley hoped to hear. "About the time the King's soldiers came... the eldest of these four sons, Kunta, went away from his village to chop wood...and he was never seen again..." (Haley 2007 [1976]: 875). Haley rushed to confirm the work:

> I managed to fumble from my dufflebag my basic notebook, whose first pages containing my grandma's story I showed to an interpreter. After briefly reading, clearly astounded, he spoke rapidly while showing it to the old griot, who became agitated, he got up, exclaiming to the people, gesturing at my notebook in the interpreter's hands, and *they* all got agitated... Later the men of Juffure took me into their mosque built of bamboo and thatch, and they prayed around me in Arabic. I remember thinking, down on my knees, "After I've found out where I came from, I can't understand a word they're saying." Later the crux of their prayer was translated for me: "Praise be to Allah for one long lost from us whom Allah has returned." (Haley 2007 [1976]: 875, 877)

To Haley's ears, the Mandinka griot echoed the oral tradition told on the Henning porch a continent away. "The African," Haley's "furthest-back person," now had a name—Kunta Kinte.

In Haley's recollection, his return to America marks the moment when *Before This Anger* expanded into a definitive telling of the nation's history. In a 1981 speech to the Cumberland Valley Writer's Conference, Haley said:

> On my return to the U.S., I got the heartbreaking news that Cousin Georgia had passed away. Later, studying the hospital death report—including the specific time—I calculated; with a jolt I realized that in Kansas City, Cousin Georgia had died literally on the day I had walked into Juffure Village. Please understand that to me it can only seem that as her generation's last survivor, Cousin Georgia's mission had been to see me into our ancestral village, whereupon she went to join Grandma and all the others.

Haley went on to say:

> Back home, I knew that what I must write, really, was our Black saga where any individual's past is the essence of the millions [*sic*]. So this book had to be the saga of a people. And since it was such, it was up to me to give it every possible thing that I, as a symbol of us, who happened to be a writer could bring to that book. I had to do everything, to find every thread that could have any bearing of us as a people. (Haley, Lecture to the Cumberland Valley Writer's Conference, Vanderbilt University, August 7, 1981, cited in McCauley 1983: 129)[14]

Jan Vansina came to play a key role in Haley's translational rootwork. When and why depends on the type of history one seeks to tell concerning *Roots*.

In some respects, Haley understood Vansina as an orientating figure. Haley's synchronic account—sparsely-dated memories spliced with affective first-person commentary—places the meeting before he met Ebou Manga or visited Africa. This account, recorded in the *Roots* tradition and in Vansina's memoir, *Living with Africa* (1994: 150), suggests that Haley came to Vansina with African terms preserved

---

14 The quotations come from McCauley's transcription of an audiotape of the August 7, 1981 speech.

in his family's southern register, words including *ko,* meaning "guitar," *Kamby Bolongo*, referring to some sort of river, and "Kin-tay," some sort of family name for The African (Haley 2007: 868). Vansina did his best to make sense of them. "*Kambi bolongo* as a putative 'the River Gambia' did not conflict with the other remembrances," he said. "Kambi" was a cognate for the name of the territory. "Bolongo" was identifiably a term for "river" in tongues of the area. But "Kinte" was problematic. "Did this American pronunciation stand for Kante, a famous clan, or Kente?" (Vansina 1994: 150). After consulting with colleague Phil Curtin by phone, Vansina advised Haley to speak with Gambians familiar with the Mandinka tongue, in which the phoneme "k" was ubiquitous. Those familiar with the language "might be able to confirm the clan name and thus establish an African ancestry, even if a somewhat generalized one, given the size of such clans in West Africa" (Haley 2007 [1976]: 869). In the final form of the search, Vansina provides the clue that leads Haley to seek out Gambians like Ebou Manga to assist in the search.

Critical histories of the period tell a different tale. In other accounts, Haley sought Vansina out for authentication. Haley had tried to connect with Vansina in spring of 1966, but the professor was away on research (Vansina 1994: 149). According to Delmont and Norrell, the meeting with Vansina happened in 1967, after Haley had met with Ebou Manga, visited Africa the first time with Ebou Manga's contacts, and after the famed second visit to Africa where Haley met with members of the clan Kinte (Norrell 2015: 126; Delmont 2016: 26–7). As such, the anthropologist could only reiterate what Haley had hoped and had taken to be true.

Furthermore, whatever Haley took as scholarly confirmation exceeded Vansina's own views about the difficulty of oral history. After reading the published accounts of Haley's search, the anthropologist would admit his reservations about Haley's dependence on folk historians whose stories may simply report what listeners want to hear, especially given the channels through which the search for the griot came about. But Vansina "kept out of it" during the height of Haley's Comet (Vansina 1994: 210).

Delmont substantiates Vansina's apprehension, explaining that were the Gambian elite to grant Haley's wishes, the media attention could bring considerable tourism to the new African nation, especially the dollars of other diasporic Black persons searching for roots (Delmont 2016: 40–7). Haley promised as much in his letters to Gambian officials, even speaking about Elia Kazan's interest in making a film—shot on location in The Gambia—about Haley's great search.[15] The only caution Haley exhibited was against jinxing his chances at a Pulitzer Prize. In a letter to Paul Reynolds just after the Vansina visit, Haley boasted, "I make you a prediction, friend. I won't come right out and call the *name* of the Prize. I just say to you: you just *watch* what we are going to win! Because just ain't never *been* a book like this one!" (2.25—Alex Haley to Paul Reynolds, October 29, 1966, Anne Romaine Collection).

Haley already had a sense of the potential before setting foot in Africa, but the coming together of so many loose historical ends culminated in a "peak experience" that only enhanced his grand vision for the book, himself, and America (Haley 1973: 13). The proposed book would not only recover a race's lost history, but it would fill a blatant lacuna in America's national imagination (Anderson 2006 [1983]: 6).[16]

> You can't tell American history without including the Negro.
> In a country of immigrants Blacks were the only unwilling
> immigrants. Others found the American dream, but it is a
> simple historical fact that the Blacks were brought here as
> implements of agriculture. They were not intended to share
> the dream. This book would be the legacy of a particular
> human deprivation. (Haley, Lecture to the Cumberland Valley

15 Delmont's argument is built upon Haley's preliminary correspondence with officials who can secure his passage to The Gambia (3.10—Alex Haley to Dr. and Mrs. John Mahoney, March 16, 1967, Alex Haley Collection, University of Tennessee; 3.10—M.D. N'Jie to Alex Haley, March 23, 1967, Alex Haley Collection, University of Tennessee, cited in Delmont 2016, 43).

16 I am thinking here of Benedict Anderson's understanding of nationalism as an "imagined community," a corporate consciousness "invented" from the discursive exchanges necessary to maintain similitude and a sense of belonging. It is dependent not simply upon proximity, but—and perhaps more so—on the mediation of social, economic, and physical boundaries.

Writer's Conference, Vanderbilt University, August 7, 1981,
cited in McCauley 1983: 129)

Haley's family was the contrapositive example. In the four generations following the Civil War, they had managed to climb the
socio-economic ladder and live relatively peacefully among White
people. And they had done so, Haley believed, because they knew
who they truly were and what America could be for them, a "home."
Having traversed the Atlantic chasm, Haley could also reverse
the logic of racism. The Murray-Palmer-Haley family did not rise to
prominence in spite of negritude, but because they were firm in their
Kinte roots. And this was knowledge affirmed by elite and folk ways,
substantiated by print and oral traditions, and planted on two sides
of the sea. More than that, Haley's stock was sustained by the same
pride he says to have felt in leaving Africa. Recalling his Gambian
safari in 1967, Haley took seriously the shouts of "'Meester Kinte!
Meester Kinte!' In their eyes I was the symbol of all Black people in
the United States whose forefathers had been torn out of Africa while
theirs remained" (Haley 2007 [1974]: 92).

> I was just bawling, as I hadn't since I was a baby... I just felt like
> I was weeping for all of history's incredible atrocities against
> fellowmen, which seems to be mankind's greatest flaw...
>   Flying homeward from Dakar, I decided to write a book. My
> own ancestors' would automatically also be a symbolic saga
> of all African-descent people—who are without exception the
> seeds of someone like Kunta who was born and grew up in some
> Black African village, someone who was captured and chained
> down in one of those slave ships that sailed them across the
> same ocean, into some succession of plantations, and since then
> a struggle for freedom. (Haley 2007 [1976]: 879)

In Haley's mind, Black people's civil rights struggle was in large
part a historiographic problem. As De Certeau explains, "historiography" exists at the influential conjunction of "history and writing"
(De Certeau 1988 [1975]: xxv). It is "the paradox—almost an oxy-
moron—of two antinomic terms, between the real and discourse. Its
task is one of connecting them and at the point where this link cannot

be imagined, of working as if the two were being joined" (De Certeau 1988 [1975]: 30). On this Haley subscribed to the logic of his mentor, James Baldwin, who wrote:

> The American Negro can have no future anywhere, on any con-
> tinent, as long as he is unwilling to accept his past. To accept
> one's past—one's history—is not the same thing as drowning
> in it; it is learning how to use it. An invented past can never be
> used. (Baldwin 1993 [1962]: 81)

Haley was convinced that despite the enslavement of his "furthest-back person," generations of his family were able to move
beyond anger and take part in the American Dream alongside White
people. The novel would explain, in his words, how "[he and his]
brothers today, the seventh generation [after Kunta Kinte, became] an
author, a lawyer/high government official, and an architect (quietly
saying that this too, happened in America)" (2.25—Alex Haley to
Michael Blow, Assistant Editor of *Reader's Digest*, November 30,
1973, Anne Romaine Collection). With *Roots*, Americans might learn
to reinterpret slavery not only as a shaming and shameful chapter in
the nation's history, but as a plot point to be resolved through integration. This was the story of a man who conscripted elite and folk
experts on two continents in search of the knowledge to root himself.

"The Man Who Traced America's Roots"

Although Haley proffered the idea of *Roots* as a solution to America's
racial problems, he was still, if not more so, subject to the mundane
realities of historiography. Haley insisted on completing his research
before formally writing a draft. He lacked documentary evidence to
support the griot's tale about Kunta Kinte, whose disappearance from
The Gambia coincided with the nebulous arrival of the king's soldiers. Atop of these issues, Haley would need to collect background
information to supplement his knowledge of the generations between
his "furthest-back person" and himself. Even with moving the estimated time of completion to 1968, the deadline proved less plausible
than the task (3.27—Ken McCormick to Paul Reynolds, January 18,

1967, Anne Romaine Collection). The financial, familial, and editorial costs delayed the book's release to the tail-end of 1976. They also made *Roots* the story with which Haley and much of America would identify themselves. Appraising *Roots* as a scripture requires recognition of why readers see the book as not only a relatable read, but also a near-impossible book to write.

Before This Anger was a project beyond Haley's monetary means (McCauley 1983: 131). Haley's rootwork was to declare for himself and its readers an identity of independence, but the project's expenses indicate that he was in fact increasingly bound to creditors and financiers of his estate. As of October 20, 1966, Haley owed $5,100 in delinquent income taxes (3.27—Paul Reynolds to Alex Haley, October 20, 1966, Anne Romaine Collection). To appease the IRS, Paul Reynolds was managing Haley's publishing earnings. Reynolds' February 24, 1967 letter shows the financial hardship that Haley was facing:

> The government served a new subpoena on us prohibiting us from paying you any money until your 1963 income tax is paid. I am ignoring this service, and will continue to send you a check each month from the Digest money, and undoubtedly the money we are withholding from the Digest money will pay this off. I hope I don't go to jail [or something]. The reason I feel that I can still pay you some money is that the Digest contract is sure to be enough to pay the government off. I would appreciate it however if you don't mention to a soul that I am doing this, and don't write any letters about it. Once this gets paid off you will be relatively on top of things and feeling [like] a free man. (3.27—Paul Reynolds to Alex Haley, February 24, 1967, Anne Romaine Collection)

Until its 1976 publication, Haley would struggle to finance the research and writing of *Roots*, and the choices he made between 1967 and 1976 would greatly affect his legacy. To cover living expenses, Haley continued lecturing on Malcolm X, the Civil Rights Movement, and Haley's own writing career, but both Reynolds and Haley knew this would not be enough to move Haley out of the research process and into actually writing the book (3.25 Alex Haley to Paul Reynolds,

February 9, 1966, Anne Romaine Collection, cited in Delmont 2016: 53–6). On March 17, 1967 Haley reached an agreement with Dell Books to publish the paperback version of the novel with an immediate signing bonus negotiated by Paul Reynolds (3.27—Ken McCormick to Paul Reynolds, March 17, 1967, Anne Romaine Collection). A month later, Reynolds would prod Haley toward modest progress. "Your experience in Africa is magnificent. The time must come very soon when you'll be doing the weary labor of sorting out your notes and organizing them, and start writing. When can you promise me the first 10,000 words?" (3.27—Paul Reynolds to Alex Haley, April 25, 1967, Anne Romaine Collection). Delays would become a running theme for the master storyteller.

Haley's inertia at the typewriter was partially a repercussion of his mythology's unwieldy growth. What had started as the story of a Black American family was becoming the saga of an "African American" family in a time when that phrase signified a debated reading of heritage and history that more often than not questioned *whether* rather than *how* the continent should factor into the self-understanding and self-determination of "American Slave Descendants"[17] (Baugh 1999: 86–99; Wilkerson 1989). In locating his "furthest-back person" in a griot's history, Haley had reason to pursue an African connection. But he would have to substantiate such a link through a rationale recognizable to his intended audience.

Money from the Dell Books agreement funded another trip to London to learn more "about the time the king's soldiers came" to the Kamby Bolongo region (McCauley 1983: 131). Searching through British Parliamentary records, Haley found mention of "'Colonel

---

17 In terms of propriety, identifiers for American-born descendants of African slaves are debated with, within, and outside of that community. By 1990, African-American (with a hyphen) became an identifier of choice, especially because of the activism of civil rights leader, Jesse Jackson (Wilkerson 1989). It gained currency—though not universal adoption—over other terms, such as "American Slave Descendants," in academe, primary and secondary school, and Black-operated media (Baugh 1999). The hyphen has largely dropped out of favor in an effort to emphasize national integration (i.e. "Americanness") over ethnicization (i.e. "Africannness"), in which the latter is reserved for recent immigrants from the African continent.

O'Hare's forces,' which had been sent up the Gambia River in 1767 to guard the then British-operated James Fort, a slave fort" (Haley 2007 [1974]: 92). Interpreting this as "the king's soldiers," Haley matched the year, 1767, with maritime records archived at Lloyds of London. One ship was catalogued that met Haley's criteria, the *Lord Ligonier*.

Haley justified his confidence in his amateur archival search because of another supposed detail held by his grandmother and cousins-once-removed. "The African," as Haley's later accounts would put it, had landed at "Naplis" and was sold under the name "Toby" (Haley 2007 [1974]: 86–8; 2007 [1976]: 880). The *Lord Ligonier* "had sailed directly from the Gambia River to America in 1767... and she had arrived at Annapolis (Naplis) the morning of September 29, 1767" (Haley 2007 [1974]: 92–3). In the 1974 *Reader's Digest* essay, "My Search for Roots," Haley says he made sure to go to the Port of Annapolis on September 29, 1967, two centuries after Kunta Kinte's arrival, to pay homage to his "great-great-great-great-grandfather." And while in Annapolis he was able to locate a microfilmed record of the October 1, 1767 edition of the Maryland *Gazette*, where on its third page, he found "an advertisement informing readers that the *Lord Ligonier* had just arrived from the River Gambia, with 'a cargo of choice healthy slaves' to be sold at auction the following Wednesday" (Haley 2007 [1974]: 93). The 1974 essay ends with a deduction that "The African" was sold then and there.

There are a number of reasons to question the validity of Haley's method. Academic historians Gary B. Mills and Elizabeth Shown Mills famously questioned Haley's connection of "Kunta Kinte" to "Toby," an enslaved man owned by the Waller family (Mills and Mills 1981: 3–26). And as will be discussed later in this chapter, many other scholarly elites question Haley's prowess as well. More important than his methodological precision is observing the effects of deploying the Waller fact. In the synchronic search account in *Roots*, Haley writes that he had found even more documentary evidence during a trip to Richmond, Virginia, including a September 5, 1768 deed from Spotsylvania County, Virginia that outlined a transfer of ownership from John and Ann Waller to a William Waller (a wealthy doctor and brother to John). Included in the list of goods and property was "one Negro man, a slave named Toby" (Haley 2007 [1976]: 882).

The "Waller" family and their ownership of Toby are missing from accounts in two letters written by Alex Haley—one in 1969 and one in 1973, pre-dating the 1974 *Reader's Digest* essay—which make no mention of Haley's further genealogical certitude. If Haley had indeed found a bill of sale and been able to identify "Toby" as likely having been purchased by the Wallers, then the omission from his "search" of such a gripping and well-documented detail is curious.

While he did not share the last link in the genealogical chain with *Reader's Digest* readers, he did do so with the editorial staff of the magazine to stave off concerns about his fledgling draft. In a letter to *Reader's Digest* editor, Fulton Ousler Jr., Haley wrote:

> I have found, and we are good friends, John Waller's seventh-generation descendant, as I am the seventh-generation descendant of Kunta Kinte. Waller Wiser (descendant via his mother) is the Dean of Simpson College, Indianola, Iowa. [The parenthetical note comes after the chapter summary with Kunta Kinte's kidnapping.] (2.25—Alex Haley to Fulton Ousler, Jr., editor of *Reader's Digest*, July 29, 1969, Anne Romaine Collection)

Similarly, in a November 30, 1973 letter, Haley thanked Michael Blow, Associate Editor of *Reader's Digest*, for a newspaper account of one "1710-constructed Benjamin Waller House." Blow was mentioned as a descendant of the Wallers, with Haley writing, "It still grabs me to reflect upon how you are of the Waller family. When *Roots* is out and doing its thing, maybe we'll get all get together in some whale of a reunion!" (Alex Haley to Michael Blow, Associate Editor of *Reader's Digest*, November 30, 1973, Anne Romaine Collection). Whether nepotism, falsehood, or coincidence was at work here, the Waller connection presented Haley a way to assure concerned readers—in the above cases, gatekeeping editors and benefactors—that his rootwork was a worthy investment for them, too.

According to *Roots*, it was only after linking the Waller's Toby to his Kunta Kinte that Alex Haley was even able to entertain the task of writing *Before This Anger* (Haley 2007 [1976]: 883). Between the fall of 1967 and 1974, Haley claimed to have done extensive research in 50 or so libraries, archives and repositories on three continents...spent a year combing through countless documents to learn about the culture of Gambia's villages in the 18th and 19th centuries...[flown] to Africa and boarded the freighter *African Star*...stripped to my under-wear, lying on my back on a rough, bare plank. (Haley 2007 [1976]: 93)

The prolonged preparations contributed to broken promises about deadlines, but as he explained to *Reader's Digest* in 1973, it was nec-essary to put Haley in the historical frame of mind to draft *Roots*.

As you know, literally for years I have been dropping notes, saying I'm in this or that process with the book, until I know that it was starting to sound almost mythical. Essentially what I was doing was bringing into an exacting chronology a really massive amount of very specialized research, so that this book would/will sweep across two centuries, telling in a quiet, cumulatively powerful, see-touch-taste-hear-smell manner, the evolution of simultaneously, a people and a culture, and hope-fully also in a manner that isn't precedented [sic]. (2.25—Alex Haley to Malcolm Blow, November 30, 1973, Anne Romaine Collection)[18]

Haley was never free to simply write the book. He needed an extraor-dinary amount of money to put himself in the physical and mental space to produce. It was a costly investment that Haley had to cover, sometimes resorting to questionable means. Haley was partially funding his chronicle by dubiously contracting to write more works (2.25—Alex Haley to Paul Reynolds, March 9, 1967, Anne Romaine Collection). In a 1970 letter to Paul Reynolds, Haley described how his friend and mentor, James Baldwin, would sign to write "nine

18 Haley hints at writing a short, companion book called *My Search for Roots*, which would detail his cross-continental research. He and Paul Reynolds hoped *Reader's Digest* would publish it after *Roots'* release, but the magazine published the content under the same title as a feature in its May 1974 issue. This content is repeated in the final three chapters of *Roots* (Haley 2007 [1976]: 854–99).

books, just for the very minor advances [publishers] would give him" (2.25—Alex Haley to Paul Reynolds, November 28, 1970, Anne Romaine Collection). Haley adopted the practice, promising publishing house William Morrow a book he tentatively called *The Imaging*, the saga of his paternal family (2.25—Alex Haley to Paul Reynolds, August 5, 1967, Anne Romaine Collection).[19] As discussed in Chapter 1, it would focus on his "half-Black, half-White" grandmother, Queen, and the story behind her Irish heritage. For Grove Press, Haley agreed to work with writer Niven Busch on a biography of Hollywood lawyer and friend, Melvin Belli (2.25—Alex Haley to Paul Reynolds, November 28, 1970, Anne Romaine Collection). He would lend his name—marketable from his journalistic career and the *Autobiography of Malcolm X*—and Busch would "do the writing," and receive "the real lion's share [of the profits] for motivational purposes...because it's fair." The book did not come to fruition as either a Haley or Busch project. And in 1970, Haley signed a contract with Viking Books to write a Black history book for children, which was the last straw for his agent (2.25—Alex Haley to Paul Reynolds, November 28, 1970, Anne Romaine Collection). To borrow from a previous mea culpa, Haley eventually felt the need "to confess that "one's sins, they say, will find one out...I simply was broke" (2.25—Alex Haley to Paul Reynolds, April 23, 1967, Anne Romaine Collection). Reynolds helped Haley to dissolve two of the contracts and eventually pay back all the advanced funds.

And yet the most zealous commitment was in an entirely different medium. In April 1967, Haley sold the film rights for a movie adaptation of his unfinished book (2.25—Alex Haley to Paul Reynolds, April 23, 1967, Anne Romaine Collection). On a social occasion, director Elia Kazan—whose work *America, America* had inspired Haley's own rootwork, was enchanted by Haley, who had passionately shared with him the idea for *Before This Anger* and his search

19 As will be discussed later, the book would eventually be published by William Morrow under the name *Queen: The Story of an American Family* in 1993, two years after Alex Haley's death. British author David Stevens would use Haley's notes to compose the book (Haley and Stevens 1993).

for "The African." Kazan approached Haley with the suggestion of optioning production and direction rights—an idea Haley did not hesitate to mention when in talks with Gambian officials in 1965. Once formalized, Haley signed a deal with Columbia Pictures, but the company lost interest in the delayed novel. Haley's professional clout was only as good as his publication record, which had gone stagnant.

His interpersonal relationships also appeared to suffer during this dry spell. In February 1968, Haley taught Black history as a visiting lecturer at Hamilton College upon the invitation of rhetoric professor Charles Todd (2.25—Alex Haley to Paul Reynolds, August 5, 1967, Anne Romaine Collection). Todd had been instrumental in connecting Haley to the Gambian student Ebou Manga, who had been working with the Committee on Racial Equality (Haley 2007 [1976]: 868–9; Delmont 2016: 40). According to Todd, Haley had been a role model to the Black students on campus and helped them develop its Black Student Union. He was a well-liked teacher—imparting wisdom, telling great stories, grading generously, and cancelling classes on account of his rootwork (Todd 1978: 133). For Haley, teaching and mentorship were secondary to his chief objective, writing his much-anticipated book. He insisted on teaching two days a week so that he could properly focus. In 1969, Haley grew frustrated, complaining that Hamilton College "had become simply too familiar to sundry people who would just drop in" (2.25—Alex Haley to Paul Reynolds, June 13, 1969, Anne Romaine Collection). By June 1969, Haley ended the lectureship and retreated to the guest home of the World Press Summit in St. Paul, Minnesota, where he had addressed journalists the previous year. Haley's career seemed to be regressing.

History was repeating himself. Haley had chosen the typewriter over his first wife Nannie Branch and their children. In 1964, he had officially divorced her and married Juliette Collins, the mother of his third child, Cynthia (Romaine 1.31: Alex Haley Book Outlines and Book Draft: 58–9). Haley's devotion to the saga kept him away from his young family. For instance, he left them behind in New York, when he retreated to Minnesota. On December 9, 1969, Juliette threatened legal action against Alex for failing to financially support her and their daughter (3.27—Law Offices of Monica & Feury to

Alex Haley, December 9, 1969, Anne Romaine Collection). The couple would ultimately divorce in 1972 (Pace 1992).[20]

Haley blamed his writer's block on the burden of other people. But the fact of the matter is that the success or failure of *Before This Anger* had consequences for his colleagues and his children. Just as he had the help of George Sims to help him research his roots, he needed others to shoulder the task of writing. In 1970, Haley invited his former *Playboy* editor Murray Fisher to help with "clinical expertise," an ambiguous term Haley used to describe copyediting, proofreading, and "structur[ing]...a seeming [sic] impassable maze of researched materials" (2.25—Alex Haley to Paul Reynolds, December 29, 1970, Anne Romaine Collection). [21] Fittingly, Haley uses the same medical metaphor to describe his own work on the *Autobiography,* where Malcolm required "a writer...not an interpreter" (X and Haley 1999 [1965]: 463). In this matter, Haley saw himself as doing "a purely clinical job of shaping a great volume of Malcolm X's printed and taped material into the form of a book" (3.24—Alex Haley to Oliver

20 Divorce proceedings were scheduled to begin as early as June 21, 1971 (2.25—Alex Haley to Paul Reynolds, June 8, 1971, Anne Romaine Collection). It is worth noting that Juliette was "committed to a psychiatric hospital [for] severe depression" in August 1973, and doctors recommended that she receive "continued in-patient" care. Haley was in Jamaica, working on *Roots*, while Cynthia was with her maternal grandmother. In order to provide for Juliette's care and child support, Haley requested an additional $10,000 advance from Doubleday (2.25—Alex Haley to Paul Reynolds, August 15, 1973, Anne Romaine Collection). Reynolds replied sympathetically but noted that Doubleday had grown weary of Haley's missed deadlines and that the author was beginning to develop a negative reputation for being unprofessional (2.27—Paul Reynolds to Alex Haley, August 16, 1973, Anne Romaine Collection). Doubleday continued to support Haley, giving him the amount piecemeal. For instance, he received "$2000 as part of the advance due...for *Roots*" (3.27—Ray Watkins, Doubleday to Oliver G. Swan, Paul R. Reynolds Inc., September 20, 1973, Anne Romaine Collection). Juliette would be released into outpatient care as of late November (2.25—Alex Haley to Paul Reynolds, November 30, 1973, Anne Romaine Collection).

21 Fisher's "clinical expertise" is elaborated upon in 2.25—Alex Haley to Paul Reynolds, February 19, 1971, Anne Romaine Collection.

G. Swan, Paul Reynolds & Son, August 5, 1963, Anne Romaine Collection). Of course, Haley greatly shaped Malcolm's story to fit his own needs. Fisher similarly had a heavy hand in shaping the *Roots* that readers would come to identify with Haley.

In 1975, Haley came close to firing Fisher, feeling that his input had crossed the boundary of clinical editing to co-authorship, a transgression that demanded a strong reprimand (3.23—Alex Haley to Murray Fisher, October 9, 1975, Anne Romaine Collection). Ultimately, Haley realized how much he needed Fisher's help and repaired their relationship. In the acknowledgments to *Roots,* Haley summarizes Fisher's assistance saying, "After we had established *Roots'* pattern of chapters, next the story line was developed, in which he then shepherded throughout. Finally in the book's pressurized completion phrase, he even drafted some of *Roots'* scenes" (Haley 2007 [1976]: vii–viii). With Paul Reynolds, George Sims, and Murray Fisher, Haley had reassembled the same team that helped him launch a career in journalism.

Doubleday took notice of Haley's renewed focus and was determined to see the project to completion, having previously forfeited the publishing rights (and profits) related to the *Autobiography*. Lisa Drew, a senior editor at Doubleday, approved Haley's 1971 request to travel on a sea-freighter so long as he progressed with his drafts (2.25—Alex Haley to Paul Reynolds, copied to Lisa Drew, May 18, 1971, Anne Romaine Collection). Evidence of his efforts came by way of published promotional excerpts—such as a July 1972 essay for *TIME* called "My Furthest-Back Person, The African"—and the 1973 submission of *Roots'* first section—the third of the book detailing Kunta Kinte's life in Africa (Haley 1972; 1973). *Reader's Digest* published two of four excerpts from the latter in 1974 (the others were published in 1977 following the book's release) (Haley 2007: 96–156). In Doubleday's eyes, he was making just enough progress that they continued to support him. But things were not as smooth as they seemed. For instance, Haley admitted to appeasing Drew with mammoth drafts consisting of notes heaved between a solid beginning and ending, for he counted on her not being able to read the manuscript in its entirety. Doubleday and Haley were in this endeavor together, with the company agreeing to support a 1973–1975 writing retreat in Jamaica (Bell 1977: 50–1, cited in McCauley 1983: 151; 2.25—Alex Haley to Paul Reynolds, July 11, 1973, Anne Romaine Collection).

While Haley plodded along with the book in Jamaica, anticipation for *Roots* grew in the United States. In 1974, director David Wolper and producer Stan Margulies secured the rights to develop *Roots* into a miniseries for the American Broadcasting Corporation. Wolper began pre-production in January 1976 while Haley was completing the novel (McCauley 1983: 151).[22] The book's Fall 1976 release would be followed up by the miniseries' epic January 1977 premiere. Doubleday had mixed feelings about the film venture that Haley had independently struck. Adaptation would bring profits, but they had still yet to receive a serious draft.

The completion of *Roots* was tied intimately to Haley's budding relationship with Myran (My) Lewis. In 1975, Haley enlisted the help of this scholar and admirer with a newly-minted PhD in communication and Black studies from The Ohio State University. Lewis lent her expertise on issues related to "story, history-weaving, character, and color" (Lewis Haley 2013). When Haley invited her to join him in Jamaica, she estimated that he had only completed "the first third of *Roots*...Kunta Kinte had just arrived in Annapolis." She, along with Fisher, helped him close the Kunta Kinte arc and finish writing the later generations, which ironically had been the focus of Haley's initial idea for *Before This Anger*. *Roots* was growing closer to completion. Haley and My were growing closer to each other (3.25— Alex Haley to Murray Fisher, October 18, 1975, Anne Romaine Collection).[23]

According to reporter Marty Bell, it was Drew's prompting that brought the long-awaited completion of *Roots*. In February 1976, she issued Haley a one-week ultimatum to finish the novel, reserving a

22 For a useful presentation of the production history of the *Roots* miniseries, as well as study of the TV miniseries as a genre, see the "Miniseries" episode of the documentary series, *Pioneers of Television* (Public Broadcasting Service 2013).

23 Alex describes both his positive professional impression and his amorous intentions regarding the Ohio State University graduate.

room in New York's Barclay Hotel as a cloister for him (Bell 1977: 50–1, cited in McCauley 1983: 151). Haley was to focus intently on the novel, but Bell reports that he left the Barclay Hotel to receive an honorary degree from The Ohio State University, the same institution from where Lewis took her degree. Haley told both Bell and biographer Mary Seibert McCauley that he had a friend deliver the final manuscript to Doubleday. And Lewis claims to have been the person to do so (Lewis Haley 2013). How "clinical" Lewis was in her handling and handing in of *Roots* is unclear. Haley demonstrated her importance through marriage in 1977, but her contributions went unmentioned in the book's acknowledgments—unlike George Sims; Mrs. DeWitt Wallace and the *Reader's Digest* editorial staff; Paul Reynolds; Lisa Drew, Doubleday Senior Editor Ken McCormick; and "the griots of Africa" (Haley 2007 [1976]: vii–viii). Also unnamed in the acknowledgments were any of Haley's family members despite their role in helping him learn how to live in America unimpeded by resentment. This was the story of a man who was no longer writing about family. He had identified something more vital than blood and more precious than kinship—the power of being read the way he had long dreamed (Haley 2007 [1991a]: 74–8).

"A Fraud's a Fraud?"

As far as Haley was concerned, the saga's allure was to be its facticity. He had touted *Roots* as the culmination of twelve years of unprecedented research—perusing rare archival records, consulting with scholars, and visiting the world's most prestigious libraries. To make palpable all the knowledge he had uncovered, he reserved literary license and, when pressed, described *Roots* as "faction" (Fisher 1993 [1977]: 431; Haley 2007 [1977]: 431). But the public was to understand, as booksellers had, that *Roots* was not just a story but a history. On a number of levels they took it to mean this and something more. In 1976, *Roots: The Saga of an American Family* became an unqualified success. Bookstores immediately sold out its 200,000 advance prints. With only three months remaining in the year, the novel was among the most popular "non-fiction" books in America, second to

Woodward and Bernstein's Nixon feature, *The Final Days* (H. Taylor 1995: 48; Moore 1996: 195).[24]

There was a prophetic quality to *Roots'* arrival. For over a decade, Haley had not only been researching and writing the book, but also promoting its message around the country. At Spelman College's 1970 commencement, he proclaimed himself "blessed with a strong sense of Black history, Black culture, and Black heritage." His intentions were clear. With "the picture, the book, the whole thing I hope to project around and to the world is not just an emotional cry but it is documented fact, that it is true that 'Black Is Beautiful'" (Haley 2000 [1970]: 4–5). In a reference reminiscent of the wolf that dwells with the lamb in Isaiah 11:6, Haley recounts to Reynolds how his lectures on *Roots* captivated Black Panthers to listen quietly with White college students (2.25—Alex Haley to Mr. Fulton Ousler, Jr. Book Editor, *Reader's Digest*, After August 10, 1975, Anne Romaine Collection; 2.25—Alex Haley to Paul Reynolds, September 20, 1975, Anne Romaine Collection).[25] The same year he told *Reader's Digest's* Fulton Ousler that audience reactions to these *Roots'* previews suggest that Americans would find the book to be every bit as profound and as convincing as *Uncle Tom's Cabin* (2.25—Alex Haley to Mr. Fulton Ousler, Jr. Book Editor, *Reader's Digest*, after August 10, 1975, Anne Romaine Collection). The reports from the media tour helped publishers and production companies imagine the money to be earned from *Roots*, but its significance was much deeper than mammon. Leslie Uggams, the actor who portrayed Kizzy, the daughter of Kunta Kinte, was in Las Vegas rehearsing the show *Guys*

24 Taylor and Moore concur on the quantitative data regarding *Roots'* initial publication and ratings. Haley would sue Doubleday, claiming the publisher's high print-runs of paperback editions had affected sales of the higher-priced (more profitable) hardback. The matter was settled amicably, Haley conceding that given his tardiness he should be grateful that the book ever got published (Stephens 1995: 147, n. 11).

25 English readers of the Bible may misremember Isaiah 11:6 as describing the "lion lying down with the lamb." This actually collapses three similar clauses in the verse. The first clause features a wolf; the second, the verb "lie"; the third, a lion. All of the clauses involve the peaceful grouping of predator and prey.

and Dolls when the miniseries aired. She recalled how "[t]he casinos were absolutely empty while 'Roots' was on… And once 'Roots' was over, then everyone could come downstairs and gamble" (Scripps Howard News Service 2002). *Roots* showcased the transcendent power of possessing history and how, in relating the truths of the past, one could rightly elucidate and improve the present.

While an embarassed Alex Haley shrugged off the "almost worshipful" response audiences had to *Roots*, he was wholly aware of the scriptural form *Roots* was taking (Fisher 1993 [1977]: 389). In a January 1977 *Playboy* interview conducted by Murray Fisher, Haley shared how a young Black woman "came rushing up to [him], grabbed [his] hand, and fell to her knees." Rather than being flattered, he considered her devotion a misinterpretation of what he and "what *Roots* is saying—to Black people, especially—…that once you find out who you really are, you don't have to go down on your knees to anyone anymore" (Fisher 1993 [1977]: 389). On other occasions, Haley was less humble. By May 1977, the groundbreaking miniseries adaptation had aired and the phenomenon media commentators dubbed "Haley's Comet" was at its peak (Marmon 1977: 14). Haley relished in the literary and historical reception of *Roots*.

> Some have wondered why I let *Roots* take twelve years of my life. Rather than *taking*, the book has *added* years—and brought me incomparable rewards. In Los Angeles, more than 3,000 people, White and Black, lined up for hours, waiting to get inscriptions in their copies of *Roots*. Exactly five persons had only one copy; the average was three, the peak eight. "This is not a book," one Black woman told me, "this is my history." A pregnant woman handed me two copies to sign. "One," she said, "is for me; the other is for him" and—with that she patted her belly…
>
> To me, the overwhelming affirmation can be explained only by something that is beyond ordinary comprehension, something spiritual. I think that we as people—and I am talking about the world—*badly need uplifting*. We all have lineage and forefathers. If I have become a symbol of the shared search for ancestral roots, then indeed am I blessed [sic]. (Haley 2007 [1977]: 162, emphasis added)

This was not simply the legendary reception for which he had hoped. It was the change he had spent a dozen years working for. The *Roots* moment was not without its critics. Jan Vansina, the scholar with whom Haley had consulted, had not heard from Haley since their initial meeting in 1966. As Haley published word of his successful search, Vansina wondered whether the griot's confirmation was just too good to be true. In *Living With Africa*, Vansina reflects, "I thought that the story could well be a fabrication foisted on him by local entrepreneurs, for Haley had been imprudent enough to let it be known what it was that he wanted to discover" (1994: 210). Vansina was not particularly vocal about his concern; others were less reticent in speaking out. Haley was excoriated by many of the recognized gatekeepers of American letters in whose fields he had trespassed (H. Taylor 1995: 51).

In 1977, African American author-historian Margaret Walker accused Haley of plagiarizing her novel *Jubilee* (1966), a fiction-alized tale about Walker's grandmother through slavery, the Civil War, and Reconstruction (Bonetti 1992: 112–31). From its pages, she claims, Haley lifted no less than fifteen passages—including the idea of Chicken George. The ruling judge noted the similarities as insub-stantial and dismissed Walker's grievance.

In 1978, a White author-anthropologist named Harold Courlander brought suit against Haley, claiming that *Roots* shared 81 passages with his 1967 book, *The African.*[26] Throughout the case, Haley main-tained that he had never read Courlander's novel, but expert testimony and literary analysis pointed otherwise. Joseph Bruchac, a professor at Skidmore College interested in Native American storytelling and comparative literature, signed a sworn affidavit saying that he had lent Haley a personal copy of *The African* (Rucker 2010: 791–2).

After five weeks in court, Haley settled with Courlander for a pur-ported $650,000 (Chideya 2007). Haley said that he and his assistants were researching such an abundance of materials that the finer proto-cols of citation and organization fell by the wayside. He consistently maintained that there was no duplicity involved. His legal counsel

---

26 See a side-by-side comparison of select passages in 1.37—*Roots* and *The African*, Anne Romaine Collection.

closed with the following statement, "Alex Haley acknowledges and regrets that various materials from *The African* by Harold Courlander found their way into his book, *Roots*" (Combine Services 1978).

Independent of the juridical proceedings in America, a British reporter named Mark Ottaway began his own investigation into *Roots*. Like Jan Vansina, Ottaway was suspicious of Haley's contact with a knowledgeable griot. On April 10, 1977, "Tangled *Roots*" went to press in London's *The Sunday Times* (Ottaway 1977). The article described Haley's portrayal of an eighteenth century Juffure as anachronistic, noting that although the African village may have become rural by Haley's 1967 visit, its proximity to Fort James Island would have made it a bustling settlement. He added that Kebba Fofana was not actually a griot but a man of questionable character who had forsaken the path of his fathers—Muslim scholars—to become a drummer. Furthermore, the article suggests that Fofana's recitation of Haley's lineage was premeditated, inaccurate, and inauthentic—not the work of a wise sage but a conspiracy with Gambian government officials.

Within the accusatory article, Ottaway includes a response from Haley, who was humbled yet defensive regarding *Roots*' historicity. "You must understand this book is also symbolic. I know Juffure was a British trading post and my portrait of the village bears no resemblance to the way it was. But...I, we, need a place called Eden. My people need a Pilgrim's Rock [sic]." Ottaway also includes Haley's admission about the questionable authority of Kebba Fofana:

> Alex Haley admitted to [Ottaway] that, at one point, he found the African end of his inquiries so confusing, so obscured by contradictory elements from different sources, that he very nearly decided to make the African section, if not the entire book, a mere historical novel. He conceded that, in retrospect, his reliance upon Fofana, the "griot" of Juffure, was perhaps an error, "and that it's possible I was misled. I have since discovered that he was something of a playboy." (Ottaway 1977)

Ottaway's primary source was a man named Bakari Sidibe, who had worked in the Gambia Cultural Archives. Sidibe had outlined to Haley the institution of griot and had arranged the meeting with

Fofana. Sidibe had also told Haley that although Fofana was the elder patriarch of Juffure, he was not a griot in the traditional sense. Fofana was colloquially understood as a griot because the Mandinka word for "drummer," *jalli*, is the same term used for griot on account that the oral histories are recited in concert with drumbeats. Sidibe took umbrage with Ottaway's accusatory article and wrote a public statement to clarify that Fofana suspended his studies as an imam to pursue his passion for music (1.6—Bakari Sidibe, "An Answer to Mark Ottaway's Critique of *Roots*," April 14, 1977, Anne Romaine Collection). Fofana, he said, was a respected sage because of his age, his hereditary return to the role of *imam* later in life, and his familiarity with tribal customs. Sidibe rebuffed Ottaway's sensationalist account, insisting that Haley's genealogical account was as good as, if not better than, the genealogical documentation in the archives.

Sidibe's words went unnoticed by Ottaway and Haley. Sidibe had expected Haley to do more research to confirm the account provided by Fofana (1.36—Barkari Sidibe to Alex Haley, n.d. [c. 1965], Anne Romaine Collection). Typically, those seeking historical information through oral means confer with multiple griots from various villages. Having consulted griots from different branches of the Kinte family along with those of other families, the archivist had found "some glaring contradictions…in names, places, and generations" between accounts that would "have to be ironed out" in order to verify Haley's lineage. Sidibe did not seem deterred by Haley's project, suggesting a large-scale ethnographic study replete with recordings, transcriptions, and comparisons. All of this would require time and money that Haley was not inclined to oblige with. Both writers—Ottaway and Haley—were more interested in harnessing the momentum behind *Roots*.

In response to Ottaway's article, *The New York Times* concurrently ran a response article entitled "Some Historians Dismiss Report of Factual Mistakes in 'Roots'" (Shenker 1977). The headline is rather misleading. A panel of Ivy League historians agreed with Ottaway about Haley's dubious history, but they varied on their appraisal of *Roots*' legacy. None of their estimations were positive given Haley's desires. Harvard professor Robert G. Fogel called *Roots* "the best historical novel on slavery," but maintained that it could not be judged

by the same standards as a "researched history." His Harvard colleague Oscar Handlin, who had written an esteemed history about
American immigrants called *The Uprooted*, was not nearly as gen-
erous, saying "a fraud's a fraud." He saw no saving grace in Haley's
multidisciplinary strategy:

> The historians say, "Well, the anthropology must be correct,"
> and the anthropologists say, "Well, the history must be correct."
> But if you add them together there are a lot of interesting ele-
> ments which raise the question of how a book like this became
> successful. (Shenker 1977)

Yale's Edmund S. Morgan, who had written the acclaimed *American
Slavery, American Freedom*, provided the most incisive answer
regarding the anthropology of scriptures. For him, reading Haley and
his *Roots* required attention to genre and effect. That is to say, the
issue came down to categories. *Roots* was quite clearly "a statement
of someone's search for an identity." He added, "It would seem to
me to retain a good deal of impact no matter how many mistakes
the man has made. In any genealogy there are bound to be a number
of mistakes." "If they [critics] can prove willful mistakes," he went
on, "I guess I wouldn't draw very many conclusions, because I don't
think the book will have a great impact on historians anyway. You can
point out errors to your heart's content and it won't affect people's
attitudes. It'll just make them mad." Generally speaking, Morgan's
theory about people's attitudes has proven correct. The elite commentary on Haley's miry work failed to impact the mass audience touched
by *Roots*. At most it has minimized *Roots'* reception into the canon of
literature worthy of scholarly attention.

With few exceptions, the American intelligentsia have only spoken
in hushed tones regarding Haley and his *Roots*. In 1977, the Pulitzer
Prize Award Committee gave Haley a "special citation" for *Roots*,
recognizing its social significance but sidestepping the questions of
genre (i.e. non-fiction, history, fiction). And despite calls from critics, the committee has never rescinded the prize (H.B. Taylor 2001:
75–6). The impact of *Roots* was indeed bigger than the story of its
creation or creator, and so the nation chose to look the other way
at Haley's (in)discretions, all the while keeping their *Roots*. The

"Publisher's Note" in Vanguard Press's recent e-version of the novel makes the defense that:

> ...none of the controversy affects the basic issue: *Roots* fostered a remarkable dialogue about not just the past, but the then present day and how America has fared since the days portrayed in *Roots*. Vanguard Press feels that it is important to publish *Roots: The Enhanced Edition* to remind the generation that originally read it that there are issues that still need to be discussed and debated, and to introduce a new and younger generation, a book that will help them understand, perhaps for the first time, the reality of what took place during the time of *Roots*. (Haley 2007: i)

Discursively this was of little consolation because Haley had so heavily signified the universality of his *Roots*, particular in terms of its factuality. He could have written off these dismissals in light of racialized historical standards, leaning into the notion that even the most erudite portrayals of a Black past must rely on "faction." But this would require support of the Black literati, which he did not fully have. Besides friends like religion scholar C. Eric Lincoln and Haley's mentor, James Baldwin, Haley had few vocal allies among established Black writers.[27] And even their regard for Haley was indifferent to the historicity of *Roots*. For instance, Baldwin's *New York Times* review, released at the time of publication and before

27 A noteworthy example is Harvard University neurology professor, Dr. S. Allen Counter, who wrote to Haley personally and believed that the criticisms would prove to be meritless (3.28—S. Allen Counter to Alex Haley, April 25, 1977, Anne Romaine Collection). He also encouraged scholars like African American historian John Hope Franklin to voice his support of Haley (3.28—S. Allen Counter to Dr. John Hope Franklin, May 10, 1977, Anne Romaine Collection). Franklin would speak on the matter with other Black historians in *Jet* Magazine (West 1977: 17). Franklin conceded that historians may "nitpick" with components of Haley's historiography, but in his opinion the symbolic power supersedes those issues. Similarly John Henrik Clarke said that griots are as dependable as the traditional standards of Western history and that the English critiques (cf. Ottaway) are an effort to distract from the British Empire's explicit commodification of Black bodies.

Ottaway's article, commends *Roots* "as a study of continuities, of consequences, of how a people perpetuate themselves, how each generation helps to doom, or helps to liberate the coming one." It lauds the books' portrayal of reality while making no mention of the novel's historicity. Lincoln would defend Haley's plagiarism as the product of an author and researcher, George Sims, untrained in the values and techniques of academic protocol (3.28—Anne Romaine interview with C. Eric Lincoln, September 29, 1991 [transcript]: 9. Anne Romaine Collection).

Black academics debated how to respond. Many distanced themselves from *Roots* by remaining silent (a move likely informed by their own struggles for legitimacy within the predominantly White academy) while others accomplished this in established publications. A month after Ottaway's article, the May 1977 issue of a scholarly journal, *The Black Scholar*, featured a roundtable debrief titled, "Forum: A Symposium on *Roots*." Like *The New York Times*, the journal invited "a number of Black intellectuals, media workers, and scholars" to comment on the imbroglio. Poet and cultural critic Clyde Taylor argued that *Roots* merely extended the legacy of minstrel spectacles in American media (C. Taylor 1977: 37–8). This was in no small part due to Haley's characterizations of the noble slave Kunta Kinte, the American-born bondsman "Fiddler," and the cock-fighting freedman, "Chicken George." When juxtaposed to antebellum sensibilities and a color-conscious interpretive world, such figures make for relatable archetypes as much as they do racialized stereotypes. Robert Chrisman, editor of the journal, noted:

> *Roots'* mixture of helpless Blacks and brutal Whites recalls *Uncle Tom's Cabin* which, after its success as an abolitionist novel, became the most successful, longest running play in U.S. history, being performed continuously in various ways from the 1860s on into the early twentieth century. It is an ironic possibility that after emancipation *Uncle Tom's Cabin* served to entrench those racist stereotypes that had sustained the vanquished institution of slavery—that of the meek, frightened and submissive slave, and in this fashion has a reactionary as well as a progressive propaganda function... But *Roots'* image of hapless Blacks is a regression to a less heroic, less dignified,

Black image than that we saw and projected during the 1960s.
(Chrisman 1977: 42)

The symposium rejected the idea that Haley's amateur scholarship resulted in a resource for Black uplift. On the contrary, they argued that it was pulling Black people back into subservience. They distinguished popular spectacle from political strength.

Although Haley introduced many Americans to Black history and literature, relatively few published scholarly works have explored *Roots* in any detail, and of those, even fewer mention the scandals. Black public intellectuals, such as literary critic Henry Louis Gates, have commented that *Roots'* significance is not in its historicity but in its symbolism of a larger truth, that Black people are not without a history (Beam 1998). Gates explains that although few scholars would maintain the coherence of Haley's genealogical claims, their historical significance was nevertheless seismic.

At the same time, Gates' edited *Norton Anthology of African American Literature* only names *Roots* in passing, and neither Haley nor *Roots* is listed in the index (Gates and McKay 2012 [1996]: 2012 and 2622). No excerpt or analysis of the book is included. However *Roots* is listed within a section of post-civil-rights era works that popularized the study of slavery and on a timeline for winning a Pulitzer Prize citation. The charges of plagiarism also go unmentioned.

Gates himself has confessed to "*Roots* envy," leading to the launch of his popular African American news website, *The Root*, and his DNA-analysis television show, *Finding Your Roots—with Henry Louis Gates, Jr.* (Conan 2012). With twenty-first century technology, Gates and a Black geneticist named Rick Kittles boast they "c[an] do Alex Haley one better…Alex Haley in a test tube." The show is one among the many examples of the genealogy boom spurred by *Roots*. Haley had convinced Americans of various backgrounds of their need to recover lost roots.

Being "The Man Who Wrote Roots"

As will be discussed in the fourth chapter, Americans' pining for *Roots* has not gone away. And the critiques leveled against Haley did not result in public outcry so much as quietude. After all was said and done, Haley welcomed the silence of insignificance and even engineered it in some respects. Just prior to the highly-anticipated novel's release, he confessed to a reporter how he would like nothing more than to be just a writer.

> I had always wondered what a million-dollar author was like... Now I've met two of them,...and it seems I'll be one myself. I shan't make whoopee with the money. It just seems I'll have the funds to finance travel and research for the writing I want to do. And in the future, I'd like not to have advances anymore. If they're small, they're not enough, and then if you get a track record, they're too big and that pressures you. The main thing is to be free, and that's something I've always wanted to be. (Shirley 2005: 72–4)

He did have a sense of the high cost of freedom and came to realize that his newfound wealth would not be enough. Between his personal financial dues, back taxes, and mounting legal costs, money continued to be a problem. In September of 1977, Haley sued Doubleday, complaining that the publisher oversaturated his consumer base with paperback editions of *Roots*, resulting in a low demand for the more expensive (read: profitable) hardback. But all parties amicably agreed that Haley should be grateful that the much-delayed book even got published.[28]

Roots gave way to several spin-offs. In 1979, Haley gave ABC the rights to produce *Roots: The Next Generations*, a sequel miniseries centered on the Palmer's arrival in Henning up to Haley's sit-down with the griot, Kebba Fofana. In 1988, he permitted ABC to release *Roots: The Gift*, a television movie where Kunta Kinte and Fiddler (again portrayed by LeVar Burton and Louis Gossett, Jr., respectively) selflessly aid a slave escape during the Christmas holiday. The two programs feature a brief clip of Haley expounding on the show's resonance with *Roots*, but he had a limited role in penning both of

---

28 On the publication history of *Roots* see Robert O. Stephens, *The Family Saga in the South: Generations and Destinies* (1995: 147, esp. n.11).

their scripts (McCauley 1983: 202–4).[29] He had more of a direct hand in the short-lived television series, *Palmerstown USA* (CBS 1980–1981). Set in the eponymous fictional 1935 Tennessee, a Black boy named Booker T. Freeman and a White boy named David Hall struggle to stay friends under racial and economic pressures. Despite picking up a few awards, the show failed to merit a second season.

When not in Los Angeles, Haley stayed busy on the lecture circuit, discussing genealogy, oral history, and *Roots*. In 1972, he established a non-profit (and tax-deductible) foundation. He also gave to numerous charities and sponsored a number of projects to promote tourism and community development in The Gambia. But in 1980, Haley was dismayed to learn that a village mosque he had promised to fund went unbuilt (Shirley 2005: 85). Some locals assured him that the project was slowly getting underway, others accused him of not paying the sum that he had promised, still others suggested the money had been embezzled by those involved in the construction (Boyd 1993). The frustration went both ways. Many Gambians believed Haley had exploited them and done little to support their efforts. This has not kept the country from hosting a *Roots* festival or encouraging visits to Kunta Kinteh Island (International Roots Festival).

By 1987, Haley had worked himself into severe exhaustion and decided a change was in order. He moved from Los Angeles to Knoxville and slowed his schedule dramatically. He oversaw the renovation of an early nineteenth century farmhouse that he had purchased in 1983. "Alex Haley Farm" became a retreat center for him to host creative persons, celebrity friends, and other guests (Gonzales 1994: 93–4). The State of Tennessee purchased Palmer House from Haley (which he had previously reacquired) and had it restored in accordance to the memories of him and his brothers. It would later open as a museum and genealogical center. Fame and wealth proved no substitute for the unfettered life he truly wanted to lead, so Haley spent the remainder of his life in Tennessee, the state he called

29 Haley describes having given producers audiotapes that expanded upon the final biographical chapters in novel *Roots*. Haley did not receive a writing credit for *Roots: The Gift.* That belonged to D.M. Eyre, Jr. with Haley receiving acknowledgment via a "based on…" credit.

"home," away from the urbanity that brought his celebrated rise and ignominious fall.

Haley's post-*Roots* literary output gave people little reason to continue to think with and about him. In 1988, he wrote *A Different Kind of Christmas*. The short story follows Fletcher Randall, a Southerner attending Princeton who converts to abolitionism while in the company of Quakers. The tale climaxes with Randall helping a dozen slaves, some belonging to his father, escape in a holiday ride along the Underground Railroad. Besides some magazine articles and small features, *A Different Kind of Christmas* would be his last solo work (Haley 2007 [1976]: 892). Haley did, however, license his name and ideas to other writers, such as the British author, David Stevens, who penned much of the posthumously published *Mama Flora's Family* (1997) and *Queen* (1993).[30] The latter derived from Haley's research into his paternal grandmother's family. The former was a fictional novel about a poor Tennessee matriarch, her children's exploration of Black identity, and their grasping for the American Dream. The two stories were also adapted as television movies. And in 1992, he served as general editor of a children's book series called *Stories of America*. The twenty-six book series highlights the stories of women and ethnic minorities in America (Alex Haley Roots Foundation 2017). Ironically, many of these works hearken back to the projects he had contracted to finance his rootworking. Now they were sustaining his post-*Roots* life.

Haley was not without book ideas. In addition to *Mama Flora's Family* and *Queen*, Haley had started work on a biography of Madame C.J. Walker; a collection of short stories on people from Henning; a novel called *Appalachia*; and a collaborative memoir on childhood friend Fred Montgomery. None came to print the way Haley had originally intended. Haley's estate commissioned Tananarive Due to write the Walker biography from Haley's mountain of notes. She received sole authorial credit but shares the copyright with his estate

---

30   Alex Haley and David Stevens, *Alex Haley's Queen* (1993) and *Mama Flora's Family* (1997). According to Petri Liukkonen (2008), "Alex Haley" has a writing credit in the Blaxploitation film, *Super Fly T.N.T.* (dir. Ron O'Neal, 1973).

(Due 2000). Germinations for *Henning* may have found their way into *Palmerstown USA*. And the research begun for *Appalachia* was released as part of a documentary film project.[31] The Fred Montgomery piece, however, was continued by Lucas L. Johnson II, an Associated Press correspondent (Johnson 2003: 203) and the book was published eleven years after Haley's death in 1992.

In one of his final interviews, Haley complained that:

> *Roots* was so successful that it's been just about near impossible for me to find the time to write the way I used to. For the last decade, I haven't been a writer. I've been the author of *Roots*, and I need to turn that around. I've got to write. (Baye 1992: 91)

For the student of scriptures, the root of Haley's literary silence merits further consideration. Prior to *Roots*, Haley had approached writing as a means of strengthening his family. He had spent his childhood on his elders' porch, listening to their stories. When on tour with the Coast Guard, writing letters helped him fight off boredom and stay connected to his family. Journalism had brought him a sense of purpose. For so much of his life, Haley had written to improve his circumstances. Writing was how he paid the bills and put food on the table for his children.

After Haley's Comet and its subsequent controversies, his work was subject to the conextual interpretation of the family relations he all but sacrificed for the cause of his book. I suspect that caused his writer's block. In 1972, while in the throes of writing *Roots*, Haley's marriage to Juliette Collins ended. At about this same time, he courted Myran Lewis, the researcher who accompanied him to Jamaica. The two married in 1977, but evidence suggests that this relationship was as rent as his others. More often than not they lived apart, and Myran had little connection to Haley's other family members. She rarely joined him at Haley farm. And when the two did converse, the conversation

---

31 Haley believed *Appalachia* would be published in December 1985 by Associated Press. Sometime before his death, Haley recorded an audio track that was used as narration for a 2008 documentary project called "Once Upon a Vision: The Story of Berea, 1854–1903" (Despoil 2017b).

frequently revolved about ending the relationship. The only barrier holding them back was the legal details regarding ownership over Alex's assets—including his written works (T. Greene 1992).

In an October 1, 1990 letter, Haley begrudges "My" for holding "hostage" an undisclosed book's "vital visceral material." It appears that the couple were collaborating on some level until the rise of some disagreement. When Haley received word that her lawyer would be holding on to the book's materials, Haley reminded her that they had "pledg[ed] things to each other" and that he would finish the book without her "however brilliant help." She could keep the materials as her "trophy" (3.23—Alex Haley to Myran Lewis Haley, October 1, 1990, Anne Romaine Collection).

With matters never completely resolved, the two remained married until his death. The mysterious book—likely *Queen*, the Madame C.J. Walker project, *Henning*, or the penultimate version of *Roots* (in which she had a hand)—was not published in Haley's lifetime.[32] "Writing is a jealous mistress," Haley had said in a 1987 interview. "If you don't pay the muse year in, year out, if you stay around and do what I do, you become a talking writer. ... I give so many interviews about writing. I don't write" (Associated Press 1985). Haley was clearly speaking from experience.

Haley's familial problems may have gone further back than his professional career. Throughout his life, he maintained a relatively good relationship with his father, Simon, but it suffered under the concern that Haley failed to meet his academic potential. This, in part, was why he found refuge in his grandfather Will Palmer, who let him be a child. Time would heal wounds, and Haley stayed in touch with his father through telegrams.[33] But even in adulthood, Haley felt the burden of parental expectation (T. Greene 1992). Simon enjoyed *The*

---

32   Haley had been working with My on the research for these books at the time of their dispute (T. Greene 1992).

33   One such telegram is on display at the Alex Haley Museum and Interpretive Center. Alex congratulates Simon on retiring from a thirty-five year career in the college professoriate. The telegram was sent from San Francisco on May 14, but the year is not given. It was likely sent during Alex's service in San Francisco between 1951 and 1954.

Autobiography of Malcolm X enough to consider it an "equivalent of [Alex] getting [a] PhD" (Alex Haley, 1.3—"Anecdotes about Dad," notecard, n.d. [c. 1974], Alex Haley Collection, Goodwin College, CT, cited in Delmont 2016: 34; T. Greene 1992).[34] But whether it was a true substitute for the scholarly credentials and training his father had wanted was debated heavily after the publication of *Roots*. As much as Haley relied on the work of historians and anthropologists, he was self-deprecating in their presence (3.23—Alex Haley to C. Eric Lincoln, January 22, 1971, Anne Romaine Collection; Delmont 2016: 73). Simon did not live to see *Roots'* completion, but it's worth speculating what he would have made of Haley's Comet (2.25—Alex Haley to Paul Reynolds, November 30, 1973, Anne Romaine Collection). Would a father have been proud of his son's accomplishment, or would Professor Haley have rebuffed the work for its historiographic and plagiaristic woes? To what extent was Alex haunted by this question of acceptance?

To be sure, Alex Haley's authorial aspirations made for difficult relationships with his own offspring. Just as he equated writing to marriage, he likened his books to his kids, commenting that he "look[s] at [his] books the way parents look at their children. The fact that one becomes more successful than the others doesn't make [him] love the less successful one any less" (Wansley and Armstrong 1976). His son, William, would admit that with *Roots*, the world gained a grandfather, but he felt at times like he lost a dad (Henneberger 1993). Both William and Alex justified the sacrifice by weighing patriarchal duties against the needs of Black uplift. William even joked, "One day, it hit me that Jesus had it harder than I did. I was just the son of Alex Haley" (Daemmrich 1992). Alex, speaking about his role as America's grandfather, explained that "[w]e have choices. I would rather be the writer and affect many people than the grandfather who's successful on the porch with his grandchildren" (Associated Press 1985). Shortly after *Roots*, when *People* magazine asked him if he followed his grandparents' tradition of passing on the family's stories, he said "flatly" to the interviewer, "They have

---

34 This is recounted within the narrative of *Roots: The Next Generation*.

the book" (Wansley and Armstrong 1976). *Roots* may have transfigured Haley into the nation's Will Palmer, but at times, Haley's own
children could relate more to Palmer Haley, the boy bereaved by the
absence of his deceased mother and his itinerant father.

In 1990, Alex Haley was diagnosed with lung cancer, and on
February 10, 1992, he died of a heart attack in Seattle, where he had
been lecturing (Daemmrich 1992). His body's Tennessee homecoming
was a gala affair with dignitaries, relatives, and admirers converging
to make sacred the event. Reflections on *Roots'* significance punctu-
ated the eulogies. Haley's own remarks made for a more poignant last
word on the potential of scriptures. On the eve of the *Roots* moment,
journalists had raced to Haley to ask what it was like for him to be
finally living his American Dream. Reporters were stunned to learn
that Haley's story was not a "rags-to-riches" tale, for he had rewarded
himself with only a few luxury items. One account describes him as
having purchased a TV, VCR, and stereo so that he might savor the
miniseries' debut in his Los Angeles apartment (Shirley 2005: 74).
In another interview, he added, "I did go out and buy the fanciest
IBM typewriter I could find. *It even erases my mistakes*" (Wanly and
Armstrong 1976, emphasis added).

Equally astounding is how Haley concluded his life. He owned a
nineteenth century farm home where he—with the help of at least one
White staffer—would host the country's elite artists, politicians, and
entertainers. The staffer, Gertie Brummitt King, had owned a small
grocery store in town and recalled her son describing Haley as "the
man who wrote" when the author first began retreating to Clinton,
TN. She also overheard an older White gentleman at the store call
him "the head nigger" (G.B. King 2012: 1). But few did not know
the name Alex Haley. A combination of philanthropy and failed
property investments forced his debt-strapped estate to auction his
personal effects, including his farmhouse and manuscripts (Bowers
1992: 2–5). But as Haley's son William proudly remarked, "you can't
destroy his legacy just because things went up for DTC [Depository
Trust Company] sale... It goes so much deeper than that. Dad was a
storyteller, and you can't destroy his story" (Daemmrich 1992).

Since Alex's death, journalists have tested Will Haley's theory.
On February 23, 1993, investigative reporter Philip Nobile published

an article entitled "Uncovering *Roots.*" After visiting the Alex Haley
Papers, an archival collection at the University of Tennessee-Knoxville
that month, Nobile concluded that "Haley invented 200 years of family history. All of Haley's ripping yarns about his search for Kunta
Kinte and his ten-year struggle to write *Roots* were part of an elegant
and complex make-it-up-as-you-go-along scam" (Nobile 1993: 32)
Like Ottaway's 1977 article before it, Nobile's piece was criticized as
slanderous in nature (McMahon 2004; Braun 2012; Crouch 2002). In
an op-ed entitled "More on the *Village Voice*'s Hatchet Job on Alex
Haley," Herb Boyd (1993) wrote:

> Perhaps Haley was not the consummate master of prose—
> though a gifted storyteller—rather sloppy in his research and
> clearly guilty of plagiarism, as Nobile quotes. But to extrapolate
> from this that the basic core of *Roots* is a fabrication is to exag-
> gerate the matter. Indeed, Haley's excesses were not necessary;
> but given the historical denial of the Black experience and our
> contributions, the invisibility of our presence, these egregious
> mistakes are forgivable. There was no need for Haley to utter
> one white lie in his desire to establish what he would later call
> a "symbolic truth." It is too bad that this "symbolic truth" and
> several others [are] viewed as an attempt to pull a fast one on
> the American people.

In Boyd's quote, we see a point relevant to reading *Roots* in light of the
anthropology of scriptures. The power associated with the text does
not stem from historical veracity alone (though that claim is indeed a
common and strategic move in the development of an identity). Texts
become scriptures vis-a-vis the meaning and experience generated
around their engagement and the identities they in turn reflect.

As much is reflected in the deference or leniency shown toward
scriptures and the people most closely linked to them. In 1996, the
British Broadcasting Company (BBC) produced a documentary based
on Ottaway and Nobile's articles, called *The Roots of Alex Haley*. It
aired in England in 1997, but "[u]nnamed U.S. broadcast executives
told the *Times* of London [that] they feared the documentary could
cause racial tension, especially in parts of the country where Haley

is most revered, such as the Deep South and urban centers" (Sosin 1997).

The "Griot from Tennessee" was not only beloved in the South. Some of the most profound and telling rebuttals to that wave of criticism come from Upstate New York, where Haley constructed much of his *Roots*. Charles Todd, who had hired him at Hamilton College, maintained his friendship with Haley through written correspondence (Hamilton College Archives). Jack Behrens, a journalism professor at Utica College, noted that the controversies stirred were common to the liberties taken by those relying on oral history. Bob Woodward and Carl Bernstein, reporting on the Watergate affair, also drew upon questionable oral sources (Dudajek 1993). If they were not reflective of the time, then they became the paradigm for journalistic source work. And Woodward and Bernstein's book was the only one to outsell *Roots* in 1976.

To what extent was Haley's work different, especially in light of its arguable contribution to some public good? Chris Johnson, Hamilton College's coordinator for Higher Education Opportunity Programs, placed her friend and colleague's censure in a broader context. She compared the situation to the inquisition of William Shakespeare's corpus, another foolhardy attempt by historians and investigative journalists to question the authorship and authority of pivotal texts:

> I think Alex took a grain of historical seed and it grew into a forest of imagination... If Nobile is trying to destroy Alex's myth or how we feel about it, he's not going to succeed. I feel it was a great work for me and other who feel a need for it and who question their roots. (Dudjaek 1993)

Deep down, friends, loyal readers, and unknowing inheritors learned that in America, Alex Haley's *Roots* are not only worth knowing, but ultimately maintaining. This was the story of a man who rooted himself so as to be remembered as an American. And he knew America so well that he made sure he could not be forgotten.

Conclusion

Creating and then identifying with a scripture is high-risk and high-reward. Scriptures inform how people evaluate the stakes of their choices as well as the worth of those impacted by them. They provide the base for weighing the needs, methods, and concerns of living a worthwhile life. Alex Haley determined that these delibera-tions—rooted in the concept of a possessable past—could not remain in the private domain of the author if they were to make a difference beyond personal esteem. To orient others, the text had to be legible to those who could give Haley the respect that he wanted. And to bring about the order of change he desired, it needed to be more than just a book. It needed to be *the* book.

Scriptures, in their orienting operational acts of identification, cor-respond to the harnessing of content and form to mediate effective social reading in a cultural context. As we have maintained here as well as in Chapter 1, Haley seems to have understood history and writing as the optimal content and form of identification, respectively. We witnessed how his personal authorial quest was also a commu-nal enterprise that involved the considerable efforts of friends like George Sims, his then-partner My Haley, and literary brokers like Murray Fisher and Paul Reynolds. *Roots* as an extension—or better said, commodification and embodiment—of Haley's identity came about from the collective chaos and social synergy.

We can just as vividly see how scriptures, in their orienting opera-tional acts of identification, present in the gatekeeping of the content and form that a culture assumes to be integral. Thus, we saw Haley's credentials and *Roots'* merits scrutinized by academic historians and literary experts. This scrutiny, and the fall-out that it can bring to those found wanting, is also part of what make scriptures work in a communal setting. They provide a sense of place and a metric for declaring who is out of place.

Studying scriptures is complicated. Phenomena like *Roots* appear to be phenomena unto themselves, but texts are always signified by people. That signification happens with the author and with read-ers, and between the author and readers. In Chapter 3, we will use the literary criticism technique of Close Reading to examine how

Haley manufactured a text with which people could identify. Then, in Chapter 4, we will use discourse analysis to examine how audiences in the thirty years following *Roots* have made Haley's text their own. In giving due attention to both authorial exploits and audience reception, we will behold scriptures as roots of identification—the presumptive "how" we know what and who we know.

3 "The Saga of an American Family"

In an intellectual age marked by authorial death, the idea of literary analysis may strike some social theorists as passe. Neither the writer nor the words written on a page are ultimately determinant, so what analytical good could come of trying to reconstruct an author's influences or intentions?

Although the author may be dead, the author did play a role in setting the stage where actors perform, even if parts of the script were later jettisoned or improvisation occurred. Furthermore, as readers develop their own understanding of a text's conventions and provenance, the author of their imaginations can become a cipher for broader discourses worthy of attention. In these acts, the author has an afterlife.

In the anthropology of scriptures, our redescriptions of the author's work are not ascriptions; they are admittedly our own reconstructions of possible rhizomatic routes that nurture the roots that an author presents a reader. We know there is a story before the book. And so far as readers continue to identify with and through the book, there is a story afterward. Literary analysis provides us with the opportunity to examine the techniques and strategies possibly responsible for authors' and readers' centering of the root-book—even when the methods of centering diverge.

In this chapter, I argue for a critical reading of *Roots* as Alex Haley's ambitious attempt to name himself as a genuine American. The dominant immigrant nation narrative—as an overarching framework for presenting oneself as American—seemingly left little with which descendants of those who survived the Middle Passage could constructively identify. After all, it was not created with them in mind (T.A. Smith and O'Connell 1997: 19). But rather than disregarding it, Haley would refashion it to meet his and their psycho-social needs. With *Roots*, Haley offered an explanation of Black people's origin in

Africa, yes. But it just as importantly made an argument for Black people intrinsically belonging in America. Furthermore, his readership at some level identified *Roots* and Haley as evidence for linking the notions of origin and American belonging together. Chapter 4 will consider this from the perspective of audience reception. In this chapter, I will use the technique of Close Reading to provide some literary and historical context for Haley's operational acts of identification.

By his own admission, Haley understood "the whole business of family quest, which is the wellspring of *Roots*," as "a great common denominator, a leveler in which a king is no more than a peasant" (Haley 2007 [1977]: 159). To borrow from poet and cultural critic Ishmael Reed, Haley was teaching the nation a "Neo-Hoodoo" historiography where "every man [sic] is an artist and every artist a priest" (Reed 1972: 21).[1] He was not simply trying to provide Black Americans with a route for subsistence within the nation. To affirm himself and other Black people in the nation, he laid claim to the archival techniques of contemporary history. *Roots* was Haley's foray into the West's scriptural legacy as a discursive tradition consisting of "writing that conquers" (De Certeau 1988 [1975]: xxv).

Historian James Stuart Olson's discussion of Whiteness during the post-civil-rights era illuminates Haley's vision of and for America. Olson comments that "[o]ver the years Americans have tried to cope with the heterogeneity of their society, seeking ways to fulfill egalitarian ideals while preventing ethnic conflict." He continues, "By rejecting and then forgetting their backgrounds, new immigrants and Indians would blend into the larger society and ethnic conflict would disappear" (Olson 1979: xxii). In turn, the social construction of "Whiteness" sublimates the complex and violent history in which:

> Northern Europeans (especially Protestants) have usually been readily accepted by the White majority, and discrimination

---

1   Vincent Wimbush presses Reed's Neo-Hoodoo manifesto "into the service of representing heightened collective criticism, sharply cut articulations of identity, and efforts at self-making, self-naming, reformation, reformation, and re-orientation among African Americans, as well as negotiation with the outside world" (Wimbush 2000: 26).

against them has been comparatively mild. Discrimination against darker-skinned southern Europeans, such as the Italians or the Greeks, has been more pronounced, as it has been for Chinese, Japanese, and Filipino immigrants. And for the darkest skinned people—Blacks, some Puerto Ricans, Native Americans and Mexican-Americans—the road to success has been strewn with obstacles. (Olson 1979: xxii–xxiii)

"The unprecedented popularity of Alex Haley's novel *Roots*," Olson writes, is part of a historical moment when "Whites as well as Blacks turned toward personal histories in search of their origins" (1979: 430).

Haley may have shown America a promising form of rootedness, but not all were taken with its ramifications. What often separated readers was their perspective on Haley's use of "faction"—the seamless weaving of fiction and fact. Haley received the mixed reception as indicative of the politics that accompany writing and history. In his words:

> History is three different things. It is what you research and collect as material, how you interpret it, and then how you write it. It is secondly how I do exactly the same process along with umpteen other people who may do the same; and thirdly, history is what really happened which none of us ever really will know. That's the truth of history. But it is assumed that somehow it has a word—the word has been given as near as if it's emblazoned in bronze. That's it. ... All this is saying is that history is not constant. (Alex Haley, [Interview], September 12, 1979, cited in McCauley 1983: 81)

In trying to write American history anew, Haley believed himself to be engaged in a war of words, powerful words to be certain. He came to realize the crucial truth argued by Henry Louis Gates, "that the immediate concern of the 'politics of interpretation' is generally the politics of interpreters" (Gates 2002: 183). Haley's critics did not simply dismiss *Roots* as one man's routing; they took offense at Haley's attempt to root the nation in his audacious version of history (H. Taylor 1995: 67). Their actions neither destroyed Haley nor his book, but the self-proclaimed writer of American history has slowly been forgotten in the annals of academics, preserved only by the "root-book" he left behind and the memories of those it has affected (Deleuze and Guattari 1987 [1980]: 5).

Even still, *Roots* was not an ineffectual narrative. With it, Haley helped the country imagine a community where "African American" identity would have bona fide importance. His history writing further cultivated a sense of nationhood and kinship. Adam Hastings theorizes that for a national history to take hold, "a range of [a community's] representatives [must] hold it to exist—clergy, farmers, lawyers, merchants, writers, as well as members of a court or cabinet" (1997: 24). Haley's legacy continues because Americans have not simply interpreted *Roots*; they have both positioned themselves against it and interpolated themselves into it (Althusser 2014 [1971]: 191). This is what Wilfred Cantwell Smith describes as the relationality of scriptures, "that a text becomes, and continues as, scripture by being related in certain ways to certain people, at certain times and places" (1993: 21). In critically reading *Roots* as what David Chioni Moore likened to a "sacred text," and Helen Taylor, a "sort of Black family Bible," the anthropologist of scriptures can derive a framework for better understanding the ascription of rootedness in light of two particular aspects of identification (Moore 1996: 198; H. Taylor 1995: 54).[2]

First, to recognize *Roots* as a "Black family Bible" is to notice it as a site for orienting one's self in relationship to a larger, more encompassing story. I am reminded here of the Bible of my maternal

---

2   In regard to ascription, Ann Taves' use of attribution theory is a helpful corollary. Taves applies the term in order to theorize about the phenomena of "religion" in light of social psychologists' attribution theory. Ascription refers to the act of attributing a "special" status to objects, experiences, and practices. Rather than labeling human activities as either sacred or profane, Taves distinguishes between "simple ascriptions (things deemed special) and composite ascriptions (methods deemed efficacious for engaging with things deemed special)" (2009: 28). Her preference for the latter reflects an interest in studying "the building blocks that can be incorporated into more complex socio-cultural formations," of which scriptures, cultures, religions, and race would be prime examples.

grandmother, Lucille Rice (1907–2002). In her Bible were not only the canons of "Old and New Testament," but also a brief biography with information about herself such as the names she had gone by, where she had lived, and her relatives—that is, the parameters by she could be identified:

> [sic] My maden name was Miss Lucille A Kemp... I grew up and met <u>Silas</u> <u>WP Rice</u>... We married and had a big family, 5 boys and 4 girls. I always lived with my family until my husband past away! I am <u>old</u> <u>now</u> but I can get around very <u>well</u> thanks to <u>Jesus</u>... I call on him and <u>he</u> <u>ances</u> <u>my</u> <u>prayers</u>...thanks to Jesus the <u>Lord</u> Jesus... This Bible I have had a long time. I got it when I lived in Missouri <u>in</u> <u>a</u> <u>Book</u> <u>Club</u>. My home is 2[###] E. Houston, San Antonio, <u>Texas</u>...<u>Topeka</u>... Mrs. Lucille A Rice... Miss Lucy <u>Kemp Rice</u>

My grandmother believed the words of the Bible to hold great importance. But its scriptural importance was in the act of locating herself in proximity to it and even within it. When reading *Roots* anthropologically, we should similarly recognize its significance less in the specific content-meaning of the text (though that is an important part for a great many readers) but perhaps more so in the meaning-filled ways that humans turn to Haley's words.

Secondly, to consider *Roots* "a sacred text" is to view how humans locate power within its binding. As a devout Methodist, my grandmother believed the Bible to be set apart from other writings. Nevertheless, for her, the Bible also appeared to be a means of setting apart words she found worth knowing. In its folds, she would tuck away devotional materials, prayer lists, newspaper clippings, greeting cards, and personal reminders. I remember peeking through her Bible as a youth, astounded by the number of tracts from Jehovah's Witnesses and other groups that I had been taught, also in the Methodist church, to see as "heretical." Immediately, I had reasoned that, to her untrained eye, the vocabulary and iconography of the groups must have appeared orthodox. In hindsight, I now recognize that she was selecting for herself what would be of use and placed these materials in the Bible for safekeeping. While I was "being taught," she had been defining orthodoxy for herself and making her own sacred text (Wimbush 2007: 43–53).[3]

The Bible of Alex Haley's maternal grandparents, Will and Cynthia Palmer, served a similar function. In the museum restoration of their bedroom a small Bible lies open upon a mantel.

As Loren Lambert, a writer for the Department of Tennessee Tourism Development explains, "Its presence symbolized deep faith and belief in the right to an education. To Black families in the 1800s and 1900s, an education was the real ticket to permanent freedom, and the Bible was often the first book read if not the only book available" (Lambert 1988). Having grown up in "Palmer House," Haley would not only have seen this Bible but would also have learned to internalize "education" as sacred.

These Black family Bibles surface some of the tensions, questions, anxieties, and assumptions that should accompany thinking of *Roots* as a sort of American scripture. I concur with W.C. Smith about the need "to understand how the forming, modifying, enriching, limiting, come about; and in what the appropriating and the being involved consist" (1993: 21). More poignantly, I am challenged by Velma E. Love's query in her essay, "Scriptures as Sundials in African American Lives." "How, then, might a reading of scriptures in America also reflect a reading of America? What can the script-(ure)s of a people tell us about who they are, where they have been, and where they are going?" (Love 2012: 86).

In previous chapters, I argued that Haley eventually had great confidence in the power of his text. I began with the qualification that his story was not just an author's "routes" or attempt at meaning-making, but also an offering of "roots," a scripture by which Americans are to

3   In my high-school years, I had aspired to become a pastor and biblical scholar in the United Methodist Church, and I took Sunday School with the utmost seriousness. But contrary to the exegetically-minded, text-centered, and commentary-driven enterprise that I had been studying, my grandmother was interested in, what Wimbush calls, "weaving meaning" or in "retextualiz[ing] (in the original sense of that term) 'scriptures' in critical/signifying relationship to other 'scriptures'" (2007: 51–2). She was not complacent with the "social therapy" afforded by any one party. Rather, she was wont to pursue that rootedness on (some of) her own terms.

know and be known. Given the manner in which Americans identified and struggled with Haley's *Roots*, I observed how late twentieth
century Americans take very seriously the writing of their histories.[4]
Whether one identifies as having landed on Plymouth Rock or as
one upon whom the rock landed, *Roots* is a version of American history and a conjunction of "America" with "history."[5] For Haley, being

4 I am following the lead of Vincent L. Wimbush who has called for
a "plumbing" of the conjunction between instantiations of scriptural discourses (e.g. history, writing, the Bible, etc.) *and* peoples as the object of
theorizing social world formation (2000: 11, 22). Thus, the focus of an
anthropology of scriptures is *"sacred text[s] and social texture[s]."* See also
Wimbush's "Cycle of Life-in-Marronage Based Upon the African American
Lag" which presents a framework for understanding social engagement with
"scriptures" in terms of De-formation, Re-Form[u]lation, and Formation
(2000: 21). The model of scriptural engagement that I am presenting here
has resonances with Wimbush's cycle. Wimbush's theorizing is concerned
with a broader survey of African Americans, the Bible, and other scriptural
texts. My grounded theory is derived specifically from scripturalizing in and
around *Roots*.

5 See Malcolm X's March 29, 1964 speech, "The Ballot or the Bullet,"
delivered in Washington Heights, NY. In this version of the speech, Malcolm
says:

> One of the reasons that it is bad for us to continue to just refer to our-
> selves as the so-called Negro, that's negative. When we say so-called
> Negro that's pointing out what we aren't, but it isn't telling us what
> we are. We are Africans, and we happen to be in America. We are not
> Americans. We are a people who formerly were Africans who were kid-
> napped and brought to America. Our forefathers weren't the Pilgrims.
> We didn't land on Plymouth Rock; the rock was landed on us. We were
> brought here against our will; we were not brought here to be made
> citizens. We were not brought here to enjoy the constitutional gifts that
> they speak so beautifully about today. Because we weren't brought
> here to be made citizens—today, now that we've become awakened to
> some degree, and we begin to ask for those things which they say are
> supposedly for all Americans, they look upon us with a hostility and
> unfriendliness… You and I need something right now that's going to
> benefit all of us. That's going to change the community in which we
> live, not try to take us somewhere else. If we can't live here, we never
> will live somewhere else.

American is about interpreting that history as a prelude to a better life. Were Americans to better know their roots, Haley believed, Black persons, White persons, and others could understand that they share a common ground, a desire to make America "home." For Haley, being a true American is about successfully writing one's self into the nation's triumphant history. In this chapter, I approach the book as a testament to his operational acts of identification as an American and a case study with which we may begin to enumerate these acts, especially as they present in and around cultural texts.

My analysis begins with a summary outline of Haley's tome, *Roots*, focusing on the narration of identity formation through Haley's characters. Because of my interest in how Haley understands these processes to work, I have preserved his diction within the main text. Discussion of wider historical and literary concert are presented within the footnotes. My intent is that this will serve not only as the raw materials to develop your own critical edition of *Roots*, but more importantly as a case study for students of identity—particularly those who have not read the novel—to engage it. Chapter 4 focuses on how these dynamics manifest in later reception and signification of *Roots* in other media forms. In both chapters I maintain that the story presents readers with three archetypal relationships to America: (1) America as a source of *uproot*; (2) America as a place to *route*; (3) America as a home wherein to take *root*.

These positions are denoted by Haley's patterned use of the terms "rooted" and "routed" as well as his symbolic portrayal of "history" and "writing," axial discourses central to Haley's understanding of America. By grounding this theory in a Close Reading of the text, I argue that a study of the characters' *uproot*, *routing*, and *taking root* can help readers learn about Haley's orientation to America and the psycho-social logic of scriptures. Thus, "roots" becomes a vocabulary for naming our "operational acts of identification," with *uprooting*, *routing*, and *taking root* serving as a grammar for parsing "the work we humans make scriptures do" for ourselves and to others (Wimbush 2010: 358).

Though *Roots* spans three continents and three centuries, the novel begins and ends in 1976 America. I refer to the bookends of this frame story as the Prologue and Epilogue for two reasons. First, they are representative of what many of those in the *Roots* moment already knew via Haley's Doubleday, *Reader's Digest*, and ABC pre-promotion of the story. Second, they encapsulate Haley's agenda for *Roots*.

THE HISTORIOGRAPHIC STRUCTURE OF *ROOTS: THE SAGA OF AN AMERICAN FAMILY*

GENERATIONS, DATES, AND LITERARY DIVISIONS

A. Prologue—A Bicentennial Celebration

Dedication

Acknowledgment

B. Body—Enslavement to Reconstruction

Kunta Kinte/Toby Waller (1750–1806)	**Ch. 1–83**
Kizzy Lea (née Waller) (1790–1861)	**Ch. 68–108**
Chicken George Lea (1806–1890)	**Ch. 85–115**
Tom Murray (née Lea) (1833–1893?)	**Ch. 97–114**

C. Epilogue—A Bicentennial Reflection

Cynthia (b. 1871) & Will Palmer (d. 1926); Cousin Georgia (1884?–1967)	**Ch. 115–16**
Bertha (1895–1931) & Simon Haley (1892–1973); Alex Haley (1921–)	**Ch. 117–20**

Figure 3 The Historiographic Structure of *Roots*.
NOTE: The dates indicate years either explicitly noted or deducible from the novel's internal timeline. Haley's headings and divisions have been marked in bold. When not specified, I have placed question marks—even if the dates can be found from outside of the text—in order to suggest that chronology was not always a focus for the author.

A. Prologue—A Bicentennial Celebration

Roots starts with Haley setting himself apart as an expert in American identity by virtue of his efforts at understanding the nation's story and the cultural significance of the book's publication. From the beginning the reader is given a basic model of rootedness. The Prologue commences with the Dedication, where Haley recognizes the prolonged, twelve-year journey of *"Roots'* researching and writing" (Haley 2007 [1976]: v). He prefaces the novel by describing it as worth the wait, adding that the resulting publication date, 1976, is "just by chance...the Bicentennial Year of the United States." For him, the kismet release makes a befitting "birthday offering to [his] country within which most of *Roots* happened" (v). Following the Dedication, Haley presents an Acknowledgments section with a sequence that shifts attention to a primordial Africa. He alternates between thanking those involved in the search for "his furthest-back person" and detailing his research resolve (vii–viii).[6] This braiding of history and writing reinforces Haley's authority to tell a profound story about America.

The Acknowledgments begins with George Sims, Haley's boyhood friend from Henning, Tennessee who researched "particularly

---

6   Haley's strategy of using history and writing to reinforce each other is at least part of the reason why literary critics disregard *Roots*. George B. Handley (2000), for instance, criticizes the "degrees of nostalgia, if not for slavery, at least for origins" characterized by "genealogy, as an intergenerational and frequently oedipal drama." For him, "the best postslavery writing...wrestles with the contradictions of depending on a reprehensible history for establishing new postslavery life and identity and warns against any simple or hasty solutions" (Handley 2000: 4).

My issue is not whether Handley's assessment of post-slavery narrative genre is correct. What is of interest here is the politics surfaced about the conjunction of history and writing. *Roots* is a complicated and creative engagement with American readers' hyper-familiarity and hyper-dependence with genealogy. The critical student of scriptures should pause to reflect why some novels appear simple (e.g. *Roots*) and the postmodern approaches that Handler lauds (the works of Toni Morrison and Ishmael Reed among others) do not. The data is the reader and the reading of the text, not the text itself.

in the U.S. Library of Congress and the U.S. National Archives [and] supplied much of the historical and cultural material that [Haley wove] around the lives of the people in the book" (2007 [1976]: vii). Then Murray Fisher, Haley's editor at *Playboy*, is mentioned for his "clinical expertise" in editing, structuring, and drafting parts of the novel (vii). Next Haley credits "Mrs. Dewitt Wallace and the editors of *Reader's Digest*" for enabling him to "explore if [his] maternal family's treasured oral history might possibly be documented back into Africa where all Black Americans began" (vii–viii). Their beneficence helped finance his conference with "librarians and archivists in some fifty-seven different repositories of information on three continents" (viii). Additionally, "Paul R. Reynolds, doyen of literary agents" and "Doubleday Senior Editors Lisa Drew and Ken McCormick" are commended for their patience with Haley's protracted writing schedule (viii). The section concludes with a nod to "the griots of Africa," rootwork incarnate:

> Finally, I acknowledge immense debt to the griots of Africa—where today it is rightly said that when a griot dies, it is as if a library has burned to the ground. The griots symbolize how all human ancestry goes back to some place, and some time, where there was not writing. Then, the memories and the mouths of ancient elders was the only way that early histories of mankind got passed along...for all of us today to know who we are. (Haley 2007 [1976]: viii)

Twentieth century Americans, in Haley's view, needed a reminder of who they are and where they came from, but the nation lacked these knowing sages. Having documented the oral histories of his maternal grandmother and a modern Mandinka griot, Haley presents his own *Roots* as a replacement for the historical record—in "African" and "American" registers alike.

B. Body—Enslavement to Reconstruction

Roots' Body section tells the story of how Alex Haley's family not only came to America but also—having seized opportunity and risen the ranks—became America exemplified. It commences with the birth of Kunta Kinte (Ch. 1) and extends to Haley's great-grandfather, Tom Murray, his settling in Henning and his leading the construction of New Hope Colored Methodist Episcopal Church (Ch. 114). The narrative explicates the tragedy that brought Haley's family to America and how it was a prelude to the family's realization of the American Dream. In total, it provides an amendment to the canonical version of the immigrant nation narrative with which new audiences (e.g. Black people) can identify. And it drew attention to socio-historical conceits that all Americans (especially White people) would need to acknowledge while negotiating their relationship to the nation and those in it.

Ch. 1–83: Kunta Kinte/Toby Waller (1750–1806)

The Body section begins with the narrative arc of Kunta Kinte, the ancestor Haley characterizes as the personification of the way one comes to identify with America. In following him we will see America transform from a site of doom to a place of possibility. But these ideas about the nation are always held in contrast to the ultimate site of rootedness, the Africa homeland of Haley's historiographic fabrication. This serves as a metaphor for *Roots'* large role as a baseline against which readers can measure their own rootedness.

Haley begins his story *in media res,* conjuring a specific vision of the world which locates Eden in a primeval Africa. Chapter 1 opens with the birthing of the story's protagonist and mythic patriarch. While the mother is in the throes of labor, Haley quickly shares the importance of what we are witnessing.

> According to the forefathers, a boy firstborn presaged the blessings of Allah not only upon the parents but also upon the parents' families; and there was the prideful knowledge that the name of Kinte would thus be both distinguished and perpetuated. (Haley 2007 [1976]: 1)

After the "chatterings" of the elderly women who delivered him and "before the first crowing…the first sound the child heard was the muted, rhythmic *bomp-a-bomp-a-bomp* of wooden pestles [of] the other women…preparing the traditional breakfast." Day breaks and the "men of the village filed briskly to the playing place, where the alimamo led the worship: *Allahu Akbar! Ashadu an Laila ha laila-halala!* (God is Great! I bear witness that there is only one God!)" (Haley 2007 [1976]: 1).[7] *Roots'* Juffure is best understood as a mythical and timeless paradise to symbolize rootedness (Laist 2013: 2), for through the newborn's awakening senses, Haley introduces details about how this world is ordered.

Eight days after the child's birth, the father, Omoro Kinte, invites every household in the village of Juffure to attend a naming ceremony for the boy. He would be known as Kunta Kinte:

> As everyone knew, it was the middle name of the child's late grandfather, Kairaba Kunta Kinte, who had come from his native Mauretania into The Gambia, where he had saved the people of Juffure from a famine, married Grandma Yaisa, and then served Juffure honorably till his death as the village's holy man… All of the people exclaimed their admiration and respect at such a distinguished lineage. (Haley 2007 [1976]: 4)

Kunta's very name evoked remembrance of Juffure's *marabout* and a line of Mauritanian forefathers that "went back more than

---

7   Haley's historical characterization of the village Juffure is an amalgamation of different periods of Gambian history. This eighteenth century portrait of a Muslim village is consistent with the spread of Islam in the region (Quinn 1972: 54–5). However, Haley's depiction of an agricultural village is not historically accurate. Juffure had been subject to European colonialism since 1650. James, Duke of Courland and godson to James I of England, made the King of Barra his vassal. Juffure's location next to the River Gambia made it a potential site for a military and economic port. Compared to his Dutch and French rivals, the Duke of Courland was of limited means and struggled to develop his holdings. Throughout the eighteenth century, the Duke of Courland entreated the British for support and England's Royal African Company increasingly took control of the region. By 1800, Juffure was a British trading post used for the acquisition of goods and slaves (J.M. Gray 1966: 38, 40, 99).

As shown in the mentioned secondary sources, the discrepancy is unlikely a result of unavailable research. After all, Haley mentions the King of Barra and his vassal relationship with European powers (2007 [1976]: 75).

two-hundred rains"[8] (Haley 2007 [1976]: 4). The ritual, designed to teach Kunta who he is, concludes with Omoro walking to the edge of the village, lifting the baby toward "the moon and the stars," and saying, "Behold—the only thing greater than yourself" (4). According to Haley, the rite took place "early in the spring of 1750, in the village of Juffure, four days from the coast of The Gambia, West Africa" (1). The specific date and place denote Kunta Kinte's birth, but the cosmic and elemental features (i.e. "the moon and the stars," "two-hundred rains") root Kunta in a way of life that has borne fruit for ages.

Readers join the young Kunta in learning to count the moons, seasons, and rains. They follow the adolescent Kunta in "Koranic" schooling (Ch. 10), manhood training (Ch. 23), puberty (Ch. 27), and his first steps as an adult (Ch. 33).[9] The challenge of tracking Kunta Kinte's early years disrupts a historical imagination accustomed to

---

8   See Charlotte A. Quinn's *Mandingo Kingdoms of the Senegambia* (1972: 53–8). "Marabout" refers to a teaching and clerical class of Muslims. According to Quinn, the term is "associated with the saint cults of North Africa" and a label for all who "accepted a purified form of Islam," in contrast to the traditional *Soninke*, "a term for animists or Muslims who failed to observe Islamic practices." Marabouts understood the Soninke as synonymous with "the Arabic *kafir* (unbeliever)" (53).

Marabouts were trained in the schools of North Africa and welcomed throughout The Gambia for their "skills in education, magic, and medicine." In the eighteenth century, northern Islamic states sent missionaries to West Africa and West African tribes sent select male children north for clerical training. "By the middle of the nineteenth century Muslim clerics had established themselves in nearly all of the Mandingo states of the Gambia" (Quinn 1972: 57).

In *Roots*, Kunta Kinte's namesake, Kairaba Kunta Kinte, is the marabout who brought Islam and much-needed rain to Juffure (Haley 2007 [1976]: 18). In testament to the village's saint and their level of devotion, Haley describes how "pagan traders hurried on past Juffure, not even stopping, for their wares of tobacco and snuff and mead beer were for infidels only, since the Moslem Mandinkas never drank nor smoked" (48).

9   I have retained Haley's spelling of "Koran," "Moslem," and other Arabic terms in order to preserve the conventions of Haley's time for critical consideration.

Western calendrics. The first thirty-three chapters overcome readers with the childlike innocence of Kunta Kinte, Haley's furthest-back person, born free and untouched by America's "original sin" of slavery (Madison 1820).

Haley then contrasts this timeless, idyllic image of Africa with a chaos from beyond its shores. Kunta was kidnapped at "seventeen rains" of age (Haley 2007 [1976]: 247), endured a "four and a half moon" journey upon the *Lord Ligonier* (250), and found himself in a strange new world (Ch. 40; 246, 250).[10] And at the port of Annapolis he was sold at auction to the Waller family of Spotsylvania County, Virginia (Ch. 41; 258).[11]

Kunta is puzzled by the relationship between American-born Black people and their White slave-masters. Too few Black people, he feels, even attempt to resist the "inhuman" toubob, and too many Black people are insolent of their African heritage (Haley 2007 [1976]: 282).[12] Not until he befriended his fellow slaves did he realize that the former was the result of the latter, that they had little frame of reference for understanding Black peoples' inherent right to freedom. In Chapter 46, Kunta begins to wonder whether he was destined for a greater purpose in America. He starts:

> …feeling that Allah had somehow, for some reason, *willed* him to be here in this place amid the lost tribe of a great Black family that reached its *roots* back among the ancient forefathers; but unlike himself, these Black ones had no knowledge whatsoever

10 The African portion of the narrative is longer than the character arcs of Kunta Kinte's descendants (i.e. Kizzy, Chicken George, Tom, etc.). This is partially why many Americans remember *Roots* for its depiction of Africa. However it is important to note that *Roots* is an American story. As Haley writes, it is in America, "*my country within which most of* Roots *happened*" (2007 [1976]: v).

11 Kunta Kinte is first sold to John Waller. The two have little interaction. After Kunta's foot is cut off (Haley 2007 [1976]: 312), Waller's brother, John takes ownership after salvaging the remaining leg (331).

12 Kunta is able to discern the tribal origins of many American-born Black people, identifying traits such as "distinctly Wolof features" (Haley 2007 [1976]: 255).

of who they were and where they'd come from. (2007 [1976]: 290, emphasis added)

Having seen Black slaves entertain their White masters with music, Kunta considered whether:

> in some strong, strange, and very deep way, the Blacks and the toubob had some *need* for each other…it had seemed to him that the toubob were at their happiest when they were close around the Black ones—even when they were beating them. (2007 [1976]: 294)

This passage is indicative of the debate in Black cultural criticism of whether *Roots* accurately presents and challenges the institution of slavery or whether it appropriates the commonplaces of Southern plantation myths and their portrayal of docile slaves.[13] In the presumption of Black rootlessness and White people's dependence on Black people, Kunta sees a synergy, if not the potential for racial cooperation, but he is ill-positioned to affect change.

In 1775—the first time Haley dictates the year according to Western convention since Kunta's birth, Kunta sees stark evidence of colonial America's most troubling paradox (Haley 2007 [1976]: 355). He cannot fathom events like "'De Boston Massacree'!" where "some a dem Boston peoples got so mad 'boud dem king's taxes dey marched on dat king's soldiers. Dem soldiers commence to shootin', an' firs' one kilt was a nigger name a Crispus Attucks" (353). Similarly, Kunta notices the "exclaiming about some Massa Patrick

13   Literary critic Tim A. Ryan reframes the conversation in a more helpful manner in *Call and Responses: The American Novel of Slavery since Gone with the Wind* (2008). He observes that docility is presented as an embodied reality and as an act that Black people perform to negotiate the slave institution (Ryan 2008: 120). Though Haley is inconsistent and perhaps haphazard with his characterizations, Ryan sees this as an opportunity to theorize about the institution. If Kunta's militant defiance, Ryan ponders, can be pushed beneath a surface of apparent passivity in just a few years, what might have been the psychic impact for subsequent generations of slaves. Americans have used *Roots* as a sort of scripture to explore these questions even when *Roots* as literature does not.

Henry having cried out, 'Give me liberty or give me death!' Kunta liked that, but he couldn't understand how somebody *White* could say it; White folks looked pretty free to him" (356). White slavecatchers had chopped off Kunta's foot in order to end his pursuit of freedom (Ch. 49; 313). He was not free to answer to his "real" name, only to the slave name, "Toby Waller," the appellation belonging to his owner (275). The ignorance of Black people's roots is paralleled by colonial America's naive understanding of freedom.

Kunta's options were limited, but he was not without aspiration. "Though it shamed him to admit it, he had begun to prefer life as he was allowed to live it here on this plantation to the certainty of being captured and probably killed if he tried to escape again" (Haley 2007 [1976]: 342). In Chapter 52, he begins participating in the conversations of "slave row," befriending an elderly, violin-playing slave called "the fiddler."[14] In the course of their relationship, the fiddler challenges Kunta's misgivings about American Blacks. "What put me out with you African niggers, looka here! ... You git over here figgerin' niggers here out to be like you is! How you 'spec we gon' know 'bout Africa? We ain't never been dere, an' ain't goin' neither!'"

As Haley explains, "the fiddler had taken off his mask; that meant he was beginning to *trust* Kunta"[15] (357). The fiddler's candor not

14 Ethnomusicologist Jacqueline Cogdell Djedje has shown that in The Gambia and other regions, the musicians' accompaniment is integral to expressions of "place (the geographical and sociocultural environment); ethnicity (the ethnic identity of the people and their relationship with those around them); religion (the belief system and its role in society); and status (the social standing of performers in relation to others in society) of teaching, divining, healing, and other manifestations of power" (Djedje 2008: 8). The fiddler's violin acts as a symbol to speak authoritatively on similar matters in America.

15 The fiddler's simultaneous rejection and longing for African roots speaks to Frantz Fanon's argument that "the Black man is *comparaison*" (Fanon 2008 [1952]: 185). Fanon uses the Creole term to underline how Black people are "preoccupied with self-assertion and the ego ideal" and how "whenever he is in the presence of someone else, there is always the question of worth and merit" (186). Fanon helps us understand that Fiddler's mask is a symbol to ward off White punishment and his own self-doubt. The

only helps Kunta grow in empathy for his estranged kin, but it marks the first time since coming to America that Kunta "was actually beginning to *know* someone" (347).

For Haley, "slave row" designates not only the slave quarters on a plantation, but also the site where Black people form new social ties while working out their differences. Political scientist Gayle T. Tate writes, "Forging kinship and fictive ties that enabled them to withstand a common oppression, slaves from disparate tribes and areas of the African continent became a people" (Tate 2003: 40). And within these surrogate tribes, Black persons distinguished themselves along the lines of class, race, and authority.

"The fiddler," Edward M. Jackson writes, is "the pragmatic realist" whose task it is to "Americanize" Kunta and "[tell] him what America is like" (1987: 73). The fiddler arrogates himself as the aged sage, having survived because of his wisdom. His violin reminds Kunta of the *kora* and other stringed instruments from his homeland (Haley 2007 [1976]: 49, 293).

As Kunta "ease[s] into acceptance of their ways," he begins to build a new home in America alongside his own New World griot (344).

As Kunta becomes more accustomed to life in America, Haley narrates Kunta's experiencing a sort of double-vision—one where the protagonist sees a scene in America while imagining a similar scene as it would take place in Africa. At "thirty-nine rains," Kunta courts Bell, the enslaved, big house cook who reminds him of the women from Juffure (Ch. 64; 415).[16] Once when she cooked him a hoe cake

---

fiddler's advice to Kunta is not selfless. As long as Kunta holds on to his African roots, the fiddler will see a stark reminder of that which he himself sacrificed in order to survive.

16 Bell's name is emblematic of her role as the "big house cook," answering to the master's every need (e.g. servant's bell). In *American Slavery and the American Novel, 1852–1977*, Edward M. Jackson characterizes Bell as a "house nigger" (1987: 73), one "who accepts White categories" and "operates on the principles of compromise and accommodation" (76). While I agree with Jackson's larger thesis that *Roots* evinces a struggle to articulate the self between poles of accommodation and resistance, I think his description of Bell and other house servants is too simplistic. As she tells Kunta, "I

using meal she had made in the mortar and pestle he had carved for her, Kunta was watching her in his mind's eye beating the couscous for breakfast in some African village. He saw his reality more clearly when she explained that hoe cakes got their name from slaves cooking on the flat edge of a hoe when they were working out in the fields (412).[17] In inducing this sort of vision, Haley presents *Roots* as a homeopathic remedy for dealing with an otherwise painful reality.

Kunta abhorred her worship of "a large, framed picture of the yellow-haired 'Jesus,' who seemed to be a relative of their heathen 'O Lawd,'" but "he couldn't feel too harshly about someone, even a pagan Christian, who was so good to one of another faith, even someone as worthy as he was" (Haley 2007 [1976]: 413–14).[18] Requiting each other's affections, Kunta and Bell receive permission from "Massa Waller" to "jump de broom" before the Waller household and slaves (Ch. 65; 417).[19]

---

keeps my ears sharp on little things gits dropped. I knows whole lo' more'n anybody thinks I knows" (Haley 2007 [1976]: 408). Bell uses her proximity to the big house to learn about the Master's family history, his temperament, and any news that has demanded his attention. Her agency should be taken into account.

17 This literary technique is a creative illustration of "a peculiar sensation" that Du Bois describes as "two-ness,—an American, a Negro; two souls, two thoughts, two unreconciled strivings; two warring ideals in one dark body, whose dogged strength alone keeps it from being torn asunder" (Du Bois 2014 [1903]: 2).

18 In describing Christianity as "pagan," Kunta is participating in religious apologetics to separate the "purity" of his African Moslem heritage from the "sullied" disposition of American-born Blacks. Haley may also be engaging in this hermeneutical exercise for his own purposes, critiquing White people's biblical defense of slavery as a misappropriation of the Christian scriptures. For an example of similar apologetics, see James H. Cone's contemporary treatise, *Black Theology and Black Power* (2012 [1969]).

19 "Jumping the Broom" is a courtship ritual that was performed by Black Americans, especially in the antebellum South where Black marriage was outlawed. Though many scholars have argued that it has origins in Africa, this thesis has been called into question. There is also evidence that the practice has connections to Europe—particularly a Romani wedding

Kunta's American family continues to grow: in September of 1790, Bell and Kunta have "a *girl*child [sic]" (Ch. 68; 436).

> [H]e couldn't stop staring at the face of the infant...almost as black as his, and the features...unmistakably Mandinka. Though it was a girlchild—which must be the will of Allah...he felt a deep pride and serenity in the knowledge that the blood of the Kintes, which had coursed down through the centuries like a mighty river, would continue to flow for still another generation. (437)

Kunta had wanted a son to carry on the Kinte patriline, but this desire fades immediately upon seeing his daughter. He is content that, despite everything he had endured, his lineage would continue.

Roots as a scripture similarly supports the hopes of those readers who want to identify as American but struggle to know whether it is possible or worth it. Haley answers in the affirmative through the example of Kunta Kinte, who is presented as having no option but to make the best of the situation while also possessing the knowledge of how to do so. Haley makes a similar claim as his route is relayed as the blueprint, the root.

Ch. 68–108: Kizzy Lea (née Waller) (1790–1861)

The second part of the Body section of *Roots* dwells in the risk and struggle that mark a life without roots. We follow Kunta's offspring who embraces Kunta's hopes but struggles to operationalize them in the midst of a contentious social reality. This part of the narrative

---

tradition practiced in Scotland and England (Dundes 1996). Folklorist Alan Dundes is careful to point out that the issue of origins is an afterthought to the history that made the practice and the question of origins meaningful. He notes that the "jump de broom" scene in *Roots* (both the novel and miniseries) reified the idea of the ritual's African origins (326). This is despite the fact that Haley does not analogize the scene with anything from Africa. Kunta recognizes the ceremony as something American-born Blacks do. Dundes similarly contends that whatever the ritual's origins, it is a statement about Black people's complicated history in the United States.

elaborates on the bewilderment, pain, and fear that Haley associates with a rootless life.

Kunta tries to root his offspring from the start. He takes seriously the duty of naming the child, "for he knew that what a child was called would really influence the kind of person he or she became" (Haley 2007 [1976]: 437). He knows that she will carry the last name of "the massa," but he "vowed before Allah that this girlchild would grow up knowing her own true name, 'Kinte.'" Like his father before him, Kunta takes the girl to the edge of his village "slave row," and raises her to the moon and stars, whispering her name, "Kizzy." Kunta had explained to Bell that "in Mandinka 'Kizzy' meant 'you sit down,' or 'you stay put,' which, in turn, meant…this child would never get sold away" (441).[20] And so, as Omoro had said to Kunta, Kunta says to Kizzy, "Behold, the only thing greater than yourself!" (441).

Kunta and Bell would work fervently to ensure that Kizzy stay rooted with her family. For Kunta, this meant teaching Kizzy as many "Africanisms" as he could without drawing suspicion. Kunta knew that White people—and more than a few Black persons—had little tolerance for outward displays of African customs or identity (including presumptions of freedom), and he only feigned docility to survive.[21] Secretly, Kunta continues to count "moons" with a jar of pebbles, hiding them in the slave quarters. And he reveals the calendrical rocks to Kizzy so that she may have a proper reckoning of history (Haley 2007 [1976]: 466). He tells her that their story did not begin in America, but rather that their roots lie under the heavens in Africa (Ch. 74).

20 Prior to working on the Waller plantation, Bell had served another master who had sold away her two children (Haley 2007 [1976]: 435).

21 Kunta's performance as the domesticated "Toby" is a layered riff on Western constructions of Africans. "Toby" is a persona adopted to pacify the slave-master, but Kunta insists that Blacks call him by his African name (Haley 2007 [1976]: 275, 280, and 327). This is a reversal of another naming practice where European slave-masters used the African names "to underline cultural distinctions…and help justify enslavement." For instance, the Hausa word, "Sambo," "evolved into a derogatory term for a Black man indicating laziness or stupidity" (L.M. Harris 2003: 26).

Kunta continues to teach Kizzy while running errands for Massa Waller. Massa Waller "trusted" Kunta enough to let him work as a carriage driver, granting Kunta a traveling pass to conduct business unsupervised and permission to take young Kizzy along (Haley 2007 [1976]: 466). When Kunta and Kizzy are alone, he points out nearby sites—for instance, the Mattaponi River— and likens them to places near Juffure—such as the Kamby Bolongo, "the life-giving river [that] was revered by his people as a symbol of fertility" (480). He teaches her "the Mandinka names of things," like *Fa* (father) in order that she might know that family "b'long to one 'nother" in a manner stronger than the bonds of slavery (483). Kunta does not just relate a family history; he imparts geography and philology *as* a family history by which she can identify herself in relation to those around her.

Neither Kunta nor Kizzy dares to imagine that those relationships could change. When discussing the possibility of being sold and separated, Kizzy says, "Aw, Pappy, I couldn't never leave you an' Mammy," to which Kunta replies, "An' chile, speck we couldn't never let you go, neither" (Haley 2007 [1976]: 484). By remembering Kunta's teachings, Kizzy would always have a way to draw near to her family. She would know her "source-place," just in case (439).

Bell focuses on more terrestrial methods of warding off the possibility of the family's division. In Bell's experience, slaves who worked in the field had less of an attachment to their masters and were thus more likely to be sold away (Haley 2007 [1976]: 479). As the house cook, Bell believes she has a relatively special position with Massa Waller. It was on account of this "closeness," for instance, that Massa Waller appointed her then-boyfriend, Kunta, a carriage driver. Similarly, Bell has convinced Massa Waller to allow her to have Kizzy assist with household duties, for it is better "dan her growin' up a fiel-han' young'un" (461). Though this limits Kunta's opportunity to teach Kizzy, he raises little objection. Massa Waller had sent Noah, a boy only two years older than Kizzy, to work in the fields, "pullin' weeds an' totin' water" (461–2). Kunta has seen how field hands live "the life of a farm animal…and would rather die than be responsible for sentencing his daughter to such a fate" (461). Bell and Kunta are in agreement that they must do everything in their power to help Kizzy "stay put."

Bell and Kunta's efforts are complicated by the visits of Massa Waller's young niece, "Missy Anne," who treats Kizzy, four years younger, as her own "l'il nigger doll!" (Haley 2007 [1976]: 443). Neither parent is keen on the children's games, like "playing nigger, bursting open a ripe watermelon and jamming their faces down into its crisp wetness." They know that this play practices the norms of the slave system without teaching Kizzy how to properly negotiate them. Thus, Kizzy does not understand the danger of having shown Missy Anne "Kunta's gourd of pebbles." When Massa Waller demands an explanation, Bell underplays the pebbles' expression of self-determination and resistance. The rocks, she says, "ain't no voodoo. Ol' African nigger I got jes cain't count, dat's all. So every new moon, he drop l'il rock in de gourd so all dem rocks say how ol' he is!" (467).

Bell's fear increases when Missy Anne and Kizzy start playing school. What begins as an innocent game results in Kizzy's budding ability to read and write (Haley 2007 [1976], 524).[22] Bell has secretly acquired some skill with letters from a lifetime of working in the big house, but this is surpassed by Kizzy's literacy. Bell knows the laws against slave literacy and the penalties of disobeying White people, and prays saying, "Ain't no game no mo'…I jes' hopes it be's awright, Lawd have mercy" (524). The fear partially subsides when the childhood playmates become divided by adolescence. Missy Anne's visits become fewer and far between. By Missy Anne's sixteenth birthday, she has "suddenly acted as if she didn't even know the starchly uniformed aproned Kizzy" (525). Bell and Kunta are neither surprised nor dismayed. Their daughter is realizing her rightful place alongside them, as well as her place within the presumptive racial hierarchy.

22 Eighteenth and nineteenth century restrictions on Black literacy were the result of Western interpretations of the meaning and potential of Black bodies (Cornelius 1992). In this post-Gutenburg era, literacy was not simply a means of communication but, increasingly, a human right (11). To train Blacks in Western letters was to risk upturning the anthropological presumptions that justified slavery—the premise that Blacks were not human (16). Prohibiting literacy was one strategy to limit Blacks from interpreting themselves as equal members in the "kingdom of God." Articulating "true meanings" of legal and biblical pronouncements was another.

With Missy Anne increasingly absent from the Waller plantation, Kizzy's attention turns toward the field hand, Noah (Ch. 82).
Hardworking and reserved, Kunta sees himself in Noah and approves
of Kizzy's romantic interest in the eighteen-year-old (Haley 2007
[1976]: 529). But when Noah asks Kunta about how to run away,
Kunta becomes anxious. The two men agree that any plot would be
too dangerous for Kizzy. Kunta also recognizes that were Noah to be
successful in escaping, "it would yet again crush utterly Kizzy's trusting faith that already had been wounded so badly by Missy Anne...
the lives of all Black people in the toubob land seemed so full of
suffering, but he wished he could spare her some of it" (535). Noah
insists, "when I gits Nawth, I means to work an' buy her free" (534).
Kunta "would ask Allah to grant Noah good luck" (535). And in
October 1806, Noah flees the Waller plantation, a week after Kizzy's
sixteenth birthday.

Six days after Noah's flight, the sheriff returns to the Waller plantation with news of Noah's capture.[23] Bell and Kunta search immediately for Kizzy, only to find her in the sheriff's custody (Haley 2007
[1976]: 541). Bell beseeches Massa Waller for an explanation and
learns that Noah has "severely knif[ed] two...road patrolmen who
challenged a false traveling pass he was carrying." Under duress, Noah
has implicated Kizzy as the forger, and Kizzy confesses her role to
the sheriff (542). When the sheriff chains Kizzy into his patrol wagon,
Kunta and Bell rush to her aid. Kizzy screams out "Save me, Fa!"
while the sheriff throws Bell aside and butts Kunta in the head with a
pistol (544–5). Kizzy continues to cry out for help, "'Missy Anne! ...
Missy Annnnnnnnnnnnne!' ... 'Missy Annnnnnnnnnnnnnnnne!' Again
and again the screams came; they seemed to hang in the air behind
the wagon swiftly rolling toward the main road" (545). Mother and
father are unable to save their daughter, and her mistress is unwilling
to help her servant.

23 Haley may have named Kizzy's lover "Noah" to reference the biblical
prophet said to take a remnant on an ark during a cataclysmic flood. If this is
the case, then the Noah of *Roots* is a tragic twist, for his ark crashes amidst
the waves of the Black Atlantic.

In Chapter 84, Kizzy awakens "weak and dazed," lying on burlap sacks in a dark cabin (Haley 2007 [1976]: 547). As she tries to muster the strength to escape, the cabin door opens to:

> the figure entering furtively, with a cupped hand shielding a candle's flame. Above it she recognized the face of the White man who had purchased her, and she saw that his other hand was holding a whip, cocked ready for use. But it was the glazed leer on the White man's face that froze her where she stood.[24] (547)

The sixteen-year-old Kizzy's only frame of reference for the White man's intentions is "what Pappy did with Mammy" and "what Noah had urged her to do" (547).

He rapes her (Haley 2007 [1976]: 548–9). Through the brutal ordeal, she wonders what came of Noah and her parents and Missy Anne—concluding there will be no rescue (549–50). Her wounds are treated by Miss Malizy, "de big-house cook," who explains that Kizzy has been sold to a "massa, who had grown to adulthood as a po' cracker, bought a twenty-five-cent raffle ticket that won him a good fighting rooster, which got him started on the road to becoming one of the area's most successful gamecock owners" (552). His name is "Massa Tom Lea" of "Caswell County in North Ca'liny" (553).

Miss Malizy schools Kizzy in the differences between Massa Waller and Massa Lea, and the institution of slavery in the two regions. Doctor John Waller came from an aristocratic family with large plantations throughout Virginia. Tom Lea's eighty-acre "planation" was a simple house for him and his wife, with an even simpler "slave row" for their five slaves and a coop for his one hundred chickens (533).

---

24 Haley's description of the "cocked" whip is, in my estimation, a euphemism for the phallus but also a connection to the character's later-revealed hobby of "cockfighting" (Haley 2007 [1976]: 552). On one level, Haley presents the White man's dependence on rape and cockfighting for power as a foil against the hard-working Kunta and Noah, who embody genuine masculinity. On another level, the gendered discourse points to Haley's dependence on the "the arithmetics" of the Black masculinist narrative, in which Black male protagonists are defined by their difference from White males" (J.L. Greene 2008: 113–14).

The Wallers added to their fortune by growing tobacco, cotton, and other cash crops (303–4). But Tom Lea was a subsistence farmer. His remaining energies were devoted to the raising of one hundred gamecocks for competitions at local tournaments. John Waller had the distinction of being a relatively benign master, caring for Kunta's amputated foot and keeping obedient slave families together. Massa Lea, Miss Malizy tells Kizzy, "will have you hunted down wid dem blood dogs, an' you in a worser mess" (552). The Waller plantation in Spotsylvania County, Virginia was the only home Kizzy had known. To her, Caswell County, North Carolina seemed like a place to die.

In being sold deeper into the South, Kizzy is thrust deeper into the horrors of the slave institution. Miss Malizy is awestruck by Kizzy's relatively mild experience as a slave, exclaiming, "Lawd, ain't many us gits to know *both* our folks fo' somebody git sol' away!" (Haley 2007 [1976]: 553). Kizzy is "speechless" when Miss Malizy says she has been purchased to serve as a "breeder…[to] bring 'im free pickaninnies." Miss Malizy goes on to say, "Fact, I wouldn't o' been surprised if massa stuck you in wid one dem stud niggers some rich massas keep on dey places an' hires out. But it looks like to me he figgerin' on breedin' you hisself" (555). On a winter evening in 1806, Kizzy gives birth to a boy whose "skin seemed to be almost high-yaller." After acknowledging his son's arrival, Massa Lea deems that a "weekend will make enough time off" and that Kizzy can return to the field the following Monday (559). Massa Lea rapes Kizzy again and decides to name the child "George—that's after the hardest working nigger I ever saw" (559). Kunta had named his daughter in an effort to protect her. Her son's name has all but sealed his doom.

Kizzy is "unsure which outrage to be most furious about" (Haley 2007 [1976]: 559). She had wanted to name the child "Kunta" or "Kinte," for she remembered learning from her father how "in his homeland, the naming of sons was the most important thing of all, *'cause de sons becomes dey families' mens!*" (559).[25] The

25 Sonship is an important concept in Mandinka society. Tribal authority is patrilineal, with the most ambitious men establishing villages under their own names and initiating dynastic rule. As Charlotte A. Quinn explains, "With some exceptions, families with traditions of direct descent

freedom-minded Noah was to have been to her what Kunta Kinte was to Bell (547). As "her mammy had told her," "De reason yo' pappy took holt of my feelin's from de firs'...was he de proudest Black man I ever seed!" (559). But "Kizzy decided that however base her baby's origins, however light his color, whatever name the massa forced upon him, she would never regard him as other than the grandson of an African" (559).

Kizzy's resolve to reject her George's paternity dramatizes how Haley would have readers resist claims of Black people's inability to be identified as tried and true Americans. If Kizzy can endure family separation, rape, and exploitation and resolve to claim an African origin, then Haley's readers can continue the struggle to find their roots. Kizzy has symbolically paid the dues. Alex Haley, by way of his relative success, has claimed the prize of American identity. Readers are challenged to further follow Haley's footsteps that they might redeem struggle for certitude.

Ch. 85–115: Chicken George Lea (1806–1890)

Kizzy's son, George, is a cautionary tale in Haley's thesis on identity formation. Under his mother's thumb, he is imbued with the pride of the Kinte line—learning that there is strength in where he ultimately comes from. But as he grows older and begins to show an interest in his father, he becomes more like his father—foolish, listless, rootless. But young George is never so far gone that his roots cannot bring him back to what Haley says matters—the story of where one comes from and where one belongs.

In Chapter 87, George becomes the pride of slave row. "By George's third year, he had begun to demonstrate a determination to 'help' the slave row grown-ups" (Haley 2007 [1976]: 570). A precocious child, he frequently takes on tasks beyond his strength or coordination. The

---

from founder-settler ancestors claimed paramount rights to land ownership through the [Mandinka] state and the economic, social, and political assets associated with it" (1972: 37). In *Roots*, Kunta Kinte's uncles, Janneh and Saloum Kinte, have established a new village (Haley 2007 [1976]: 81). Kunta carries on this tradition by establishing a new people in America.

doting affection he receives combined with his incessant questions about his parentage "frazzled" Kizzy (570). But she takes his "inquisitiveness" as a sign that he is ready to learn about the truth of who he is, the son of an African, who "had come on a ship from Africa to a place my mammy said dey calls 'Naplis,'…an' when he kept on runnin' 'way, dey chopped off half his foot" (570–1). George struggles to understand "what ['niggers'] was runnin' from" and "what de White massas done to 'em," which exasperates Kizzy, yet "even beyond what she had hoped," George internalizes her father's "different, funny-soundin' words"—"*ko*" for a "fiddle" and "*Kamby Bolongo*" for a "river" (571). This semi-successful transmission of the family tradition brings Kizzy much needed relief, hope that the boy might move out from under his father's influence.

George also cultivates a "gift for mimicry," at first drawing him closer to his slave-row family, but eventually bringing him under his father's influence (Haley 2007 [1976]: 576). During the War of 1812, George works with Miss Malizy to keep slave row apprised of the news being discussed in the big house, even bringing comic relief with his own version of the Star-Spangled Banner: "Oh, hey, can you see by dat dawn early light…an' dem rockets' red glare…oh, dat star-spangle banner wavin'…oh de lan' o' de free, an' de home o' de brave" (575–6).[26] The slaves are especially amused by George's

26 Although the Lea plantation was far from any battles, the effects of the War of 1812 were felt across the nation. Debate over the meaning of republicanism resurfaced as Americans worked to distinguish themselves from the British. Manumission and expatriation were discussed by Black and White people alike. Leslie M. Harris explains that northern Blacks who had previously "participated in public displays of politics and culture [prior to the war]…felt increased pressure…to move out of public space and indeed with the formation of the American Colonization Society, out of the United States all together" (2003: 5).
On the Lea plantation, the members of slave row are divided regarding the "'Merican Colonize Society." Kizzy and George admire the idea of returning to a homeland, but Sister Sarah "wouldn't go to no Africa wid all dem niggers up in trees wid monkeys—" (Haley 2007 [1976]: 581). Massa Lea dismisses "free niggers" as the downfall of the country, wishing that tales of "bacon trees" tempt all of them to "Liberia" (580–1).

impression of the itinerant preachers Massa Lea would invite to harangue the slaves. Slave row turns fearful when Massa Lea catches George in the act:

> "What do you do to earn your rations around here, boy?" The four grown-ups all but collapsed as nine-year-old George, squaring his shoulders confidently and looking the massa straight in the eye, declared, "I works in yo' fields an' I preaches, Massa!" Astounded, Massa Lea said, "Well, let's hear you preach, then!" With five pairs of eyes upon him, George took a step backward and announced, "Dis dat White preacher you brung down here, Massa—" and suddenly he was flailing his arms and ranting, "If you specks Uncle Pompey done took massa's hog, tell massa! If you see Miss Malizy takin' missis' flour, tell missis! 'Cause if y'all's dat kin' o' good niggers, an' doin' well by yo' good massa an' missis, den when y'all die, y'all might git into de kichen of heab'n!"

Massa Lea is doubled over with laughter even before George finishes—whereupon, flashing his strong White teeth, the boy launches into one of Miss Malizy's favorite songs, "It's me, it's me, it's me, O'Lawd, a standin' in de need o' prayer!" None of the adults have ever seen Massa Lea laugh so hard. Obviously captivated, he claps George across the shoulders, "Boy, you preach around here anytime you want to!" (578–9).

After this, whenever the Leas entertain wealthier guests, Massa Lea calls George inside the big house to perform the preaching routine. George adds an additional dimension to the hospitality that the Leas could show to members of the next socio-economic class. Miss Malizy scoffs that they are using the boy for "puttin' on airs, tryin' to act like dey rich White folks!" (Haley 2007 [1976]: 579). Kizzy dislikes that the eleven-year-old George "spent hardly half of his time out with the [slaves] in the fields anymore" and fears the effect that Lea will have on George (580).

George is torn between the lessons of his Black mother and the example of his White father. Like Kizzy, George finds importance in knowing his African heritage. In Chapter 88, he says to Kizzy:

"Mammy…one time you tol' me gran'pappy give you de feelin' dat de main thing he kep' on his mind was tellin' you dem Africa things…Mammy, I been thinkin'. Same as you done fo' me, I gwine tell my chilluns 'bout gran'-pappy." Kizzy smiled, it being so typical of her singular son to be discussing at twelve his children of the future. (Haley 2007 [1976]: 582)

Kizzy is happiest when George shows an interest in her tales about Kunta Kinte. But George pays similar attention to "Uncle Mingo," the slave in charge of Massa Lea's chickens. George spends Sunday afternoon breaks learning to "rub dey backs an' necks an' legs, to help 'em fight de bes'!" (Haley 2007 [1976]: 582).[27] Impressed by the boy's handling, Uncle Mingo asks Massa Lea to appoint George to the chicken coop permanently. A slave named "Sister Sarah" turns silent when Kizzy mentions the likelihood that George will be leaving the fields and joining Uncle Mingo. Calling upon her "gift of fortune-telling," Sarah divines that "he ain't never gwine be what nobody would call no ordinary nigger! He always gwine keep gittin' into sump'n new an' different jes' long as he draw breath" (583). Kizzy is certain of this but wonders whether George is fated for good or ill.

In Chapter 89, Massa Lea decides to move George out of slave row and into Uncle Mingo's shack, next to the chicken coop on the edge of the plantation. Separated again from her family, Kizzy is inconsolable. George tries to soothe his mother, but reveals himself to be obtuse to the root cause of Kizzy's concern. "'Massa feel like he bein' good to me, Mammy. He treat Uncle Mingo an' me nice, ain't like he acts to fiel' hands—' Too late, he gulped sickly, remembering that his mammy was a field hand" (Haley 2007 [1976]: 588). George sees himself as special, not because of his roots but because a White man has valued him as such. This is a far cry from the pride instilled in a child by a loving parent. Kizzy is incensed:

27   "Mingo" is a name with West African origins and present in records about enslaved Black persons in America (L.M. Harris 2003: 36). Haley makes no mention of the character's memory of Africa, but the name may signify his role as George's wise elder (read: "African") sage. In this regard, he would be comparable to (though less developed than) the fiddler.

Jealousy and bitterness twisted her face as she grabbed George and shook him like a rag, screaming, "Massa don't care nothin' bout you. He may be yo' pappy, but he don't care nothin' 'bout dem chickens!" ... "Its true! An' jes' well you know it fo' you's figgerin' he doin' you sich favors! Only thing massa wants is you's helpin' dat ol' crazy nigger take care his chickens dat he figger gwine make him rich!" (588)

George's visits to slave row become less frequent as his responsibilities increase. He resists "putting on any airs" or discussing how "the massa was his daddy, or his daddy was the massa, whichever it was" (Haley 2007 [1976]: 596). But "everyone on slave row by now was openly awed by his new status, though they tried to seem as if they weren't" (591). At fourteen years of age, George accompanies Massa Lea to gamecock competitions throughout the region. On their wagon rides, he sees more of the world and speaks more freely with Massa Lea than any slave has. This is similar to the wagon rides Kizzy enjoyed with her father, Kunta Kinte—the difference being that George will emerge less rooted.

The adolescent George becomes Massa Lea's protégé—even adopting his father's questionable behavior. Tom Lea is a legend among the poor Whites envious of the gamecocker's relative wealth. Similarly George is "respected" as a talented chicken fighter, earning the title, "Chicken George" from Tom Lea and the other poor White tournament participants (Haley 2007 [1976]: 629). Like Tom Lea, Chicken George indulges in "White lightning" and "tomcatting" (610–11, 618, 662, and 671). By the age of seventeen, Chicken George proves to be what Kizzy had feared—his father's son.

In Chapter 91, Kizzy tries to re-educate George but with mixed results. On a Sunday morning in 1822—after a Saturday evening tryst—George walks toward slave row when Kizzy pulls him into her cabin.

"Lawd, boy! Massa got word some free nigger over in Charleston, South Ca'liny, name o' Denmark Vesey, had hunnuds o' niggers ready to kill no tellin' how many White folks right tonight, if dey hadn't o' got caught. Massa ain't long lef' here actin' like he gone wild, a-wavin' his shotgun an' threatenin' to kill anybody

missy see outside dey cabins fo' he git back from som big orga-
nizin' meetin'!" (Haley 2007 [1976]: 608)

George refuses to worry, reluctantly returning to the chicken coop
while saying, "Awright, Mammy... But I ain't slippin' through no
bushes. I ain't done nothin' to nobody. I'se gwine back down de road
jes' same as I come up it." After George arrives at the chicken coops,
Massa Lea rides up on horseback, armed with a shotgun and brim-
ming with anger.

> "Plenty good White people would be dyin' tonight if one nigger
> hadn't told his massa just in time. Proves you never can trust
> none of you niggers! ... Ain't no tellin' what's in y'all's heads
> off down here by yourselves! But you just let me *half* think any-
> thing funny, I'll blow your heads off quick as a rabbit's!" (Haley
> 2007 [1976]: 609)

Reflecting on his mother's concern and his father's threat, George
questions his past mistakes and his present trajectory.

> After all these years, George wondered what his mammy really
> felt about the whole excruciating thing, for by now, as far as
> he could see, she and the massa acted as if they were no lon-
> ger aware that the other existed, at least in that way. It shamed
> George even to think about his mammy having been with the
> massa as Charity—and more recently Beulah—would be with
> him on those nights when he slipped away from the plantation.
> (Haley 2007 [1976]: 611)

In this moment, George begins to consider his father's complicity in
the suffering of Black people and, in turn, re-evaluates how best to
relate to him.

Haley is using class as one indicator of a character's roots or relationship to America. And hackfighting will serve as an ideological
battleground between those most desperately grasping roots. Haley
describes "hackfights" as contests:

> ...for those who were able to fight only one or two or three usu-
> ally second- or third-rate birds—the poor Whites, free Blacks,

or slaves whose pocketbooks could afford bets ranging from twenty-five cents to a dollar, with as much as perhaps twenty dollars being bet only when some hackfighter went out of his head and put on the line everything he had in the world. (Haley 2007 [1976]: 620)

As is demonstrated later in Chapter 103, Tom Lea finds himself in a position where he bets all of his possessions and loses, proving that he had not actually risen from the station of "po' cracker."

Even still, Massa Lea understands himself as above the hackfighters, a category that would include Chicken George. His ability to hold authority over George and others reiterates how rootedness—that is, identity—is not just about meeting some abstract textbook social criteria or definition. It is about brokering power relations and the media used to do so.

Case in point, as a slave, George cannot stop working for Tom Lea, but he can capitalize on his master's dependence. George now recognizes what "Uncle Mingo knew well," "That the name of Tom Lea, throughout the length and breadth of Caswell County, symbolized the rise of a poor White man to eminence and a major gamecocker who started out as a hackfighter with one good bird" (Haley 2007 [1976]: 619).[28] George is able to extract various benefits by preying on Tom Lea's desire to climb the social ladder. In Chapter 92, Tom Lea agrees to further invest in George's cockfighting ability, splitting "half of any winnin's" (623). While Tom Lea prides himself as a magnanimous, genteel "massa," George plans on "winnin' an' savin' enough from hackfightin' to buy" his family's freedom (622).

In Chapter 93, Massa Lea derides Chicken George for "slippin' off" at night, but offers to "write out a travelin' pass [for him] to go chase tail *every* night." George is such a valuable investment that Massa Lea cannot afford to lose him, reasoning "I don't want that road patrol maybe shooting you like happened to that Mr. Jewett's trainer nigger" (Haley 2007 [1976]: 640). And when courting a slave

---

28 On this score, Tom Murray and Will Palmer would represent the zenith—Black persons of relatively high (i.e. uplifted) socio-economic status yet firmly rooted by the knowledge of where they came from.

woman named Matilda from another plantation, George convinces Massa Lea to purchase her saying, "Nothin' but a *high*-class massa do dat!" (641). Chicken George and Matilda marry in "August of 1827" (645). George uses Tom Lea to advance his family's cause.

After the birth of his firstborn, Virgil, in 1828, George shows signs of maturity. He makes good on a boyhood promise, exclaim[ing] to Kizzy, "Mammy, 'member what I tol' you, I gwine tell my young'uns what you tol' me?" (Haley 2007 [1976]: 652). Taking the newborn, George "made a little ceremony of seating himself before the fireplace...sp[eaking]...in grand tones 'bout yo' great-gran'daddy...a African...Kunta Kinte." Virgil hears that "he call a guitar a *ko*, an' a river 'Kamby Bolongo,' an' lot mo' things wid African names" (653–4). This is George at his most rooted.

But as Tom Lea's prized chicken trainer, Chicken George is often away from his family and his roots. He misses the birth of his next three children—Ashford in 1830 (Ch. 95), George in 1831 (Ch. 96), and Tom on September 20, 1833 (Ch. 97). Matilda understands his absence, but she takes issue with George's ignorance of the slave condition. On one visit to slave row, Chicken George tells of having seen "a mile long o' niggers bein driv along in chains!" (Haley 2007 [1976]: 660). He adds that "great big cotton plantations steady bein' cleared out'n de woods in Alabama, Mississippi, Louisiana, Arkansas, an' Texas" to be worked by slaves from North Carolina, South Carolina, but "mainly out'n Virginia" (661).[29] Kizzy is brought to tears when she thinks about what may have become of her parents in Virginia. Yet Chicken George cannot determine "What come *over* her?" Matilda has

29 Sugar and cotton were profitable crops that enticed Southerners (and those willing to move South) to develop large-scale plantations in the early nineteenth century. The economics are intimately tied to the anthropology of race so far as "Whiteness" was equated with land-ownership. This equation, historian Neil Foley argues, was particularly convoluted as plantation workforces included enslaved Blacks, free Blacks, indentured Whites, Mexicans, European immigrants and others. But Blacks were the typical standard for non-Whiteness. The more "Black"/less "White" one was, the harsher the working conditions (Foley 1997: 20–1).

become convinced that for all of his worldliness, he was sorely lacking in sensitivity about too many things. "You knows well as I does Mammy Kizzy been sol' herself! Jes' like I was! ... Anybody ever sol' ain't gwine never forgit it! An' won't never be de same no mo'! You ain't never been. Dat's how come you don't understan' no massa cain't never be trusted—includin' your'n!" (661)

Matilda uses the Bible to reprimand Chicken George when the scent of rosewater perfume betrays his continued tomcatting.

> "Naw, George, you *listen*! Look here, long as I'se yo' wife, an' mammy to our chilluns, I be here when you leaves an' I be here when you gits back, 'cause ain't us much as yo'self you's doin' wrong. It right in de Bible: 'You sows what you reaps'—sow single, you reaps double! An' Matthew sebenth chapter say, 'Wid whatsoever measure you metes out to others, dat shall be measured out to you again!'" (661–2)

George tries to appease her with gifts purchased with his winnings, but as Matilda explains, the problem is Chicken George's lack of vision (658). In the eyes of Kizzy and Matilda, the more time Chicken George spends with his father, the more he seems to forget his *true self*.[30]

---

30 Matilda and Kizzy are what Gayle T. Tate refers to as "nexus women." She highlights that

> Black female slaves played a pivotal role in the creation and sustenance of slave culture. As culture bearers, they passed the oral history on from generation to generation… Memories of Africa were also cast in a deeply spiritual context… Coupled with their role as culture bearers, female slaves also occupied the political role of nexus women, utilizing the culture to continuously transform the environment into a climate of resistance (Tate 2003: 41).

While their influence on the slave community is noteworthy, in the world of *Roots*, their power over and in the presence of men—Black and White—is limited. Their lessons do not truly *take root* in Chicken George, the acting patriarch. This is largely because of Tom Lea's domineering affections. And while their teachings do *take root* in Tom the blacksmith, he learns them as a child. Once he becomes an adult, he himself supplants their symbolic

"You's a good man, George," said Kizzy softly. "Don't never let anybody tell you no different! An' don't never git to feelin' we don't love you. I b'lieves maybe you gits mixed up 'bout who you is, an' sometime who *we* is. We's yo *blood*, jes' like dese chilluns' great-gran'pappy." (672)

Matilda identifies Chicken George's essence in his family, "his blood." The flaw in her argument is that his blood also includes his namesake's. But Matilda quickly uses the Bible to qualify her statement—an effort complemented by their son's remembrance of The African.

"It's right in de Scriptures—" said Matilda... "Everything in de Bible' ain't sump'n hard. De Scriptures have plenty 'bout love." (672)

And as a young Virgil reminds Chicken George, "Gran'mammy say de African make us know who we is!" So, Chicken George can find his way if he remembers who the Bible and The African say he is. These sources will tell him to whom he truly belongs—his family and not his enslaving father.

In Chapter 98, Chicken George rethinks his role as the family patriarch. Uncle Mingo's death in 1833 required that George divide his time between raising chickens in the coop and competing at tournaments with Massa Lea (Haley 2007 [1976]: 679–80). At the coop, George has time to reflect on his roots without the intrusion of his wife, mother, or father. In 1838, he tells Matilda that the combination of solitude and the anticipation of their eighth child spurred his "thinkin', if'n us could save 'nough dese nex comin' years, maybe us

---

authority as a paragon of rootedness. This gendering of power is predicated on a patriarchal organization and prioritization of knowledge within the scriptural economy (Ortner 1972: 8–19, 17).

31 Purchasing one's freedom was an economic avenue of which some enslaved Blacks were able to avail themselves. Even so, freedom was not absolute, as receipt of self-purchase was always subject to the interpretation of local authorities. Federal, state, and local sovereignties frequently differed on the enforcement of manumission. For a history of jurisprudence and the honoring of manumission see Baker (2012: 1136–7).

could buy ourselves free" (692).[31] In his adventures with Tom Lea, Chicken George has ignored this aspiration, such that he is embarrassed to bring it up with Matilda. But she blesses the plan with "...sump'n out'n de first chapter o' Ruth. Tol' you, 'Whither thou goes', I will go, an' where thou lodgest, I will lodge; they people shall be my people...'" (696). This is the version of George for whom Matilda and Kizzy had long hoped.

George's freedom is entwined with Massa Lea's own American dreaming. Were George to earn enough money, Massa Lea would still have to agree to the sale, but George remains hopeful because of Massa Lea's desire to "git 'nough together to buil' de fine big house he want, wid six column crost de front" (Haley 2007 [1976]: 693). At around sixty-three years of age, Lea has "five, six years" with which he could reasonably continue to cockfight, according to George. By then, "he really might let us buy ourselves, an 'specially if we be payin' him 'nough would he'p 'im buil' dat big house he want" (694).

In order to purchase themselves, their eight children and Kizzy, George and Matilda would need to save around $7000 (Haley 2007 [1976]: 713). George worries that his meager earnings alone could never amount to the needed total. In Chapters 100 and 101, George notices that his fourth son, Tom, has a talent for metal work, having crafted a watering can for Kizzy and an "S-curved pothook" for Miss Malizy (697, 699). On his travels, George has met enslaved blacksmiths who had brought considerable profits to their masters. To raise the family's earning power, he convinces Massa Lea to lease Tom as a blacksmith's apprentice.

George succeeds in doing this by accurately reading Massa Lea to determine the pitch required—a picture of the financial advantages.

> "Massa, every year money you's spendin' on blacksmithin' you could be savin'! Ain't none us never tol' you how Tom awready been savin' you some, sharpenin' hoe blades an' sickles an' different other tools—well as fixin' lot o' things gits broken roun' heare... If he was to learn, Massa, ain't jes' he could do ever' thing we needs roun' here, but he could be takin in' work to make you plenty money." (Haley 2007 [1976]: 698)

Massa Lea agrees, seeing a chance to realize his dreams of retirement. The boy, Tom, is happy, "realiz[ing] that his dream had actually come true" (700–1). And George leads the family toward a chance at freedom.

By 1848, Chicken George and Tom have a contentious father-son rivalry. Tom, now sixteen years old, has apprenticed for nine months and has "never been treated so much like a man." The young man meets the "outpouring of his slave-row family's love and respect" with a measure of dignified silence (Haley 2007 [1976]: 704). In contrast, the outspoken and flamboyant Chicken George teases Tom before the residents of slave row with questions such as, "What kin' of blacksmith you is ain't makin' no money?" and mocking that there "sho' ain't money in [blacksmithing] like fightin' chickens!" (704 and 708). Kizzy makes her preference known, retorting, "Well, it's sho' plenty mo' use o' blacksmithin' dan it is dem chickens!" (707). His reserve and work ethic resembling that of Kunta Kinte and Noah, Kizzy believes Tom to be the more rooted of the two.

George is not without roots, but he uses the persona of "Chicken George" to blunt the pain of his regretful paternity and the harsh realities of slavery. In private, George shows his vulnerable, conflicted self to Tom, saying,

> "Looka here, reckon you know I ain't meant no harm jes' teasin you a l'il at dinner… Massa ain't bad as yo' mammy an' gran'mammy an' dem likes to claim. He got 'is ornery ways, sho' is! You jes' have to learn how to git to massa's good side, like I does—keep 'im b'leevin' you considers 'im one dem high-class massas what do good by dey niggers" (Haley 2007 [1976]: 711–12).

Chicken George has not forgotten whose he is or where he has come from. Rather he recognizes that making those roots work for him is complicated. But, as he shares with Tom, he has a plan.

> "Lissen here, boy!" The urgency increased in Chicken George's tone. "If'n I keeps winnin' 'bout de same as in de past few seasons, I oughta have three, fo' hunnud mo' stashed away time you starts blacksmithin' fo' massa." Tom was eagerly nodding his head. "An', Pappy, wid *bofe* us makin' money, mammy could bury maybe five, six hunnud a year." (714)

Tom reasons that, together, they could buy the family's freedom in "bout fifteen years!" George concurs, saying "Wid two us, I *knows* we can do it! ... Make dis family *'mount* to sump'n! Us all git up Nawth, rasin' chilluns an' gran' gran'chilluns *free*, like folks was meant to!" (713). Family brings out George's roots and sense of purpose (714). But that purpose is not his own. It is an aspiration planted genera- tions ago by the people and stories that the family used to define their destiny.

But Chicken George succumbs to his sanguine flaw, trusting Massa Tom Lea at the expense of his true family. In Chapter 103, a wealthy plantation owner named Massa Jewett and his English guest, Sir C. Eric Russell, host a large-scale cockfighting tournament. As a local legend among the "po' crackers," Massa Lea cannot resist partici- pating in the high-stakes competition. Chicken George accompanies him, bringing along the family's savings to place on side bets. George performs well, as does Tom Lea, but the pair's success garners the attention of Sir Russell. The gentleman challenges Massa Lea to an extravagant wager. The cheers of the local po' crackers spur Tom Lea to accept, but Sir Russell is victorious. Unable to pay the purse, Massa Lea must settle the wager with his cash-on-hand, two house mortgages, and a two-year lease on George, who will serve as Sir Russell's personal cockfighter (Haley 2007 [1976]: 734–5). Chapter 103 ends with Chicken George's abrupt exit. Kunta Kinte's family is once again separated on account of White people's disregard for Black life.

Ch. 97–114: Tom Murray (née Lea) (1833–1893?)

If Chicken George is a warning to readers who do not heed Haley's commending of rootedness, George's son Tom is the standard for emulation. A commitment to family, a sense of origin, practical opti- mism, and a strong work ethic: these are the traits Haley attributes to Tom. Readers are invited to identify these values as beneficial beyond the protagonist's journey. They can support generations to come.

In George's absence, the mantle of family leadership falls to Tom the blacksmith. In Chapter 104, Massa Lea makes arrangements to sell the remainder of his slaves in order to "pay two mor'gage notes on dey house" (Haley 2007 [1976]: 742). Tom shares his mother's and grandmother's valuation of family unity, but like his father, Tom tries to interpret the needs of White slave-masters for the family's gain. He reasons that "wid some different massa we jes' might fin' ourselves better off." This optimism, however, is rooted not in a gamble on another Massa's quality (a la Chicken George), but in the belief that the family could handle anything "long's we all stays together" (742). The "big worry" for Tom is that Massa Lea might further divide the family, selling members off to different plantations (742).

Tom's concern proves well-founded, but he works cunningly to keep the family together. In 1857, nearly two years after the cockfight, Massa Lea contracts with a slave trading company to locate Matilda and her children on "a tobacco planation ain't too far from here! Right near the North Carolina Railroad Company over in Alamance County" (Haley 2007 [1976]: 746). The rest of slave row—including Kizzy—is left behind. Kizzy protests to Massa Lea, "You done sent off yo' own boy, can't I *leas'* have gran'chilluns?" Her outburst is followed by similar pleas from Miss Malizy and Sister Sarah, but Massa Lea remains unmoved. The slave trader intervenes to reprimand the women, yelling "SHUT UP! … I'm tellin' you the last time! You find out quick I know how to handle niggers!" (747). But like George, Tom the blacksmith knows how to handle Massa Lea.

> Tom's eyes sought and locked for a fleeting instant with those of Massa Lea, and Tom hoarsely fully chose words, "Massa, we's sho' sorry you's met bad luck, an' we knows only reason you's sellin' us is you got to—" Massa Lea seemed almost grateful before his eyes again bent downward, and they had to strain to hear him. "Naw, I ain't got nothin' 'gainst none of y'all, boy—" He hesitated. "Fact, I'd even call y'all good niggers, most of y'all born and bred right up on my place." "Massa," gently Tom begged, "if dem Alamance County peoples won't take our family's ol' folks, ain't it some way you lemme buy 'em from you?" (747).

With Alamance County being next to a railroad, Tom the blacksmith hints that he likely could earn enough money to pay Tom Lea, who was hemorrhaging funds and lacking pride after the aforementioned cockfight. Massa Lea agrees to sell the elder slaves once he receives "three hundred dollars apiece." Just as Chicken George had frequently done, Tom gains an advantage by appealing to Massa Lea's desire to climb the socio-economic ladder.

But the blacksmith's hope is not only in the agreement procured, but in the encouragement of Kizzy's admonitions. As the family parts in tears, she tells Matilda and the grandchildren:

> "Don' y'all take on so! Me an' [the elders] jes' wait here for George 'til he gits back. Ain't gwine be dat long... If'n he ain't got de money to buy us, den I 'speck won't take much mo' time fo' Tom an' res' y'all boys will... 'Nother thing...any y'all gits mo' chilluns fo' I sees you ag'in, don't forgit to tell 'em 'bout my folks, my mammy Bell, an' my African pappy name Kunta Kinte, what be yo' chillun's great-great gran'pappy! *Hear* me, now! Tell 'em 'bout me, 'bout my George, 'bout yo'selves, too! An 'bout what we been through 'midst differn' massas. Tell de chilluns all de res' about who we is!" (Haley 2007 [1976]: 748).

Tom and the rest of the family reply with a "a snuffling chorus of 'We sho' will' ... 'Ain't gon' *never* fo' git, Gran'mammy'" (748). Tom's optimism is fortified by an appreciation of where he came from in a manner that it took years for Chicken George to realize.

The narrative abruptly shifts backs to Chicken George, showing the like-mindedness of father and son. In 1860, Chicken George returns to Caswell County where he finds a destitute Tom Lea and a mentally unstable Miss Malizy. George learns that "Missis Lea," Kizzy, and the remaining elderly slaves have died and that Matilda and the children have been sold to a Massa Murray of Alamance County (Haley 2007 [1976]: 783). When George comes for his promised "freedom papers," Massa Lea refuses to hand them over, pleading for George to stay and work for him (783-4). The fifty-four-year-old George knows better, now seeing his father as the untrustworthy, violent man of whom Kizzy would speak. Haley narrates, "[i]t flashed through Chicken George's mind. *Ain't changed none...still tricky an' danger-ous as a snake...got to keep from gittin' 'im real mad*" (782). George is single-minded in purpose. He must find the freedom papers that he saw before he left, and locate his family in Alamance County. To ease his search, George reminisces with Massa Lea over whiskey. Massa Lea succumbs to his own alcoholism while George drinks just enough to feign participation (786). When Tom Lea falls unconscious, George finds his father's strongbox and removes the freedom papers (787).[32] Liberated from his father-son/master-slave relationship, he rushes to find his true family in Alamance County.

In Chapter 109, Chicken George briefly reunites with his family on the Murray Plantation in Alamance County. George regales them with fantastic tales of his travels in Europe. The family introduces him to Tom's wife, Irene, and their son, Uriah. Matilda "beam[ed] with satisfaction," not only at the sight of her husband's return, but at his passing on the family story to Uriah (Haley 2007 [1976]: 796). George learns that Massa and Missis Murray are relatively kind slave-owners—"good Christian peoples," as Matilda describes them (750). The Murrays permit George to live on the plantation freely until J.D. Cates, the local sheriff, grows annoyed at the freeman and gives notice of a sixty-day limit on emancipated slaves in the county (798). George must choose either to leave the county as a freeman or become Massa Murray's slave. The ultimatum weighs heavily on George, but Matilda challenges him to think about the future. "'Cause you de firs' one us ever free. You got to *stay* free, so us have somebody free in dis family. You jes' can't go back to bein' a slave!" (799). She helps George realize that his familial roots are not just about who he has come from and where he has been, they are also about where he is going and the possibilities for those that come after him. George decides to leave, charging his twenty-seven-year-old son, Tom, to carry on the family's story.

Tom continues his leadership of the family. As a full-fledged blacksmith, he works the county's forge. Whites and slaves come to his shop when in need of various repairs, and while working on their orders, he overhears the news of the day in "November of 1860," which he relays to Matilda (Haley 2007 [1976]: 800). Rather than

---

32 When Chicken George returns to the Lea plantation, Miss Malizy is the only slave living, but he does not take her to Alamance County because "her mind had weakened" (Haley 2007 [1976]: 780). When he arrives, he tells the family that she was in no condition to make the journey. Miss Malizy does not seem to mind being left behind.

a chance at freedom, Tom presents the election as a portent to violence, explaining how "his White customers [were] fuming that they would be 'wadin' knee deep in blood' before they'd give in to the North on something they called 'states' rights,' along with the right to own slaves" (802).[33] Tom advises the family to "act dumb as we can, like we ain't even heard 'bout what gwine on" (803). By playing ignorant, the family might safely distance itself from the disputes of White people.

Despite their best efforts, the violence of the Civil War comes to Tom's family. In 1862, J.D. Cates, now a Major in the Confederate Army, presses Tom into service as his unit's blacksmith (Haley 2007 [1976]: 811). Late one evening while at camp, Tom stumbles upon a White boy rummaging for food in the garbage. The boy bolts when Tom confronts him, but a Confederate night watchman investigates the commotion and accuses Tom of stealing supplies (814). Tom tries to explain to Cates the situation, but the Major is incredulous: "Now you got a White man eating garbage! You forget we've met before, plus I know your kind, nigger! Took care of that no-good free nigger pappy of yours, but you slipped loose. Well, this time I got you under the rules of war!" (815). Cates beats Tom with a braided whip, "lashing like fire across Tom's shoulders, again, again…" (815). Once back at the blacksmith tent, Tom "seized his kit of tools, sprang onto his mule, and did not stop until he reached the big house," telling a sympathetic Massa Murray that he would not return (815).

The whipping at the hands of J.D. Cates is a blow to Tom's pride. As he tells Massa Murray, "I ain't hurt none, 'cept in my mind" (Haley 2007 [1976]: 815). But even the psychic wounds Tom experiences cannot inhibit his strength of character. By "spring of 1862," Haley writes, "there seemed no question that the Yankees were losing most of the major battles." Descriptions of the war's great casualties disturb Irene such that she no longer wants to stay abreast of the conflict, telling her husband, "Tom, I jes' don't want to hear no mo' 'bout dis terrible war" (816).

33 Haley is referring to Southern arguments based upon the Tenth Amendment to the Constitution. Because slavery had not been federally outlawed, Southern states maintained that adjudication of manumission was a state matter.

The family's resilience is again tested when Tom discovers that the "scrawny po' White boy" who had scavenged for food in the Confederate camp was now begging for scraps on slave row (Haley 2007 [1976]: 817). After feeding the boy, Tom and the family alert Massa Murray. The boy asks for work, introduces himself to the Massa as

> "George Johnson. From South Carolina, sir. The war pretty near tore up where I lived. I tried to join up but they said I'm too young. I'm just turned sixteen. War ruint our crops an' everything so bad, look like even no rabbits left. An' I left, too, figgered somewhere—anywhere else—had to be better. But seem like the only somebody even give me the time of day been your niggers." (818)

Taking pity on the boy, Massa Murray hires the boy as "an overseer, even though my niggers do a good job raising my crops." The slaves take umbrage at the need for supervision, questioning their initial show of generosity. But George Johnson validates their beneficence.

> "I can't blame y'all none for hatin' me, but I can ask y'all to wait a little to see if I turn out bad as y'all think. You the first niggers I ever had anything to do with, but seem like to me y'all got Black same as I got White, an' I judge anybody by how they act. I know one thing, y'all fed me when I was hungry, and it was plenty of White folks hadn't." (819–20)

George Johnson's comments illuminate how the Civil War tested the mettle of many in America—Black and White, slave and free, rich and poor. But it also presents a teaching moment, an opportunity for members of the nation to reconsider how they relate to each other. Massa Murray's empathy for an impoverished White man leads to a Christ-like act of kindness—the hiring of George Johnson. The slaves' compassion for the boy hints at the possibility of racial reconciliation.

Haley commends these acts of mercy as the seeds of a new America, in contrast to the concurrent war. "Y'all fed me when I was hungry" may be a reference to Matthew 25:35—"For I was an hungred, and ye gave me meat: I was thirsty, and ye gave me drink: I was a stranger, and ye took me in" (King James Version). If so, George Johnson would not only be blessing the Black family for showing mercy, but also cursing those White persons who failed to show him mercy. The biblical passage (25:45–6) ends, "Then shall he answer them, saying, Verily I say unto you, Inasmuch as ye did it not to one of the least of these, ye did it not to me. And these shall go away into everlasting punishment: but the righteous into life eternal." This would be among Haley's strongest rhetorical condemnations of White racism.

Furthermore, the contrast should be read as a critique of race relations in the contemporary readers' context. Even Black people's most blunt demands for civil rights appear gracious, for the callous and criminal behavior of nearly all White people in *Roots* deserves a multigenerational reckoning. And yet, instead of an equal and opposite reaction to White hatred (cf. the Nation of Islam's "hate that hate produced"), Haley begins to model a different sort of reconciliation.

Haley's message invites White people and Black people to see each other's differences as a chance to complement—and not compete with—each other. And while this may seem like a passive accommodationist gesture, Haley is making a calculated statement about race in America for Black people and White people. Toward the end of Chapter 112, "ol' George," as the slaves nickname him, is portrayed as a failed overseer. He works cooperatively with the slaves in the field, never reprimanding or striking them. The slaves go so far as to teach "ol' George" how to more convincingly act "White" in order to avoid suspicion (Haley 2007 [1976]: 821). That "ol' George" had to be taught to yell, "'Git to work, you niggers!' an' sich as dat," led the family to appraise him as "de only White man we ever gwine meet dat's jes' plain honest 'bout hisself" (821–2). The slaves not only have an amenable relationship with "ol' George," but also his pregnant wife, Martha. Irene makes a special effort to tend to Martha during the pregnancy and after a hunger-induced miscarriage (824–5). In the midst of a war-torn nation, Haley commends slave row as symbol of a rooted, integrated community—one whose people are honest about themselves and, in difficult circumstances, work together to create a home.

In Chapter 113, "the Black Murrays" hear that "Pres'dent Lincoln done signed 'Mancipation Proclamation dat set us *free*!" Although

signed on "1863 New Year's Day...the presidential order had acti-
vated nothing" in Alamance County and "the steadily more bloodied,
ravaged Confederacy" continued (Haley 2007 [1976]: 826). When
the Confederacy surrenders in 1865, the Black Murrays permit themselves to dream vividly about the meaning of freedom. But "Tom
Murray" cautions, "Freedom ain't gwine feed us, it just let us 'cide
what we wants to do to eat... We ain't got much money, and 'sides
me blacksmithin' an Mamy cookin', de only workin' we knows is in
de fiel's" (828).[34] After much debate, the family agrees to continue
to work for Massa Murray as sharecroppers, saving any profits to
"git [them]selves ready" (828). The family is relieved when Chicken
George returns and brings word of a "promised lan,"..."a western
Tennessee settlement whose White people anxiously awaited their
arrival to help build a town" (830, 833).

> "Lemme tell y'all sump'n! De lan' where we goin' so Black an'
> rich, you plant a pig's tail an' a hog'll grow...you can't hardly
> sleep nights for de watermelons growin' so fas' dey cracks open
> like firecrackers! I'm tellin' you it's possums layin' under 'sim-
> mon trees too fat to move, wid de 'simmon sugar drippin' down
> on 'em thick as 'lasses..." (830)

Chicken George's good news spreads among all the Black families
of Alamance County, and all of them come to the Black Murrays,
demanding to join the caravan out West. "They were [the] Black
Holds, Fitzpatricks, Perms, Taylors, Wrights, Lakes, MacGregors, and
others" (Haley 2007 [1976]: 830).[35] Chicken George supervises the

---

34   Tom Murray's reserve is well-founded and reflective of what historian LaWanda Cox calls "the reflections on the limits of the possible." She
argues that "a comparative approach to Reconstruction also suggests that
there is an inherently stubborn difficulty to providing a road out of poverty
for a dependent, subservient agrarian people, most especially for non-White
laborers of a plantation economy" (Cox 1981: 159).

35   Haley's literary tone switches from narrator to chronicler in this
line, reminding readers that he is both author and historian. The shift re-
emphasizes the certainty he has about the truth and significance of this event
of exodus.

families' preparations. Tom Murray builds the families' "Rockaway" wagons. The newly-freed Americans are poised to write the next chapter of their lives. George and Martha Johnson are equally also poised for a new beginning and ask to join the caravan of twenty-eight wagons to Tennessee, explaining "y'all the only folks we got." The matter is voted upon by the Black families, with a majority saying the Johnsons can come after "someone spoke quietly, 'He can't help it if he White'" (831). Haley establishes the scene as America at its root, the story of people—Black and White—freely choosing to join with one another to build a new life together. And by choosing to dwell on deepening the reader's empathy for Black people rather than the horridness of White people, Haley spins integration into a matter of indebtedness. White readers will see the goodness of Black people as praiseworthy and realize that extending civil rights is a bargain when reparations and retribution are due.

Even still, Haley is quite conservative so far as he continues to portray Black people working to prove their worth. In Chapter 114, the caravan arrives in Lauderdale County, Tennessee where the formation of a new town called Henning is underway. The White settlers are reluctant to accept the arrival of the Black families and tell Tom that he cannot blacksmith "unless…[a] White man owned the shop" (Haley 2007 [1976]: 835). But the Black families persevere. They take up residence at the edge of town, and Tom transforms a wagon into a mobile forge. He becomes the county's premier blacksmith, "so indispensable around town that [Henning] couldn't afford to raise any objections even if they'd wanted to."

However little use the White community had for them—and vice versa—Tom and the others knew very well that the town's tradesmen could hardly contain their elation at the brisk increase in business they'd been responsible for. Though they made most of their own clothes, raised most of their own food, and did most of their own labor, the quantities of nails, corrugated tin, and barbed wire they bought over the next couple of years testified to the rate at which their community was growing (Haley 2007 [1976]: 837–8).

By 1874, the family turns its attention to the construction of a church "to replace the makeshift brush arbors that had been serving as their place of worship" (Haley 2007 [1976]: 838). In a year's time, the Black families pool their resources and establish the New Hope Colored Methodist Episcopal Church (838).[36] Chicken George, Tom, and his brothers would serve as the church's stewards, and Tom's youngest child, Cynthia, would attend it not only for church, but also for school (840). The aptly named institution would equip Black people with some of the tools necessary to contribute to American Reconstruction and Black uplift.

C. Epilogue—A Bicentennial Reflection

The novel concludes with Haley recounting his search and intentions for *Roots*. I mark Chapter 115 as the beginning of the Epilogue, where Haley's grandparents, Will Palmer and Cynthia Murray, marry and build the home in Henning that shaped Alex Haley. After this point, readers learn of Alex Haley's own biography, the oral tradition he learned on the porch of Palmer House, the writing of the *Autobiography of Malcolm X*, and the researching and writing of *Roots*. Though the section details three generations of Haley's family, it appears as an afterthought to the body of the novel, the three generations of history that Haley did not previously know but took twelve years (1964–1976) to rediscover. The close of the book turns around a question that "naturally now and then someone asks, 'How much of *Roots* is fact and how much is fiction?'" (Haley 2007 [1976]: 884). Haley answers by revisiting his position in the beginning of the book:

> To the best of my knowledge and my effort, every lineage statement within *Roots* is from either my African or American families' carefully preserved oral history, much of which I have been able to corroborate with documents. Those documents, along with the myriad textural details of what were contemporary indigenous lifestyles, cultural history, and such that give *Roots* flesh have come from years of intensive research in fifty-odd libraries, archives and other repositories on three continents. Since I wasn't yet around when most of the story occurred, by

---

36 The Colored Methodist Episcopal Church would change its name to the Christian Methodist Episcopal Church in 1954.

far most of the dialogue and most of the incidents are of necessity a novelized amalgam of what I *know* took place together with what my researching led me to plausibly *feel* took place. (883–4)

The response here is not just a thought experiment. He has prepared this defense after having fielded this question while on the pre-*Roots* lecture circuit. That audiences—scholarly and non-scholarly—were preoccupied with his historiographic technique provides some indication of the importance of history and writing in the larger scriptural economy in which Haley was trading. So as in the Prologue, Haley ends the book with both historical and literary justifications for his portrayal of America.

In Chapter 120, Haley again presents *Roots* as an ancient story. Whereas the Prologue featured the griots as human libraries and the embodiment of rootedness, the Epilogue confers the position on Haley's own family as the modern equivalent. The comparison hinges around death and its effect on the living. In the Acknowledgments, Haley wrote that "when a griot dies, it is as if a library has burned to the ground." *Roots* ends with Haley eulogizing his father, Simon, who had devoted his life to "forty years of educating" and "had fathered—members of the seventh generation from Kunta Kinte" (Haley 2007 [1976]: 887–8), although Simon was formally part of Bertha's lineage. Simon had encouraged Alex to learn to type and to enlist in the Coast Guard.[37] And "on [a] cargo-ammunition ship plying the Southwest Pacific, [Alex] stumbled onto the long road that [took him] finally to the writing of this *Roots*" (860). In Alex Haley's mind, this parental guidance earned Simon a place among the rooted. "I think now that not only are Grandma, Cousin Georgia, and those other ladies 'up there watchin,' but so are all of the others: Kunta and Bell; Kizzy; Chicken George and Matilda; Tom and Irene, Grandpa Will Palmer; Bertha; Mama—and now, as well, the most recent one

---

37 In the miniseries followup, *Roots: The Next Generation*, Simon lifts Alex to the night sky, further affixing Alex's birth into the Kinte lineage. While solidifying the generational motif, the event does not take place in the novel—likely because Simon is not in the Kinte bloodline.

to join them, Dad… " (885). In the final two-sentence paragraph of *Roots*, Haley makes clear what these persons enabled him to do:

> So Dad has joined the others up there. I feel that they *do* watch and guide, and I also feel that they join me in the hope that this story of our people can help to alleviate the legacies of the fact that preponderantly the histories have been written by the winners. (887)

Alex Haley believes that, like the griots, his forebears had entrusted him with the power "for all of us today to know who we are" (viii).

Living with Scriptures in America: Three Archetypal Configurations

As shown above, the body of *Roots* is framed by an Epilogue, a five-chapter conclusion that brings the story back to a Prologue acknowledging and in dedication to the American Bicentennial. It is a version of American history centered on Haley's ancestors' praiseworthy pursuit of America's ideals in a nation that had yet to accept them as full-fledged members. (Ch. 118). The enduring roots of his family are published and presented as a birthday gift to his country, a reminder of how far both his family (from Africa to America) and the nation (from slavery to integration) had come (Ch. 119).

To critically read *Roots* as an American scripture is to theorize about Haley's construction of a different kind of frame story. The subtitle, "the saga of an American family," hints at the political nature of the text. If Haley's family is understood to be a paradigmatic example of "an American family," what then is at the root of being American? In this sense, the "saga" is not only about Haley remembering his roots, but Haley tutoring readers how to understand his vision of America at the bicentennial. Beyond a literary Close Reading, an anthropology of scripture endeavors to model this framing of American identity with explanatory nuance. Haley's *Roots* shows that being American means situating oneself in a past that will not let you take that sense of home for granted. But the past to be held is signified in the authoritative sources—the roots—of the moment that are ironically taken for granted as meaningful in their provenance. The closer one is to "home," the more rootedness and the expressions one uses to identify oneself as rooted become routine. Likewise, little is more jarring than being reminded about the precariousness of being rooted. For scholars, *Roots* can keep us from forgetting the social dynamics involved in identity formation.

Haley's use of the "root" metaphor—including the homonym, "route"—offers an evocative handle for enumerating his configuration of America—potentially (1) as a source of *uproot*, indeed (2) as a place to *route*, but ultimately (3) as a home wherein to root or *take root*. By highlighting Haley's diction and imagery, Kunta Kinte serves not only as Haley's patriarchal figure, but as an axial figure whose *uprooting*, *routing*, and *taking root* characterize the efficacy of rootedness in America.

Additionally, a deep understanding of Kunta's roots—especially their expression in symbologies of history and writing—show how Kizzy, Chicken George, and Tom the Blacksmith each personify a different archetypal configuration. The combination illustrates the struggle for these roots as central to American life (especially African Americans) and how the American Dream belongs to those who know where they came from (history) and can convey (i.e. write) a convincing version of the nation to themselves and others.

A. America as a Source of Uproot

As previously mentioned, Haley dedicates *Roots* "as a birthday offering to [his] country within which most of *Roots* happened" (Haley 2007 [1976]: v). However, these pleasantries are duplicitous. The majority of the harrowing drama not only takes place in America, but largely because of America. Historian of Religion Charles H. Long describes these polar situations as "both inhering within the epistemological valence of civilization" (2004 [1986], 95). He goes on to contend that "the symbol civilization is…the context for a necessary lie (the appearance of crude and debased cultures and the demonstration of the superior power of the Europeans) [and] a new sacred power in the world (the bringing of all cultures into communication with one another and the beginnings of the possibility for a new meaning

Power Dynamics	Character-(ization)s	Symbologies of History and Writing	Textures
Uproot	Kunta Kinte & Kizzy	Enslavement/Branding (Ch. 33–4) Slave Names/ Deed of Sale (Ch. 44 and 84) Dispersion of Calendrical Stones (Ch. 83) Mandinka Prohibition against Women's Literacy (Ch. 76, 83)	Fear Pain Assault Estrangement from Family and Community Isolation Hopelessness
Routes	Kunta Kinte & Chicken George	Virginia House of Burgesses & Outlaw of Africanisms (Ch. 51) Biblical Exegesis (Ch. 43) Traveling Passes (Ch. 93) Parameters of Freedom Papers (Ch. 109) Chicken Handling as Mandinka Taboo (Ch. 15, 103)	Panopticon The Gaze Secrecy Subject to Authoritative Interpretation Fate as Gamble/ Subject to Chance Frustration/ Disappointment
Roots	Kunta Kinte & Tom Murray	Griots/Oral History (Ch. 24, 74, 104) Family History (Ch. 57, 60, 68) Blacksmith as a Vocation in Kinte Lineage (Ch. 24, 104) Muslim Faith and Community (Ch. 1, 61) Emancipation Proclamation (Ch. 113) New Hope Colored Methodist Episcopal Church and School (Ch. 114–15) Sears Roebuck Catalog (Ch. 114)	Freedom Optimism Destiny Rememory Pride Investment in the Future

Figure 4 An Anthropology of Scriptures Derived from *Roots: The Saga of an American Family*.

of human freedom in the world)" (95). That is to say, the story of a nation requires a sort of negative background reconstruction in which the past must be a nightmare from which the present constitution allows one to wake. "America, the Beautiful" can only be a prescient refrain if the chorus pledges to remember all prior homes (e.g. the émigré's point of departure) or scenarios (e.g. British colonialism or frontier life).

Haley takes pride in his country, but he does so with recognition that his very existence as a Black American is the result of a violent and complicated history. What is intriguing—if not compelling, for some of his readers—is that his patriotic orientation does not preclude him from identifying White Americans as descendants of creators—if not creators themselves—of a nightmare scenario for Black people.

Though this is but one grim stage in Haley's triumphal saga, we can isolate it to register the devastating power of scripture-making— the ability of one symbol civilization "to reduce [another] to the semantics of tribes and primitives" (Long 2004 [1986]: 95). Vincent L. Wimbush elaborates on the violence that can be done with the fraught symbols of a "language world."

> The experience of being *uprooted* from their African home-land and forced to labor in a strange place produced in the first African slaves what has been termed a type of disorientation... Certainly part of what it means to be fully enslaved was to be cut off from one's cultural *roots*...including their languages and religious heritage. (Wimbush 1991: 82–3, emphasis added)

While Kunta Kinte's initial capture in Africa is a gripping scene, Haley most poignantly illustrates America's potential for uproot in the chopping of Kunta Kinte's foot and the sale of Kizzy to the Lea plantation (Haley 2007 [1976]: 49, 84). These scenes relate the estrangement, isolation, and excommunication that result from being without roots in (and because of) America.

Kunta Kinte experiences colonial America not as a land of opportunity but as "*Jong Sang Doo*...a land where slaves are sold to huge cannibals called *toubabo koomi*" (Haley 2007 [1976]: 78). With the exception of his father and a few others, hardly anyone in Kunta Kinte's village had even seen a toubob (76). In Juffure, the toubob were spoken of in cautionary tales and parental threats given to disobedient children (27). Kunta Kinte's manhood training uses the specter of the toubob to delineate the rite of passage.[38] Captured by persons in frightful masks, boys of the third kafo are hooded and forced to walk to a new village, where they are tested over Mandinka history and trained as warriors. The year-long training culminates with the circumcision of the boys' *foto*, marking them as men (52). The traumatic ordeal is designed to prepare the men to stand strong, rooted in the face of the most frightful circumstances.

The psychological distress experienced in the ceremony should be seen in relationship to Kunta's enslavement. While "trapped like a leopard in a snare...he remembered sitting in the darkness of the manhood-training hut after being taken blindfolded to the *jujou* [man-hood-training camp] so many rains before, and a sob welled up in his throat, but he fought it back" (Haley 2007 [1976]: 194–5). The difference between Kunta's training and his capture is that the former was intended to transform Kunta into a Mandinka man; the latter was designed to uproot and emasculate him.

The contrast is drawn most comprehensively in Chapter 49 when slave-catchers have caught Kunta on his fourth and last flight from the Waller plantation.

> Kunta stood there wild-eyed, his body shaking, his brain flash-ing a memory of toubob faces in the wood grove, on the big canoe, in the prison, in the place where he had been sold, on the heathen farm, in the woods where he had been caught, beaten, lashed, and shot three times before. (Haley 2007 [1976]: 312)

For Kunta, the sight of the toubob induces a flashback to a series of upooting incidents. "The wood grove" outside of Juffure where Kunta was kidnapped (Ch. 33); "the big canoe" that brought him across the Atlantic (Ch. 35–9); the "prison" where he was held cap-tive until he was "sold" to a "heathen farm" owner (Ch. 40–1); and

38 Merrill Maguire Skaggs emphasizes that the mythology of *Roots* is not simply that of a Black hero but a male hero. Hence it is Kunta's manhood training that foreshadows the terrors that he will face in America (Skaggs 1978).

"the woods" where his previous escapes had been foiled (Ch. 42, 43, 47)—America is the unspoken metonym for the source of Kunta's uproot. The psychic and physical violence increases and the lessons of Kunta's manhood training prove futile. The one defiant blow he lands only makes matters worse.

> He knew from their faces that he would die now, and he didn't care. One lunged forward and grabbed him while the other clubbed him with the gun, but it still took all of their strength to hold him, for he was writhing, fighting, moaning, shrieking in both Arabic and Mandinka—until they clubbed him again. Wrestling him violently toward a tree, they tore his clothes off him and tied him tightly to it around the middle of his body. He steeled himself to be beaten to death. (Haley 2007 [1976]: 312–13)

A Mandinka warrior, Kunta valiantly fights the two toubob but to no avail. He has been bested and has no hope of escape.

Kunta had faculty in Arabic and Mandinka but knew nothing of the toubob tongue. Even still, his punishment needed no translation because Haley communicates its effects by using the root metaphor. While Kunta stood bound to a tree, one of the toubob "chopped a rotting tree trunk away from its *roots* and pulled it over next to Kunta" (Haley 2007 [1976]: 313, emphasis added). In addition to the arboreal imagery, Haley uses the adjective "rotting" to evoke a syllogism between Kunta and the uprooted trunk. In Chapter 37, the "rot and stink" of an enslaved African led the toubob of the *Lord Ligonier* to perform an amputation that resulted in death (216–17). Kunta realizes that he too would experience death at the hands of the toubob, but Kunta's death would come in a different manner. "Making gestures," the toubob forced Kunta to choose between the cutting of his genitals with a hunting knife or the chopping of his foot with an ax. "When Kunta understood, he howled and kicked— and was clubbed again."

This violence is not only physical, but psychosocial in nature. "Deep in his marrow, a voice shouted that a man, to be a man, must have sons. And Kunta's hands flew down to cover his foto. The two toubob were wickedly grinning." For modeling an anthropology of scriptures, the psyschosomatic imagery, particularly "deep in his marrow" is evocative because it is consistent with Haley's prescription of the novel for Americans. In his 1977 retrospective essay, "What *Roots* Means to Me," he frames the novel as an attempt to satisfy rootlessness: "in all of us lies a hunger, *marrow deep*, to know our heritage... Without this enriching knowledge, there is a hollow yearning no matter what our attainments in life" (Haley 2007 [1977]: 159). Kunta's uproot culminates in the toubob's ax "severing skin, tendons, muscles, bone...as bright red blood jetted from the stump as he plunged into Blackness" (Haley 2007 [1976]: 313). Having experienced the difficulties that accompany Blackness in America and feeling cut off from ones roots, Haley presents Kunta Kinte as a reminder of the violence for which symbol civilizations, like America, are culpable.

Although Kunta's progeny prove that he was not totally without roots, Kizzy's birth further represents the extent to which America uprooted Kunta from the scriptures of his homeland. Her character arc reiterates how dismal America can be. The contrast is conspicuous when registering the patrilineal, patriarchal, and patrilocal textures of Kunta's preconceived expectations for his Mandinka sons and how those are stymied by Kizzy's experience of America. Mandinka sons carry on the mantle of culture (Ortner 1972). Just as "only the sons of griots could become griots" and preserve the history of their people, sons are the heirs of familial knowledge (Haley 2007 [1976]: 133). As Kunta put it, "*de sons becomes dey families' mens*" (560). As he waited expectantly for the birth of his son in Chapter 68, "it saddened him to know not only that [his parents in Juffure] would never see his man-child—or he them—but also that they would never know he'd had one" (436). The birth of a "*girl*child [sic]" meant that Kizzy would not truly be suited to continue the bloodline without breaking with tradition, which is precisely what Kunta is forced to do (436–7).

In America, Kizzy is burdened not only with undue physical hardship, but also with another kind of burden that Kunta interprets as unbefitting of a daughter—literacy. In addition to the "talking drum" and their tribal language, Mandinka boys are trained in the Arabic "marks that talk" (Haley 1976 [2007]: 29).[39] This facilitates fuller participation in "Koranic" study and other Moslem devotional acts as well as being a medium for communicating with men of the wider Islamic world or *ummah* (195). Haley narrates that successful examination in Koranic recitations and in the writing of Arabic "…would bear heavily upon their being formally advanced into the status of third *kafo*" or last stage of boyhood (40). Because Kizzy becomes the heir of the Kinte line, Kunta passes on to her knowledge of various Mandinka customs such as the calendrical rocks and oral stories. In Chapter 76, however, Kunta refuses to teach her how to write in Arabic.

> "Would you learn me to write like you does?" Kizzy asked. "Wouldn't be fittin'," said Kunta sternly. "Why not?" She sounded hurt. "In Africa, only boys learns how to read an' write. Girls ain't got no use fer it—over here neither." "How come mammy can read an' write den?" Sternly, he said, "Don't you be talkin' dat! You hear me? Ain't nobody's business! White folks don' like none us doin' no readin' or writin'!" "How come?" "'Cause dey figgers less we knows, less trouble we makes." (493–4).

Literacy, as a site of power, is a gendered barrier that Kizzy is not supposed to trespass. But Kunta cannot fully guard her from it. He himself had "shrunk away from any closeness to toubob writing, thinking it contained some *toubob greegrees* that might bring him harm," but Missy Anne demanded Kizzy to be schooled in English letters (Haley

---

39 The ability to read the "marks that talk" is also a sign of schooling. During school, Kunta and his classmates "had all wished writing was as easy to understand as the talking drum, which even those of [his little brother's] age could read" (Haley 2007 [1976]: 112). "The talking book" is a motif throughout the Black American literary tradition, especially in slave narratives and the genres that mimic them (Gates and McKay 1996: xxvii–xxviii). Haley contributes to this tradition as a historiographer, placing the writing of the self (i.e. "the marks that talk") before enslavement. Kunta's descendants are not learning to imitate their enslavers, but recovering lost agency.

2007 [1976]: 424).[40] When Kizzy is caught having forged a travelling pass, she is sold away from her parents, despite Kunta's prayers that she do as he named her and "stay put." In raising Chicken George, Kizzy "took great care never to mention writing or reading, which she felt had forever scarred her life…she kept her sworn pact with herself never to write again" (575). The trauma turning around Kizzy's literacy not only conveys her *uproot* from the Waller plantation but the accompanying isolation she feels with "the absence of news about what was happening in the world beyond the plantation" (575). Too frightened to read newspapers in secret, she remains cut off from the world around her.

Kizzy's distance from letters parallels her separation from her family. Had Kizzy been born in Juffure, she would have lived with her father's family until she had married. At that point she would consummate her marriage and move in with her husband. Kizzy's experience in America is wholly different than the Mandinka's patrilocal practice. She is sold to and raped by Tom Lea while she is an unmarried, sixteen-year-old girl (Haley 2007 [1976]: 547). Haley communicates the wider narrative and psychosocial ramifications of this event. When Kizzy is taken from the Waller plantation in Chapter 83, Kunta "bursts through [his] cabin's door" and pulls up his calendrical rocks from under the floorboard.

> Tears bursting from [Kunta's] eyes, snatching his heavy gourd up high over his head, his mouth wide in a soundless scream, he hurled the gourd down with all his strength, and it shattered against the packed-earth floor, his 662 pebbles each month of his 55 rains flying out, ricocheting wildly in all directions. (547)

This scene is similar to one in Chapter 96 when Chicken George describes seeing "chained-up Virginia niggers [being sent] down to New Orleans!" Kizzy "bolt[s] toward her cabin in tears" after telling

---

40   The discussion of how to raise Kizzy—as a Mandinka child, a house servant, or a White girl's pupil—should be understood as "a literacy crisis" (Fernandez 2001: 4–5). It brings to the fore the question of who polices ways of knowing and what are the consequences for being trained or not trained according to certain systems.

him to "Jes' *heish!* ... HEISH!" (Haley 2007 [1976]: 660). America as a source of uproot speaks to scriptures' ability to make one completely uncertain about one's world, the events to come, and how to make sense of it all. *Roots* dangles the prospect of a narrative to reinforce the pride Americans can have in their nation. That it does so through the historical mire of Black experiences brings a novelty too enticing to ignore. But taking hold of *Roots* requires admission of America's unimpeachable role in uprooting masses of people to make room for those wanting to identify as belonging to the nation.

B. America as a Place to Route

Thinking with sociologist Paul Gilroy, *Roots* could be read as an example of "a process of movement and mediation that is more appropriately approached via the homonymn routes." The novel is a product of "modern Black political culture's interest in the relationship of identity to roots and rootedness...a nationalistic focus that is antitheitcal to the rhizomorphic, fractal structure of the transcultural, international formation" that more aptly characterizes what he calls "the Black Atlantic" experience (Gilroy 1993: 19). While Gilroy's "routes" framework is a useful way to contextualize *Roots*, it prematurely flattens Haley's cartography of the Black struggle for identity in America. Even whilst Black people have levied critiques against America, they have also pined for it, worked for it, and died for it such that they have not identified the dynamics of routing and the longing for roots as intrinsically mutually exclusive. Scholars might redescribe that duality as politically untenable, nevertheless that paradox is the very site of so many Black American cultural productions.

Anthropologist Stuart Hall's engagement of Gilroy's *The Black Atlantic* helps us to nuance the relationship between "roots," "routes," and "identification." People signify all three to invoke an origin in a historical past with which they continue to correspond. For Hall, identity is best understood as the product of questioning, the interrogation of cultural resources such as history and language in the process of social development. Identity is "not 'who we are' or 'where we came from' so much as what we might become, how we have been represented, and its bearing on how we might represent ourselves" (Hall 1996: 4). Like Gilroy, Hall is interested in the liminality involved in identity formation, but he emphasizes that the "narrativiziation of the self" is not about "the so-called return to roots but a coming-to-terms-with our 'routes.'" To arrive at an identity is less about solidifying oneself with an ideal sense of self or community than finding sites where one becomes complacent in negotiating selfhood and community.

In this I see Hall as more forthright about "the question of agency and politics" (1996: 4).

> It seems to be in the attempt to rearticulate the relationship between subjects and discursive practices that the question of identity recurs—or rather, if one prefers to stress the process of subjectification to discursive practices, and the politics of exclusion which all such subjectification appears to entail, the question of *identification*. (2)

Hall's theory provides for a more complicated rendering of the relationship between roots and routes. Rather than being oppositional, "routing" prompts questions about the terms on which identification can occur in a social space. As anthropologist Rachel Reedjik comments, "'identities are construed in a constant interplay of one's orientation to the past and the future...roots *and* routes" (2010: 18).

While *Roots* is indeed a reflection of Black routing through America, the novel's title also reflects that bicentennial Americans identify themselves and others in terms of "roots." Thus Haley, believing himself to be an American, boldly participates in this discourse which Gilroy describes as "marked by its European origins" (1993: 19).[41]

Hall's discussion of routing also draws attention to the learning of that discourse. To borrow from Hurston, routing in America is to observe, for instance, how the descendants of enslaved Africans learned that "colored folks is branches without roots and that makes things come round in queer ways" (Hurston 1998 [1937]: 16). An

---

41 For another cultural critique of Black racial ontologies as derivations of "White genius cults," see Victor Anderson's study of the grotesque in Western history (1995: 118–58).

anthropology of scriptures must take into account the complications encountered while routing—moments such as when Kunta Kinte (Ch. 50 and 57) and Chicken George (Ch. 93, 103, 109) discover that their appeal to roots is subject to "de law" of the land.

After Kunta Kinte recovers from the chopping of his foot, he silently observes the other Black people on slave row. His comprehension of English has increased such that he understands their conversations, but he does not even attempt to speak "the toubob tongue" (Haley 2007 [1976]: 324). Those on slave row see him as an "African nigger" and his silence is the only way he can protest, "At least, I'm Black, not brown like you" (324). In Chapter 50, the fiddler comes to Kunta's cabin, "beckon[ing] with his head for Kunta to follow him" (324). "It was so totally unexpected—and disarming—that Kunta found himself following the brown one back to his cabin without a word. Obediently, Kunta sat down on the stool the brown one pointed to and watched as his host seated himself on the other stool" (325). Haley notes that the fiddler is sitting quietly, "plaiting cornshucks" in a manner Kunta recognizes as distinctly African, a comparison further showing that Kunta is beginning to make sense of America.

These efforts at sense-making are tempered by the fiddler's disheartening rant. The "brown one" explains the limits under which Kunta can route in America, and the "African stuff" is expressly forbidden:

> "I been hearin' 'bout you so mad. You lucky dey ain't kilt you. Dey could of, an' been inside de law. Jes' like when dat White man broke my hand 'cause I got tired of fiddlin'. Law say anybody catch you 'scapin' can kill you and no punishment for him. Dat law gits read out again eve'y six months in White folks' churches. Looka here, don't start me on White folks' laws. Startin' up a new settlement, dey firs' builds a courthouse, fo' passin' more laws; nex' buildin's a church to prove dey's Christians. I b'lieve all dat Virginia's House of Burgess do is pass more laws 'gainst niggers. It's a law niggers can't carry no gun, even no stick that look like a club. Law say twenty lashes you get caught widdout a travelin' pass, ten lashes if'n you looks White folks in dey eyes, thirty lashes if'n you raises your hand against a White Christian. Law say no nigger preachin'

lessen a White man dere to listen; law say can't be no nigger funeral if dey claim you lied twice. Law say you *kill* anybody White, you hang; kill' nother nigger, you jes' gits whipped. Law say reward a Indian catchin' a 'scaped nigger wid all de tobacco dat Indian can carry. Law 'gainst teachin' any nigger to read or write, or givin' any nigger any book. Dey's even a law 'gainst niggers beatin' any drums—any dat African stuff." (Haley 2007 [1976]: 325–6)

The fiddler speaks as one well-versed in the "language-game" in which Kunta has found himself a part (Wittgenstein 2009 [1953]: 28–9). The speech maps a panopticon in which all Black routing is subject to a White "gaze" (Foucault 1995 [1975]: 184). As Haley later sets up the fiddler to function as an African griot in occultation, Kunta's routing with and through him fails, convincing Kunta that African roots (at least, in and of themselves) will not work in America. Further experimentation, adaptation, and improvisation will be needed to salvage any use they may yet have.

Routing for new roots, Kunta discovers, is a dangerous proposition. Prior to becoming Massa Waller's wagon driver in Chapter 57, Kunta's predecessor, Luther, was arrested, jailed, and sold for helping a "runaway housegirl" (Haley 2007 [1976]: 364). The girl "admitted under a lashing that her crude escape *route* had been drawn by none other than the massa's driver, Luther" (364, emphasis added).[42] While this leads to an opportunity for Kunta, Haley is clear that the arrangement is problematic. Kunta would have to be "loyal" and "a man" in a manner contrary to how he had been trained in Africa (365). Under the massa's gaze, he would have to actively demonstrate subservience.

> "You know what happened to Luther?" the massa asked.
> "Yassuh," said Kunta. *The massa's eyes narrowed*, and his voice

---

42 In her discussion of "underground railroads" to Black freedom, Katherine McKittrick writes that "disclosure of routes and places would curtail, often violently, Black freedoms. The subversion was a radical spatial act, an explicit reconfiguration of the spaces of White supremacy and a socio-spatial resistance that, if discovered, would incite death, bodily violence, and a return to enslavement" (2007: 100).

turned cold and hard. "I'd sell you in a minute," he said. "I'd sell
Bell if you two had no better sense." (365)

The sense-making that Kunta must do in America is not apolitical.
It requires a complicated regimen of accommodation and resistance,
risk and sacrifice.

Kunta Kinte typifies the familial struggle to continually reconceptualize what "roots" means in the American context. When he turned
thirty-four years old, he was unsure of who he was and what he had
become:

> He had been in the White man's land as long as he had lived in
> Juffure. Was he still an African, or had he become a "nigger," as
> the others had called themselves? Was he even a man? He was
> the same age as his father when he had seen him last, yet he had
> no sons of his own, no wife, no family, no village, no people, no
> homeland, almost no past at all seemed real to him anymore—
> and no future he could see. It was as if The Gambia had been a
> dream he'd had once long ago. Or was he still asleep? And if he
> was, would he ever waken? (Haley 2007 [1976]: 363)

In eventually having Chicken George as a male descendant, Kunta
transitions from one dream state to another. Chicken George could
be the patrilineal carrier of Mandinka identity that would validate all
of Kunta's New World strivings. The fulfilled wish would allow the
Kintes a chance at truly *taking root* in America.

Yet Chicken George represents the antithesis of the Mandinka man
Kunta Kinte was reared to be. Under the tutelage of his father Massa
Lea, George was a "tomcattin'" drunkard (Haley 2007 [1976]: 671).
Even in America, Kunta resolves himself to abstain from alcohol and
abstain from extramarital sex according to his Moslem (sic) training
(365). When Kunta arrives in America, he is greatly disturbed by the
sight of cockfighting, for the Mandinka believed touching a rooster's spur to bring illness and bad luck (65, 178, 248). In Chapter 93,
Chicken George, however, takes relish in the act, justifying it as a
means toward a biblically-sanctioned value of self-reliance that had
been passed on from father to son:

> Massa Lea looked at Chicken George. "You know anything
> about the Bible?" "'Not—well, nawsuh, not to speak of."
> "Bet you wouldn't of thought I know nothin' about it either!
> It was from the Psalms. I've got that place marked in my own
> Bible. It says, 'I have been young and now am old, yet have I
> not seen the righteous forsaken nor His seed beggin' bread.' ...
> Everything I saw in my family just translated to beggin' bread.
> We didn't have nothin', and we wasn't goin' go *get* nothin'.
> Finally it seemed like that sayin' meant if I made myself to get
> righteous—in other words, if I worked hard, and lived the best
> I knew how—I'd never have to beg for bread when I was old."
> (635–6)

Kunta Kinte also came of age in an agricultural society that valued
hard work as a sign of manhood. But Chicken George's White father
passes on a perverted expression of this sign of rootedness.

> "Boy, you hear what I tell you, I worked shoulder to shoulder
> alongside that George nigger, we slaved from can to can't *roo-
> tin'* up stumps and brush and rocks to plant my first crop. It
> wasn't nothin' but the Lord that made me buy a twenty-five-cent
> lottery ticket, and that ticket won me my first gamecock. Boy,
> that was the best bird I ever had! Even when he got cut bad,
> I'd patch him up and he went on to win more hackfights than
> anyone ever heard of one rooster doin'" (636, emphasis added).

The child of a Black slave woman and a poor White man, George
depicts an American dream yet to be realized.[43] Genetically—or more
appropriately, sanguinely—he is a sign of integration, but not the kind
that signified liberation, for he was very much subject to the politics
of a racially and economically stratified state.

In modeling an anthropology of scriptures, it is important to note
that Chicken George's routing does not result in an ability to take root.

---

43 The effects of Chicken George's mixed race on his actions is representative of nineteenth century debates—by Blacks and White people
alike—regarding "questions of progress and change, stability, anarchy, and
decline, in terms of supposed laws of racial entities, especially supposed
laws of the benefits or perils of race mixing" (Dain 2002: 227).

As I will discuss in the next section, George inherits roots from his son Tom Murray, who more so resembles Kunta Kinte. But Chicken George's character personifies the difficulty of routing through the laws of the land. When George devises a plan to secure the family's freedom with cockfighting money, he loses the savings on account of Massa Lea's greed (Ch. 103). "'Massa,' he said quietly, 'I was gwine *buy* us all free! Now all I had gone an' you sendin' *me* off crost de water somewheres 'way from my wife an' chilluns besides. How come you can't leas' free *dem* now, den me when I gits back?'" (Haley 2007 [1976]: 735). George's failed attempt at negotiating the release is reminiscent of Massa Waller's warning to Kunta about disloyalty. Just as Kunta was scrutinized by Massa Waller's gaze, George's own options for routing are limited.

> *Massa Lea's eyes narrowed.* "I don't need you tellin' me what to do boy! Ain't my fault you lost that money! I'm offerin' to do too much for you anyhow, that's the trouble with niggers! You better be careful of your mouth!" The massa's face was reddening. "If it wasn't for you bein' all your life here, I'd just go ahead an' sell your ass!" George looked at him, then shook his head. "If all my life mean anythin' to you Massa, how come you's jes' messin' it up mo'?" The massa's face set into hardness. "Pack whatever you intend to take with you! You leave for England Saturday!" (735)

Haley notes that George's return to the United States does not signify rootedness. Even when bearing freedom papers, George is prohibited from interpreting them. After reuniting with his family in Alamance County, Sheriff J.D. Cates and Massa Murray inform him that "North Carolina law forbids any freed Black from staying within the state for more than sixty days, or he must be re-enslaved." George's response—especially with his eyes and silence—highlights a frustration with the terms on which he can route:

> It took a moment to sink in. *Chicken George stared* disbelieving at Massa Murray. He couldn't speak. "I'm really sorry, boy. I know it don't seem fair to you." "Do it seem fair to you, Massa Murray?" The massa hesitated. "No, to tell you the truth. But the law is the law." He paused. "But if you would want to choose

to stay here, I'll guarantee you'll be treated well. You have my word on that." "Yo' word, Massa Murray?" *George's eyes were impassive.* (Haley 1976 [2007]: 798–9).

The lament relays the constructed nature of the scriptural economy and its structuring of power relations.

George finds routing to be a disheartening activity in which to engage. "That night George and Matilda lay under their quilt, hands touching, both *staring* up at the ceiling. ''Tilda,' he said after a long while, 'guess ain't nothin' to do but stay. Seem like runnin's all I ever done'" (Haley 2007 [1976]: 799). George does not stay, instead continuing to route for a better life for his family. America as a place to route speaks to scriptures' perpetuation of difference. Those whose interpretations carry legal authority define the markers and stakes of that difference. As a result, they can sit relatively complacent in the world. But those overdetermined by the culturally-governing scriptures must route in order to survive.

C. America as a Home Wherein to Take Root

Thus far, I focused on the psychosocial turns that have taken place around the concept of roots. America, as an instantiation of the European colonial project, was a source of uproot for "the African," Kunta Kinte. He and his progeny, especially Kizzy, were severed from the family, customs, teachings, and rituals that would otherwise root them. This set in motion a scenario in which Kunta, Chicken George, and other American Black persons would need to *route* for new roots to survive. As the novel advances, Haley's family ultimately finds a way *to take root* in America. But what does this entail on an anthropological level? What form do these roots take?

In Chapter 2, I pointed to Toni Morrison's discussion of "rootedness" as the orienting power of ancestral understanding (Morrison 1984: 343). For her, rootedness "suggests what the conflicts are, what the problems are. But it need not solve the problems because it is not a case study, it is a recipe" (341). Rootedness is a potential to see the world differently *and* to see one's world as having potential. A claimed rootedness is not necessarily a sign of transformation but the forceful articulation of a desire for change. Thus, rootedness is also a concession. It is an acknowledgment, in the words of philosopher Leonard Harris, that there is "no route of escape...no redemption...at best, [it] provides psychological solace, voice, and for some sense of authentic self-authorship. At its worst,...a useful method for voicing self-hatred and self-mutilation" (L.H. Harris 2008: 207). For this reason, Harris questions the utility of scriptural engagement in the form of what I have called "rootwork."

But Morrison's concept of "rememory"—the reconstitution of a harrowing past for present need—addresses what makes rootedness compelling (Morrison 2007 [1987]: 43).[44]

> By juxtaposing the open-ended dimensions of the past...with its material traces in the present (rememory), Morrison maintains a conception of historicity and creates a text that resists the abstraction of violence in the gothic and the limitations of traditional narrative history. (Spaulding 2005: 66)

It unveils the possibilities concealed by *uproot*. It makes intelligible present uncertainty, an interpretive act that translates past uproot into a promising—though not necessarily actualized—future. Kunta Kinte (Ch. 57, 61, 68) and Tom Murray (Ch. 114, 115) are able to experience America as home because they have managed, in Pierre Bourdieu's terms, to exchange "the cultural capital" of one scriptural economy, Haley's Africa, for another (Bourdieu 1997 [1986]: 46). Both characters show how *taking root* lays a groundwork from which

---

44 Morrison introduces the concept in the 1987 novel *Beloved*. The story is based upon the life of Margaret Garner, a fugitive slave who, when recaptured, killed her two-year old daughter in an effort to shield the child from the horrors of slavery. Like Garner, Morrison's protagonist Sethe kills one of her daughters. In discussing the matter with a friend, Sethe says, "I was talking about time. It's so hard for me to believe in it. Some things go. Pass on. Some things just stay. I used to think it was my rememory. You know. Some things you forget. Other things you never do" (43). In the course of the novel, Sethe is visited and haunted by a girl named Beloved. Their joyous and torturous relationship becomes a vehicle for Sethe to work out the consequences of her actions and the trauma of slavery.

to re-form the past so as to construct a better or at least more manageable vantage for viewing one's future.

Kunta begrudges *routing* around as Massa Waller's chauffeur. The task keeps him away from his surrogate family on slave row, but the job's mobility brings an alternative perspective on America. On one of his first excursions in Chapter 57, Kunta passes by a "a lonely old oak or cedar in the middle of a field...[that] would send his mind back to the baobabs of Africa, and to the elders' saying that wherever one stood alone, there had once been a village" (Haley 2007 [1976]: 367–8).

Reminiscence turns into inspiration when another trip leads Kunta to Enfield, the majestic home of Massa Waller's parents. While the Wallers' take part in frivolity, the big-house maid gives Kunta a secret tour of the mansion. Kunta is disturbed by her commentary and her frequent use of "'usn's' and acting as if she owned the plantation she lived on instead of the other way around" (Haley 2007 [1976]: 370). The maid took Kunta into the home's inner sanctum, "a small room within the big house" and "making a great show of unlocking the door with one of the keys at her waist, she led him inside and pointed to one wall." There hung the "Waller's coat of arms, their silver seal, a suit of armor, silver pistols, a silver sword, and the pray book of the original Colonel Waller" (369). Haley describes Kunta's "ill-concealed amazement" as she "'read' the long since memorized inscription: 'Sacred to memory of Colonel John Waller, Gentleman third son of John Waller and Mary Key, who settled in Virginia in 1635 from Newport Paganel, Buckinghamshire'" (369).

Kunta is unable to "read" the inscription, but he recognizes that the articles' value as symbols of "accumulated history," what Bourdieu would identify as the currency of this "social world" (Bourdieu 1997 [1986]: 46). But this knowledge is of little benefit to Kunta because America's laws have all but locked away the symbols of his roots— what the fiddler dismissed as the "African stuff" (Haley 2007 [1976]: 325).[45]

---

45 The mystical/mystifying power of literacy is important to recognize in and around the world of the text.

Kunta learns how to convert this symbolic capital on a trip to Enfield in Chapter 61. Kunta walks its slave row and meets an elderly Ghanaian man of the Akan people named Boteng Bediako. Boteng— or "Pompey," as his owner has named him—was the messenger boy for an Akan chief and had been captured by "de White mens" while on an errand (Haley 2007 [1976]: 389). He had since lived on "six White folks' plantations [with] hopes dis de las' one" (388). The man has been dejected from years of *routing* but encourages Kunta with the following words.

> "Well, I's been here longer'n you been born. Wishes back den I could'a knowed sump'n dat I's learned now. But you still young, so I tell it to you."... "Dis is what I wants to pass on to you, dat I's learned in de White fols' land. What you needs most to live here is patience—wid a hard shell." (391)

Kunta listens dutifully while the elder man speaks. "In my country," Boteng regrets, "whilst we was talkin', I'd been a carvin' somethin' out of a thorn to give to you." Kunta reciprocates, saying that he would have been doing the same with "a mango seed," but Boteng interjects,"You's young. Seeds you's got a-plenty, you jes' needs de wife to plant 'em in" (Haley 2007 [1976]: 391). Fearful that the Wallers' party will soon end, the two Africans close their meeting with a warm embrace, sealed by the Arabic salutation. *"Ah-salakium-salaam."* *"Malaika-salaam."* Haley writes that "No evening of [Kunta's] life had ever meant more to him" (391).

In *The Autobiography of Malcolm X*:

> literacy is about possibility and power, a means of writing a way into a society that had written him off and working toward changing that society. It is an entrance to the worlds of knowledge that were closed off to him... And it is a means of constructing identity and claiming agency in a way that had been denied him. (Yagelski 2000: 45)

Literacy works much the same way for Kunta Kinte. He is being denied access to the means of recognized self-definition in both scriptural economies—Africa and America.

After meeting with Boteng, Kunta appears less bothered by the fact that he is no longer in Africa and more focused on rooting himself in America. Unlike the Waller family, Kunta is apart from the trappings of his family's history. At the same time, his encounter with Boteng enables him to approach America with a deeper sense of rootedness, one that personifies the lessons he learned from a griot during manhood training:

> "How else could you know the great deeds of the ancient kings, holy men, hunters, and warriors who came hundreds of rains before us? Have you met them?" asked the old man. "No! The history of our people is carried to the future in here." And he tapped his gray head. (Haley 2007 [1976]: 133)

Kunta *takes root* in America by remembering Africa as best as he can. This act makes a place for Kizzy to see the world and see herself better than she otherwise would. He becomes a stand-in for the griots that his *uproot* prohibits her from meeting. But because of his rootwork in America, Kizzy becomes "the first person to know who she was" (Haley 2007 [1976]: 441).

Similarly, Haley presented Tom Murray as the embodiment of the Kinte clan. Tom knew the family story transmitted orally by his father, George, and his grandmother, Kizzy (Haley 2007 [1976]: 748). He shared "their solemn *duty* to become griots," passing on the knowledge to the next generation (133). Tom's occupation as a blacksmith further associates him with the Kinte lineage, for in boyhood Kunta had learned that "[h]undreds of rains ago in the land of Mali…the Kinte men were blacksmiths" (111). Tom's Christian faith—denoted by his role as a founder, builder, and steward of Henning's New Hope CME church—parallels that of Kunta Kinte's grandfather and namesake. Kairaba Kunta Kinte was a marabout responsible for bringing Islam and rain to a drought-stricken Juffure. The cumulative symbolism of "marabout," "blacksmith," and "griot" is deliberate on Haley's part, for in manhood training, Kunta and his classmates:

> …were that taught during any wars, neither enemy should ever do harm to any traveling marabouts, griots, or blacksmiths, for

an angered marabout could bring down the displeasure of Allah; an angered griot could use his eloquent tongue to stir the enemy army to greater savagery; and an angered blacksmith could make or repair weapons for the enemy. (130)

Tom's African roots do not protect him from a beating by J.D. Cates (Ch. 111) nor do they assuage the prejudice of Henning's White business leaders (Ch. 114). Yet this is not to say that his roots are worthless. In Bourdieu's terms, Tom "liquifies" his African "cultural capital" into "social" and "economic capital" in America (Bourdieu 1997 [1986]: 55). In Chapter 115, he puts forward "the money to buy pencils, tablets, and primers on 'readin', writin', an' 'rithmetic'" when a graduate of nearby Lane College offers to educate Henning's Black children at New Hope CME (Haley 2007 [1976]: 840). He is "among the more prosperous men in town" (841). With his roots, Tom is able to build a home for his family.

Tom's family embodies what historian David W. Blight describes as the "emancipationist vision" of the Civil War. It is the "complex remembrance of their own freedom, in the politics of radical Reconstruction, and in conceptions of the war as the reinvention of the republic and the liberation of Blacks to citizenship and Constitutional equality" (Blight 2001: 2). The construction of a business, church, and school portray a family that sees America as a land of future opportunity. In Blight's words, "Remembering the thrill of emancipation, experiencing the pride of citizenship, witnessing the growth of Black education and intellectual achievement, and building new Black institutions all afforded the emancipationist vision fertile ground *to take root*" (304, emphasis added). The Murrays remember being uprooted from Africa and routing through America. And they are poised to write their next chapter in America's history.

In regard to the anthropology of scriptures, *taking root* is best symbolized in Chapter 114 and the "$250 stained-glass window [the Murrays] ordered from Sears, Roebuck" for the church (Haley 2007 [1976]: 838). The Sears, Roebuck, and Co. Catalog here serves as a codified zeitgeist, "a mirror of [America's] times, recording for future historians today's desires, habits, customs, and mode of living" (Sears

News Graphic 1943, cited in History of the Sears Catalog 2012).[46] Here it helps to convey Haley's understanding of Reconstruction. We are told that the purchase of the window, as well as the building of the church, "took almost a year, and much of their savings...[but] was well worth the time, effort, and expenses it represented" (Haley 2007 [1976]: 838). The family no longer had to worship in the "makeshift bush arbors" (838). They were no longer commodities to be bought and sold by White people. They were now traders in the nation's economy. The stained-glass window—refracting and coloring their "new hope"—exalted the family's efforts to shape a vision of America as well as how they wished America would see them.

Conclusion

In May 1977, after the publication and airing of his saga, Haley characterized *Roots* and America in the following way:

> With the exception of American Indians, we are a land of immigrants. All of us ancestrally come from somewhere across the ocean. Our roots with our immigrant forebears touch the deepest chords within us. When you look at slave-ship scenes, as horrible as they were, you also have to remember the long lines of immigrant ships, with their passengers huddled in steerage, desperately trying to learn a few words of a language that was to be their adopted tongue forever. (2007 [1977]: 160)

In this articulation of America, history and writing represent the ways by which people know and are known. Americans work out their sense of origin and belonging against these two discourses. Alex Haley wrote *Roots* in response to the anxiety that he and other Black

---

46 According to the *The Sears Archives*, "the roots of the Sears catalog are as old as the company." The first such proto-catalog, then called "The R.W. Sears Watch Co," was printed and mailed in 1888 (History of the Sears Catalog 2012). However in *Roots* the church is completed in 1875. The anachronism is a powerful example of Haley writing history to suit his psychosocial and narrative needs.

people felt about their social location in Bicentennial America. *Roots: The Saga of an America Family* assured them that the nation could indeed be their home if they remembered and read its story properly. The future of his characters could be their future too. In this chapter, I have sketched the literary and narratival turns of the novel in order to frame the identificatory strategy Haley commends to readers.

My Close Reading of *Roots* did not intend to strictly capture authorial motivations or method. It did strive to account for the means and ends of his argument. For all the cultural critics who would proclaim his writing to be just another example of social routing, Haley's literary choices suggest that he took a harder stance regarding the import of his book, as if there could be no substitute for rootedness. *Roots* is a frame story that bookends family history with discussions of the extraordinary historiographic work and Haley's confidence in his Americanness.

Roots' success was not dependent upon readers' wholesale comprehension of each line. But its details read enough like those of previously established American histories, epics, and descriptions so that it registered for audiences. Haley appears quite conscientious in making his America the idealized one of prior accounts while fashioning its ideals according to his integrationist purposes.

Haley's strategic American dreaming made *uprooting and routing* the preamble to *taking root* in the nation. Only after Americans join him in coming to terms with historical facts—as redefined by Haley's faction—may they feel free to write their own futures. As the saga of his family, Alex Haley presents his *Roots* as a model for identifying the self and others under America's "scriptural" conditions or obligatory modes of legibility within a cultural context. The novel qualifies the notion that America can be a haven for the rootless, but it adds that the nation requires its people to actively form new roots. In this way, the plot may be redescribed as a multigenerational tale about a family trying to make sense of how identity works in America. The family's relative success was a product of their ability to salvage the past and negotiate their antagonistic surroundings until they could seamlessly articulate themselves as beneficially membered to the nation.

In addition to developing an analytical grammar for parsing operational acts of identification—that is, the *uprooting*, *routing*, and *taking root* that occur when people claim belonging in a social setting—my Close Reading of *Roots* displays how social theorists can trace the edges of the texts that seem to envelop us and inform our actions. This chapter focused on the author's role in fostering culturalism. The next chapter will focus on how readers reinforce this culturalism by continuing to enage the author's book as a sort of scripture.

Readers do not do this by strictly adhering to authorial prescriptions or adopting wholesale the author's perspective. For, as we will see in the next chapter, once *Roots* left Haley's hands, the details and purposes behind the text became secondary to the social concerns of the readers. They would spend the next thirty years explicitly alluding to *Roots* in ways with which Haley would scarcely identify. Nevertheless, they continued to assume the text as worthwhile and engage it, rooting their own ideas about America in a foundation he laid. This is the irony and legacy of a scripture like *Roots*. Roots are the routes we come to privilege because of their local expedience and proven effectiveness. By reading closely a cultural text as influential as Alex Haley's *Roots*, we can begin to sketch the ways identity is assumed.

4 Kunta Kinte in American TV, Film, and Music

Scriptures do not belong to any one person. If they have indeed proven to be effective for a user, then they will be taken up by different people and even for different purposes than those intended by the cultural texts' authors. What makes text scripture, again and again, is the dynamism that envelops and alters the social order around it. Lives are changed because of it. But texts are changed because of that potential, too. Sometimes this is literal; other times, figurative.

To examine *Roots* as a scripture, we must understand how and why the story has not only found popularity but also influence in the lives of its readers. We need to examine the ways this cultural text has met and even exceeded its author's intent while paying attention to the subtle and conspicuous ways that readers retrofit it for what Elizabeth A. Castelli calls scriptural "afterlives" (Castelli 2010: 654). This demands sustained attention to the human activity mediated through "text and temporality, materiality and authority, disciplinary practices and intellectual/religious lineages" (Castelli 2010: 655). In reading Alex Haley's *Roots* in light of the anthropology of scriptures, we abstain from the canon wars and authorial autopsies in order to relearn people's penchant for filling texts with worlds of meaning. This critical distance affords us the space to identify patterns within the diverse ways people identify themselves and others through scriptures.

In the case of *Roots*, Americans learned to reinterpret slavery not only as a shaming and shameful chapter in the nation's history, but also as a plot point to be worked out. *Roots*' serendipitous release in 1976—the nation's two-hundredth anniversary year—showed Haley to be a consummate American, one who had so dutifully given a "birthday offering to [his] country" (Haley 2007: vi). As sociologist

Michael Eric Dyson observes, *Roots* "convince[d] the nation that the Black story is the American story...that Black humanity is a shining beacon that miraculously endured slavery's brutal horrors" (Dyson 2007: ix). Its popular reception reflects Americans' acknowledgment that *Roots* is not simply a narrative about the nation, but a national narrative. It is a canonical account of the American mythos. Those who dutifully study *Roots* can move from *being uprooted* and *routing* frustratingly in America to *taking root* in the nation as a promised land. Haley's birthday gift to America is also what Jacques Derrida terms "an oblique offering" in demanding reciprocation in "the language of ritual and the language of duty" (Derrida 1995 [1993]: 7). It was proof that Black people, if sufficiently rooted, could indeed achieve the American Dream. To take root here means to celebrate the progress made on the integrationist front, but doing so by means that champion the past, obligating all Americans—including White people—to demonstrate their own rootedness. Celebrating U.S. history and committing to a more inclusive American future became a package deal.

Whatever role *Roots* played in furthering integration, it cannot be said to have ended racism. As I write this book, Americans are debating the national utility of Confederate monuments and Southern Gothic narratives (Coates 2017). In these counter-stories we begin to see another element of scriptures as living cultural texts. They are works in progress. Complete fulfillment and fully requited promises would render a scripture obsolete. A scripture's final signification would penultimately spell its death. For *Roots* or any cultural text to be a scripture, its future cannot truly be now. It must always remain at "not yet."

By honing in on this aporia we can more clearly observe the manner in which people identify with scriptures. The late Kendall Folkert teased out two ways this works in his posthumously published "The 'Canons' of Scripture" (1989: 170–9). Thinking about the identification of religious texts as scriptural, he posits that one of two canonical criteria are being evoked. The first is that the text is "being carried" or being vectored "by some other form of religious activity" and its "significance for a tradition cannot be grasped fully without reference to its carrier and to the relationship between the two" (173). The second is that the text itself is a "vector of religious authority…a carrier of ritual iconolatry and/or individualist piety" (173). If we qualify the modifier "religious" as indicative of some *a priori* signification or attribution of "specialness," we see Folkert's insightful appreciation of scriptures' economics (Taves 2009: 26–31). Communities identify texts as scriptural when people—who do already-identified important activities—engage a mundane text or because already-identified important texts speak to mundane people. Both "being vectored" and "vectoring" involve the discursive claim of *rooting* or imbuing an essential significance to a sign and mediating the social order in relation to it.

Thus far my analysis has focused primarily on the first canonical type, the way Alex Haley has vectored *Roots* through the already-identified important activity called historiography. While I have only nodded to the ways in which Haley's *Roots* has come to vector or root the American experience, it is this second canonical type that originated my interest in *Roots* as an American scripture. If the paradox of historiography (cf. De Certeau) preoccupies the first canonical type, then the second type, as I see it, is absorbed in the paradox of the individual self—that one must somehow turn to a cultural narrative outside oneself to understand what is essential to it.

In the course of informally discussing my research, I have heard countless stories of where people were when the *Roots* miniseries aired. The recall of these Americans—of any number of racial backgrounds—matched those tracing their steps to pivotal national moments like September 11, 2001, November 22, 1963, and December 7, 1941. To be certain, the bicentennial publication and January 1977 airing were not as memorable as the 9/11 attacks, the assassination of President John F. Kennedy, or the attack on Pearl Harbor. But as LeVar Burton put it in a retrospective interview, "there was before *Roots* and there was after *Roots*" (*Roots One Year Later* 2012). What now could happen (and happen again and again) because of the *Roots* moment? With little difficulty one can think about *Roots* as potential paradigm or resource in popular late-twentieth century reflexive pursuits including genealogy and counseling psychology (Gavazzi 2011: 77–9).

Michelle Hudson, a research librarian and archivist, is among the many to observe Americans' growing interest in genealogy following the *Roots* moment.

> Endorsed by the American Educational Association, the printed and filmic versions of *Roots* enthralled more readers and more viewers than any saga in publishing or cinematic history. Besides coining new words, America's best known family tree has come to symbolize a new era in genealogical research and has served as a foundation for a host of educational courses and genealogical lectures. (Hudson 1991: 325)

She notes that in addition to acquiring resources on African American history, libraries had to expand the number of trained staff members to assist the volume of persons—across racial lines—searching for their roots (1991: 323, 335–6).

In *Roots Too: White Ethnic Revival in Post-Civil Rights America*, Matthew Frye Jacobson details this effect, probing its wider socio-political implications.

> *Roots* is important as a national phenomenon not only because the book and the miniseries were so eagerly devoured by millions across the country, but because, over time, the roots idiom revised the vernacular imagery of the nation itself… *Roots* speaks *to* all of us, certainly; but *for* all of us? … Haley's narrative was quickly appropriated as a moveable template for considering *anyone*'s familial origins in *any* distant village. (Jacobson 2006: 42–3)

The trends recorded by Hudson and Jacobson describe just some of the ways that Haley had re-set the terms on which one may be American. "Roots" had become a (if not *the*) commonplace for knowing oneself—where one has been and where one may go—within the nation. This scripture has afterlives because of its persistent utility in enabling various users to constitute a renewed and updated version of self.

In providing a theoretical language to parse "operational acts of identification," the explanatory power of the anthropology of scriptures is its usefulness in explaining the role of cultural texts in identity

formation. Rootedness provides a vocabulary for redescribing identity claims, while *being uprooted*, *routing*, and *taking root* present a
grammar for analyzing the consequences of these claims in a social
context. Similarly, the anthropology of scriptures articulates how cultural texts mediate social relationships and how those texts are not
only routinized (that is, referenced repeatedly) but also *rootinized*
(that is, referenced without question). James W. Watts' rubric of
"Three Dimensions of Scriptures" assists us in sketching the "forms
of ritualization [that] are intrinsic to scriptures and necessary to their
nature and function" (Watts 2006: 140). It is the combination of what
he calls iconic, semantic, and performative engagement that mani-
fests scriptures' effective, comprehensive quality.

The present chapter examines the identity claims embedded
in interpretations of Kunta Kinte It starts by outlining iconic and
semantic readings of Haley's originary protagonist and how these
readings broker self-understandings in the post-*Roots* moments. It
concludes with a discourse analysis of the character's appearance
in television and film performances in the three decades following
the *Roots* moment. Attention to these dimensions will underscore
how Americans have mediated the problematics of social difference
through *Roots*, their modern scripture. It will also display how the
vocabulary and grammar of rootedness can bring critical attention
to bodies, meaning, and the media through which they are identified.

Iconic Identifications with Kunta Kinte

To attribute *Roots*' significance solely to its narrative script is to over-
look its iconic importance for Americans. "The *iconic dimension* of
scriptures," Watts explains, "…finds expression in the physical form,
ritual manipulation, and artistic representation of scriptures" (2006:
142). Americans transferred Haley's charisma onto the physical book,
making his appeal available to anyone in possession of the tome.

Doubleday & Co. capitalized on this by releasing five hundred
autographed first edition copies of *Roots*. With dark leather covers
inlaid with gold lettering, the visage hearkens to an iconography usually reserved for the Holy Bible. Scores more purchased the hardback,

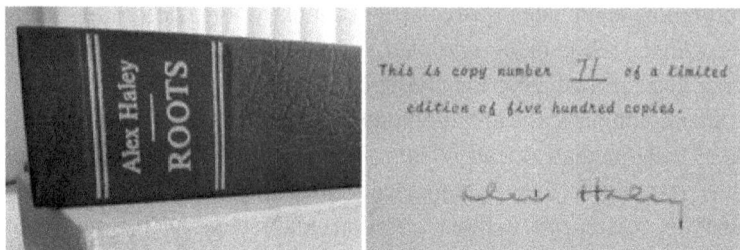

Figure 5 Leather Bound, Autographed, Limited First Edition of *Roots: The Saga of an American Family*, 1976 (Edwards 2010).
Source: The Collection of Ben Edwards, used with permission.

first edition run of the novel. The reverence and rush for the book speak to the owner's investment in what *Roots* says—between the lines—about the owner. It is potentially a personal window onto a more rooted life.

Similarly, the nondescript, unlined, empty-paged book bronzed at Knoxville's Haley Heritage Square reminds us that *Roots* functions as a literal and symbolic text. The thirteen-foot statue and the activities it hosts are "the final chapter in Alex Haley's life, written by people he never met, living the lesson they learned from him, that 'you can never enslave somebody who knows who he is'" (Despoli 2015).

Enshrined is a useable past, ideas worth remembering about life in America. How that past should be remembered is ultimately at the discretion of the viewer, but *Roots* acts as a prism through which the world may be seen. Though, as written imperfectly on an adjoining plaque, scriptures like *Roots* "provide an imaginitive [sic] place for children to play," the stakes of these games can be quite substantial. Figuratively speaking, the misspelling of "imaginative" conceals the manner in which a rooted worldview (cf. imagining) can help one be at home (cf. native) in an otherwise strange land.

This is the dream taking shape in Atlanta at the Martin Luther King, Jr. National Historic Site. Visitors enter a hallowed space where they may pay their respects at his graveside and study the events, philosophies, and strategies that led to his martyrdom. The complex is a liminal space, situated between grief and conviction, but its purpose is clear. King's work is a mantle to be taken up. The direction

Figure 6 "Sculpture of Alex Haley" by Tina Alley (1998), Haley Heritage Square, Morningside Park, Knoxville, Tennessee.
Source: Richard Newton.

onward is just fifty meters away in front of Ebenezer Baptist Church in a courtyard installed with Patrick Morelli's *Roots*-inspired sculpture entitled, *Behold*.

Behold is a three-meter-tall bronze statue of a father raising his newborn skyward. "One sees the strong, uplifted profile of the father," Morelli explains, "and the face of his sleeping infant, unaware of the sacrifices and suffering endured by the father, tranquil and serenely oblivious to all the joy and sorrow the future holds" (Morelli 1990). The muscular Black father, shorn of nearly all clothing, returns the viewer to the Edenic sensibilities that Haley sought to bring through *Roots* (Fisher 1993 [1977]: 430). The world that could have been becomes *the world that could still be*.

The *Roots* imagery raises the optimism for an integrated America. Morelli stages the exaltation of the child in a pose expressed in the film and novel in which Omoro Kinte names his newborn son Kunta

Figure 7 *Behold* by Patrick Morelli (1990), Martin Luther King Jr. National Historic Site, Atlanta, Georgia.
Source: Richard Newton.

Kinte, and "raises his face to the heavens…saying, 'Behold—the only thing greater than yourself'" (Haley 2007[1976]: 4). Yet, instead of "the moon and the stars," this child is elevated against a different scene, for *Behold* is "silhouetted against a broad expanse of sky and raised above the towering skyscrapers of downtown Atlanta's commercial district…symboliz[ing] Dr. King's hope that one day all Americans would share, significantly, in the cultural and materials [sic] as well as the spiritual riches of our great nation" (Morelli 1990). Atlanta is unashamedly held as a site for King-dom building.

Behold acts as a temporal lodestone that orients visitors toward a fuller vision of history. One cannot forget that Atlanta's brand of cosmopolitan progressivism palls in the face of a history of slavery. Yet the statue points out the powerful transformation that has taken place. "The father holds his hope for the future, his infant, facing the tomb of Dr. King and its inscription, 'Free at last, Free at last, Thank god, Almighty, Free at last'" (Morelli 1990). The failure of Reconstruction is recast as a time of trial. Deliverance comes to those guilt-laden Americans willing to revisit the moment through Haley's *Roots*. Iconic engagement with it will enable them to find the good in America and praise it.

The stories surrounding *Behold*'s construction further represent a vision of an integrated, reconstructed America in progress. To begin with, sculptor Patrick Morelli racially presents as White—a significant demographic point that reiterates that *Roots* is not solely an African American story, but an American story about African Americans. Second, *Behold* belongs to a genre of Kingian depictions despite the fact that it is not—at least on the surface—a picture of King himself (Sabourin 2014). Rather, it is a sculpture that testifies to Kingian values through the countenance of the Kunta Kinte tradition. Its strategy is not to duplicate the Civil Rights leader, but more poignantly to change the grounds on which we recognize him.

This last point touched a chord with King's son, Dexter Scott King. The younger King begins his autobiography by remembering the day he saw *Behold* unveiled. He recalls what "Omoro Kinte said to baby Kunta [and] Kunta repeated to his daughter, Kizzy, 'Behold, the only thing greater than yourself,'" saying to himself that "it reminded me of Daddy and me" (D.S. King 2003: 2). "For years," King writes, "I'd looked in the mirror and seen my father's face trapped in mine." But it was after beholding the statue and reading its inscription that he took time to stop and ask "Free at last. Was I? Were we?" And it is with those questions that he goes back now, "in memory, to try and find the answers" (2003: 3). Through the icon of Kunta Kinte, the young King found his roots.

Semantic Identifications with Kunta Kinte

Broadly speaking, the story of Kunta Kinte persists as a hermeneutical favorite for determining how best to be Black in America. This reflects:

> the *semantic dimension* of scriptures [which] has to do with the meaning of what is written, and thus includes all aspects of interpretation and commentary as well as appeals to the text's contents in preaching and other forms of persuasive rhetoric. (Watts 2006: 141)

Since the novel's publication, *Roots* has acted as a scriptural lexicon with which one can better articulate the American Dream.

Naming Black children "Kunta" and "LeVar" (after the actor who portrayed the young protagonist in the miniseries) abounded in the years immediately following *Roots*. In 1977, "Kunta" and "Kinte" were among the top 1,000 most frequent names given to children in America ("Pride in 'Roots' Inspiring Blacks to Name Babies After Characters," *Morning Record and Journal*, March 19, 1977, cited in Man 2012). Sociologists Stanley Lieberson and Kelly S. Mikelson explain that the rise in Afrocentric names, including those from *Roots* are "an excellent example of how innovations are grounded by an existing set of cultural practices" (Lieberson and Mikelson 1995: 944). As they note, *Roots* presented Black parents with a resource for spelling out their intentions for the children of the post-civil-rights era (940).

The underlying rationale surfaces within the novel's pages when Kunta's American-born daughter, Kizzy, recalls learning how "in his homeland, the naming of sons was the most important thing of all, "'cause de sons becomes dey families' mens." (Haley 2007 [1976]: 560). Carrying on these names outside of the text lays claim to the promises foretold within, "the special blessings of Allah not only upon the parents but also the parents' families" (1). To be made in the image of Kunta Kinte is to be set apart for greatness.

Spoken word artist J. Ivy echoes this understanding of rootedness in the 2004 hip hop anthem "Never Let Me Down." I've excerpted two key stanzas here:

I'm not just another individual. My spirit is a part of this.
That's why I get spiritual. But I get my hymns from Him. So it's
not me, it's He that's lyrical...

Vibrations is what I'm into. Yeah, I need my loot by rent day.
But that ain't what gives me the heart of *Kunta Kinte*.
I'm trying to get us free like Cinqué.
(West 2004, emphasis added)

J. Ivy is one of many to believe that Kunta Kinte's example can translate America into a promised land. The metaphoric "heart of Kunta
Kinte" beats with a call to arms, charging Black people to reckon
themselves within the ongoing generational struggle for freedom.
Kunta Kinte became the definition of the "inspiration" and "motiva-
tion" required to make America home.

While Haley intended the name to convey a social uplift impera-
tive, African Americans also interpret Kunta Kinte as a descriptor of
savagery. Speaking with Alex Haley's son, William, in 2007, journalist Farai Chideya remarked:

One of the things I remember [about *Roots* is] that people
would...take great pride in the miniseries, in the book, but...
young Black kids—at least where I grew up—had also used
Kunta Kinte as a kind of put down...still dealing with the complex reality of our relationship to our own ancestry and to the
Middle Passage. (Chideya 2007)

William Haley concurred, responding:

[Kunta Kinte is] to a lot of folks, uplifting because we had often
thought of our African ancestors as savages. And I think what
Roots did was dispel many of those perceptions. So some folks
really took Kunta to heart and others, as we do in our community from time to time, we thrust things in reverse. Where all
things that we admire, we put down in a sense. (Chideya 2007)

After the *Roots* moment, African Americans signified the name
"Kunta Kinte" to mediate inter-racial and intra-racial differences.
By signification, I am not simply referring to either the semiotics
expressed, or the politics of meaning-making, but what Henry Louis

Gates Jr. famously historicized as the "Afro-American rhetorical strategy of signifying…unengaged in information giving" (1988: 688). Signifying, whether in literature, hip hop, or profane conversation, is a matter of Black cultural performance (Gates 1988). *To call* oneself Kunta Kinte is to express the roots or racial pride necessary to gain entry into the melting pot. It is to have arrived in America (seemingly) on one's own terms. On the other hand, for a Black person *to be called* Kunta Kinte is to be reminded of one's outsider status by those more firmly rooted in America. It is to fall victim to racial "conjure" (Chireau 2008: 124). It is to practice a spellbinding interpretive obfuscation that Wimbush historicizes as "White men's magic" (2012: 20–2). Thus, *Roots* has a propensity for blessing and cursing those in its "textual field." This field, as Wesley Kort has argued, speaks to scriptures' capacity to "orient persons and groups and provide them with resources for direction, identity, and reconstitution" (Kort 2008: 220). But mastery of identifying with *Roots* requires more than just semantic literacy. It demands skill in a sophisticated racial hermeneutic.

Performative Identifications with Kunta Kinte

Roots may signify a stumbling block in realizing the American Dream. It can represent just how far one still has to route. But if actively engaged, one may use the narrative to demonstrate a sense of rootedness. Successfully acting out *Roots* can prove one's American quality. The American film tradition offers a sort of catechesis in which the performative dimension of scripture dramatizes not simply the "words…and contents" of *Roots* (i.e. the miniseries), but more potently, the politics of rootedness (Watts 2006: 141–2). As George Lipsitz theorizes:

> Culture can seem like a substitute for politics, a way of posing only imaginary solutions to real problems, but under other circumstances culture can become a rehearsal for politics, trying out values and beliefs permissible in art but forbidden in social life. Most often however, culture exists as a form of politics, as a means of reshaping individual and collective practices for specified interests, and as long as individuals perceive their interest

as unfulfilled, culture retains an oppositional potential. (Lipsitz 1990: 16–17)

The frequency with which the American media cites *Roots* and Kunta Kinte is difficult to determine; however, references to Kunta Kinte steadily have appeared in television shows, movies, music videos, and viral Internet clips since the miniseries' debut. In these instances, word plays on Kunta Kinte mediate racial power dynamics. This is not to argue that Haley's work has some ultimate, *sui generis* importance or is forever codified in America's memory. Rather, the ubiquity of these references insists that a cursory familiarity with *Roots* is in the cultural curriculum of many persons (of African descent or otherwise) studying to be bona fide Americans in the post-civil-rights era.

In this section, I present twelve television/film clips that reference Kunta Kinte. The selections span from 1977 to 2011 and portray how—since the *Roots* moment—Americans have debated their rootedness in terms of the Kunte Kinte mythology. Each excerpt is comedic in tone, for as psychologists Moniek Buijzen and Patti M. Valkenburg have documented, humor in audiovisual media often signifies fluctuating power dynamics (Buijzen and Valkenburg 2004: 147–8). Laughter is an instinctual, precognitive response and a sympathetic indicator that we are approaching the edge of our cultural formation. The performance of jest facilitates the layered psychosocial engagement that enables critique, communion, and confession—often at the same time. Hence, historian of religion Charles H. Long stresses the resonances between the jocular "signifying" practices he and many African Americans learned in their youth (e.g. "colloquial and slang expressions...a very clever language game") with the politics of semiotics underscored by Saussure and Derrida (Long 2004 [1986]: 1, 9). These twelve clips—"bound" by their use of *Roots* to work through the paradoxical commitments entailed in African American identity—exemplify the performative license a social actor may take with it as scripture (Newton 2017a).[1]

---

1 In "The African American Bible: Bound in a Christian Nation," I discuss the way Black people in America similarly have been "*bound in* (i.e. the enchained, the castigated, the conquered)" and "*bound for* (i.e. the invigorated, the cheered, the conquerors)" as a product of scriptural engagement of the Bible within the United States (Newton 2017a: 22).

Returning to the grounded theory sketched in Chapter 3, I use discourse analysis to frame each Kunta Kinte statement in light of its usefulness for *uprooting*, *routing*, or *taking root* against America's post-civil-rights backdrop. This is in part modeled on the work of anthropologists James S. Bielo (2009b: 157–75) and Brian Malley (2009: 194–205) who have employed discourse analysis as a means of diagramming the constitution of scriptures and scripturalizing. Beyond rhetorical analysis, they examine the "ethnopsychological assumptions" or cultural presuppositions represented within the discussed habitus (Strauss 2005: 205–7). Their work challenged me to consider the question of how, once we understand social conventions—and the cultural texts in which they are rooted—to be anything but cohesive, we surface the complexities of identification. I argue that *uprooting*, *routing*, and *taking root* act as analytical categories through which we can elaborate on the inter- and intra-racial performance that happens around *Roots* and more broadly on the political work of scriptures.

In his pivotal monograph, *What is Scripture? A Comparative Approach* (1993), W.C. Smith explores the relational nature of scripture formation in macro-historical terms, taking religious traditions as coherent blocks. Though appreciated, anthropologist James S. Bielo contends, "this line of inquiry has failed to follow up by empirically demonstrating how these practices of ratification unfold" (Bielo 2009a: 4).

A. Uprooting Kunta Kinte

"Uproot" designates people's ability to use scriptures to displace and disorient an other. It evokes the disorientation that came to Kunta as he was uprooted from his African home. Enslaved in America, the New World's customs, traditions, norms, and religion bewildered him. The sights and sounds of this foreign land reminded him just how out of place he was. But even more devastating was the feeling that the roots of his homeland—his prodigious naming and other cultural commonplaces—seemed ineffectual. Americans can provoke similar sentiments of displacement by derogatorily using his name.

1. Richard Pryor: *Here and Now* (1983)

A poignant instance of uproot rests in one of comic Richard Pryor's standup routines. Pryor's sharp, post-civil-rights' critiques alleviated the pressures of race-blind consciousness while also bringing to the fore the Black community's extant inter- and intra-racial concerns. Communications scholar Larry G. Coleman reads Pryor's persona as part of a cultural lineage of African tricksters, particularly the "'Negro slave" archetype of the "revolutionary trickster... He is the combination of the classical 'badman' or 'bad nigger' of folk history and real life and the 'high John the Conqueror' type trickster" (L.G. Coleman 1984: 69). Through stock characters, improvisation, and storytelling, Pryor cunningly unsettles the well-situated. His 1976 bit, "Bicentennial Nigger," embodies his oeuvre.

> Ise soo happy cause I been here 200 years... I'm just thrilled to be here... I used to live to be a hundred and fifty. Now I dies of high blood pressure by the time I'm fifty-two... That thrills me to death. [Chuckle] They brought me over here on a boat. There was 400 of us come over [chuckles and snorts] 360 of us died on the way over here [chuckle] I just love that...it just thrills me to death... You White folks are just sooo good to us... We got over here and another twenty of us died from disease...split us all up...I don't know what I'm gonna do if I don't get 200 more years of this [silence]. Y'all probably done forgot about it [with a threatening voice] but I ain't gon never forget. (L.G. Coleman 1984: 75)

Pryor would appear to play the minstrel, but with each shuck and jive, he lured audience members into a position where he could prey on their politically incorrect fears. In this case, he exposed White guilt as a tactic of appeasement, the placating of a potentially vengeful Black population.

Sometimes audience members interpreted Pryor's lively act as giving them license to fight back. In the middle of Pryor's recorded 1983 performance, *Here and Now* (2002), his set was interrupted by a Black man who was seated in the back of the hall. Never one to cede control in a performance, Pryor called the man to the front row for an inconspicuous tête-à-tête. Pryor demanded to know what the heckler wanted, to which the man meekly responded, "an autograph." The comedian graciously obliged, though only feigning an advance onto the moral high ground. When the man asked for the autograph to be addressed to "Joe," Pryor pounced, roaring with displeasure.

> You brought your big ass all the way up out from here [pointing to the rafters], and for all this your name is Joe? God damn it! "To Joe," pauses, presumably taking time to scribble a message down on a napkin]. Fuckin'... I thought your name would be Kunta Kinte or something.

The audience's laughter was a tribute to Pryor's prowess, and it came at the heckler's expense. The camera panned to record the multiracial crowd's raucous allegiance. A lesser-skilled comedian might have surrendered to Joe's interruption, but the veteran was unfazed. The devastating blow came by way of Pryor's comparison of Joe to Kunta Kinte. The American post-*Roots* crowd recognized Joe as a dark-skinned man who had come a long way from home (in this case, his seat) and was vulnerable to all the shaming that comes from being uprooted from a place of comfort. The two jovial Black men were stratified by an allusion to a shared text. That which was an obstacle for Joe was a stepping-stone for Pryor to further connect with the audience.

2. *Coming to America* (1988)

Pryor's brand of comedic social commentary inspired a generation of humorists. Actor Eddie Murphy's penchant for character work (sometimes playing multiple parts within a single film scene) bears resemblance to Pryor's persona, as does the content and subject matter of his jokes. The themes of Murphy's 1988 film, *Coming to America*, resonate with the discursive uproot in Pryor's "Bicentennial Nigger" and *Here and Now*. *Coming to America* is a film that has fun with the arbitrary rules of identifying as "African American." The story revolves around Murphy's Prince Akeem, heir-apparent to the throne of the wealthy (and contrived) African nation of Zamunda. In a stunning break with tradition, Prince Akeem rejects his arranged betrothal and leaves Zamunda in search of a woman who "is going to arouse

[his] intellect as well as [his] loins." The prince jilts his royal title and comes to America, more specifically Queens, New York, where the audience can enjoy watching Murphy's character struggle to survive the urban jungle.

African scholar Tejumola Olaniyan points out that the film belongs in the tradition of racial uplift given its contrast of a regal and opulent Africa with not only America's dilapidated streets, but also "the standardized images of poverty, decay, death, and devastation" too frequently associated with "Motherland" Africa (Olaniyan 1996: 92). The film, in part, commends Africa's firm roots as an antidote to Black America's newfangled civil-rights. But despite the benign tenor of uplift, Olaniyan maintains that *Coming to America* belittles Africa in order to succor Black Americans' racial anxieties.

A stark example is when Akeem seeks to groom himself in preparation to pursue an African American woman. Akeem opens the door to a Black barbershop with four older gentlemen inside: three Black barbers (Sweets, Morris, and Clarence) and a dawdling, White Jewish man named Saul. Akeem catches the door as a Black customer exits, ignoring Akeem's gesture and friendly nod. The three barbers similarly continue milling about while Saul reads his newspaper. Akeem entreats the men saying, "Excuse me…" The (faux) African accent captures Saul's attention, who looks to the barbers and announces, "Hey, It's Kunta Kinte!" The barbers laugh exuberantly while the joke passes by Akeem. Shilpa S. Davé's work on accents clarifies the boundaries expressed by the punch line. Akeem's vocal distinction betrays his ignorance of "the socially nuanced and…socially constructed reality" that is Americanness (Davé 2013: 5). The introduction of a foreign accent implies that even though someone may live in America, they are in fact not fully American.

The humor here works on multiple levels, none of which favors Akeem. The Kunta Kinte reference underlies the fish-out-of-water scenario upon which the film is premised. Akeem expects to share some kinship with the Black barbers, as well as the other Black customer, but comes into a situation that negatively reinforces his singleness. Similarly, viewers are led to expect Saul's own affected speech (e.g. Yiddish loanwords, faux Ashkenazic accent) and fair skin color to demarcate difference, but the reference to Kunta Kinte enables

American rootedness to trump African ethnicity. Like Kunta, Akeem has come to an America that rejects his being.

3. *Diary of a Mad Black Woman* (2005)
Roots enables a similar role reversal in Tyler Perry's 2005 film, *Diary of a Mad Black Woman*. The film is the first in the controversial universe of Mabel "Madea" Simmons, an elderly, Black matriarch portrayed by Perry in a number of movies. The series usually revolves around Madea's descendants, whose lives in Atlanta have gone into disarray. These relatives find respite in Madea's suburban home, her absurd antics, and sage advice. *Diary* revolves around the trials of Madea's granddaughter, Helen, the wife of a wealthy lawyer. The film begins with Helen learning of her husband's extra-marital affair and children. The husband makes clear that Helen must move out to make room for his other family. Late into the night, a disheveled and distraught Helen arrives at Madea's door. Madea opens the door and welcomes Helen in without hesitation. But Madea's brother, Joe (also portrayed by Perry), can be heard yelling about the late-night inconvenience. Though off-camera, his complaints draw the viewer's attention.

> **Joe**: [Yelling] I'm getting tired of all these people…
> **Madea**: [Talking over him] Shut up, Joe! I got dis.
> **Joe**: [Continuing] …coming over this late at night I'm going to have to put my foot down.
> **Madea**: Kunta Kinte put his foot down; it got chopped off. Now shut the hell up and go back to sleep!

The gendered sibling rivalry makes the exchange particularly heated, and household authority is far from settled. Robert J. Patterson, an English scholar and student of Perry's films, sees Madea as an exemplar of the "*strong* Black woman" (Patterson 2011: 16).[2] The

---

2   For feminist and womanist scholars' deconstructions of Tyler Perry's films and the politics of their success among Black women and Black communities, see *Womanist and Black Feminist Responses to Tyler Perry's Productions* (Manigault-Bryant, Lomax, and Duncan 2014).

typology stands at a complex intersection between gender and race. She is not the nemesis of patriarchy but the exception that proves the rule of Black people's backwardness—that because Black men are not man enough to rule the household, Black women must compensate. In turn, Black women's strength undercuts their femininity. Madea may have the power to keep a family together, but her displays of strength come with an admittance of "surrogacy" and "mammification" (Patterson 2011: 16).[3]

Madea's power over Joe comes by way of another social paradox. She aligns herself with the slave-catcher who cut off Kunta Kinte's foot. By using Kunta Kinte as a cautionary tale, she informs her brother of his subservient role while naming herself as the master of the house. Tyler Perry has received criticism for his portrayal of Madea, but he likens his portrayal to a mother's fierce love for her children (Ulaby 2010). In *Diary*, Perry is willing to express that fierceness by comparing it to a White person's ability to violently harm and uproot a Black person during slavery.

4. *Everybody Hates Chris* (2008)

African American comedian Chris Rock joked about an instance where he was put in his place by a White man using a Kunta Kinte reference. In a 2008 episode of his autobiographical sitcom, *Everybody Hates Chris*, a nerdy "Chris" attempts to raise his social standing by doing the homework of football star, Walter Dickerson (*Everybody Hates Chris* 2009). The White teacher, Coach Thurman, uncovers the scheme when the dunce signs the too-good-to-be-true paper with Chris's name. Coach Thurman calls the two Black perpetrators to his office and shares his disappointment. Thurman benches Dickerson from the next game so that he can use detention and the time off to make up the paper. Thurman has other plans for Chris.

---

3   Donald Bogle explains that the mammy archetype is defined "by her sex and her fierce independence," adding that "she is usually big, fat, and cantankerous." He traces the mammy's film debut to a 1914 blackface comedy, entitled *Coon Town Suffragettes*, "[which] dealt with a group of bossy mammy washer-women who organize a militant movement to keep their good-for-nothing husbands at home" (Bogle 2001: 9).

Coach Thurman: And you...

Chris: No [mumbling]...detention.

Thurman: No! Detention is way too easy. You turned your back on easy when you did his paper, Cool Breeze. So Lincoln goes to all this trouble to issue the Emancipation Proclamation, frees your people from slavery, and what do you do? You run around doing other people's work for them. You're killing me. *Et tu* Kunta Kinte?

Chris: [Innocently] I'm sorry.

Thurman: No, I'm sorry. [Determined] But I'm going to help you out. Maybe Lincoln couldn't get to you. but I can!

Chris: [Fretfully] What are you going to do?

Thurman: Oh, wouldn't you like to know. [Laughs maniacally]

Thurman operates under what sociologists Maragaret M. Zamudio and Francisco Rios describe as "colorblind racism" (Zamudio and Rios 2006: 484). The position presumes that race is "a thing of the past," and that, thanks to Civil Rights legislation, people of all races vie for the American Dream on a level playing field (2006: 484–5). Accordingly, subtle expressions of racism go unchecked because social policing only registers the most blatant forms.

Thurman unknowingly turns the uplifting power of *Roots* for Black people into a tool for discrimination and uproot. The coach's erudite inflection of Kunta Kinte places Rock as a traitor (cf. Brutus) to the freedom-loving Kunta Kinte and the nation's abolitionist martyr. Rock's lament is met by a backhanded compliment gloved in a White savior complex, and he is ultimately knocked back down to the position of social outcast. The humor turns around Thurman's presumption that he is helping, even speaking to the Black character in terms that should be clear. But even the tradition of Lincoln and the language of *Roots* can be tools of oppression.

B. Routing Kunta Kinte

Whereas "uproot" speaks to scriptures' role in domination, "routing" connotes scriptures' utility for conveying ambivalence and uncertainty about one's place in a social world. Kunta Kinte's first moments in America were full of despair. Though the character found intermittent spaces for respite, these recesses from hopelessness should not be interpreted as successes. Each attempt to run free leads to yet another capture. As demonstrated in the following scenes, African Americans play with "Kunta Kinte" in order to point out the unnerving liminality of the Black experience and the persistent need to route to somewhere better.

1. *A Different World* (1990)

The television show *A Different World* centered on the struggle of African Americans to root themselves in America's promises. Running from 1987 to 1993, the show followed a group of college students at a historically Black college in the post-civil-rights era. The theme song artfully discloses the premise of the situational comedy.

> I know my parents love me, stand behind me come what may.
> I know now that I'm ready because I finally heard them say,
> "It's a different world from where you come from."
>
> Here's a chance to make it, if we focus on our goals.
> If you dish it, we can take it, just remember you've been told,
> "It's a different world from where you come from."
> "It's a different world from where you come from."
> (Means Coleman and Cavalcante 2012: 39–40)[4]

The show presumed that Black people's historic struggle for civil rights had created new opportunities for the community's next generation. But these opportunities came with new challenges, the solution to which was the same as those for previous generations: roots, knowledge of "where you come from."

A Different World explored this rootedness as a discourse diffused through various faces of the African American experience. Television scholar Herman Gray situates the 1980s show in an era that consciously dismantled monolithic claims of what Blackness should or must signify.

---

4 The lyrics to the theme song were composed by Bill Cosby, Stu Gardner, and Dawnn Lewis.

At the heart of these debates were...visions of nation, community, authenticity, masculinity, and heterosexuality. Points of
contention in such debates often centered on sexuality, inter-
racial relationships, mixed-race heritage and social class. (H.
Gray 1995, 97)

The show drew dramatic tension from the characters struggling—and
often, competing—to make their Black roots work for them in an
ever-new America.

In the episode, "Perhaps Love," a romantic couple grapples with
maintaining their relationship while pursuing their respective career
goals. Thus far, their bliss derives from their mutuality. The fair-
skinned, well-to-do, and sometimes pretentious pair stood out from
their peers at Hillman College. The few differences between them
only added to their complementarity. Whitley Gilbert came from
a southern family and attended the Virginia school for her entire
undergraduate education. Julian Day came to Hillman by way of an
exchange program with Georgetown University. As the school year
was coming to a close, Whitley anxiously anticipated her beau's proposal, a commitment that would reinforce their bonds in spite of their
diverging professional paths. The couple dines over Italian food when
Julian proposes that Whitley follow him back to Washington D.C.—
sans ring. Whitley is forced to choose between accepting a local
internship or following Julian's dreams. The deliberation devolves
into a contest of rootedness.

> **Whitley:** No, I can't go to D.C. with you this summer. I have
> that internship with E.H. Wright.
> **Julian**: E.H. Wright is here in town. You can work for them next
> semester. Besides I can find you some kind of office job
> at Pan-Africa.
> **Whitley**: I don't know, Julian. I already accepted that job. It's
> kind of unprofessional not to show up.
> **Julian**: Sweetheart, before you go into the corporate world, I'd
> love for you to get some real life experience. I mean learn
> how to make it without the credit cards, Gucci pumps, the
> Cartier watch.
> **Whitley**: Why?
> **Julian**: Because you're a little sheltered and out of touch.

Whitley: Out of touch with what?

Julian: The community, the way most people live.

Whitley: I'm not most people, Julian. Neither are you, Mr. Exeter prep school, summers on the Vineyard.

Julian: I'm talking about developing your survival skills. Honey, you can't even walk through certain areas of the town without thinking you're going to be attacked.

Whitley: Oh, please.

Julian: Remember that time you took the bus.

Whitley: Julian! Why don't you just ship me off to the Peace Corps?

Julian: Because I'd miss you too much.

Whitley: Then why don't you spend the summer here in Virginia?

Julian: My job at Pan-Africa is critical to my future in the diplomatic corps.

Whitley: And my job is critical to my career as a corporate art buyer. Manning a stamp sponge in some Pan-African office looking like a Mother Teresa wannabe is not. Plus you don't care about that. That's just *my* career.

Julian: I'm thinking about your career. I don't want to see you go through life as a pampered bougie princess.

Whitley: Pampered? Bougie? Princess?

Julian: I'm only telling you the truth because I care about you.

Whitley: Well, you and your truth can kiss my Cartier—all 18 karats. And the next time you call me a pampered bougie princess, be prepared to throw down, homie. That's right. I know that expression, too.

Waiter: *Allora*, we're finished? A little coffee, dessert?

Julian: No no. The check please.

Whitley: Yes, *la cuenta*! And fast!

Julian: It's, "il conto."

Whitley: *Conto, cuenta*, Kunta Kinte. Just bring the ding dang check!

To borrow from H. Gray, Whitley and Julian's hopes are "firmly rooted in African American social experiences and cultural sensibilities," so their lovers' spat unsurprisingly turns into a quarrel over rootedness (1995: 97). For Julian, the Pan-African cause will afford them further opportunity. Whitley thinks this disingenuous since both of them were raised in bourgeois luxury. The two can concur, however, that their relationship is a failure.

A Different World uses Kunta Kinte to make clear the elusiveness of life, liberty, the pursuit of happiness, and "Perhaps Love" for African Americans. Whitley names her frustrations through an exaggerated demonstration of her roots, proof that she knows where she comes from. When Julian declares that the meal is over, she appeals to her learned cosmopolitanism, uttering "*la cuenta!*" The display is comical because she confuses the Italian phrase with its Spanish cognate. When Julian pedantically shames her, she bests him with a show of vernacular mastery— "*Conto, cuenta,* Kunta Kinte." But the reference punctuates the futility of the contest. Whitley loses the battle for worldliness but proves more rooted in Blackness. Even so, the win is a pyrrhic victory, for she had to align herself with a slave to redeem her ignorance. And pursuit of her internship is of little consolation. To take her "chance to make it," she had to forfeit her relationship and continue to route further to find herself.

2 & 3. *The Fresh Prince of Bel Air* (1991, 1992)

Whitley was not unique in her struggle to lay hold of the American Dream whilst remaining Black. The sitcom *The Fresh Prince of Bel Air* exploited the dilemma to further lengths. A mother's worry over urban decay sends a Black teenager packing from his home in West Philadelphia to swanky Bel Air, California. Exiled to the mansion of his rich uncle, aunt, and cousins, he flounders trying to maintain his 'hood-hardened Blackness (i.e freshness) and manhood (i.e. princedom). From 1990 to 1996, audiences looked on as Will Smith, the pop-rapper turned actor, played a character of the same name and became Hollywood royalty.

The show pivots around the cost for Black people to join the bourgeoisie. West Philadelphia is just one of many Black enclaves that gave way to urban ills following the mixed results of the Great Migration (Omi and Winant 1994: 20).[5] Smith's mother has decided

---

5   Sociologists Michael Omi and Howard Winant describe how "the Bootstraps Model" did not work for the "great waves of the 'Atlantic migration' of the nineteenth and early twentieth centuries" because of "structural

that there is little good for him in the 'hood, so she sends Will to find safety elsewhere. Media critic Robin R. Means Coleman observes a second crisis that the show sets before African Americans: the trade-off of Black uplift. "[H]igh socioeconomic status meant an absence of Blackness. The Black upper-middle class had to *also* be assimilated African Americans who must be brought back 'in touch' by ghettocentric characters" (Means Coleman 1998: 115, emphasis added). According to Means Coleman, for each episode, the situational backdrop changed in order to shuffle who could restore whom. Whatever the configuration, the show's cast remain shackled to liminality, never free from rooting out each other's incomplete conceptions of Blackness.[6] Will twice alludes to Kunta Kinte's amputated foot as a means of underlining—and undermining, Haley might argue given his own leanings—the continued struggle for Black uplift.

In a 1991 episode, "Will Gets a Job" (*The Fresh Prince of Bel Air* 2005a), Will learns that the Bel Air Preparatory homecoming dance costs considerably more than the parties hosted by his school in Philadelphia. He admits to having enjoyed his lavish surroundings,

---

barriers." These frustrations gave way to two different responses to identity politics among Black people. Omi and Winant describe these as the *racial* model, "which demanded group rights and recognition" and the *ethnic* model, "which emphasized the dangerous radicalism (and in their view) anti-democratic character of 'positive' or 'affirmative' antidiscrimination policies. State activities should be restricted, they argued, to guarantees of equality for individuals" (Omi and Winant 1994: 20).

6   Will exhibits what Omi and Winant describe as the racial model of blackness. He displays this with hanging a Malcolm X poster in his room. Will's cousin Carlton is a Young Republican and Reagan-admirer, and typifies the ethnic model, which Omi and Winant link to "neoconservatism" (Omi and Winant 1994: 20). Will's Uncle Phil is more difficult to typecast. He is a Princeton-trained lawyer and California Superior Court judge, credentials that he reiterates throughout the series. But in Phil-centric episodes, the audience learns that he was raised in the rural, segregated, South and attended Malcolm X speeches. In this situational comedy, one character's understanding of Blackness is featured as the salve for the episode. Each of these examples can be seen in the pilot episode (*The Fresh Prince of Bel Air*, Season 1, Episode 1, originally aired September 10, 1990).

but he refuses to ask his uncle for money on this score. Being unable to pay his own way or that of his date would shred the last of his masculine dignity. So unbeknownst to his Aunt Vivian and Uncle Philip, Will takes a part-time job as a waiter. When the truth catches up to him, his Uncle Phillip refuses to believe that his nephew has such a work ethic.

> **Uncle Phil**: Will, we have to talk.
>
> **Will**: Yeah, sure Uncle Phil. What's the problem?
>
> **Uncle Phil**: You missed basketball practice. You've been falling asleep in class. And you missed curfew twice this week. I want an explanation.
>
> **Will**: And you deserve an explanation. And I have an incredible one that I'd like to give you next week.
>
> **Uncle Phil**: [Silent, patience thinning from his face]
>
> **Will**: … But then again, I'd like to see next week. So maybe I should give it to you now? I got a job!
>
> **Aunt Vivian**: Well, why are we just now hearing about this?
>
> **Will**: I wanted to surprise you.
>
> **Uncle Phil**: Look! I wasn't born yesterday. I expect you to honor your commitments. And I expect you to be honest. Now until you can tell me the truth, you are grounded. No TV. No phone calls. And no visitors. [Storms off]
>
> **Will**: [Perplexed] But Unc… [Yelling] Why don't you just do me like Kunta Kinte and chop off my foot?

Will's outburst encompasses numerous anxieties emblematic of the unsettled nature of the African American experience. Success in one realm (e.g. economic) requires sacrifice in another (e.g. school activities). Even something as benign as showing one's initiative or industriousness can lead to punishment. Will is doing his best to mature into manhood, but Uncle Phil has dismissed these efforts as yet more evidence of his nephew's petulant deviance. Uncle Phil believes himself to be simply rooting out any vestige of the streets. Will reads the resulting disciplinary measures as alienating him further from the Black world and its masculine values. Will is as good as Kunta Kinte, a Black man standing before a White enslaver, forced to choose between castration or amputation.

Histrionics aside, Will is not beyond empathy with Uncle Phil, for he finds himself playing slave-master to his cousin, Carlton. Carlton, more than any other character, embodies a loss of ontological Blackness. For all his bookishness and social graces, he lacks the street-wise charm of the Fresh Prince. In a 1992 episode "Mama's Baby, Carlton's Maybe" (*The Fresh Prince of Bel Air* 2005b), audiences and cast are shocked to learn that the teenaged Carlton may have fathered a child out of wedlock. Will, Uncle Phil, and Aunt Viv agree that until confirmed by a pregnancy test, Carlton should withhold accepting any responsibility. Carlton disagrees and tries to join the mother's side, throwing caution and his grounding to the wind. He attempts many escapes, only to be foiled by Will each time. After promising Will he will not try to flee again, Carlton scales down an improvised rope-ladder. Will awaits him below to yet again foil the escape.

> **Will**: Give me your car keys.
> **Carlton**: You know, Will, I gave you my word. I thought that would be enough.
> **Will**: Well, you're lucky I don't do you like Kunta Kinte and chop off your foot.
> **Carlton**: [Begrudgingly hands Will the car keys and walks back inside the house]

The Fresh Prince of Bel Air added a pop hip hop beat to the familiar rags-to-riches fairy tale. Its predominantly African American cast worked out the meaning of Blackness before a largely White viewing audience. Media scholars have debated the show's arguable resort to minstrel tropes and thinned social criticism, but even these critiques have not diminished the show's apt display of Black liminality (Dates and Stroman 2001: 216–23).[7] On the contrary, the combination of steps and missteps toward rootedness is characteristic of this intermediate stage where persons struggle to make their scriptures work in a

---

7   Dates and Stroman also argue that the engagement of these themes worked well for *The Fresh Prince*, but it did not work well for Haley's short-lived collaboration with Norman Lear, *Palmerstown U.S.A.*

new situation. Will vents about his difficulty through the exclamation, "Kunta Kinte."

When Carlton acts out as the well-intentioned deviant, Will is quick to channel his Uncle Phil and discipline accordingly. The reference to *Roots* here echoes Will's attempt to make sense of the quandary. Will has deputized himself to keep Carlton from acting chivalrously. And though Will has not gone so far as to chop off Carlton's foot or report him directly to Uncle Phil, he is doling out discipline instead of "brotha'-ly" support. Will has lost a bit of the roots he so frequently bandies about, and Carlton's repeated attempts also delimit Will's impotence. Unlike the slavers that stopped Kunta Kinte from running, Will cannot keep Carlton from fleeing the mansion. Even in accommodating his Uncle's sensibilities, the Fresh Prince stands uprooted from Philadelphia yet not rooted in Bel Air.

4. *Boyz n the Hood* (1991)

The late twentieth century genre of hood films wrestles with the circumstances of African American identity formation, albeit in a grittier fashion. Movies like the Hughes' brothers *Menace II Society* (1993) and John Singleton's *Boyz n the Hood* (1991) delighted in the uncensored rhetorics of Gangsta Rap. Paula J. Massoud explains that the genre is part of a century-long tradition of irresolution:

> ...a legacy in which the city has been mythologized as both a utopia—as a space promising freedom and economic mobility —and a dystopia—the ghetto's economic impoverishment and segregation. In this manner, the city as a signifying space has performed a dual function, both real and imaginary. (Massoud 1996: 88)

In the city, competing approaches to Black uplift collide into a mélange of confusion about what persons, values, and behaviors properly comprise a community.

The film follows Tré Styles as he comes of age in Los Angeles. It opens with Tré misbehaving in an Inglewood school despite his obvious intelligence. His mother intervenes by having the boy join his father, Jason "Furious" Styles, in South Central. The parents had Tré while teenagers and had since separated amicably. But the mother concedes that the boy needs a strong father figure, and she cannot suitably parent while finishing her nursing degree. "Furious" promises to raise Tré into a respectable young man while the city grows more dangerous. Many of Tré's friends lack a positive role model, in turn succumbing to urban perils such as gang violence. In maturity, Tré learns to appreciate the opportunities afforded to him, but the adolescent Tré is torn between obeying his father and connecting to his friends, Chris and Doughboy.

Mr Styles: So, Doughboy, are you staying out of trouble?

Doughboy: Troubles? I ain't got no troubles. You got some troubles?

Mr Styles: I got some lawn trouble. Why don't y'all rake these leaves up for me?

Chris: How much?

Mr Styles: I'll give you five dollars for the whole lawn with not one leaf on it.

Chris: [Laughs] Five dollars? Man, that ain't shit. I can make more doing nothing.

Mr Styles: Oh, yeah? Doing what?

Doughboy: He works for his uncle.

Mr Styles: Oh well, that's too bad. I guess I just have to get my son to do it for me.

Tré Styles: Do what?

Mr Styles: I want you to rake up these leaves off the lawn.

Tré Styles: [Grumbles]

Mr Styles: Hey, boy! Don't look at me funny if I ask you to do something. Here, take this. There's two trash bags right there on the ground. See y'all later [exits].

Doughboy: [Exhales deeply] Damn, your daddy mean! He's worse than the bogeyman himself. You gotta do all these leaves. Who he thinks you is, Kunta Kinte? [Shakes his head in disbelief] Later, Tré. [Walks off].

Chris: Later [Walks off with Doughboy].

In so many words, Doughboy has called Mr Styles a slave-master, but the allusion to *Roots* signifies the difference between how the two characters interpret the city. Doughboy is oblivious to the criminality that adults in the neighborhood intuitively fear and that, as narrated in the film, he will witness himself later in life. His ignorance enables him to enjoy the city as a utopian paradise in no need of landscape or upkeep. By calling Tré "Kunta Kinte," Doughboy understands himself as free of burden. Mr Styles, on the other hand, sees the city in dystopic terms, a difficult place to grow up. Thus, he takes it upon himself to give Tré (and his friends, if they choose to avail themselves of this) the roots needed to survive. In either case, Tré represents the anxious Kunta Kinte, *routing* for a midpoint between a city where he can be close to friends and a city where he can be close to family.

5. *The Wire* (2003)

According to *The Wire*, being rooted in America is not as simple as being in a respectable position or on the right side of the law. This police drama depicts the corrupt streets and institutions of Baltimore. The city's police department deploys wire taps in order to neutralize the criminal work of drug dealers, dock workers, bureaucrats, public school administrators, and local journalists. Through the wire, audience members learn that all these entities are similarly tainted. This voyeurism also shows how trying to make one's world a better place is a high-wire act where all eventually fall into transgression.

Law professor Bennett Capers (2011) observes that the show's realism stems largely from its rejection of White Hat/Black Hat—or better said, "White skin/Black skin"—dichotomies that oversimplify crime dramas.

The cops, prosecutors, and defense attorneys are mostly White, as is the one judge that has a recurring role, while Avon Barksdale's (drug) crew is all Black. What are the politics of identification here? Or for that matter, what are the politics of identification when one senses that the smartest person on the show is Avon Barksdale's lieutenant in the drug organization, Stringer Bell, who attends business school at night, tries to explain microeconomics to his subordinates, and occasionally invokes Robert's Rules of Order to keep drug consortium meetings organized?

And how is identification further complicated by the many similarities between the cops and the drug dealers? Both groups share an obsession with the chain of command and getting paid. Both groups are plagued by nepotism and internal corruption. One quickly realizes the drug dealers have a code of ethics and a sense of retribution and deterrence as strong as the cops have, indeed stronger. For too many of the cops, making arrests is simply going through the motions. Drug dealers think about why they punish (Capers 2011: 460).

The show is by no means post-racial. Rather, it is occupied with asking when, how, why, and for whom race matters. Capers is taken by the routine instance of a Black police detective choosing the badge—and the White partner with whom he shares it—over racial solidarity. Detective Carver does not give a second thought to "describing their 'assailants' as 'fucking project niggers'" (Capers 2011: 463). Skin color is but one possible sight for finding commonality, but as a *Roots*-inflected joke underlines, there are plenty of others.

During a 2003 episode "Hot Shots" (*The Wire* 2005), the Baltimore Port Authority come upon a cargo container with thirteen asphyxiated women inside. With the help of the police department, they track the ship of origin to the port of Philadelphia. Through some interdepartmental cooperation, *The Atlantic Light* and its crew sit detained until the Baltimore Police Department can interrogate them.[8] The investigation goes south when Detectives Lester Freamon and Bunk Moreland (both Black) discover that the crewmembers cannot (or will not) speak English.

A montage splices each of the motley crew speaking a different native tongue while the detectives sit in frustrated silence. Their notepads and pens go unused. The scene ends with the detectives interrupting the lone Black crewmember's rant in an African tongue.

> **African Crewmember**: *English?* [Continues speaking in an African language]…
> **Bunk**: [Raises his hand to interject] Kunta Kinte, *yabba dabba dabba do.*
> **African Crewmember**: *Huh?* [Speaks softly, presumably asking a clarifying question in his language]…

---

8   Four months before his death, Alex Haley gave a lecture to *Reader's Digest* about the time he purchased a ticket aboard a freighter called the *African Star* in order to better empathize with Kunta Kinte's transatlantic journey (Haley [1991b] 2007: 80–5). The Atlantic-oriented mythology is unavoidable because it is rooted in this scriptural economy.

Lester: Ha! [Exclaiming false comprehension] Mishy gishy gushy gushy mishy mushy mooshy motherfucker.

African Crewmember: [Leans back and expresses bewilderment] Eh?

Lester: Eh? [Reciprocates loudly]

African Crewmember: [Replies calmly with some explanation]...

Lester: [Interrupts] Negro! ...

Bunk: [Bows his head, laughing silently while feigning to take notes]

Lester: ... You cannot travel halfway around the world and not speak any motherfuckin' English.

African Crewmember: [Begins speaking apologetically]

Lester: [Interrupts and hammers his index finger into the desk] English, motherfucker!

The epigraph to the episode quotes a Port Authority officer, who upon seeing the sex slaves in the container remarked, "What they need is a union." Stripped from its context, it also signifies the unified effort of *The Atlantic Light*'s crew as well as the different police agencies. Though the police works together to apprehend the criminals, the crew's solidarity—as non-English-speaking, non-compliant suspects—proves more effective.

The detectives work out their frustration by acting out a burlesque of *Roots*. The slave ship, poignantly named *The Atlantic Light*, is apprehended for shipping humans as chattel. The ship's crew are interrogated by two Black men named Freamon (cf. *free man*) and Moreland (cf. *more land*), surnames befitting the descendants of emancipated slaves awaiting their forty acres and a mule. The lone African, here called Kunta Kinte, again becomes the whipping boy, and the detectives hold forth in disbelief that he cannot speak English. However cathartic the jest may have been, it ultimately comes off as a lament, demarcating the stalemate and rooting out any premature celebration of having cracked the case. The African American detectives have more in common with the detained African than they care to admit.

C. Rooting Kunta Kinte

As cathartic as routing may be, humans return to the phenomenon of scriptures because they perceive themselves as more rooted when scripturalizing than when not. Scriptures bring a sense of arrival. Kunta Kinte can make a home out of America because he finds purpose and strength in passing his African roots on to his descendants. Kunta Kinte's example is never more compelling than as a jubilant finale to racial strife.

1. *Saturday Night Live*'s "Weekend Update" (2002)
Since its founding in 1975, the National Broadcasting Company's *Saturday Night Live* (SNL) has been the gold standard in American satire. The popularity of the sketch comedy program waxes and wanes, but its brand consistently intrigues television viewers keen on ending the week on a humorous note. Audiences have counted on the segment "Weekend Update" to bring a touch of parody to current events. The bit features one or two suited correspondents behind a news desk, riffing on actual headlines. As communications specialist Aaron Reincheld has noticed, for nearly five decades "actors and actresses have sat behind the "Weekend Update" desk to tell the world what it is doing wrong" (2006: 190). The "news anchors" entertain millions in lampooning the missteps of the most powerful figures in the public eye. Celebrities, politicians, and corporate executives mentioned can expect a blow to their credibility.

Rival network the American Broadcasting Company (ABC) learned this after passing on a twenty-fifth anniversary retrospective of their *Roots* miniseries. Producer David Wolper (the miniseries' show runner) and Director Judy Leonard pitched the special to ABC, but Programming Executive Andrea Wong rejected it saying, "There's no market for it." Network Chairman John Braun tried to spin the decision, explaining that "we obviously all deeply value what 'Roots' has meant to our network…[but] when [the special] was pitched to us, quite candidly, we just didn't feel creatively what we heard was that strong." John Carman (2002), media reporter for the *Los Angeles Times*, commented: "From a programming perspective, ABC probably made the right call. From a public-relations perspective, it shot itself in the foot." On various fronts, NBC understood what ABC did not and chose to run the special the next Friday evening but not before *SNL* cast member Jimmy Fallon would skewer ABC on "Weekend Update" (originally aired January 19, 2002).

> **Fallon**: This week, ABC declined to air a twenty-fifth anniversary special on their groundbreaking miniseries, *Roots*. The decision not to run the special was made by ABC Programming Executive, The Man.
> **Live Studio Audience**: [Breaks into laughter]
> **Fallon**: For those of you who don't remember *Roots*, it follows the saga of Kunta Kinte from young African tribesman, to slavery, to becoming literate, and eventually the top of his class at Starfleet Academy.
> **Live Studio Audience**: [Erupts into even stronger laughter]

Burton made his acting debut as the young Kunta Kinte, going on to develop and host the award-winning children's educational program, *Reading Rainbow*, as well as to play the prodigious engineer Geordi LaForge on *Star Trek: The Next Generation*. Burton's meta-narrative rise to fame symbolizes the work that *Roots* makes possible. Fallon's discussion of Kunta Kinte colors ABC as particularly obtuse—making a smart financial decision when the subtext called for a culturally savvy one. To return to the proper side of historical memory, ABC rushed to feature a multipart tribute to *Roots* on its flagship weekday morning program, *Good Morning America*. Still, "Weekend Update" places ABC and *Roots* at opposite ends of America's civil rights struggle. ABC becomes the face of overbearing, greed-driven, hegemony (i.e. "The Man"). Meanwhile NBC stands with a body politic wanting to believe that Black people are rooted in the nation, American Dream in hand, evidenced by LeVar Burton's storied career.

2. *Chappelle's Show* (2003)

African American humorist Dave Chappelle adds another dimension to America's optimistic reading of *Roots*. His sketch comedy show, *Chappelle's Show*, parodied the 25th anniversary release of the miniseries with a reel of pseudo-outtakes and DVD bonus footage. Chappelle's penchant for the absurd enables his critique to enjoy the gains of the post-civil-rights and post-*Roots* era (cf. Richard Pryor's "Bicentennial Nigger" and Kunta Kinte riff) and yet mock America's attempt to interpret *Roots* as carte blanche for a post-racial national myth (cf. *Everybody Hates Chris* and *SNL*'s "Weekend Update"). Thinking with Stuart Hall, communications scholar Lisa Glebatis Perks attributes this to the "polysemic scaffolding" of *Chappelle's Show*. She explains that "the egregious stereotypes transpose inferential racism, which disguises the discriminatory predicates of the stereotypes, into overt racism that can be more readily critiqued" (Perks 2010: 276). In other words, Chappelle magnifies prevalent stereotypes to the nth degree in order to expose their more subtle aspects. And with the enlarged textual field, he can point his barbs at multiple interpretive communities simultaneously.

In Season 1 Episode 3 (originally aired February 5, 2003) Chappelle spoofs the commemorative DVD commercial made to help America do a doubletake on their embrace of the *Roots* miniseries. The spoof commercial begins with stock footage of Black slaves working on a plantation—faceless and unassuming. A legato orchestral score accompanies the scene, and a basso profundo, perhaps mimicking James Earl Jones, narrates:

> Twenty-five years ago, an epic motion picture was unleashed on America. Considered one of the most important films in history. We are now proud to release this masterpiece on DVD for the very first time. This one of a kind twenty-fifth anniversary commemorative edition features extras—including cast interviews, director's commentary, and never-seen-before outtakes.

The description brings the *Roots* moment to the audience's mind as a DVD cover floats into view. But instead of the familiar iconography of Burton's young, enchained Kunta Kinte, Dave Chappelle is pictured. A laughing studio audience interrupts the somber narration of the disc's contents.

The scene transitions to an older Kunta Kinte raising the infant Kizzy to the starlit heavens, but as he begins the familiar benediction, "Behold!...," the baby urinates and falls from her father's arms. The audience's laughter is accompanied by a folksy, electric blues shuffle. The camera then pans left alongside a chain gang of Black men bellowing the spiritual, "Swing Low, Sweet Chariot." The audience's silence reflects recognition of the song's poetic expression of Black slavery. But the audience returns to laughing when an Asian man's accent betrays the chain gang's heterogeneous composition. The audience's vocalized surprise echoes Matthew Frye Jacobson's question about *Roots*, "Whose story is it? If America is indeed a melting pot's tale, then how can *Roots* remain solely in the purview of Black people?" (Jacobson 2006: 42–3).

Chappelle answers with the last scene. The music switches back to the orchestral score and the camera returns to Chappelle's Kunta Kinte, who is portraying the now-famous whipping scene. A White man whips Kunta Kinte while asking, "What is your name?" Kunta is to answer with the name Toby, but he resists, conceding nothing except for "Kunta Kinte." In the original, the whipping goes on until Kunta finally says "Toby" and forfeits consciousness. Chappelle's rendition has Kunta turn from the gallows (with lumbar padding now visible) as if to beat the overseer. The White actor apologizes for whipping too hard and cowers before Chappelle. The electric blues shuffle returns and the cast members (Black and White people alike) fall into hysterics before sliding back into character.

The joke cuts differently depending upon one's position in relation to racial reconciliation. Chappelle mocks the expression of White guilt by those with a deep-seated fear and mistrust of Black people while, at the same time, extending comic relief. The sketch encourages the audience to take past racial prejudices seriously and in its stride in order to move and take root past them. The sentiment is more than just a platitude, for Chappelle sees himself as having accomplished this. His production company's title card shows Chappelle enchained as Kunta Kinte but holding a stack of dollar bills in each hand. The comedian leaves the audience, exclaiming, "I'm rich, biatch [sic]!"[9] He affirms that he can and has done the previously unimaginable—he has taken a dominating racial discourse and made it work in his favor.

---

9   The audio clip is in fact from a sketch in the next episode where a parody newscast brings breaking news of the United States government granting African Americans reparation. One citizen, exclaims " I'm rich, biatch" (originally aired February 12, 2003).

Just as Kunta Kinte created an African family in America, Chappelle can make a joke of race.

3. *Community* (2011)

On a guest spot on the NBC sitcom *Community*, Burton enjoys the luxury of mocking America's (post-)racial discourse. *Community* centers on the hijinks of a flawed study group at a community college. The show has received acclaim for its unique blend of highbrow, intertextual sensibilities and pedestrian humor. In a 2011 episode called "Intermediate Documentary Filmmaking," the study group learns that a middle-aged, craven member named Pierce is dying from a drug addiction. On his deathbed, he requests that the hyper-attentive Abed document his final days as he bequeaths gifts to the rest. But unbeknownst to the group, Pierce has contrived the entire situation to reveal that he is no more flawed than they, for the documentary records all of the characters at their worst. For instance, were Abed not distracted by the artistic possibilities and paradoxes of the documentary genre, he would have easily seen through Pierce's scheme (Sander 2012: 72). The episode experiments with the documentary as an unwieldy lens on reality and one's prejudices. Pierce is especially cruel to Troy, the lone African American group member.

Pierce recollects Troy's obsession with actor-educator, LeVar Burton. Troy admired Burton as a paragon of Black achievement (cf. *SNL*'s "Weekend Update") but refused to meet the star, longing only for an autographed picture. In Troy's words, "you can't disappoint a picture." When Pierce invites Burton to the community college, Troy spends the entire episode fleeing the guest's presence. The episode wraps with Burton and a catatonic Troy sharing a meal. Ashamed of his inability to speak, Troy runs out of the room. Burton, a little puzzled, looks at Troy's plate and quips, "Mo' fish for Kunta."

By playing into profane stereotypes of slave dialect, Burton actually masters America's post-racial discourse. His affected speech contrasts the eloquence and articulateness for which he is known. Within the larger context of *Community*, he shows himself as also being able to document and disrupt seemingly ontological realities like race and the *Roots* legacy. He is secure enough with his roots that he can manipulate the harrowing story of Kunta Kinte in whimsical ways. When a fan asked why Burton can take such liberties with the character, he replied, "I embrace him" (Burton 2013). By calling himself Kunta Kinte, Burton declares that he can *act Black* on his own terms.

Conclusion

Roots has served as a resource for trying to make sense out of American history. Alex Haley presented Kunta Kinte as a personage to which Americans can aspire. The twelve references to Kunta Kinte above offer dramatic examples of how Americans express their prospects for rootedness in the nation. But these measures also draw attention to a mutual sense of discontent with the nation and their place in it. Since 1977 audiences have twisted Haley's meaning and used Kunta Kinte as a way of labeling outsiders. Americans deployed the name to *uproot* those Black persons understood to be lacking the proper (read: American) etiquette, accent, or values. Intra-racially, Blacks have called each other Kunta Kinte to *route* difference and critique another's performance of American-ness. Inter-racially, Kunta Kinte reminds Americans how far Black persons have come in the United States—from Africa, from tragedy, from strife—and how far other Americans have to go in extending liberty and justice to all. Despite the differences in inflection, they share an underlying hope that *Roots* will enable each performer to recite a pledge of allegiance to the America that Haley ultimately called "my country."

In parsing how Kunta Kinte has been made to work, it becomes clear that Haley has had an enduring influence on what it means to be rooted in America. And though *Roots* is a saga through which Americans continue to search for meaning, Haley's readers are not wholly bound to his conclusions. They are free to determine whether Kunta Kinte represents a problem to transcend or a source of transcendence. And yet, his protagonist and root metaphor provide the vocabulary (i.e. roots) and grammar (i.e. uprooting, routing, taking root) for a national discourse. Haley's *Roots* is one person's interpretation of American history. Decades after its release, Americans have used it to write their own cultural commentaries. *Roots* is a national scripture with its own history of interpretation and, as outlined here, traditions of racial identification.

Critically speaking, this anthropology of scriptures surfaces fundamental insights about how meaning is inscribed or *rootinized* into bodies. Humans must first identify the roots of a (con)textual field in order to make substantial claims about themselves and others. And the most effective acts of identification not only can become routine within a (con)textual field, they can become the very terms that define meaning and substance. They can become the identificatory lens through which we identify who matters, how they matter, and why they matter. The next chapter calls for scholars to remain vigilant in not essentializing scriptures or the work they do, since to blithely associate scriptures with the transcendent is to miss their raison d'être, the social scenarios upon which we conjure them to transcend the plights and even the people we read as problems.

5 Root-Work in the Academic Study of Religion

Scriptures are not cultural texts with a unique essence. This should not be a provocative statement to make within the field of religious studies or any other human science. Yet I am fully aware that in identifying *Roots* as a "scripture," I am pushing upon the canonical privileges of those who would reserve that category for what they identify as "sacred" or "religious" texts. I understand the convenience of the status quo argument, but such an approach to scriptural study falls short of reaching the critical horizon that Wilfred Cantwell Smith, a foundational scholar in this emerging field, had set out to meet.

In his monograph, *What is Scripture? A Comparative Approach,* W.C. Smith limited his driving question to the textual resources of the world religions. The Qur'an, the Bible, the Torah, the Vedas, the Sutras, and the Analects populate his data set. And though he initiates his book by positing "scripture" as a "bilateral" relationship between "people" and "texts" (W.C. Smith 1993: 17), he concludes the project with an amendment of a third locus, "transcendence" (228).

This is a curious addendum for a thesis that challenged scholars to reconceptualize scripture as an anthropological potentiality rather than an ontology. At book's end, his proposed relational understanding of scriptures doubles down on a phenomenological premise. "Reality transcends us, and we do well to be constantly mindful of this fact even while we marvel at the richness, yet finitude, of human capacity to apprehend it" (W.C. Smith 1993: 229). Smith is uncomfortable leaving the symbolic "it" undefined. He suggests that humanists will interpret transcendence as the realization of "ideals" and that theists will associate these ideals with "God" (240–1). Thus, his hypothesis of scriptures as the powerful and volatile relationship between people and texts becomes a problematic that he can only satisfactorily resolve through a *deus ex machina* appeal. "Transcendence," W.C. Smith writes, "is at the heart of involvement with scripture" (228).

His conclusion, however, begs his initial question since scripturalizing, as a human potentiality, creates the terms that define ideals. On some level, Smith recognizes this, observing, "It seems, then, perhaps defensible that this presents itself as a book about 'scripture.' Yet it must be recognized that calling it that could be part of the very problem that it ostensibly is trying to solve" (W.C. Smith 1993: 237). The assuming inclusion of transcendence undercuts one of Smith's most poignant interventions into the field of critical scriptural study. In his 1971 essay "The Study of Religion and the Study of the Bible," he challenges the antiquarian veneration of the historical-critical method by advocating a study of "scripture as a generic phenomenon." Using the Bible as the subject of his case study, he outlines the following guiding questions for a course of study:

> The course that I envisage would be concerned with the Bible as scripture. It would begin with some consideration of scripture as a generic phenomenon. The questions to which it would address itself would be questions such as these: What is involved in taking a certain body of literature, separating it off from all other, and giving it a sacrosanct status? What is involved psychologically; what, sociologically; and what, historically? How and where did it first come about? How did the Christian Church happen to take up this practice? What attitudes, magical or otherwise, towards writing are involved? And—once this is done— what consequences follow? (W.C. Smith 1971: 132)

Here Smith charts out on an analytical enterprise that adopts the appearance of the unchanging, timeless, and evergreen relevance of certain texts as data rather than gospel. He knows that behind this visage is the work of human signification. For this reason, the historian of religion Jonathan Z. Smith tries to "defend W.C. Smith from W.C. Smith" and "the same sort of reification, the same sort of concreteness, [W.C. Smith] has elsewhere warned against" (J.Z. Smith 1992: 100).

J.Z. Smith is better read as an interlocutor than an outright opponent of W.C. Smith. I interpret the former attempting to keep the latter honest about where the "magic" dwells in the scholar's study (J.Z. Smith 1982: 21–2). In "Scriptures and Histories," J.Z. Smith goes so far as presenting a thesis regarding the New Testament that directly responds to W.C. Smith's probing questions:

> For, in the hands of the sixteenth-century Christian reformers (as with the nineteenth-century Jewish reformers), historical criticism was introduced precisely to serve a mythic project, the reactualization of the original "purity" of the "primitive, apostolic church." (One of the rare, positive uses of the term "primitive" in Western religious discourse). That is to say, the earliest reformers used the New Testament as a standard to judge the degree to which Roman Catholicism had degenerated into "paganism." What they did not anticipate was that the following generations would take the very same techniques and apply them to the New Testament itself, thereby judging the degree to which some parts had degenerated from, or accreted to, the "original, pure faith." I know of no "native" myth more wedded to a cyclical view of history and to a recovery of pristine first times that than that of the Reformation." (J.Z. Smith 1992: 100)

J.Z. Smith's brief excursus gives a glimpse of the observable dynamics between people and texts. Furthermore he highlights a key point regarding canon politics. When people exalt a text as "scripture," they have created a measure for comparing people's worth and from which people can derive other scriptures for other purposes (even challenging the standard and standards of its originators). "Transcendence" mystifies this complex human creativity with *sui generis* claims such that the label of reductionism becomes a stupefying irony. The ingenuity of human interpretive activity requires no god in the gaps.

To be fair, W.C. Smith, attempts to meet so-called reductionists halfway by acknowledging that what is being studied is "the presumption of transcendence," but he finds that verbiage unsatisfactory because the phenomenon in which he is interested—the great rootbooks of the world's religions—appears to promise something akin to transcendence (W.C. Smith 1993: 232). In an endnote on that remark, he also reiterates that such transcendence is not the result of people seeking out a text, but with the text's proven and persistent ability to find people in a host of situations within a cultural context (363–4, n. 44). W.C. Smith believes that applying an analytical qualifier to transcendence is unjust and unnecessary.

But what about people's latent, unconscious, suppressed, or routine engagements with texts and the politics that inform cultural amnesia? What about the negligence that accompanies the gothic nostalgia for "good ol' days" that may not have actually been all that good for users—let alone the used? More attention is due to the study of people transcending themselves, other people, and supposed forces that they identify as obstacles. Therefore J.Z. Smith acknowledges W.C. Smith for this very initial intellectual challenge which ultimately pushed him to engage in a study of scriptures that would rightly include "a larger world of texts that he [J.Z. Smith himself] probably would not have read, texts which raise issues he would have never thought about" (J.Z. Smith 1992: 104). He has in mind a breadth of texts (i.e. "lectionary systems," "concordances and harmony systems," "iconography") and people (i.e. the "lay-reader," Christopher "Columbus" and the Millenarian, Pre-Adamite Rationalist philosopher Isaac La Peyrère) worthy of study. Who and what is being transcended in their contexts? As such, Jonathan Z. Smith's articulation of scriptures is a more compelling continuation of W.C. Smith's anthropological trajectory than, at least, the essentialist trope found at the end of *What is Scripture?*

Russell McCutcheon's comparison of the two Smiths leads to an even more forceful dismissal of ontological appeals in the study of "religion" and deeper recognition of how far the discourse for which "religion" is an abbreviation extends. His metaphor of choice—the "fabrication" of origins—points to the artisanal, even industrial labor involved in keeping up the appearance of a stable, stalwart reality. Thus, those who

> "uncritical[ly]" conscript a community's interpretive mechanism (e.g. for transcendence) for explanatory purposes erect a facade over routine claims of, for instance, diaspora, which makes no sense without positing a static, original homeland, a prehistoric source from which the subsequent scattering supposedly took place, thereby providing a standard against which

degrees of purity, significance, and membership can be measured. (McCutcheon 2015: 70)

The same should be said of applying a descriptor like "religious," which historians of religion (cf. Long 2004 [1986], Chidester 1996, Masuzawa 2005, Nongbri 2013) have shown to be a "modern western metric for manning proximity to Protestant Christianity" (Newton 2017c). In rejecting the notion of scriptures as "religious" texts, I am reiterating Brent Nongbri's caution that "we have to be honest about the category's origins and not pretend that it somehow organically and magically arises from our sources" (Nongbri 2013: 153). We must instead draw due attention to "the social life of scriptures" that are more potent and more complicated than some have given them credit for. We must also explain how scholars' particular reticence on this score is a reflection of the rootwork that would have them forget the rhizomatic nature of human's most meaningful social constructions (Bielo 2009a: 2).

It is not my ambition to alter a speech act (i.e. De Saussure's "parole") with which we have come to be familiar (De Saussure 1966 [1916]: 15). I suspect the world will continue calling the scripture of Islam "the Qur'an" regardless of what I write here. Rather, I am challenging scholars of religion to consider the history and assumptions behind this slip of the tongue (i.e. De Saussure's "langue"). The "social product of the faculty of speech" is our avenue into the "collection of necessary conventions adopted by a social body to permit individuals to exercise that faculty" (De Sassure 1966 [1916]: 9). These social facts together constitute the phenomenon of "language…a self-contained whole and principle of classification" (9). The problem for the semiotician is shared by the anthropologist of scriptures. "As soon as we give language first place among the facts of speech, *we introduce* a natural order into a mass that lends itself to no other classification" (9, emphasis added). Those firmly within a scriptural economy are rewarded by leaving convenience unquestioned. The scholar's task—and the plight of the underclass—is to never know such satisfaction. In fact, questioning "the presumption of transcendence" need not be a gesture of callousness, as W.C. Smith intimates (1993: 232). The unrootedness of uncertainty may be the most genuine expression of empathy we can imagine.

In this final chapter, I caution those tempted to intimate that my classification of *Roots* as scripture and scriptures as roots is a case of reductionism for iconoclasm's sake. If scriptures properly refer to a human activity, then the *sui generis* defense of cultural texts warrants revision. This is all the more demanded, I argue, in light of the way late twentieth century liberation-minded academicians have turned to *Roots*—over and even against the Bible—to challenge the centrality of the Eurocentric and patriarchal theological regimes. That these scholars would draw on a transgressively *transcending* text rather than an established transcendent text draws attention to the relative nature of W.C. Smith's ultimate concern. Secondly, in recognizing how appeals to the "transcendent" have served as a technique for drawing social difference, we can more clearly focus on how even a "secular" text like *Roots* acts as more than a textual commonplace, but as what Alex Haley called "source-place(s)," the loci that can make a difference in people's lives by grounding them in an understanding of who they are, where they came from, and what they could become (Haley 2007 [1976]: 439). I will briefly discuss how the Alex Haley Museum and Interpretive Center in Henning, TN and the Kunta Kinte-Alex Haley Memorial in Annapolis, MD root visitors in a manner indicative of W.C. Smith's understanding of scripturalizing despite their detachment from the transcendent world religions that were his focus. Thus, it is one thing to ask someone about the texts they call "scripture," it is another—and more fruitful—enterprise to have people identify the texts they read that also manage to read them back.

Liberation Theologies Rooting Against the Transcendent

The anthropologist of scriptures takes interest in the social politics of knowing, remembering, and forgetting. Contra W.C. Smith, it is indifferent to the textbook pursuit of Rudolf Otto's *mysterium tremendum et fascinans* (1936 [1917]). As author Gertrude Stein observed in *Everybody's Autobiography* after her attempted return to her sainted childhood home of Oakland, "There is no there there" (Stein 1993 [1937]: 298). Essentialist claims should prompt us to ask questions like: Who exemplifies the authentic? What institutions delimit a tradition? For whom is nostalgia a liability? When people raise such questions, they will turn to scriptures. And where people settle on answers, there their roots lie…and from there, their identities are forged. In fact, when *rootinization* becomes the object of study, we soon realize that contrary to popular belief, scriptures are neither comprehensive nor self-sufficient. They are constantly in need of maintenance by hermeneutes. Appeals to cultural texts outside of a canonical framework belie the relativity or rhizomatic nature of the otherwise-esteemed root-book and the entities identified with it (Deleuze and Guattari 1987 [1980]: 8–9). Thus exegetical commentaries, divination schemes, newly discovered archaeological evidence, and sophisticated historical reconstructions serve to extend the half-life of depreciating scriptures. This sort of renovatory work happens not only as a matter of discursive practices (Wimbush 2008: 5–13), but also in the material preservation of scriptures (Myrvold 2016 [2010]). That said, these are an affect or accident of broader human relations. The point of studying scriptures anthropologically is to recognize the bending, breaking, and mending of canonical boundaries involved in furthering socio-cultural formations.

All this to say, there is a teleology, a utility, to scriptural engagement. Biblical scholar James Massey notes as much in *The New Interpreter's Bible Commentary*. He comments that people turn to the Bible in search of "faith, affirmation, hope, courage and wisdom for living, and a glimpse of the means by which the horizons of personal and social reality can be altered in the direction of human good" (Massey 1994: 152–3). W.C. Smith would call these either transcendental ideals or characteristics of the transcendent. But this fails to elaborate on what that transcendence represents. For our analytical purposes, transcendence is ultimately problem solving. It is the presupposition of an issue in need of a resolution. And as we center our focus on the social work of scriptures, we can see the kinds of humans a group identifies as problems to be transcended .

A scripture may make a positive difference in readers' lives, but it may make a difference in the lives of others in a way that most communities otherwise would not associate with transcendence or the transcendent were it not in their favor. Interpretations are also useful for infringing on the rights of an other and transcending an other's agency. According to Charles H. Long, this is part and parcel to history of religion in America.

> "The mighty saga of the outward acts" is a description of the American language rooted not simply in the physical conquest of space, but equally a language which is the expression of a hermeneutics of conquest and suppression. It is a cultural language that conceals the inner depths, the archaic dimensions of the dominant peoples in the country, while at the same time it renders invisible all those who fail to partake of this language and its underlying cultural experiences. The religion of the American people centers around the telling and the retelling of the mighty deeds of the White conquerors. This hermeneutic mask thus conceals the true experience of America from their very eyes. (Long 1974: 214)

It is not enough to seek proper or righteous interpretations. Scriptures are the tools we use to demarcate difference. And scripturalizing is an endeavor designed to stymie the ascendence and subdue the frontier that stands between us and the world for the taking. In so doing, it carries—or better said, contains, manages, alleviates—the burden of identifying obstacles in our way. It is little wonder why James Baldwin called *Roots* "America's first Black genuine Westerner [sic]" (Baldwin 1976). Alex Haley created his own scriptural text in order to manifest his own destiny, just as his readers have looked to it to follow suit.

The consequence of cavalier "culturalism" is not lost on the clerical class that identifies with liberation theology. The very naming of the movement by the Peruvian priest Gustavo Gutiérrez levels a critique against the assumption that the Bible has been good news for all (Gutiérrez 2000 [1971]). Its proponents read their situation in light of a Christian understanding that has more often than not spelled bondage rather than freedom. And because this stratification has been rootinized, one cannot easily reject their world's scriptures. The more tenable response is to identify the wide reach of a scripture as a vulnerability wherein the roots may be taken ahold of by those at the margins of society. Chinua Achebe encapsulates this strategy most poetically, writing:

> The price a world language must be prepared to pay is submission to many different kinds of use. The African writer should aim to use English in a way that brings out his message best without altering the language to the extent that its value as a medium of international exchange will be lost. He should aim at fashioning out an English which is at once universal and able to carry his peculiar experience. (Achebe 1997 [1965]: 347)

In the context of late twentieth century liberation theology, "tribal theologians" have conjured what they believe to be the heart of the Bible. Commonplaces include Micah 6:8 and Luke 4:18–19 (itself an evangelist's scripturalizing of Isaiah 61). These references are the kind of "fashioning" of identity that Achebe has in mind.

But through his study of W.B. Yeats, and his own experiences in Nigeria's postcolonial turn, Achebe also understood the relative nature of the most essential scriptures. When a text's bindings "fall apart; the center cannot hold, mere anarchy is loosed upon the world," and people will turn to other scriptures. And in the late twentieth century, liberation-minded exegetes saw the Bible so mired in racial and gender oppression that they turned to *Roots* for guidance on how to make sense of the Bible and locate Massey's canon of ends. Kunta Kinte's blood, sweat, and tears watered the textual field of a Christian imagination gone fallow (Jennings 2010: 13–14).

When Elisabeth Schüssler Fiorenza took biblical scholarship to task *In Memory of Her: A Feminist Theological Reconstruction of Christian Origins*, she says that instead of writing off the Bible as a wholly patriarchal text, feminists must reclaim the text and its history (Schüssler Fiorenza 1983). "Feminists cannot afford such an ahistorical or antihistorical stance because it is precisely the power of oppression that deprives people of their history," and we could add, identity. She gleans this from the work of "both Black and Latin American theologians" and lists—first and foremost—Alex Haley's *Roots* as the example par excellence next to Gustavo Gutiérrez (Schüssler Fiorenza 1983: xix). *Roots*, for Schüssler Fiorenza, demonstrates the possibility of transcending a hopeless situation through a historiographic text. On one level, the juxtaposition is curious. Haley was neither a preacher nor a preacher's son, but he was molded in a world built around "uplift," "new hope," and good books. What inspires her is not an eloquent discussion of the transcendent but the proven utility of people being able to alter their circumstances through discourse. And Haley authored a way toward liberation that biblical exegesis—save for the liberationist hermeneutics of those like Gutiérrez—did not.

In February 1977, Garrett-Evangelical Theological Seminary's Center for the Church and the Black Experience dedicated the inaugural issue of their journal to provide a "Prolegomenon to a Theological Response to *Roots*." In no uncertain terms, its essays used *Roots* to bring reckoning to the Church because "authentic Christian 'theology' is supposed to help individuals and those in corporate community come to grips with the existential question of human identity" (H.B. Taylor 1977: 1). The scholars, unsurprisingly, do not dismiss the transcendent quality of the Bible. In fact, their indictment is far more damning. By classifying *Roots* as a "prolegomenon," or a preceding discourse, they imply that traditional Christian reckoning is incomplete without its rootedness. "For *Roots* is about human lineage and real blood, about history and suffering and such a thing as the simple need to know *something* as a prerequisite before 'genuine liberation' of the *mind* and soul, and body can take place" (H.B. Taylor 1977: 1).

If Christians—identifiable by their language, credentials, institutions, and other characteristics—bear witness to the transgressive nature of their own supposed sacred texts and can find transcendence in an otherwise secular text, then the notion of transcendence should be limited to the reporting or description of interpretations. As a phenomenon postulated by the people we study, transcendence is not suited for the explanatory work that is the anthropology of scriptures.

To be clear, we can and should acknowledge with Roland Barthes that "a text is not a line of words releasing a single theological meaning (the message of an Author-God) but a multi-dimensional space in which a variety of writings, none of them original, blend and clash" (Barthes 1978 [1967]: 146). Meaning is created in a chain of a "scriptor's" momentary encounters with a text—reading, writing, remembering, invoking, dreaming, performing, etc. (Barthes 1978 [1967]: 145–7). Yet some texts—for whatever reason—exude permanence, certainty, rootedness.

Our work is the humbling task of learning how commonplaces become what Alex Haley called "source-place[s]." In *Roots*, Kunta Kinte comes to the New World as an ethnographer, observing how American-born Black people lack this source-place. And though there can be no going back home, no finding of the "there there," he appoints himself a proxy for the rootedness that will help Black people transcend "the slave institution" (Raboteau 2004 [1978]). Within the novel, this surrogacy is exemplified by the ancient tradition of "traveling trees," on the outskirts of West African villages. Each day, a different family would be responsible for greeting visitors and escorting them to a hospitality hut. The visitors received food and shelter at no cost until they were ready to continue their journey (Haley 2007 [1976]: 31). Although Kunta Kinte was a stranger in the chaotic New World, he would help his distant relations transcend their estrangement through his own transplanted rootedness.

Scriptures as roots, as source-places, lay the groundwork for new social relationships and a possible promising future. *Roots* as scripture has given way to a tradition of traveling trees, memorials for rootedness. The Alex Haley Museum and Interpretive Center in Henning, Tennessee and the Kunta Kinte-Alex Haley Memorial in Annapolis, Maryland, become sites to briefly point out the transcendence liberationists and others believed to be dormant in the foundational documents of church and state.

Alex Haley Museum and Interpretive Center

Following the success of the novel and miniseries, Haley recovered Palmer House for posterity. With the death of Cynthia Palmer in 1949, the house had long been sold. But Haley used his newfound means to reacquire it (Hinman 2009). On December 14, 1978, Palmer House was listed in the National Register of Historic Places (The Tennessee Department of Tourist Development 2016). With the help of art historians, antique dealers, and his younger brother George, Haley restored each room to its 1920s provenance (B. Johnson personal communication, July 11, 2013).

In 1986, the state of Tennessee collaborated with the family to open Palmer House as the Alex Haley House Museum (The Tennessee Department of Tourist Development 2016). Visitors could not only see the author's source-place, but also memorabilia in testament to the fruit of his labor. Though Haley died in 1992, his legacy continued to blossom at the site. By his request he was interred at a memorial on the front lawn. Docents offer directions to nearby Bethlehem Cemetery, the final resting place of Chicken George Lea. The museum itself has added a permanent exhibit with a replica slave-ship, a media room showing short documentaries on *Roots*, gift shop, and artifacts from Haley's own life. The museum sees its mission as solidifying *Roots'* impact. It hosts writers' workshops, African American history programs, and celebrations of Haley's legacy. In 2009, a new Interpretive Center was added between the House Museum and New Hope CME. The Interpretive Center invites visitors to research their own genealogy, using the Church of Latter Day Saints' "Family Search" software suite (Johnson 2009). The site acts as a gateway through which patrons may discover their own origins and, in turn, rootedness.

Haley would likely approve of the center's use of Latter Day Saint materials and his family lore for this rootwork. In a 1983 article entitled "The Secret of Strong Families," Haley commends the "weekly tradition known as 'Family Night' which is widely practiced by Mormons" (Haley 1983: 114). Despite being a "fourth-generation Methodist" he sees the benefit of "set[ting] aside an hour one night every week to get reacquainted with each other and to work and pray together and exchange candid views." Adopting this tradition might help cultivate a "useful perspective on history…broaden[ed] vistas… [and] shielding…against the racial harshnesses" that so many in America must face (112). One poignant way these lessons came to Haley was through his fifth birthday gift from his family: Grandpa Will Palmer, Grandma Cynthia, father Simon, and mother Bertha gave him a slice of a California redwood tree. It came with dates pinned on corresponding tree rings to chart key historical events.

> For me, I know a tree slice, a symbol of a family's concern and
> love, certainly did implant my boyhood concept of history as a
> drama of people…[a]nd I know that my tree slice gift had the
> further effect of getting me to read all the books that I could as
> my desire grew to find somebody else worthy of yet another
> marker's placement. (Haley 1983: 114)

Haley was learning that he had the power to define kinship and historical significance for himself. Decades after the fact, others can visit
Henning to accomplish the same. Just as Haley received a birthday
gift wrapped with great expectations, he shares his *Roots* as a bicentennial birthday gift to a nation that he expects to reform according
to his image.

Kunta Kinte-Alex Haley Memorial

On a pier at the edge of the Chesapeake Bay, visitors can come to
better appreciate Haley's vision of rootedness. In 1981, citizens of
Annapolis worked with city administrators and the Kunta Kinte-Alex
Haley Foundation to install a plaque commemorating the place's significance (The sculpture group n.d.). The foundation describes the site
as "the only memorial in the country that commemorates the actual
name and place of arrival of an enslaved African," thus "serving as a
symbolic Ellis Island for African Americans" (The Sculpture Group
n.d.; "The Original Plaque" n.d.).

Its impact is best measured by the actions of its opponents and
determination of its supporters. Two days after the dedication ceremony, the plaque was forcefully removed. The vandals only left a
note, "You have been patronized by the KKK" (Cook 2015).[1] Soon
after, the community raised funds for a replacement plaque. The con-
testation of the site itself connotes "the bondage and toil" endured by

---

1   Whether the Ku Klux Klan actually took the plaque is debated by
locals. The idea of leaving a note is not out of the ordinary for the Klan, as
print culture was central to the Christian White nationalist's evangelization
and public witness (Baker 2011: 70–97). The fear left behind is also part of
the Klan's calling card.

Kunta Kinte and countless others. At the same time, its endurance reflects the "character and ceaseless struggle for freedom" of those the plaque honors ("The Original Plaque" n.d.). Later expansion of the site would solidify this spirit.

By 1999, the replacement plaque was joined by a sculpture assemblage of Alex Haley reading a book to three children while gesturing to the Chesapeake Bay (The Sculpture Group, n.d). An interpretive panel notes that Haley is reading *Roots* to children of "diverse ethnic groups" in order to show "how the strength of the human spirit to overcome challenges comes from maintaining strong family connections and pride in one's heritage." As much as the sculpture conveys Haley's overarching message, the scene invites participation. Roughly one million people stop by the memorial as they tour the nearby United States Naval Academy and the colonial-era Maryland State House, just a stone's throw away. The juxtaposition leads visitors to consider the ways in which each is a chapter in the American

Figure 8 An image of the Kunta Kinte-Alex Haley Memorial in Annapolis, Maryland.
Source: Preservation Maryland. CC BY-SA 2.0 https://commons.wikimedia.org/ wiki/File:Kunta_Kinte_Alex_Haley_Memorial_(21601264555).jpg

story. And while one may intimate that the book on Haley's lap is his story, the absence of any inscriptions leaves visitors with the idea of re-reading and delving into their own lives.

This ambiguity is the interpretive space in which readers are to journey. In 2002, the memorial was completed with features to call visitors to action. Across the street from the pier is a courtyard park inlaid with a compass rose pointing to true north. At the compass's center is a map of North America circumscribed with directions for facing toward Europe, Africa, Asia, and South America. A curatorial panel instructs visitors to "stand there and face the direction of their ancestors." Haley lends his source-place to those needing to reconnect with their heritage.

The same curatorial panel recounts Kunta Kinte's journey on the Middle Passage and directs readers to the sculpture assemblage as well as to the "Story Wall," a set of ten ornate "Reconciliation Plaques" spaced intermittently along the pier. Each includes a quotation from

Figure 9 Dock Street Annapolis, Annapolis, MD.
Source: Small Bones. Public Domain https://en.m.wikipedia.org/wiki/
File:Dock_Street_Annapolis.JPG

Roots, a meditation on its significance, a one-word root value summarizing the meditation, and a border engraved with a guiding image. Named for the founder and president of the Kunta Kinte-Alex Haley Foundation, "The Leonard A. Blackshear Walk" provides "a pathway to reconciliation and healing." It narrates the Civil Rights saga as a psychological pilgrimage to America's democratic roots. Paramount to this is the physical walk that transports the reader from a marker of America's complicity in the institution of slavery to grounds from which to pledge to bring liberty and justice for all.

While the plaques illustrate a gripping transformation, the walk's power stems from a dramatic irony. It ends at the exact site where Kunta Kinte is said to have disembarked from the *Lord Ligonier* as well as the spot where Alex Haley peered at their mutual source-place. The memorial offers visitors an opportunity to *take root* and create an integrated America.

The Study of Scriptures and Religion Reconsidered

Roots—as Alex Haley's source-place and the traveling trees it germinated—thrived on a discourse often associated with religion, "scripture." In a post-civil-rights era still struggling to contend with racism, *Roots* at times proved more germane than the unrequited promises of the Bible. By no means did Christianity become unimportant after *Roots*. But in the instances described, Christianity's route to liberative significance had grown dilapidated just as the American Dream was renovated to accommodate the needs of a population which it was not previously designed to include. In the hands of its readers, *Roots* operated as a means to make the commonplace transcendent again.

What I have argued here is that the rhetoric of transcendence means nothing if a text does not help scriptors transcend the problems before them. Analytically, we cannot be satisfied to think of scriptures even as the self-sufficient products of social work. Instead we must press further in identifying scriptures as those ever-productive constructions people maintain to negotiate cultural circumstances—routine in that they no longer appear conspicuous, but *rootinized* in that their absence make all the difference in our worlds. In the examples

Plaque Number	Roots Quotation and Character	Meditation	Root Value	Guiding Imagery
1	"You must hear me now with more than your ears!" – Omoro Kinte	Commemoration of nameless Africans and their New World struggle.	Dedication	A village circle; slave ship; auction block; Underground Railroad; and axe beside broken chain links.
2	"The far-thest-back person they ever talked about was a man they called the 'African.'" – Alex Haley	Haley's *Roots* as an inspiration for all peoples to embrace personal histories and their mutual member-ship in the human family.	Heritage	Outlines of persons from infants to elders.
3	"Share his pain!" – Mandinka Elder	The New World as a product of the Middle Passage, Native America subju-gation, and the indentured labor of Europeans and Asians.	Servitude	Figures working in agricultural, manufac-turing, and industrial settings.
4	"We all suffer. If a man's wise, he learns from it." – Boteng Bediako (Uncle Pompey)	Finding "survival through faith, strength through family, and wisdom through forgiveness."	Perseverance	The ebb and flow of tides.
5	"Behold! The only thing greater than yourself!" – Omoro Kinte	Belief empowers people to endure hardship, succeed in the present, and build for the next generation.	Faith	*Roots*-inspired scene of a father raising a baby to the heav-ens, along with familial scenes inter-spersed with trees.

6	"Your sweet grandma and all of them–they're up there watching you." – Cousin Georgia	"…knowing our family is knowing ourselves…" Values and traditions are the product of ancestral striving.	Family	Sun, moon, heavens, and an extended line of family members.
7	"When you clench your fist, no one can put anything in your hand, nor can your hand pick up anything." – Omoro Kinte	Historical understanding leads to reconciliation and healing.	Forgiveness	Fist hitting through rock; an open hand releasing a dove; arms reaching upward.
8	"We must be in this place as one village!" – Mandinka Elder	A mandate to embrace and love one another and to understand this as connecting the past, present, and future.	Love	A bird's-eye view of numerous village plots and fields.
9	"Things don't ever get better unless you make them better." – Tom Murray	How *Roots* teaches that "only through individual efforts" can the country overcome racism and "remain a beacon of opportunity and hope for oppressed people around the world."	Challenge	New York City skyline; Statue of Liberty; a rocky coast with ocean waves.
10	"Hear me! Though we are of different tribes and tongues, remember we are the same people!" – African Elder	Diversity as America's life-blood and greatest strength.	Diversity	The word "people" translated in over fifty languages.

Figure 10 A Chart of *Roots* Reconciliation Plaques.

mentioned in this chapter, neither the promises of the Bible nor the codified themes of national aspiration seemed to mean much for Black Americans (among others). Yet we can observe how Haley's audacious *Roots* became a way to make the psycho-social spaces of a condemnable, if not hostile, religion and nation habitable.

If the transformative work traditionally associated with "scriptures" exists outside of religious canons, then are all textual engagements relative? My answer is yes. Those accustomed to identifying "scriptures" with the world's religions may throw up their hands in the face of the argument. But what religious studies scholars should acknowledge is that there is so much to understand about the complexities of relativity. In those relationships humans establish the conventions of culture that inspire, shame, parade, and conceal the trappings of our existence.

I am not closing the book on religious studies scholarship, but broadening its outlook, especially regarding the matter of cultural texts. How is it that some texts—despite their commonalities in medium, rhetorics, themes, and politics—take on greater significance for a community? Why do people identify themselves and others in light of some texts and not others? Theorizing the relativity of meaning making and the social physics of our routing is the project of the anthropologist of scriptures.

Religious studies scholars have much to offer here because our field is steeped in the study of rhizomatic branches that have proved so transcendent—relative to scriptors' contexts—that they give off the appearance of being roots—self-sufficient, self-sustaining, self-important. When we no longer take for granted the ludics and language-games of transcendence, we can critically identify the edges of our cultural production. In searching the scriptures, we will find the root of the differences humans strike between themselves and the difference humans hope to make for those people they identify as kindred. The power of scriptures lies in paradox and mystery. And lest we forget, this power, and its elusive and illusive guile, are of our own making.

Conclusion: Rooting Identity

On January 20, 2017, Donald Trump became President of the United States of America. The business mogul campaigned from a conservative, populist platform and took the oath of office with the support of two Bibles. One he had received from his mother when he was a boy. The other belonged to Abraham Lincoln, the same Lincoln Bible with which Barack Obama's second term had been inaugurated, four years ago to the day (McCann 2017). There would be no reference to Alex Haley this time (cf. Sen. Lamar Alexander's remarks noted in the introduction). But, in fact, the conjuring of *Roots* in the previous ceremony makes subsequent appeals to the roots discourse all the more conspicuous.

This Joint Congressional Committee on Inaugural Ceremonies (JCCIC) themed the occasion "Uniquely American." President Trump, who had all but launched his candidacy on a platform of disputing the validity of Barack Obama's American citizenship and Christianity, promised to "Make America Great Again." For the first speech of his presidency, he joined Woodrow Wilson and other isolationists in vowing to put "America First" in policies foreign and domestic (Delving 2017). Campaign promises to ban Muslims, get tough on crime in urban areas, and build a wall on the U.S.-Mexico border would become a cipher for patriotism. His administration's own counsel would decide who qualified as a proper American.

JCCIC member and Democratic Senator Chuck Schumer of New York leveled a subtle warning to the Trump administration's claim to represent the will of the American people. Against the subtext of a popular vote defeat trumped by an Electoral College victory, Senator Schumer referenced a previous moment of national division, the Civil War. Within glosses on the peaceful transition of power, he included an excerpt from the last letter of Union soldier Sullivan Ballou. In

1861, Ballou had taken to the page to leave parting words for his wife before entering what would be the First Battle of Bull Run:

> "If it is necessary that I should fall on the battlefield for my country, I am ready," Ballou wrote. "I have no misgivings about, or lack of confidence in, the cause in which I am engaged, and my courage does not halt or falter. I know how strongly American Civilization now leans upon the triumph of the Government, and how great a debt we owe to those who went before us through the blood and suffering of the Revolution. And I am willing—perfectly willing—to lay down all my joys in this life, to help maintain this Government, and to pay that debt. (Dockterman 2017)

Schumer, like his JCCIC and Senate colleague Lamar Alexander, was calling for Americans to unite in the face of an opposition president. This is the route demanded. But the core value of that unity was left to be signified by the hearers of the word. Under the forty-fifth president of the United States, Americans would once again need to choose with whom and with what they would identify the root of the nation. Schumer turned the country to Ballou's example just as Ballou looked to the founding fathers of the American revolution. In De Certeau's words, America was once again on the brink of a scriptural revolution. Parties were once again fighting for the past so that they might write the future. Schumer's call to save American civilization through the maintenance of a true government would be an anarchical gambit were it not part of the nation's rootinized tradition.

Of note to the anthropologist of scriptures are the conditions under which a similar strategy of laying claim to a nation's roots is not only revolutionary, but a blasphemous affront. In this cultural moment, there may be no greater display of the twisted nature of identity than around those debating the assertion, "Black Lives Matter." Coined by Alicia Garza, Patrisse Cullers, and Opal Tometi in 2012, the social media hashtag questioned the rhizomatically-unique American a priori claim that "all men are created equal." This "self-evident truth" could not ring any more hollow than against the acquittal of George Zimmerman, an ethnically Hispanic, racially White man who admittedly shot and killed an unarmed, Black seventeen-year-old child named Trayvon Martin (Garza 2014). Zimmerman claimed self-defense. Martin could not tell his side of the story. There would be no "life," "liberty," or "pursuit of happiness" for Trayvon. He—not Zimmerman—would be tried and found guilty of doing the wrong thing, being at the wrong place, and existing in the wrong body at the wrong time.

More people would call this a lynching were it not for the scriptural conceit that our founding documents have been so amended as to occlude the ways in which Blackness remains a body problematic in the body politic. Thus the movement's trinity write, "*Rooted* in the experiences of Black people in this country who actively resist our dehumanization, #BlackLivesMatter is a call to action and a response to the virulent anti-Black racism that permeates our society" (emphasis added). Though the nation may choose to remember otherwise, neither Trayvon's death nor the response of these three women could be more American.

It is unclear whether Garza, Cullers, and Tometi identified *Roots* as a resource for their mobilizing efforts, but it is telling how the issue of rootedness surfaces regarding the matter of Black life. In his 2015 hit song "King Kunta," hip hop artist Kendrick Lamar rhymes the agony of uproot and the ecstasy of taking root—in one's circumstances (Lamar 2015).

> B——where you when I was walkin'?
> …Now I run the game, got the whole world talking
> King Kunta
> Everybody wanna cut the legs off him
> King Kunta
> Black man taking no losses, oh yeah

In his read of America through *Roots*, he ascertains that all people route for meaning. Laying claim to rootedness is the privilege of the few and can leave one wounded:

> I'll probably go to jail
> If I shoot at your identity and bounce to the left.

The vulnerability, anxiety, and bravado of "King Kunta" gives respite to listeners—especially Black people—who feel ambivalent about their place in the American experiment. And it goes to show that *Roots* still mattered to a generation born long after Haley's Comet had passed over. To this very point, in 2016, the History Channel produced a reboot of the *Roots* miniseries, which critics heralded as *Roots* for the Black Lives Matter generation. Simulcast on Lifetime and A&E during Memorial Day, the new *Roots* reimagined the familiar beats of the novel. The aggregate media review website, *Metacritic*, tabulated "universal acclaim" for the series (*"Roots* 2016").

With the emergence of second-screen (computer) and third-screen (mobile devices) technologies since the 1977 miniseries, the 2016 version promoted an integrative media strategy to retell Haley's story. The show promoted itself as an experience and launched an aggressive public relations campaign across social media. On the *Roots* website, viewers could upload their own headshot to be embossed with "I am Kunta," in emulation of promotional materials featuring the show's breakout star, Malachi Kirby (History 2016). Audiences sharing real-time musings under the *Roots* hashtag (#ROOTS) spiked overall usage (i.e. "trended") on both Facebook and Twitter during the run. And the influential organic network of African American Twitter users known as "Black Twitter" devised hashtags such as #KuntasKin to proudly identify with the protagonist.

As should be expected of any reiteration of a scriptural text, producers of the 2016 miniseries wrestled with the task of revering the source material while making enhancements. This included an improvement in production techniques, greater attention to historical detail, and a more substantive role of women within the narrative. For our purposes, the most poignant change is to the root metaphor that transcends the transatlantic and generational divide of Kunta's kin.

In Haley's novel and the original miniseries, Kunta shares Mandinka words from his "source place" with his daughter Kizzy. The biological spreading of seed is joined with a semantic generation of rootedness—increasingly recessed—but present enough to find in Haley's historiographic awakening. The 2016 miniseries is more radical in its deploy of roots. Whereas Haley conveyed the essence of rootedness through the sound of mysterious Mandinka words, the reboot passed it on through its musical soundtrack, produced by Ahmir "Questlove" Thompson, co-founder of the hip hop group, The Roots ("'Roots' Cast Announced, Questlove Speaks on the Musical Theme" 2015).

As a device, a recurring, routine melody with which audiences can identify creates a commonplace for narrative direction. But *Roots* further operationalizes the musical theme to make a powerful statement about the thrust of Haley's discourse. Questlove explains how its African origins establish a baseline for a pre-scribed society, a world where Black bodies have dignity. The theme is stowed away in the Middle Passage and, through Kunta and his slave-born friend "Fiddler," finds an afterlife in uplifting the spirits of the protagonists in each generation. The heroic soundtrack plays beyond the fourth wall to help audience members face a world that would otherwise have them shaken, unmoored, and unrooted.

The series plays on the assumption of music as a universal language that transcends the rules of narrative space, time, and language. In the first act, Binta Kinte sings the melody as a lullaby to a young Kunta. In colonial America, when being "trained" for his master by Fiddler, Kunta hears the older slave fumbling his way through the tune on the violin. Kunta immediately recognizes it as the one sign that all is not lost in the New World. Fiddler explains that his own grandmother sang the song before his sale and that it has stuck with him, more or less, ever since. It also reminds him of an old man from that time that played an African-looking guitar, which Kunta tells him was likely a *kintango*. Fiddler rebukes Kunta for dredging up "too many things tucked away real deep inside." But Binta's lullaby becomes the root of their new friendship. It is a reminder that they are the sons of mothers, that they, too, are human. It is Kunta's most precious saving grace, until his wedding with the house cook, Bell, and the birth of their child.

After Bell gives birth to a *girl*child, Kunta scouts out a space at the edge of the Waller's land and invites Fiddler to join him and his daughter there under the cover of a starry night. Kunta adapts the Mandinka naming ceremony for the new terrain. Usually it is done with the father and child, but Kunta stresses the importance of familial bonds, saying to Fiddler "...if you play my mother's song, then she will be with me, too." A nearby night patrol interrupts the ceremony before it can begin. And Fiddler sacrifices his life so that Kunta and the child can return to the "safety" of Waller property. Kunta manages to perform the ceremony under duress, raising her to the heavens, saying "Behold, the only thing greater than yourself."

Contra the meaning of her name, "stay put," Kizzy is eventually sold to the plantation of Tom Lea, but not before learning her heritage and her grandmother's song. She sings the lullaby to her baby, Chicken George, so that the offspring of the slave-master's rape can become the son of a proud African. And despite George's wayward routing, he knows that its notes are rooted in something and somewhere bigger than himself. Decades later, when he is all grown and has children of his own from whom he too had been separated, the song is there.

The night that George is reunited with his family at the Murray plantation in North Carolina, the master is throwing an unrelated soiree in the big house. The guests are dancing inside, but the Southern waltz echoes outside for the slaves to hear. Chicken George turns to his wife in disbelief, "That's my mama's song." Matilda replies, "Every band in the country plays it now. It's changed some but always the same." Just as Kunta had passed it on to Kizzy, Fiddler had shared it with other enslaved Black musicians who played it until it became standard repertoire for all ensembles—Black and White alike. Chicken George's heart is warmed. "I can hear Mama Kizzy humming it." He laughs at the thought that "these folks don't know where it come from." "Well, we do, Mornin' Dove," Matilda replies.

In response to historiographic critiques of the novel and the original miniseries, the 2016 telling goes to great lengths to sharpen the precision of its portrayals. Juffure is no longer just a small Mandinka village along the Gambian River, but a massive trading port at the intersection of British trade and local kingship. Kunta Kinte only reluctantly "jumps de broom," rebuffing the ceremony as a European invention and a mockery to African culture. In this revisiting of *Roots*, the production team labors to get the history even more "right" by trying to eliminate spaces of ambivalence. The contrast between Africa and the West is made more stark. And the protragonists are the ones adept at conscientiously traversing the divide. The tune for them is not just another expression. It means something. Hence, the social theorist can redescribe Matilda and George's exchange as a metaquestion about identity: when did roots become so important and more important than routes?

The answer cannot be isolated to a single Ur-moment, but we would do well to train an eye on where *Roots* begins, the eighteenth century. While Kunta is learning to count rains, Europe is testing the waters of imperial expansion. And for all their bluster for glory, gold, and God, the emerging nations are experiencing devastating growing pains (Pagden 1995: 132–40). Their forays away from the metropolis and into Asia, the Americas, and Africa stretch the limits of their nationalist ideologies, leaving colonists with a pathology diagnosed by late Enlightenment thinker Denis Diderot.

> In proportion as the distance from the capital increases, this mask detaches itself; it falls off on the frontiers; and between one hemisphere and another, is totally lost. When a man crosses the line, he is neither an Englishman, a Dutchman, a Frenchman, a Spaniard, or a Portuguese. He preserves nothing of his country, except the principles and prejudices which give a sanction to his conduct, or furnish him with an excuse for it. Servile when he is weak, and oppressive when he is strong; eager to acquire wealth, and to enjoy it. And capable of all the enormities which can contribute most speedily to the completion of his designs; he is a domestic tiger again let loose in the woods, and who is again seized with the thrift of blood. Such have all the Europeans indiscriminately shown themselves in the regions of the New World, where they have been actuated with a common rage, the passion for gold. (Rayant 1798 [1770]: 264)[1]

Successful colonists, Adam Hastings writes, would learn to cope through their legitimizing structures of "clergy, farmers, lawyers, merchants, writers, as well as members of a court or cabinet" (Hastings 1997: 24). The importance of their interconnectedness would be made visible in the course of modern Europe's numerous civil wars

---

1   Rayant had many contributors to the multivolume series. The portion included here was written by Denis Diderot.

and revolutions—the outgrowth of people enforcing their vision of the proper mode in the present moment.

A century earlier, Thomas Hobbes summoned "the leviathan" to help England imagine the sort of culturalist beast that could evoke such fear, an entity that would draw out the loyalty and deference required by nationhood. And as Britain and other European powers tried to settle the strange New World, they doubled down on their mutually-constructed cultural constellations by orienting the entire structure toward a single north star to fill the void of identificatory uncertainty. Kunta's kin had a name for their solution to the unmeasured, unchecked, unnamed nothingness to which Diderot alludes, the rise of the *toubob*. Americans would come to know it as Whiteness. Though never separated from Hastings' offices nor discourses of the terroristic exclusionism (the outlawing of Kunta's African—Mandinka—Muslim ways in America), ableism (the maiming of Kunta Kinte), sexism (the rape of Kizzy), classism (the commodification of Chicken George), it was the presumptive logic of race that defined and ultimately identified the order of all manner of thing, including "the Negroid."

What makes Alex Haley's intervention such a fascinating case study are the means by which he over-writes the logic of Whiteness in the American experiment. His literary legacy shows a deep awareness of the construction of Whiteness, so much so that in the posthumously completed novel about Haley's paternal grandmother, *Queen*, his great-grandfather was an Irish-American Confederate soldier whose family had manifested their destiny westward with the help of a horse named Leviathan and was injured at the First Battle of Bull Run (Haley and Stevens 1993: 180, 414). In *Roots*, Haley sees White Americans' dependence on history and writing and determines that Black people—well-acquainted with the effects of loss—need more than their own route through the New World. To change their subhuman status, their routes must be rootinized into the consciousness of all those with whom they hope to integrate. Alex Haley attempted—rather successfully—to use his narrative to write a more ingenious, integrationist American history. For post-civil-rights Americans, *Roots* is a significant cultural product, one with characters many can identify with. *Roots* matters as a scripture because it exemplifies a cultural production so invasive that it often arbitrates the very terms of identity, specifically in light of the predominant discourse of race.

Roots, as an allegory for identity, is a song that has struck a chord with many, but it is not intrinsically for everyone. Discursively it operates as an anthem of the folk, the culture, the rooted. And White people can sing along and dance to it, but they can only add to its harmony if they identify themselves within Haley's narrative—an American whose transcendence is one way or another rooted in the transgression and transcendence of Black bodies. The "Negro" is no longer the problem. New Orleans' fiftieth mayor, Mitch Landrieu, made an overture toward this work in his leadership over the removal of a memorial to Confederate General Robert E. Lee from the city's public square. On this occasion he said:

> The soul of our beloved City is *deeply rooted in a history* that has evolved over thousands of years; *rooted in a diverse people* who have been here together every step of the way—for both good and for ill. It is a history that holds in its heart the stories of Native Americans: the Choctaw, Houma Nation, the Chitimacha. Of Hernando de Soto, Robert Cavelier, Sieur de La Salle, the Acadians, the Islenos, the enslaved people from Senegambia, Free People of Color, the Haitians, the Germans, both the empires of France and Spain. The Italians, the Irish, the Cubans, the South and Central Americans, the Vietnamese and so many more. You see: New Orleans is truly a city of many nations, a melting pot, a bubbling cauldron of many cultures. There is no other place quite like it in the world that so eloquently exemplifies the uniquely American motto: *e pluribus unum*—out of many we are one. (Landrieu 2017, emphasis added)

It is unclear whether Mayor Landrieu spoke with Alex Haley in mind, but his remarks were all the more compelling because of *Roots*' success. As Chicken George and Matilda say when discussing the roots melody persistence through history, "These folks don't know where it come from… Well, we do."

By studying Alex Haley's *Roots* as scripture, we come to *recognize scriptures as living narratives*. As they were for Haley and his readers, roots are how we humans come to understand ourselves within the world. With them, we establish kinship and differences with one another. With their knowledge we construct the world anew, making the human condition tenable and the human experience meaningful. Like roots, scriptures are a twisted construct that we struggle to live with and without. We live and die by our roots' effectiveness. We obsess over techniques to improve their usefulness, and then defend them from those who might cut them with criticism. And scriptures live on beyond our creative uses and intent. Just as Haley's *Roots* became America's roots, scriptures get taken up by subsequent generations to do their work in new places and moments.

Furthermore, *Roots* does not easily afford readers to remain in the dark about the power of our operational acts of identification. In analyzing the rootwork in and around Haley's text, we arrive at a paradigm for conjugating rootedness. Uprooting, routing, and taking root explain the moves postured in the identity formation. With the anthropology of scriptures, I challenge us to press our studies of culture to say more about the social effects of people's significations.

Identifying Roots interrogates the terms on which we determine what matters. It is an order of analysis unwilling to settle for truisms, commonplaces, or tradition. Instead it advances a kind of fieldwork into the very media through which we come to know anything and everything. At some level Alex Haley determined that no amount of social, economic, or psychological uplift could assure that he—as a Black person in America—could ever lay hold to "life, liberty, and the pursuit of happiness" without a caveat. As much as audiences remember *Roots* as a testament to "all men [being] created equal," one could just as easily read the narrative as generations of evidence to the contrary.

Alex Haley had grounds for a forceful jeremiad against the nation. He was a contemporary to Malcolm X, after all. And though Haley did not suffer the blunt racial discrimination against which Malcolm frequently railed, Haley knew the sting of never being quite enough in the eyes of prejudiced but well-meaning White people. In fact, it was the arbitrary sometimes-ness of racism that was the most frustrating aspect of the United States. That was the context in which Haley labored to identify and be identified with the best that America had to offer. There is an asceticism in his patriotism. If he could find good in the nation and praise it, the nation might reciprocate by finding him good and praiseworthy.

Regardless of whether one agrees with Haley's politics, his resilient commitment to a racially integrated America surfaces some of the more complicated aspects of identity formation. For instance, Haley seems hardly surprised by the ambivalence of cultural standards. He does not feign shock that White people and Black people can live in the same country and seemingly inhabit different social worlds. Also—whether in his critique of Malcolm or the advancement of his own integrationist agenda—he can imagine a scenario in which sympathetic figures (in his case Black people or Americans, in general) could act as oppressive agents. Hence he encourages people to take hold of strong roots that will be unshaken by the twists and turns of social favor. That is how one knows whether they are approaching who and what is good or who and what is praiseworthy.

Haley's boldness in identifying roots—and identifying them for the taking—reminds scholars that once we determine the scriptures at play in a setting, we should quickly prepare to observe how people will arbitrate social standing in and through them. In modern America, Haley revealed history and writing as cultural master-texts with which people make claims about important matters. Time and again, legible historiography appeared to make a difference. And in crafting a novel mythology with familiar media and tropes, Haley rooted himself in the American self-understanding. He became a nation's griot. His fame was not without controversy, nor was it without sacrifice. The words responsible for his rise were also a factor in his fall. And the work in making Haley a household name made him estranged to his loved ones. But as Haley identified for himself, the anthropology of scriptures is what makes all the uprooting, routing, and taking root worth it.

This project does not intend to be the last word on Alex Haley's *Roots* or more importantly the anthropology of scriptures. If anything, it should be read as an extended prologue to deeper questioning about the so-called "nature" of identity. I do not doubt that the same case for the study of identity formation could be made without an invocation of "scripture," just as I could have said as much about the anthropology of scriptures by focusing on some example from a world religion.

But the root of the matter has never been a definitive datum. It is the peculiar reality that we have grown so comfortable with our own identificatory categories that we have forgotten the radical claims they make on the value of human bodies. Sometimes we are longing to remember. Sometimes we are doing everything to forget.

I still wonder whether we can perceive how much stock we place in our identities unless one strikes at our roots. None of us can do well without them it seems, and it behooves us to understand the stakes. But when we find ourselves captivated in such a drama, we may realize that identifying with a scripture is not only valuable, but also comes at great price. When do we care enough to ask who will pay? The answer is, when it matters to us.

Bibliography

A Different World. 1990. "Perhaps Love," Season 3, Episode 25. Directed by Debbie Allen. Produced by Carsey-Werner Productions. Originally aired May 3.

Aberjhani. 2003. "Harlem Riots." In *Encyclopedia of the Harlem Renaissance*, edited by Aberjhani and Sandra L. West, 144–6. New York: Facts on File.

Achebe, Chinua. 1997 [1965]. "English and the African Writer." *Transition* 75/76: 342–9. https://doi.org/10.2307/2935429

Alex Haley Papers. Hamilton College Archives. Clinton, NY.

Alex Haley Roots Foundation. 2017. *Stories of America*. http://www.alexhaley.com/stories_of_america.htm (accessed July 8, 2017).

Allen, Robert L. 1976. "The Black Scholar Interviews: Alex Haley." *The Black Scholar* 8(1): 33–40. https://doi.org/10.1080/00064246.1976.11413857

Althusser, Louis. 2014 [1971]. *On the Reproduction of Capitalism: Ideology and Ideological State Apparatuses*. Translated by G.M. Goshgarian. New York: Verso.

American Anthropological Association. 1997. "AAA's Response to OMB Directive 15: Race and Ethnic Standards for Federal Statistics and Administrative Reporting." *Race: Are We So Different?* http://www.understandingrace.org/about/response.html (accessed January 15, 2016).

Anderson, Benedict. 2006 [1983]. *Imagined Communities: Reflections on the Origin and Spread of Nationalism.* London: Verso Books.

Anderson. Victor. 1995. *Beyond Ontological Blackness: An Essay on African America Religious and Cultural Criticism.* New York: Continuum.

Anne Romaine Collection. MS2032. University of Tennessee Libraries, Knoxville, Special Collections.

Anzaldúa, Gloria. 1987. *Borderlands/La Frontera*. San Francisco: Spinsters/Aunt Lute.

Appiah, Kwame Anthony. 1992. "Introduction." In *Things Fall Apart (1958)*, by Chinua Achebe, ix–xviii. New York: Alfred A. Knopf.

Associated Press. 1985. "Berea College Students Help Author Alex Haley Research His Next Book." *Daily News*, June 30.

Baker, H. Robert. 2012. "The Fugitive Slave Clause and the Antebellum Constitution." *Law and History Review* 30(4): 1133–74. https://doi.org/10.1017/S0738248012000697

Baker, Kelly J. 2011. *The Gospel According to the Klan: The KKK's Appeal to Protestant America, 1915–1930*. Lawrence, KS: University of Kansas Press.

Baldwin, James. 1976. "How One Black Man Came to Be an American: A Review of *Roots*." *New York Times*, September 26, 1976. http://www.nytimes.com/books/98/03/29/specials/baldwin-roots.html
_____. 1993 [1962]. *The Fire Next Time*. First Vintage International Edition. New York: Vintage Books.

Ball, Erica L. and Kellie Carter Jackson, eds. 2017. *Reconsidering* Roots: *Race, Politics, and Memory.* Athens: University of Georgia Press.

Barthes, Roland. 1978 [1967]. *The Death of the Author*. Translated by Stephen Heath. New York: Hill and Wang.

Bauer, Margaret D. 2005. "'[He] Didn't Come Here on the Mayflower': A Defense of Alex Haley's Roots." *Crossroads: A Southern Culture Annual*: 377–401.

Baugh, John. 1999. *Out of the Mouths of Slaves: African American Language and Educational Malpractice.* Austin: University of Texas Press.

Bayart, Jean-François. 2005. *The Illusion of Cultural Identity*. Translated by Steven Randall, Janet Roitman, Cynthia Schoch, and Jonathan Derrick. Chicago: University of Chicago Press.

Baye, Betty Winston. 1992. "Alex Haley's Roots Revisited." *Essence*, February 1.

Beam, Alex. 1998. "The Prize Fight over Alex Haley's Tangled 'Roots.'" *Boston Globe*, October 30.

Bell, Marty. 1977. "Alex Haley: Tale of a Talker." *New York Magazine*, February 28.

Benjamin, Walter. 1936. "The Work of Art in the Age of Mechanical Reproduction." Translated by Harry Zohn. *Marxists Internet Archive*. https://www.marxists.org/reference/subject/philosophy/works/ge/benjamin.htm (accessed July 7, 2017).

Bhaba, Homi. 1984. "Of Mimicry and Man: The Ambivalence of Colonial Discourse." *October* 28: 125–33. http://www.jstor.org/stable/778467

Bielo, James S. 2009a. "Introduction." In *The Social Life of Scriptures: Cross-Cultural Perspectives on Biblicism*, edited by James S. Bielo, 1–9. New Brunswick: Rutgers.

_____. 2009b. "Textual Ideology, Textual Practice: Evangelical Bible Reading in Group Study." In *The Social Life of Scriptures: Cross-Cultural*

Perspectives on Biblicism, edited by James S. Bielo, 157–75. New Brunswick: Rutgers.

Bird. J.B. 2017. *Roots: U.S. Serial Drama* [Online]. Museum of Broadcast Communications. http://www.museum.tv/eotv/roots.htm (accessed June 13, 2017).

Blackside, Inc. 1988. Interview with Alex Haley [Full Unedited Transcript]. *Eyes on the Prize 2*. October 24. Henry Hampton Collection, Film and Media Archive, Washington University Libraries.

Blackstone, Andrea. 2017. "The History of Grove Street Magazine." *The Alex Haley Roots Foundation*. http://www.alexhaley.com/grove_street.htm (accessed January 15, 2017).

Blayney, Michael Steward. 1986. "*Roots* and the Noble Savage." *North Dakota Quarterly* 54(1): 1–17. Republished in *Twentieth-Century Literature Criticism*, Vol. 157, edited by Linda Pavlovski. Detroit: Gale, 2004. Literature Resource Center. Gale Document Number: GALE|H1420056554 (accessed June 17, 2013).

Blight, David W. 2001. *Race and Reunion: The Civil War in American Memory.* Cambridge, MA: Harvard University Press.

Blyth, Caroline. 2011. "Responding to the Radical in RIOT Bible." *Postscripts* 7(3): 295–303. https://doi.org/10.1558/post.v7i3.28302

Bodnar, John. 1985. *The Transplanted: A History of Immigrants in Urban America*. Bloomington, IN: Indiana University Press.

Bogle, Donald. 2001. *Toms, Coons, Mulattoes, Mammies, and Bucks: An Interpretive History of Blacks in American Films*. Fourth Edition. New York: Continuum.

Bonetti, Kay. 1992. "An Interview with Margaret Walker Alexander." *The Missouri Review* 15(1): 112–31. https://doi.org/10.1353/mis.1992.0022

Bourdieu, Pierre. 1977. *Outline of a Theory of Practice*. Translated by Richard Nice. Cambridge, UK: Cambridge University Press. https://doi.org/10.1017/CBO9780511812507

_____. 1997 (1986). "The Forms of Capital." Translated by Richard Nice. In *Education: Culture, Economy, Society*, edited by A.H. Halsey, H. Lauder, P. Brown, and Amy Stuart Wells, 46–58. New York: Oxford University Press.

Bowers, Detine L. 1992. "Disintegrating Roots: African American Life and Culture Returns to the Auction Block." *Black Scholar* 22(4): 2–5. https://doi.org/10.1080/00064246.1992.11413053

Boyd, Herb. 1993. "More on the Village Voice's Hatchet Job on Alex Haley." *New York Amsterdam News*, March 6.

Boyz n the Hood. 1991. Directed by John Singleton. Columbia Pictures.

Branch, Taylor. 2007. *Pillar of Fire: America in the King Years 1963–1965.* New York: Simon & Schuster.

Braun, Jay. 2012. "Alex Haley—From Famous to Fraud When the Truth Came Out." *Yahoo! Voices.* http://voices.yahoo.com/shared/print.shtml?content_type=article&content_type_id=1437241 (accessed May 15, 2014).

Buijizen, Moniek and Patti M. Valkenburg. 2004. "Developing a Typology of Humor in Audiovisual Media." *Media Psychology* 6(2): 147–67. http://dx.doi.org/10.1207/s1532785xmep0602_2

Burton, LeVar. 2013. Twitter, November 6, 9:34 PM. https://twitter.com/levarburton/status/398292404950011904?s=20

Buxton, L.H. Dudley. 1935. "The 'Australoid' and 'Negroid' Races." *Anthropos* 30(3): 343–50.

Cana, Frank Richardson. 1911. "Mandingo," *Encyclopedia Britannica* [Online]. https://en.wikisource.org/wiki/1911_Encyclopædia_Britannica/Mandingo (accessed June 14, 2017).

Cannon, Reuben. 2014. Interview by Adrienne Faillace. *Archive of American Television.* North Hollywood, CA. http://www.emmytvlegends.org/interviews/shows/palmerstown-usa (accessed July 7, 2017).

Capers, Bennett. 2011. "Crime, Legitimacy, Our Criminal Network, and *The Wire.*" *The Ohio State Journal of Criminal Law* 8: 459–71.

Carman, John. 2002. "ABC Rejects Its Miniseries / NBC, Ironically, to Celebrate Silver Anniversary of Miniseries." *SF Gate*, January 16. https://www.sfgate.com/entertainment/article/ABC-rejects-its-Roots-NBC-ironically-to-2884048.php (accessed April 6, 2020).

Castelli, Elizabeth A. 2010. "The Philosophers' Paul in the Frame of the Global: Some Reflections." *South Atlantic Quarterly* 109(4): 653–76. https://doi.org/10.1215/00382876-2010-011

Chappelle's Show. 2004. Season 1, Episode 3. Directed by Bobcat Goldthwait. DVD. Hollywood: Paramount Home Video. Originally aired February 5, 2003.

"Chicken George Made Sure People Wouldn't Quit." 1977. *The News Journal*, Wilmington, Delaware, July 25.

Chidester, David. 1996. *Savage Systems: Colonialism and Comparative Religion in South Africa.* Charlottesville, VA: University of Virginia Press.

Chideya, Farai. 2007. "Thirty Years of Roots." *NPR: News and Notes*, June 4. http://www.npr.org/templates/story/story.php?storyId=10706524 (accessed July 7, 2017).

Chireau, Yvonne. 2003. *Black Magic: African American Religion and Conjuring Tradition.* Berkeley, CA: University of California Press. https://doi.org/10.1525/california/9780520209879.001.0001

_____. 2008. "Conjuring Scriptures and Engendering Healing Traditions." In *Theorizing Scriptures: New Critical Orientations to a Cultural Phenomenon*, edited by Vincent L. Wimbush, 119–27. New Brunswick: Rutgers University Press.

Chrisman, Robert. 1977. "*Roots*: Rebirth of the Slave Mentality." *The Black Scholar* 8(7): 41–2. https://doi.org/10.1080/00064246.1977.11413905

Clark, Emily Suzanne. 2016. *A Luminous Brotherhood: Afro-Creole Spiritualism in Nineteenth-Century New Orleans.* Chapel Hill, NC: University of North Carolina Press.

Clifford, James A. 1997. *Routes: Travel and Translation in the Late Twentieth Century*. Cambridge, MA: Harvard University Press.

Coates, Ta-Nehisi. 2015. *Between the World and Me.* New York: Speigel & Grau.

_____. 2017. "The Lost Cause Rides Again." *The Atlantic*, August 4. https://www.theatlantic.com/entertainment/archive/2017/08/no-confederate/535512/

Cole, Alan. 2005. *Text as Father: Paternal Seductions in Early Mahayana Buddhist Literature.* Berkeley, CA: University of California Press. https://doi.org/10.1525/california/9780520242760.001.0001

Coleman, Larry G. 1984. "Black Comic Performance in the African Diaspora: A Comparison of the Comedy of Richard Pryor and Paul Keens-Douglas." *Journal of Black Studies* 15(1): 67–78. https://doi.org/10.1177/002193478401500107

Combine Services. 1978. "Alex Haley Settles Suit Out of Court." *Schenectady Gazette*, December 14.

Coming to America. 1988. Directed by John Landis. DVD. Hollywood: Paramount Home Video.

Community. 2011. "Intermediate Documentary Filmmaking." Season 2, Episode 16. Directed by Joe Russo. DVD. Culver City, CA: Sony Pictures Entertainment. Originally aired February 17, 2011.

Conan, Neal. 2012. "Henry Louis Gates Jr.: A Life Spent Tracing Roots." *NPR: Talk of the Nation*, May 8. http://m.npr.org/news/Books/152273032 (accessed July 7, 2017).

Cone, James H. 2012 [1969]. *Black Theology and Black Power*. Maryknoll, NY: Orbis Books.

Cook, Chase. 2015. "Could Ego Alley Repairs Solve the Mystery of the Kunta Kinte Plaque?" *Capital Gazette* [Maryland], November 30. http://www.capitalgazette.com/news/ph-ac-cn-kunta-kinte-plaque-1201-20151130-story.html (accessed July 5, 2017).

Cornelius, Janet D. 1992. *When I Can Read My Title Clear: Literacy, Slavery, and Religion in the Antebellum South.* Columbia, SC: University of South Carolina Press.

Cox, LaWanda. 1981. *Lincoln and Black Freedom: A Study in Presidential Leadership.* Columbia, SC: University of South Carolina Press, 1981.

Crouch, Stanley. 2002. "The 'Roots' Of Haley's Great Fraud." *New York Daily News*, January 17. http://articles.nydailynews.com/2002-01-17/news/18200142_1_alex-haley-hoax-plagiarism (accessed May 13, 2014).

Curtis IV, Edward E. 2006. *Black Muslim Religion in the Nation of Islam, 1960–1975.* Chapel Hill, NC: The University of North Carolina Press. https://doi.org/10.5149/9780807877449_curtis

Curtis IV, Edward E. and Danielle Brune Sigler, eds. 2009. *The New Black Gods: Arthur Huff Fauset and the Study of African American Religions.* Bloomington, IN: Indiana University Press.

Daemmrich, JoAnn. 1992. "Alex Haley's Children: Haley's Children Keep the Legacy of 'Roots' Alive." *The Baltimore Sun*, September 24. http://articles.baltimoresun.com/1992-09-24/features/1992268018_1_alex-haley-haley-died-kunta-kinte (accessed July 7, 2017).

Dain, Bruce. 2002. *A Hideous Monster of the Mind: American Race Theory in the Early Republic.* Cambridge, MA: Harvard University Press, 2002.

Dates, Jannette L. and Carolyn A. Stroman. 2001. "Portrayals of Families of Color on Television." In *Television and the American Family.* Second Edition, 207–28. Mahwah, NJ: Lawrence Erlbaum Associates, Inc.

Davé, Shilpa S. 2013. *Indian Accents: Brown Voice and Racial Performance in American Television and Film.* Champaign: University of Illinois. https://doi.org/10.5406/illinois/9780252037405.001.0001

De Certeau, Michel. 1984. *The Practice of Everyday Life.* Berkeley, CA: University of California Press.

_____. 1988 [1975]. *The Writing of History.* Translated by Tom Conley. New York: Columbia University Press.

De Saussure, Ferdinand. 1966 [1916]. *Course in General Linguistics*, edited by Charles Bally and Albert Sechehaye, in collaboration with Albert Reidlinger, translated with an introduction and notes by Wade Baskin. New York: McGraw-Hill.

Deleuze, Gilles and Felix Guattari. 1987 [1980]. *A Thousand Plateaus: Capitalism and Schizophrenia.* Minneapolis: University of Minnesota Press [Online]. http://projectlamar.com/media/A-Thousand-Plateaus.pdf (accessed June 13, 2017).

Delmont, Matthew F. 2016. *Making* Roots: *A Nation Captivated.* Berkeley, CA: University of California Press.

Delving, Ron. 2017. "Trump Vows Policy Vision of 'America First,' Recalling Phrase's Controversial Past." *NPR*, January 21. http://www. npr.org/2017/01/21/510877650/trump-vows-policy-vision-of-america-first-recalling-phrases-controversial-past (accessed July 5, 2017).

Department of Religious Studies at the University of Alabama. 2017. "A Tale of Prepositions and Conjunctions." *Studying Religion* in *Culture*. https://religion.ua.edu/links/studying-religion-in-culture/ (accessed July 7, 2017).

Derrida, Jacques. 1995 [1993]. "Passions: An Oblique Offering." In *On the Name*, edited by Thomas Dutoit, translated by David Wood, John P. Leavey, Jr., and Ian McLeod, 3–34. Stanford: Stanford University.

Despoli, Darren. 2017a. *Alex Haley Tribute Site*. http://www.alex-haley.com/alex_haley_articles.htm (accessed July 8, 2017).

_____. 2017b. "Once Upon a Vision: The Story of Berea, 1854–1903." *Alex Haley Tribute Site*. http://www.alex-haley.com/once_upon_a_vision_the_berea_story.htm (accessed July 8, 2017).

Diary of a Mad Black Woman. 2005. Written by Tyler Perry. Lionsgate Films.

Djedje, Jacqueline Cogdell. *Fiddling in West Africa: Watching the Spirit in Fulbe, Hausa, and Dagamba Cultures*. Bloomington, IN: Indiana University Press, 2008.

Dockterman, Eliana. 2017. "The Story Behind the Civil War Letter Read by Chuck Schumer at the Inauguration." *TIME*, January 20. http://time.com/4641169/trump-inauguration-sullivan-ballou/ (accessed July 7, 2017).

Douglass, Frederick. 2003 [1845]. *Narrative of the Life of Frederick Douglass, an American Slave*. New York: Barnes and Noble Books.

Du Bois, W.E.B. 2007 [1903]. "The Talented Tenth." In *The Negro Problem: Booker T. Washington, W.E.B. Du Bois, Charles W. Chesnutt, Wilford H. Smith, H.T. Kealing, Paul Laurence Dunbar, and T. Thomas Fortune*, edited by Jim Manis. The Electronic Classics, Pennsylvania State University.

_____. 2007 [1920]. *Darkwater: Voices From Within the Veil*. New York: Cosimo Books.

_____. 2014 [1903]. *The Souls of Black Folk*, Dover Thrift Editions. Minola, NY: Dover Publications.

Dudajek, Dave. 1993. "Local Friends of Haley Defend Work." *Observer-Dispatch*, Utica, NY, February 29.

Due, Tananarive. 2000. *The Black Rose: The Dramatic Story of Madame C.J. Walker, America's First Black Female Billionaire*. New York: Random House.

Dundes, Alan. 1996. "'Jumping the Broom': On the Origin and Meaning of an African American Wedding Custom." *The Journal of American Folklore* 109(433): 324–9. https://doi.org/10.2307/541535

Dyson, Michael Eric. 1995. *Making Malcolm: The Myth and Meaning of Malcolm.* New York: Oxford University Press.

———. 2007. "Haley's Comet: A Special Introduction to *Roots*." In *Roots: The Saga of an American Family.* Thirtieth Anniversary Edition, ix–xi. New York: Vanguard Press.

Edwards, Ben. 2010. Leather Bound First Edition of *Roots* from the Collection of Ben Edwards. Photograph.

Eisenstadt, S.N. (ed.) 1986. *The Origins & Diversity of Axial Age Civilizations.* Albany: State University of New York Press.

Everybody Hates Chris. 2009. Season 4, Episode 5. Directed by Jerry Levine. [DVD]. Hollywood: Paramount Home Media Distribution. Originally aired October 31, 2008.

Executive Board of the American Anthropologist Association. 1998. "Statement on 'Race.'" May 17. http://www.aaanet.org/stmts/racepp.htm (accessed July 7, 2017).

Fallace, Adrienne. 2014. "Reuben Cannon Discusses Casting 'Palmerston, U.S.A.'" October 17. *Archive of American Television.* http://www. emmytvlegends.org/interviews/shows/palmerstown-usa# (accessed July 15, 2017).

Fanon, Frantz. 2008 [1952]. *Black Skin, White Masks.* Translated by Richard Philcox. New York: Grove Press.

Faucett, Arthur Huff. 1944. *Black Gods and the Metropolis: Negro Religious Cults of the Urban North.* Philadelphia: University of Philadelphia.

Federal Bureau of Investigation. 1962. "1.60—Memo from M. A. Jones to Deloach, re: Alfred Balk," October 9 [FBI File on Alex Haley]. Anne Romaine Collection, MS2032. University of Tennessee, Knoxville, Special Collections.

Fernandez, Ramona. 2001. *Imagining Literacy: Rhizomes of Knowledge in American Culture and Literature.* Austin: University of Texas Press.

Fisher, Murray. 1993 [1977]. "A Candid Conversation with the Author of the America Saga 'Roots.'" In *Alex Haley: The Playboy Interviews*, edited by Murray Fisher, 384–436. New York: Ballantine Books.

Fisher, Murray, ed. 1993. *Alex Haley: The Playboy Interviews.* New York: Ballantine Books.

Foley, Neil. 1997. *The White Scourge: Mexicans, Blacks, and Poor Whites in Texas Cotton Culture.* Austin, University of Texas Press.

Folkert, Kendall W. 1989. "The 'Canons' of Scripture." In *Rethinking Scripture: Essays from a Comparative Perspective*, edited by Miriam Levering, 170–9. Albany: State University of New York Press.

"Forum: A Symposium on *Roots*." 1977. *The Black Scholar* 8(7).

Foucault, Michel. 1994 [1963]. *The Birth of the Clinic: An Archaeology of Medical Perception.* Translated by A.M. Sheridan Smith. New York: Vintage Books.

_____. 1995 [1975]. *Discipline and Punish: The Birth of the Prison.* Translated by Alan Sheridan. New York: Vintage Books.

_____. 2010 [1972]. *The Archaeology of Knowledge and the Discourse on Knowledge.* Translated by A.M. Sheridan Smith. New York: Vintage Books.

Frankel, Haskel. 1966. "Interviewing the Interviewer: Alex Haley." *Saturday Review*, February 5: 37–8.

Frazier, E. Franklin. 1974 [1964]. *The Negro Church in America.* New York: Schocken Books.

Gaines, Kevin M. 1996. *Uplifting the Race: Black Leadership Politics and Culture in the Twentieth Century.* Chapel Hill, NC: University of North Carolina Press. https://doi.org/10.5149/uncp/9780807845431

Garza, Alicia. 2014. "A Herstory of the #BlackLivesMatter Movement." *Black Lives Matter.* http://blacklivesmatter.com/herstory/ (accessed July 5, 2017).

Gates, Jr., Henry Louis. 1988. *The Signifying Monkey: A Theory of African-American Literary Criticism.* New York: Oxford University Press.

_____. 2002. *Loose Canons: Notes on the Culture Wars.* New York: Oxford University Press.

Gates, Jr., Henry Louis and Nellie Y. McKay, eds. 2012 [1996]. *The Norton Anthology of African American Literature.* New York City: W.W. Norton & Company.

Gavazzi, Stephen M. 2011. *Families with Adolescents: Bridging the Gaps Between Theory, Research and Practice.* New York: Springer.

Gill, Jonathan. 2011. *Harlem: The Four Hundred Year History from Dutch Village to Capital of Black America.* Grove Press: New York.

Gilroy, Paul. 1993. *The Black Atlantic: Modernity and Double Consciousness.* Cambridge, MA: Harvard University Press.

Glenn, Charles L. 2011. *African-American/African-Canadian Schooling: From the Colonial Period to the Present.* New York: Palgrave Macmillan. https://doi.org/10.1057/9780230119505

Gonzales, Doreen. 1994. *Alex Haley: Author of ROOTS.* Springfield, NJ: Enslow Publishers.

Gopnik, Adam. 2010. "What Did Jesus Do? Reading and Unreading the Gospels." *The New Yorker*, May 24. http://www.newyorker.com/arts/critics/atlarge/2010/05/24/100524crat_atlarge_gopnik?currentPage=all (accessed July 7, 2017).

Gray, Herman. 1995. *Watching Race: Television and the Struggle for "Blackness."* Minneapolis: University of Minnesota.

Gray, John Milner. 1966. *A History of The Gambia*. London: Frank Cass and Co.

Gray, Paul. 1988. "Required Reading: Nonfiction Books." *TIME*, June 8. http://content.time.com/time/magazine/article/0,9171,988496,00.html (accessed March 21, 2017).

Gray, Rosie. 2017. "The Alt-Right's Rebranding Effort Has Failed." *The Atlantic*. https://www.theatlantic.com/politics/archive/2017/08/alt-right-charlottesville/536736/

Greene, J. Lee. 2008. *The Diasporan Self: Unbreaking the Circle in Western Novels*. Charlottesville, VA: University of Virginia Press, 2008.

Greene, Terry. 1992. "The Anguish of Alex Haley's Widow: With Her Husband's Literary Legacy Dispersed, She's Locked in a Bitter Probate Battle." *Phoenix New Times*, November 11. http://www.phoenixnewtimes.com/1992-11-11/news/the-anguish-of-alex-haley-s-widowwith-her-husband-s-literary-legacy-dispersed-she-s-locked-in-a-bitter-probate-battle (accessed July 5, 2017).

Gundaker, Grey. 1998. *Keep Your Head to the Sky: Interpreting African American Home Ground*. Charlottesville, VA: University of Virginia Press.

_____. 2008. "Roundtable Discussion." In *Signifying (on) Scriptures: Text(ures) and Orientations*, edited by Vincent L. Wimbush. *AAR Spotlight on Teaching* 3. http://rsnonline.org/indexf8bf.html?option=com_content&view=article&id=228&Itemid=296 (accessed July 5, 2017).

Gundaker, Grey and Judith McWillie. 2005. *No Space Hidden: The Spirit of African American Yard Work*. Knoxville: University of Tennessee Press.

Gutiérrez, Gustavo. 2000 [1971]. *A Theology of Liberation*. Fifteenth Anniversary Edition. Maryknoll, NY: Orbis Books.

Hahn, Steven. 2005 [2003]. *A Nation under Our Feet: Black Political Struggles in the Rural South from Slavery to the Great Migration*. Revised Edition. Cambridge, MA: Belknap Press.

Haley, Alex. 1943. "Alex Haley to Walter White. November 26." *United States Coast Guard* [Online]. https://www.uscg.mil/history/people/docs/1943_HaleyLetter.pdf (accessed June 14, 2017).

_____. 1963. "3.23—Alex Haley to Commandant (PS)—U.S. Coast Guard Headquarters, September 22." Anne Romaine Collection, MS2032. University of Tennessee Libraries, Knoxville, Special Collections.

_____. 1965. "3.10—Letter to Paul Reynolds, January 30." Alex Haley Collection, University of Tennessee Libraries, Knoxville, Special Collections.

_____. 1966. "3.10—Alex Haley to Maurice Ragsdale, December 14." Alex Haley Collection, University of Tennessee Libraries, Knoxville, Special Collections.

_____. 1972. "My Furthest-Back Person—'The African.'" *New York Times*, July 16: 12–16.

_____. 1973. "Black History, Oral History and Genealogy." *Oral History Review* 1: 1–17. https://doi.org/10.1093/ohr/1.1.1

_____. 1978. "38.6—Roots: The Second Hundred Years, transcript of meeting with Alex Haley, John McGreevey, and Stan Marguiles, January 9." Alex Haley Collection, University of Tennessee Libraries, Knoxville, Special Collections.

_____. 1983. "The Secret of Strong Families." *Ladies Home Journal*, February: 62, 64, 114, 115. https://doi.org/10.1029/EO064i012p00114-05

_____. 1988. *A Different Kind of Christmas*. New York: Gramercy Books.

_____. 1990 [1986]. "We Must Honor Our Ancestors." *Ebony*, November: 152, 154, 156.

_____. 2000 [1970]. Convocation Speech. *Spelman Messenger* 114 (2): 4–5.

_____. 2007. *Alex Haley: The Man Who Traced America's Roots*. New York: Reader's Digest.

_____. 2007 [1960]. "Mr. Muhammad Speaks." *Reader's Digest*, March. Republished in *Alex Haley: The Man Who Traced America's Roots*, 50–7. New York: Reader's Digest.

_____. 2007 [1963]. "The Man Who Wouldn't Quit." In *Alex Haley: The Man Who Traced America's Roots*, 42–9. New York: Reader's Digest.

_____. 2007 [1974]. "My Search for Roots." *Reader's Digest*, May. Republished in *Alex Haley: The Man Who Traced America's Roots*, 86–93. New York: Reader's Digest.

_____. 2007 [1976]. *Roots: The Saga of an American Family*. Thirtieth Anniversary Edition. New York: Vanguard Press.

_____. 2007 [1977] "What *Roots* Means to Me." *Reader's Digest*, May. Republished in *Alex Haley: The Man Who Traced America's Roots*, 158–62. New York: Reader's Digest.

_____. 2007 [1991a]. "In the Shadowland of Dreams." In *Alex Haley: The Man Who Traced America's Roots*, 74–8. New York: Reader's Digest.

_____. 2007 [1991b]. "Aboard the *African Star.*" In *Alex Haley: The Man Who Traced America's Roots*, 80–5. New York: Reader's Digest.

Haley, Alex and Alfred Balk. 1963. "Black Merchants of Hate." *The Saturday Evening Post*, January 26. Republished on the *Alex Haley Tribute Site*. http://www.alex-haley.com/alex_haley_black_merchants_of_hate.htm (accessed July 1, 2017).

Haley, Alex and David Stevens. 1993. *Alex Haley's Queen.* New York: Avon Books.

_____. 1997. *Mama Flora's Family.* Ithaca: Ithaca ILR Press.

Hall, Stuart. 1990 [1979]. "Cultural Identity and Diaspora." In *Identity: Community, Culture, Difference*, edited by Jonathan Rutherford, 222–37. London: Lawrence and Wishart.

_____. 1996. "Introduction: Who Needs 'Identity'?" In *Questions of Cultural Identity*, edited by Stuart Hall and Paul du Gay, 1–17. London: Sage Publications.

Handley, George B. 2000. *Postslavery Literatures in the Americas: Family Portraits in Black and White.* Charlottesville, VA: University of Virginia Press.

Handlin, Oscar. 1973 [1951]. *The Uprooted.* Second Edition. Boston: Little, Brown and Company.

Harris, Leonard H. 2008. "Against Signifying: Psychosocial Needs and Natural Evil." In *Theorizing Scriptures: New Critical Orientations to a Cultural Phenomenon*, edited by Vincent L. Wimbush, 206–13. New Brunswick: Rutgers University Press.

Harris, Leslie M. 2003. *In the Shadow of Slavery: African Americans in New York City, 1626–1863.* Chicago: University of Chicago Press. https://doi.org/10.7208/chicago/9780226317755.001.0001

Harrison, Faye V. 2008. *Outsider Within: Reworking Anthropology in the Global Age.* Chicago: University of Illinois Press.

_____. 2008. *Black Religion: Malcolm X, Julius Lester, and Jan Willis.* New York: Palgrave Macmillan.

_____. 2011. *Afro-Eccentricity: Beyond the Standard Narrative of Black Religion.* New York: Palgrave Macmillan. https://doi.org/10.1057/9780230118713_2

Hastings, Adam. 1997. *The Construction of Nationhood: Ethnicity, Religion, and Nationalism.* Cambridge, MA: Cambridge University Press. https://doi.org/10.1017/CBO9780511612107

Henneberger, Melinda. 1993. "The Tangled Roots of Alex Haley." *The New York Times*, February 14. http://www.nytimes.com/1993/02/14/books/television-the-tangled-roots-of-alex-haley.html (accessed July 4, 2017).

Hinman, Dave. 2009. *West Tennessee Journal with Dave Hinman* (television broadcast) WJLT 11. http://www.alex-haley.com/alex_haley_museum. htm (accessed January 5, 2016).

History. 2016. "Identity—Your Name is Your Shield," *Roots.* http://roots. history.com/identity/your-name-is-your-shield (accessed July 4, 2017).

History of the Sears Catalog. 2012. *The Sears Archives* [Online]. Last updated March 21. http://www.searsarchives.com/catalogs/history.htm (accessed July 4, 2017).

Hogan, William. 1966. "A Bookman's Notebook," *Corona Daily Independent*, January 11.

Hudson, Michelle. 1991. "The Effect of *Roots* and the Bicentennial on Genealogical Interest Among Patrons of the Mississippi Department of Archives and History." *The Journal of Mississippi History* 53: 321–36.

Humes, Edward. 2006. "How the GI Bill Shunted Blacks Into Vocational Training." *The Journal of Blacks in Higher Education* 53: 92–104.

Huntzicker, William E. 2007. "Alex Haley's *Roots*: The Fiction of Fact." In *Memory and Myth: The Civil War in Fiction and Film from* Uncle Tom's Cabin *to* Cold Mountain, edited by David B. Sachsman, Kittrell S. Rushing, and Roy Morris Jr., 269–80. Lafayette, IN: Purdue University Press.

Hurston, Zora Neale. 1998 [1937]. *Their Eyes Were Watching God*. San Francisco: Harper Perennial.

Jackson, Edward M. 1987. *American Slavery and the American Novel, 1852–1977.* Bristol, IN: Wyndham Hall Press.

Jacobson, Matthew Frye. 2006. *Roots Too: White Ethnic Revival in Post-Civil Rights America*. Cambridge, MA: Harvard University Press. https://doi.org/10.4159/9780674039063

James, C. Boyd. 2009. *Garvey, Garveyism and the Antinomies in Black Redemption.* Trenton, NJ: Africa World Press.

Jennings, Willie James. 2010. *The Christian Imagination: Theology and the Origins of Race*. New Haven, CT: Yale University Press.

Johnson, Beverly. 2013. *Alex Haley House Museum and Interpretive Center* [Tour]. July 11.

Johnson II, Lucas L. 2003. *Finding the Good.* Nashville: Rutledge Hill Press.

Joint Congressional Committee on Inaugural Ceremonies. 2013. *The 57th Presidential Inauguration: Barack H. Obama* [Online]. June 21. https://www.inaugural.senate.gov/about/past-inaugural-ceremonies/fifty-seventh-inaugural-ceremonies/ (accessed June 3, 2017).

"Julius Haley Obituary." 2010. *Washington Post*, April 14. http://www.legacy.com/obituaries/washingtonpost/ obituary.aspx?pid=141801196 (accessed July 30, 2017).

Kernstein, Andrew E. 2002. "African Americans and World War II." *Organization of American Historians' Magazine of History* 16(3): 13–17.

King, Dexter Scott. 2003. *Growing up King: An Intimate Memoir*. New York: Warner.

King, Gertie Brummit. 2012. *Alex Haley: The Man I Knew*. Pittsburgh: Dorrance Publishing.

Kort, Wesley A. 2008. "Reading Places/Reading Scriptures." In *Theorizing Scriptures: New Critical Orientations to a Cultural Phenomenon*, edited by Vincent L. Wimbush, 220–6. New Brunswick: Rutgers University Press.

Kunta Kinteh Island. 2012. Directed by Elvin Ross.

Laist, Randy. 2013. "Alex Haley's Roots and Hyperreal Historiography." *Mediascape*: 1–4.

Lalruatkima. 2014. "Taking Stock of a Rhizome." Institute for Signifying Scriptures. http://signifyingscriptures.org/signify/taking-stock-of-a-rhizome/ (accessed July 7, 2017).

_____. 2014. "Wild Races: Scripts and Textures of Imperial Imagination." PhD dissertation, Claremont Graduate University.

Lamar, Kendrick. 2015. "King Kunta." *To Pimp a Butterfly*. Top Dawg, Interscope, and Aftermath.

Lambert, Loren. 1988. "Haley's Home Tells the Story of *Roots*." *The Hour*, Norwalk, CT, August 9.

Landrieu, Mitch. 2017. "Mitch Landrieu, Mayor of New Orleans, Louisiana, Opening to a Speech on the Occasion of the Removal of Confederate General Robert E. Lee from the Public Square of New Orleans" [Transcript]. *The Pulse*, May 19. http://pulsegulfcoast.com/2017/05/transcript-of-new-orleans-mayor-landrieus-address-on-confederate-monuments (accessed July 7, 2017).

Lefler, Laura. 2008. "Laura Lefler's Thanksgiving Story: Finding the Good." *Knoxnews.com: Frank Munger's Atomic City Underground*, November 26 [Online]. http://knoxblogs.com/atomiccity/2008/11/26/laura_leflers_thanksgiving_sto/ (accessed June 13, 2017).

Legg, Sue Guinn. 2012. "Sen. Lamar Alexander tells short stories at Jonesborough Festival." *Johnson City Press*, October 5 [Online]. http://www.johnsoncitypress.com/Local/2012/10/05/Sen-Lamar-Alexander-tells-short-stories-at-Jonesborough-festival (accessed June 13, 2017).

Lewis, Miles Marshall. 2012. "'Roots' vs. 'Django Unchained': Two Generations of the Slave Narrative." *Ebony*, December 16 [Online]. http://www.ebony.com/entertainment-culture/django-unchained-review-773#axzz2ngBVGWH4 (accessed June 13, 2017).

Lewis Haley, Myran 2013. "My Contribution to *Roots*." African American Literature Book Club. http://aalbc.com/authors/my-haley.html (accessed June 21, 2017).

Lieberson, Stanley and Kelly S. Mikelson. 1995. "Distinctive African American Names: An Experimental, Historical, and Linguistic Analysis of Innovation." *American Sociological Review* 60(6): 928–46. https://doi.org/10.2307/2096433

Lincoln, Bruce. 2006. *Holy Terrors: Thinking about Religion after September 11*. Second Edition. Chicago: University of Chicago Press.

Lipsitz, George. 1990. *Time Passages: Collective Memory and American Popular Culture*. Minneapolis: University of Minnesota.

Liukkonen, Petri. 2008. "Alex Palmer Haley (1921–1992)." *Books and Writers: Author's Calendar*. Kuusankosku City (Finland) Library. http://kirjasto.sci.fi/ahaley (accessed March 8, 2012).

Long, Charles H. 1974. "Civil Rights—Civil Religion: Visible People and Invisible Religions." In *American Civil Religion*, edited by Russell E. Richie and Donald G. Jones, 211–21. New York: Harper and Row.

_____. 2004 [1986]. *Significations: Signs, Symbols, and Images in the Interpretation of Religion*. Aurora, CO: The Davies Group.

Lorde, Audre. 2007 [1979]. "The Master's Tools Will Never Dismantle the Master's House." *Sister Outsider: Essays and Speeches*, edited by Audre Lorde, 110–14. Berkeley, CA: Crossing Press.

Love, Velma E. 2012. *Divining the Self: A Study in Yoruba Myth and Human Consciousness*. New Brunswick: Rutgers University Press.

_____. 2013. "Scriptures as Sundials in African American Lives." In *Misreading America: Scriptures and Difference*, edited by Vincent L. Wimbush, 86–116. New York: Oxford University Press. https://doi.org/10.1093/acprof:oso/9780199975419.003.0003

Luders, Joseph E. 2010. *The Civil Rights Movement and the Logic of Social Change*. New York: Cambridge University Press. https://doi.org/10.1017/CBO9780511817120

Madison, James. 1820. Letter to Marquis De La Fayette, November 25. In *The Writings of James Madison, Comprising His Public Papers and His Private Correspondence, Including His Numerous Letters and Documents Now for the First Time Printed*, Vol. 9, edited by Gaillard Hunt. New York: G.P. Putnam's Sons, 1900. http://oll.libertyfund.org/title/1940/119255 (accessed August 5, 2017).

Malley, Brian. 2009. "Understanding the Bible's Influence." In *The Social Life of Scriptures:Cross-Cultural Perspectives on Biblicism*, edited by James S. Bielo, 194–205. New Brunswick: Rutgers.

Man, Nancy. 2012. "Baby Names from Alex Haley's *Roots*." *Nancy Baby Names*, April 24. http://www.nancy.cc/2012/04/24/baby-names-from-alex-haleys-roots/ (accessed 28 May 2015).

Mandell, Barrett John. 1972. "The Didactic Achievement of Malcolm X's Autobiography." *Afro-American Studies* 2(4): 269–74.

Manigault-Bryant, LeRhonda, Tamura A. Lomax, and Carol B. Duncan, eds. 2014. *Womanist and Black Feminist Responses to Tyler Perry's Productions*. New York: Palgrave Macmillan.
https://doi.org/10.1057/9781137429568

Marable, Manning. 2011. *Malcolm X: A Life of Reinvention*. New York: Viking Penguin.

Marmon, William. 1977. "Why *Roots* Hit Home." *TIME*, February 14 [Online]. Academic Search Complete, ESCOhost. http://search.ebscohost.com.ezproxy.etown.edu/login.aspx?direct=true&db=a9h&AN=5351953 8&site=ehost-live (accessed June 13, 2017).
https://doi.org/10.1108/eb023928

Massey, James Earl. 1994. "Reading the Bible from Social Locations: An Introduction." In *The New Interpreter's Bible Commentary*, edited by Leander G. Keck et al., Vol. 1, 150–3. Nashville: Abingdon Press.

Massoud, Paula J. 1996. "Mapping the Hood: The Genealogy of City Space in 'Boyz n the Hood' and 'Menace II Society.'" *Cinema Journal* 35: 85–97. https://doi.org/10.2307/1225757

Masuzawa, Tomoko. 2005. *The Invention of World Religions: Or How European Universalism Was Preserved in the Language of Pluralism*. Chicago: University of Chicago Press.
https://doi.org/10.7208/chicago/9780226922621.001.0001

McCann, Eric 2017. "The Two Bibles Donald Trump Used at the Inauguration." *New York Times*, January 18 [Online]. https://www.nytimes.com/2017/01/18/us/politics/lincoln-bible-trump-oath.html?_r=0 (accessed June 28, 2017).

McCauley, Mary Seibert. 1983. "Alex Haley, A Southern Griot: A Literary Biography." PhD dissertation, Vanderbilt University.

McCutcheon, Russell T. 1997. *Manufacturing Religion: The Discourse on Sui Generis Religion and the Politics of Nostalgia*. New York: Oxford University Press.

_____. 2015. "Writing a History of Origins." In *Fabricating Origins*, edited by Russell T. McCutcheon, 70–3. Sheffield: Equinox Press.

_____, ed. 2017. *Fabricating Identities*. Sheffield: Equinox Press.

McGuire, Willard and Marian S. Clayton. 1977. "An Interview with Alex Haley." *Today's Education*, September–October: 46–7.

McKittrick, Katherine. 2007. "'Freedom is a Secret,' The Future Usability of the Underground Railroad." In *Black Geographies and the Politics of Place*, edited by Katherine McKittrick and Clyde Woods. Cambridge, MA: South End Press.

McMahon, Tom. 2004. "Sorry Kids, But Alex Haley's 'Roots' Was A Fraud." *Tom McMahon: The Strategy of Bingo, The Excitement of Chess* [Weblog]. February. http://www.tommcmahon.net/2004/02/sorry_kids_but_/comments/page/4/ (accessed August 7, 2017).

Means Coleman, Robin R. 1998. *African American Viewers and the Black Situation Comedy: Situating Racial Humor.* New York: Garland Publishing.

Means Coleman, Robin R. and Andre M. Cavalcante. 2012. "Two Different Worlds: Television as a Producer's Medium." In *Watching While Black: Centering the Television of Black Audiences*, edited by Beretta E. Smith-Shomade, 33–49. New Brunswick: Rutgers.

Merriweather-Hunn, Lisa R., Talmadge C. Guy, and Elaine Manglitz. 2006. "Who Can Speak for Whom? Using Counter-Storytelling to Challenge Racial Hegemony." In *Proceedings of the 47th Adult Education Research Conference, Minneapolis*, May 19–21 [Online]. http://newprairiepress.org/aerc/2006/papers/32/ (accessed June 13, 2017).

Miller, Monica R. 2013. "Fabricating Origins ... One Coffee Bean at a Time." *Culture on the Edge*. October 22. https://edge.ua.edu/monica-miller/fabricating-origins-one-coffee-bean-at-a-time/ (accessed August 1, 2017).

Miller, Monica R., ed. 2015. *Claiming Identity in the Study of Religion: Social and Rhetorical Techniques Examined*. Sheffield: Equinox.

Mills, Gary B. and Elizabeth Shown Mills. 1981. "*Roots* and the New 'Faction': A Legitimate Tool for Clio?" *The Virginia Magazine of History and Biography* 89(1): 3–26.

Mitchell, Angelyn. 2002. *The Freedom to Remember: Nature, Slavery, and Gender in Contemporary Black Women's Fiction.* New Brunswick: Rutgers University Press.

Moore, David Chioni. 1994. "Routes: Alex Haley's Roots and the Rhetoric of Genealogy." *Transition* 64: 4–21.

_____. 1996. "Revisiting a Silenced Giant: Alex Haley's *Roots*—A Bibliographic Essay, and a Research Report on the Haley Archives at the University of Tennessee, Knoxville." *Resources for American Literary Study* 22(2): 195–249. https://works.bepress.com/david_moore/19/ (accessed August 2, 2017).

Morelli, Patrick. 1990. *"Behold* Monument: Sculptor Statement." *National Park Service*: *Martin Luther King Jr., National Historic Site.* https://www.nps.gov/malu/planyourvisit/behold_monument.htm (last updated April 24, 2015).

Morrison, Toni. 1984. "Rootedness: The Ancestor as Foundation." In *Black Women Writers (1950–1980): A Critical Evaluation*, edited by Mari Evans, 339–45. New York: Anchor/Doubleday.

_____. 2007 [1987]. *Beloved.* New York: Random House.

Moses, Wilson Jeremiah. 1998. *Afrotopia: The Roots of African American Popular History*. New York: Cambridge University Press. https://doi.org/10.1017/CBO9780511582837

Myrvold, Kristina, ed. 2016 [2010]. *The Death of Sacred Texts: Ritual Disposal and Renovation of Texts in World Religions*. New York: Routledge.

National Museum of The Gambia. 2017. "International *Roots* Festival." http://rootsgambia.gm (accessed May 13, 2014).

Newton, Richard. 2017a. "The African American Bible: Bound in a Christian Nation." *Journal of Biblical Literature* 136(1): 221–8. https://doi.org/10.1353/jbl.2017.0015

_____. 2017b. "Naaaaaw, You Show Me YOUR ID." In *Fabricating Identities*, edited by Russell T. McCutcheon, 99–104. Sheffield: Equinox.

_____. 2017c. "Words and Things: Happily Ever After Religion," February 20. *Studying Religion in Culture* [Weblog]. University of Alabama-Tuscaloosa. https://religion.ua.edu/blog/2017/02/20/words-and-things-happily-ever-after-religion/#respond (accessed July 15, 2017).

Nobile, Philip. 1993. "Uncovering *Roots*." *Village Voice*, February 23.

Nongbri, Brent. 2013. *Before Religion: History of a Modern Concept*. New Haven, CT: Yale University Press. https://doi.org/10.12987/yale/9780300154160.001.0001

Norrell, Robert J. 2015. *Alex Haley and the Books That Changed a Nation*. New York: St. Martin's Press.

Oakley Page, Mildred. 1995. Interviewed by Doris Dixon and Felicia Woods. Durham, NC (btvnc03029). June 1 [Transcript]. *Behind the Veil: Documenting African-American Life in the Jim Crow South Digital Collection*. John Hope Franklin Research Center. Duke University Libraries [Online]. http://library.duke.edu/digitalcollections/media/pdf/behindtheveil/btvnc03029.pdf (accessed June 28, 2017).

Obie, Brooke. 2013. "LeVar Burton on why 'Roots' Still Matters." *Ebony*, February 4 [Online]. http://www.ebony.com/entertainment-culture/interview-levar-burton-2013-495#axzz2ngBVGWH4 (accessed 13 June 2017).

Office of Management and Budget. 1977. *Directive No. 15: Race and Ethnic Standards for Federal Statistics and Administrative Reporting*, adopted May 12. Centers for Disease Control and Prevention [Online]. https://wonder.cdc.gov/wonder/help/populations/bridged-race/directive15.html (accessed June 14, 2017).

Olaniyan, Tejumola. 1996. "'Uplift the Race!': *Coming to America, Do the Right Thing*, and the Poetics and Politics of 'Othering.'" *Cultural Critique* 34: 91–113. https://doi.org/10.2307/1354613

Oliver, Myrna. 2002. "Murray Fisher, 69; Shaped Playboy Interview." *Los Angeles Times*, June 5 [Online]. http://articles.latimes.com/2002/jun/05/local/me-fisher5 (accessed June 15, 2017).

Olson, James Stuart. 1979. *The Ethnic Dimension in American History.* New York: St. Martin's Press.

Omi, Michael and Howard Winant. 1994. *Racial Formation in the United States: From the 1960s to the 1990s.* Second Edition. New York: Routledge.

Onstott, Kyle. 1957. *The Mandingo.* Daytona Beach, FL: Dendinger's Publishers.

Ortner, Sherry B. 1972. "Is Female to Male as Nature Is to Culture?" *Feminist Studies* 1(2): 5–31. https://doi.org/10.2307/3177638

Ottaway, Mark. 1977. "Tangled *Roots.*" *The Sunday Times*, London, April 10.

Otto, Rudolf. 1936 [1917]. *The Idea of the Holy: An Inquiry into the Non-rational Factor in the Idea of the Divine and its Relation to the Rational.* Revised edition. Translated by John W. Harvey. London: Oxford University Press.

Pace, Eric. 1992. "Alex Haley, 70, Author of 'Roots' Dies." *New York Times*, February 11 [Online]. http://www.nytimes.com/learning/general/onthisday/bday/0811.html (accessed June 15, 2017).

Pagden, Anthony. 1995. "The Effacement of Difference: Colonialism and the Origins of Nationalism in Diderot and Herder." In *After Colonialism: Imperials Histories and Postcolonial Displacements*, edited by Gyan Prakash, 129–52. Princeton, NJ: Princeton University Press. https://doi.org/10.2307/j.ctt7t242.9

Patterson, Robert J. 2011. "'Woman Thou Art Bound': Critical Spectatorship, Black Masculine Gazes, and Gender Problems in Tyler Perry's Movies." *Black Camera* 3(1): 9–30. https://doi.org/10.2979/blackcamera.3.1.9

Perks, Lisa Glebatis. 2010. "Polysemic Scaffolding: Explicating Discursive Clashes in *Chappelle's Show.*" *Communication, Culture & Critique* 3(2): 270–89. https://doi.org/10.1111/j.1753-9137.2010.01070.x

Pile, Steve and Nigel Thrift. 1995. "Introduction." In *Mapping the Subject: Geographies of Cultural Transformation*, edited by Steve Pile and Nigel Thrift, 1–12. New York: Routledge.

Platon, Adelle. 2012. "Spike Lee Slams *Django Unchained*: 'I'm Not Gonna See It.'" *Vibe*, December 21 [Online]. http://www.vibe.com/article/spike-lee-slams-django-unchained-im-not-gonna-see-it (accessed June 13, 2017).

Prothero, Stephen R. 2012. *The American Bible: Whose America Is This? How Our Words Unite and Divide a Nation*. San Francisco: HarperOne.

Pryor, Richard. 2002. *Richard Pryor: Here and Now* (1983). DVD. Directed by Richard Pryor. Culver City, CA: Sony Pictures.

Public Broadcasting Service. 2013. *Pioneers of Television*, "Miniseries." Season 3, Episode 4.

Quarles, Benjamin Arthur. 1973. *The Negro in the American Revolution*. New York: Norton and Company.

Quinn, Charlotte A. 1972. *Mandingo Kingdoms of the Senegambia: Traditionalism, Islam, and European Expansion*. Evanston, IL: Northwestern University Press.

Quinn, Naomi, ed. 2005. *Finding Culture in Talk*. New York: Palgrave Macmillan. https://doi.org/10.1007/978-1-137-05871-3

Raboteau, Albert J. 2004 [1978]. *Slave Religion: The Invisible Institution*. Updated Edition. New York: Oxford University Press.

Rampersad, Arnold. 1976. "Review of *Roots*." *The New Republic*, December 4.

Rancière, Jacques. 2007. *The Future of the Image*. Translated by Gregory Elliot. New York: Verso Books.

Rayant, Guillaume Thomas François. 1798 [1770]. *A Philosophical and Political History of the Settlements and Trade of the Europeans in the East and West Indies*. Second Edition. Translated by J.O. Justamond, Vol. 3, bk. IX, ch.1.

Reed, Ishmael. 1972. "Neo-Hoodoo Manifesto." In *Conjure: Selected Poems, 1963–1970*, 20–5. Amherst, MA: University of Massachusetts Press.

Reedijk, Rachel. 2010. *Roots and Routes: Identity Construction and the Jewish-Christian-Muslim Dialogue*. New York: Rodopi. https://doi.org/10.1163/9789042028401

Reincheld, Aaron. 2006. "'Saturday Night Live' and Weekend Update: The Formative Years of Comedy News Dissemination." *Journalism* 31(4): 190–7. https://doi.org/10.1080/00947679.2006.12062688

Romaine, Anne. n.d. "1.31—Alex Haley Book Outlines and Book Draft." Anne Romaine Collection, MS2032. University of Tennessee Libraries, Knoxville, Special Collections.

_____. n.d. "1.53—Book Proposal for Alex Haley's Biography." Anne Romaine Collection, MS2032. University of Tennessee Libraries, Knoxville, Special Collections.

_____. n.d. "1.56—Alex Haley Book Draft." Anne Romaine Collection, MS2032. University of Tennessee Libraries, Knoxville, Special Collections.

Roots. 2016. Distributed by The Wolper Organization and Will Packer Productions. Originally aired May 30–June 2, 2016, History. [Blu-Ray]. Lionsgate.

"*Roots* (2016)". *Metacritic*. http://www.metacritic.com/tv/roots-2016 (accessed July 5, 2017).

"'Roots' Cast Announced, Questlove Speaks on Musical Theme." 2015. *Ebony*, September 16. http://www.ebony.com/entertainment-culture/ roots-cast-announced-questlove-speaks-on-the-musical-theme-999#axzz3lwT5trEm (accessed August 5, 2017).

Roots: One Year Later. 2012. Produced by Robert Guenette. Originally aired January 23, 1978, ABC Broadcasting Company. [DVD]. Warner Home Video.

Roots: The Gift. 2012. Produced by David L. Wolper and Bernard Sofronski. Originally aired December 11 1988, ABC Broadcasting Company. [DVD]. Warner Home Video.

Roots: The Miniseries. 2012. Produced by Stan Margulies. Originally aired January 23–30, 1977, ABC Broadcasting Company. [DVD]. Warner Home Video.

Roots: The Next Generations. 2012. Produced by Stan Margulies. Originally aired February 18–24, 1979, ABC Broadcasting Company. [DVD]. Warner Home Video.

Rucker, Walter. 2010. "Alex Haley." In *Encyclopedia of African American History*, edited by Leslie M. Alexander and Walter C. Rucker, 791–2. Santa Barbara: ABC-CLIO.

Ryan, Tim A. 2008. *Call and Responses: The American Novel of Slavery since Gone With the Wind*. Baton Rouge: Louisiana State University Press. https://doi.org/10.2307/27694853

Sabourin, R. 2014. "20 Martin Luther King Jr. Monuments Around the World You Didn't Know Existed." *Complex*, January 20. http://www.complex. com/style/ 2014/01/martin-luther-king-jr-monuments/behold-monument (accessed February 2, 2016).

Sander, Johanna. 2012. "The Television Series *Community* and Sitcom." Thesis, Karlstads Universitet.

Schüssler Fiorenza, Elisabeth. 1983. *In Memory of Her: A Feminist Theological Reconstruction of Christian Origins*. New York: Crossroad Publishing Company.

Scripps Howard News Service. 2002. "Roots: The Miniseries that Changed America." *The Augustana Chronicle*, January 7. http://chronicle.augusta. com/stories/2002/01/17/ent_333364.shtml#.WU43AzOZNE5 (accessed July 6, 2017).

Shapiro, Gary. 2006. "Misprint Is Spied in Lazarus Poem at Liberty Island." *The New York Sun*, December 8 [Online]. http://www.nysun.com/arts/ misprint-is-spied-in-lazarus-poem-at-liberty/44816/ (accessed July 14, 2017).

Sharot, Stephen. 2001. *A Comparative Sociology of World Religions: Virtuosos, Priests, and Popular Religion*. New York City: New York University Press.

Shenker, Israel 1977. "Some Historians Dismiss Report of Factual Mistakes in '*Roots*.'" *New York Times*, April 10 [Online]. http://www.nytimes. com/1977/04/10/archives/some-historians-dismiss-report-of-factual-mistakes-in-roots-the.html?_r=0 (accessed July 7, 2017).

Sheth, Falguni G. 2009. *Toward a Political Philosophy of Race*. Albany: State University of New York Press.

Shirley, David. 2005. *Alex Haley: Author*. Philadelphia: Chelsea House Publishers.

Shklar, Judith N. 2004 [1986]. "Squaring the Hermeneutic Circle." *Social Research* 71(3): 655–78. https://www.jstor.org/stable/40971719

Simmons, K. Merinda. 2014. *Changing the Subject: Writing Women Across the African Diaspora*. Columbus, OH: Ohio State University Press.

Skaggs, Merrill Maguire. 1978. "*Roots*: A New Black Myth." *Southern Quarterly* 17(1): 42–50.

Smith, Jonathan Z. 1982. *Imagining Religion: From Babylon to Jonestown*. Chicago: University of Chicago Press.

_____. 1992. "Scriptures and Histories." *Method & Theory in the Study of Religion* 4(1–2): 97–105. https://doi.org/10.1163/157006892X00084

_____. 2000. "Bible and Religion." *Bulletin: Council for the Study of Religion* 29: 87–93.

_____. 2009. "Religion and Bible." *Journal of Biblical Literature* 128(1): 5–27 [Online]. https://www.sbl-site.org/assets/pdfs/presidentialaddresses/ JBL128_1_1Smith2008.pdf (accessed June 13, 2017).

Smith, Leslie Dorough. 2013. "Our Sofas, Ourselves: The Art of Selling Origins," *Culture on the Edge*. https://edge.ua.edu/leslie-dorrough-smith/ our-sofas-ourselves-the-art-of-selling-origins/ (accessed February 2, 2017).

Smith, Shanell T. 2014. *The Woman Babylon and the Marks of Empire: Reading Revelation with a Postcolonial Womanist Hermeneutics of Ambiveilance*. Philadelphia: Fortress Press. https://doi.org/10.2307/j.ctt9m0shd

Smith, T. Alexander and Lenahan O'Connell. 1997. *Black Anxiety, White Guilt, and the Politics of Status Frustration*. Westport, CT: Praeger Publishers.

Smith, Theophus H. 1995. *Conjuring Culture: Biblical Formations of Black America*. New York: Oxford University Press.

Smith, Wilfred Cantwell. 1971. "The Study of Religion and the Study of the Bible." *Journal of the American Academy of Religion* 39: 131–40. https://doi.org/10.1093/jaarel/XXXIX.2.131

———. 1993. *What Is Scripture? A Comparative Approach*. Minneapolis: Fortress Press.

Sollors, Werner. 1994. "National Identity and Ethnic Diversity: 'Of Plymouth Rock and Jamestown and Ellis Island'; or, Ethnic Literature and Some Redefinitions of America." In *History and Memory in African-American Culture*, edited by Geneviève Fabre and Robert O'Meally, 92–121. New York: Oxford University Press.

Sosin, Michelle. 1997. "BBC Documentary Causes Row." *E! News*, September 9. http://www.eonline.com/news/35146/bbc-documentary-causes-roots-row (accessed August 7, 2017).

Spaulding, A. Timothy. 2005. *Re-Forming the Past: History, the Fantastic, and the Postmodern Slave Narrative*. Columbus, OH: The Ohio State University Press.

Staff Writer. 1950. "New Palmer-Turner School is Dedicated One of Finest in Tennessee for Negroes." *Memphis World* 19(12), August 1. Digital Library of Tennessee, Rhodes College, Crossroads to Freedom [Online]. http://www.crossroadstofreedom.org/view.player?pid=rds:1231 (accessed June 15, 2017).

Star Trek VI: The Undiscovered Country. 1991. Directed by Nicholas Meyer. Paramount Pictures.

Stein, Gertrude. 1993 [1937]. *Everybody's Autobiography*. Cambridge, MA: Exact Change.

Stephens, Robert O. 1995. *The Family Saga in the South: Generations and Destinies*. Baton Rouge: Louisiana State University Press.

Strauss, Claudia. 2005. "Analyzing Discourse for Cultural Complexity." In *Finding Culture in Talk*, edited by Naomi Quinn, 203–42. New York: Palgrave Macmillan. https://doi.org/10.1007/978-1-137-05871-3_6

Super Fly T.N.T. 1973. Screenplay by Alex Haley. Directed by Ron O'Neal.

Sussman. Robert Wald. 2014. *The Myth of Race: The Troubling Persistence of an Unscientific Idea.* Cambridge, MA: Harvard University Press. https://doi.org/10.4159/harvard.9780674736160

Taneya. 2012. "From the Inbox: Finding Jim & Carrie of *Roots: The Next Generations.*" TNGenWeb Project, June 25. http://tngenweb.org/blog/from-the-inbox-finding-jim-carrie-roots-next-generations/ (accessed June 14, 2017).

Tate, Gayle T. 2003. *Unknown Tongues: Black Women's Political Activism in the Antebellum Era, 1830–1860.* East Lansing, MI: Michigan State University.

Taves, Ann. 2009. *Religious Experience Reconsidered: A Building-Block Approach to the Study of Religion and Other Special Things.* Princeton, NJ: Princeton University Press. https://doi.org/10.1515/9781400830978

Taylor, Clyde. 1977. "*Roots:* A Modern Minstrel Show." *The Black Scholar* 8: 37–8.

Taylor, Helen. 1995. "The Griot from Tennessee: The Saga of Alex Haley's *Roots.*" *Critical Quarterly* 37(2): 46–62.
https://doi.org/10.1111/j.1467-8705.1995.tb01053.x

Taylor, Hycel B., ed. 1977. "Prolegomena to a Theological Response to *Roots.*" *The Church and the Black Experience Bulletin*, February.

———. 2001. *Circling Dixie: Contemporary Southern Culture Through a Transatlantic Lens.* New Brunswick: Rutgers University Press.

"Texas Birth Certificate Lists 'Negroid' as Man's Race." 2010. *KRIV FOX 26*, January 25. http://www.myfoxhouston.com/story/18230531/texas-birth-certificate-lists-negroid-as-mans-race#ixzz2thhUKt9x (accessed June 11, 2014).

The Combahee River Collective. 1977. "Black Feminist Statement." *WSQ: Women's Studies Quarterly* 42(3–4): 271–80.
https://doi.org/10.1353/wsq.2014.0052

The Fresh Prince of Bel Air. 2004. "The Fresh Prince Project." Season 1, Episode 1. Directed by Debbie Allen. [DVD]. Burbank, CA: Warner Home Video. Originally aired September 10, 1990, NBC.

———. 2005a. "Will Gets a Job." Season 2, Episode 3. Directed by Ellen Falcon. [DVD]. Burbank, CA: Warner Home Video. Originally aired September 23, 1991, NBC.

———. 2005b. "Mama's Baby, Carlton's Maybe." Season 3, Episode 5. Directed by Shelley Jensen. [DVD]. Burbank, CA: Warner Home Video. Originally aired October 12, 1992, NBC.

"The Original Plaque." n.d. *Kunta Kinte-Alex Haley Foundation, Inc.: The Genealogy Experience.* http://www.kintehaley.org/testsite/the-original-plaque/ (accessed January 6, 2016).

The Roots of Alex Haley. 1996. Directed by James Kent. British Broadcasting Company.

The Sculpture Group. n.d. *Kunta Kinte-Alex Haley Foundation, Inc.: The Genealogy Experience*. http://www.kintehaley.org/testsite/the-sculpture-group (accessed January 6, 2016).

The Tennessee Department of Tourist Development. 2016. "Alex Haley Museum and Interpretive Center—Henning." http://www.tnvacation.com/vendors/ alex_haley_museum/ (accessed January 5, 2017).

The Wire. 2005. "Hot Shots." Season 2, Episode 3. Directed by Elodie Keene. [DVD]. New York: HBO. Originally aired June 15, 2003, HBO.

Todd, Charles L. 1978. "Alex Haley on Campus." *Family Heritage*, Brooklyn, NY, October 1 (5): 131–3.

Tyler, James. 2006. *The Geography of Malcolm X: Black Radicalism and the Remaking of American Space*. New York: Routledge.

Ulaby, Neda. 2010. "More than 'Madea': Tyler Perry Changes Course." *NPR: All Things Considered*, March 8. http://www.npr.org/templates/ transcript/ transcript.php?storyId=124459269 (accessed August 7, 2017).

United Nations Educational, Scientific and Cultural Organization: World Heritage Convention. 2017. "Kunta Kinteh Island and Related Sites." http://whc.unesco.org/en/list/761 (accessed July 7, 2017).

United States Coast Guard. 2016. "Alex Palmer Haley, Chief Journalist, USCG (Ret.)." http://www.uscg.mil/history/people/Alex_HaleyBio.asp (last modified December 21).

Valentine, Curtis. 2015. "Remembering George Haley: The Greatest American You've Never Heard Of." *Huffington Post*, May 22. http:// www.huffingtonpost.com/curtis-valentine/remembering-george-haley-_b_7418484.html (accessed June 15, 2017).

Vansina, Jan. 1965 [1961]. *Oral Tradition: A Study in Historical Africa*. Translated by H.M. Wright. London: Routledge & Kegan Paul.

_____. 1994. *Living with Africa*. Madison: University of Wisconsin Press.

Wansley, Joy and Lois Armstrong. 1976. "Alex Haley's Search for *Roots* Took Him First to the Brink of Suicide, and Now to Fame and Riches." *People*, October 18. http://www.people.com/people/archive/ article/0,,20067011,00.html (accessed August 7, 2017).

Watts, James W. 2006. "Three Dimensions of Scriptures." *Postscripts: The Journal of Sacred Texts and Contemporary Worlds* 2: 135–59. https://doi.org/10.1558/post.v2i2.135

"Weekend Update." 2002. *Saturday Night Live*. Season 27, Episode 11. Originally aired January 19, NBC.

Weiner, Rachel. 2013. "Why Lamar Alexander Quoted Alex Haley." *The Washington Post*, January 21 [Online]. https://www.washingtonpost.com/news/post-politics/wp/2013/01/21/why-lamar-alexander-quoted-alex-haley/?utm_term=.7c4b71b612ad (accessed June 13, 2017).

Weisenfeld, Judith. 2016. *New World A-Coming: Black Religion and Racial Identity During the Great Migration*. New York: NYU Press.

West, Kanye. 2004. "Never Let Me Down." Featuring Jay-Z and J-Ivy. *The College Dropout*. Def Jam and Roc-a-fella Records.

West, Malcolm R. 1977. "Black Historians Reflect On Criticisms of *Roots*." *Jet*, April 28: 16–17.

Willis, Jan. 2008 [2001]. *Dreaming Me: From Baptist to Buddhist, One Woman's Spiritual Journey*. Somerville, MA: Wisdom Publications.

Wilkerson, Isabel. 1989. "'African-American' Favored by Many of America's Blacks." *New York Times*, January 31 [Online]. http://www.nytimes.com/1989/01/31/us/african-american-favored-by-many-of-america-s-blacks.html?pagewanted=all (accessed August 7, 2017).

_____. 2010. *The Warmth of Other Suns: The Epic Story of America's Great Migration*. New York: Vintage Books.

Wimbush, Vincent L. 1991. "The Bible and African Americans: An Outline of an Interpretive History." In *Stony the Road We Trod: African American Biblical Hermeneutics*, edited by Cain Hope Felder, 81–97. Minneapolis: Fortress Press.

_____. 2000. "Introduction: Reading Darkness, Reading Scriptures." In *African Americans and the Bible: Sacred Texts and Social Textures*, edited by Vincent L. Wimbush, 1–43. New York: Continuum.

_____. 2007. "We Will Make Our Own Future Text: An Alternate Orientation to Interpretation." In *True to Our Native Land: African American New Testament Commentary*, edited by Brian Blount et al., 43–53. Philadelphia: Fortress Press.

_____. 2008. "Introduction: TEXTureS, Gestures, Power: Orientation to Radical Excavation." In *Theorizing Scriptures: New Critical Orientations to a Cultural Phenomenon*, edited by Vincent L. Wimbush, 1–22. New Brunswick: Rutgers University Press.

_____. 2010. "The Work We Make Scriptures Do for Us: An Argument for Signifying on Scriptures as Critical Orientation." In *Transforming Graduate Biblical Studies*, edited by Elisabeth Schüssler Fiorenza and Kent H. Richard, 355–66. Atlanta: Society of Biblical Literature.

_____. 2012. *White Men's Magic: Scripturalization as Slavery*. New York: Oxford University Press.

_____. 2016. "Introduction: Scriptures and Transgression." In *Refractions of the Scriptural: Critical Orientation as Transgression*, edited by Vincent L. Wimbush, 1–16. New Brunswick: Rutgers University Press.

Wimbush, Vincent L., ed. 2008. *Theorizing Scriptures: New Critical Orientations to a Cultural Phenomenon*. New Brunswick: Rutgers University Press.

_____. 2013. *Misreading America: Scriptures and Difference*. New York: Oxford University Press.

Winters, Joseph R. 2016. *Hope Draped in Black: Race, Melancholy, and the Agony of Progress.* Durham, NC: Duke University Press. https://doi.org/10.1215/9780822374084

Wittgenstein, Ludwig. 2009 [1953]. *Philosophical Investigations*. Revised Fourth Edition. Edited by P.M.S. Hacker and Joachim Schulte, translated by G.E.M. Anscombe, P.M.S. Hacker and Joachim Schulte. Oxford, UK: Wiley-Blackwell.

Wolcott, Harry F. 2005. *The Art of Fieldwork*. Second Edition. Walnut Creek, CA: Alta Mira.

Woodson, Carter G. 1990 [1933]. *The Mis-education of the Negro*. Trenton, NJ: Africa World Press.

X, Malcolm. 1963. "Message to the Grassroots," November 10. Northern Negro Grass Roots Leadership Conference, King Solomon Baptist Church, Detroit, MI. *Teaching American History,* Ashland Center at Ashbrook University. http://teachingamericanhistory.org/library/document/message-to-grassroots/ (accessed August 7, 2017).

_____. 1964. "The Ballot or the Bullet," March 29, Washington Heights, NY. *AMDOCS: Documents for the Study of American History*. http://www.vlib.us/amdocs/texts/malcolmx0364.html (accessed August 7, 2017).

X, Malcolm and Alex Haley. 1999 [1965]. *The Autobiography of Malcolm X as Told to Alex Haley*. New York: Ballantine Books.

Yagelski, Robert P. 2000. *Literacy Matters: Writing and Reading the Social Self*. New York: Columbia University's Teachers College Press, 45.

Zamudio, Margaret M. and Francisco Rios. 2006. "From Traditional to Liberal Racism: Living Racism in the Everyday." *Sociological Perspectives* 49(4): 483–501. https://doi.org/10.1525/sop.2006.49.4.483

Index

www.ingramcontent.com/pod-product-compliance
Lightning Source LLC
Chambersburg PA
CBHW050504270326
41927CB00009B/1900